GOOD
SCHOOLS
GUIDE

A HARPERS & QUEEN PUBLICATION

Amanda Atha & Sarah Drummond

GOOD SCHOOLS GUIDE

A parents' guide to over 270 schools

EBURY PRESS • LONDON

Published 1991 by Ebury Press
an imprint of the Random Century Group
Random Century House
20 Vauxhall Bridge Road
London SW1V 2SA

First impression 1991

British Library Cataloguing-in-Publication Data
Atha, Amanda
    "A Harpers and Queen" publication good schools
    guide: The bestselling parents' guide to over 270
    top schools.
    I. title II. Drummond, Sarah
    371.029

    ISBN 0-85223-971-8

Co-ordinating Editor: Sarah Bailey
Editor: Elizabeth Martyn
Designer: Gwyn Lewis

Typeset from authors' discs by Saxon Printing
Limited, Derby.

Printed and bound in Great Britain by Butler and
Tanner Limited, Frome and London

CONTENTS

The authors and publishers would like to thank the following schools and pupils for allowing them to reproduce the illustrations in this edition of the Good Schools Guide:

(Caldicott) pages 19, 158 and 205
(The Edinburgh Academy) pages 20, 38 and 51
(Millfield Senior School) pages 23 and 141
(Stonar) page 57
(Westonbirt School) pages 35, 66, 128 and 177
Ben Dowden (Lambrook) pages 62, 130 and 144
Harriet Fergusson (Westonbirt School) pages 29 and 49
Matthew Humphries (Edgarley Hall School) page 153
Joanne Hung (Streatham Hill and Clapham High) page 150
John Kulukundis (Sussex House Preparatory School) pages 116 and 138
Yasmin Mehmet (Streatham Hill and Clapham High) page 194
Christopher Moore (Edgarley Hall School) pages 86 and 199
Victoria Muirhead (Streatham Hill and Clapham High) pages 26 and 121
Sophie Newell (Streatham Hill and Clapham High) page 148
James Nicolian (Sussex House Preparatory School) page 69
Charlotte Padwick (Westonbirt School) page 91
Jay Puddy (Edgarley Hall School) pages 113 and 156
S Riddell (Westonbirt School) page 131
Mischa Scott (Sussex House Preparatory School) pages 37 and 72
Emily Sutton (Edgarley Hall School) pages 154 and 189
Edward White (Edgarley Hall School) pages 48 and 167

The authors would like to state that the information contained in this book was checked as rigorously as possible before going to press. Neither the authors nor the publishers can take responsibility for any changes which may have occurred since, nor for any other variance of fact from that recorded here in good faith.

CONTRIBUTORS
Patrea More Nisbett
Annie Coulson
Gilly Greene
Lydia Hancock
James Hughes-Onslow
Philip Lane Clark
Jane Lott
Fiona Macpherson
and numerous parents, pupils, educationalists, Heads, staff, readers and moles.

CAN YOU HELP US?
We would like to know what you think about the schools in this edition, and any suggestions for the next one. Please write to Amanda Atha and Sarah Drummond, Good Schools Guide, c/o Ebury Press, Random Century House, 20 Vauxhall Bridge Road, London SW1V 2SA.

INTRODUCTION

We are living in troubled times, educationally speaking. Schools are feeling the chill winds of demographic trends with fewer children to educate. Parents are feeling the recession. Day school numbers are still significantly increasing, and boarding numbers are considerably down, among boys especially; fee-paying Sixth Forms have also been hard hit by the recession and the perceived need to spread the wings earlier.

Most schools have been forced to join the great consumer society, laying out their wares before the public, either with the help of professional public relations people or with recruits from within. They are also having to think harder about what these wares should be: should day pupils be admitted? Would weekly boarding boost the numbers? Would a really high-tech computer centre tempt the big spenders? Or an exotic trek in the Himalayas? And shouldn't those Florence Nightingale dorms be turned into fancy studios with fans, fridges, central heating, wall-to-wall carpeting, custom built pin boards, enough plugs for ghetto blasters and hair dryers? Should Johnny be allowed to take Geog A-level, weak though he be, or is this going to jeopardize those results charts which so impress the parents? How best can the results be massaged into seas of 100% A and B passes? Some schools are finding they need to drop their standard of intake, though they would die rather than admit it (so would the parents, for that matter). Bursaries and scholarships are being more widely – and thinly – spread.

Girls are still the ace card as far as boys' schools are concerned, to keep numbers and standards up. Large numbers have gone 'co-ed' since we last went to press. Girls' schools are fighting back bravely and the best of them, with considerable success. (We even detect a slight reaction against the more half-baked versions of co-education.)

In the state sector, introduction of the new competitive element has seen, for the first time, glossy prospectuses, even 'bribes' for prospective customers in the shape of free plumbing or set squares, and a sudden willingness on the part of Heads to see the press and explain what they are up to.

For many reasons, there is an increase in the number of parents choosing private day schools and the entries in this edition of the book reflect that trend. We have also noticed lip service to Europe and even one or two steps in that direction, eg chateaux in France, satellite dishes peeping coyly from antique roofs, one or two fascinating new exchange schemes. There is however little sign of Modern Languages being more or better taught anywhere.

The National Curriculum has, of course, caused major upheavals in the state sector, but has caused little problem in the private sector (though Labour plan to make it compulsory). CDT is no longer the buzz thing, replaced by DT and IT – and some heads admit to being mystified by all three. Fierce debate continues about how important AS-levels should be, and whether A-levels are fair? There is widespread despair among parents over the wasted end of summer term, as pupils queue up to get out after exams.

Drugs are everywhere – in schools as well as out of them. Alcohol ditto, and smoking carries on despite all the propaganda. Telly continues to reign supreme in many schools, the plug-in-drug for desperate and/or lazy staff to turn on in their hours of need. We have had scores of reports of bullying, the unexpected horror story for the nineties.

There is much emphasis on educating the 'whole' child, and many schools offer so much 'stretching' that children come home exhausted – and home life is pale and flat compared with school. 'Sometimes I think I'm running a holiday camp' said one Headmistress. In most schools there is little time for reading, reflection and reasoning.

As usual, researching this book we find a carousel of Heads on the move, and increasing numbers of appointments coming from outside the traditional routes. Despite all the window dressing, we observe a depressing shortage of really inspiring staff.

Amanda Atha   Sarah Drummond
London, June 1991

ENTRANCE

PRIVATE SCHOOLS

As a rule of thumb this is what you do:

1. Register the child's name in the school(s) you have chosen. Telephone the school, and they will send you an application form.
2. Fill it in. This has to be done at the right moment or the 'list' may be 'full'. Embryos are acceptable at some schools, but you should get the child's name 'put down' as soon as possible to be on the safe side; they will tell you if it is too early – and it will cost you a registration fee (usually non-returnable) ranging from about £10 to £200 or more.
3. At the appropriate moment the school will contact you or your child's current school about the next step (it doesn't hurt to telephone and check, though, if you think they might have forgotten you – and don't forget to let them know if you change your address). They will also probably get a report from the Head of your child's current school and great attention is usually paid to that.
4. Next step is usually a visit to the school, a tour round it and a talk with the Head or Housemaster or whoever is appropriate. More money may be extracted from you at this stage to make a definite reservation, though this may be knocked off the first term's school fees in due course.
5. The child is usually, though not always, put through its paces, which might mean an exam, a test or two, or 'meaningful play' or whatever.
6. All being well, the school will then offer a firm place. You must write and confirm acceptance of this place or it may be offered to someone else.
7. Pay school fees – in advance of the term is normal practice, alas.

There are a few variations on this theme. For example, schools with an academically competitive exam – grammar schools, for instance – will often accept entries right up to the last minute, though there will be an official date of closing, from about three weeks to three terms before the exam.

For the most fashionable schools of the moment you more or less have to put the child's name down the minute you get out of the labour ward – and even this only guarantees that your child gets a chance to sit the exam.

London and other inner cities are special cases because too many candidates are chasing too few places. It can be frantically complicated, many schools set their own exams. It is quite normal to be trying for several schools more or less at the same time.

Entry at Sixth Form level depends on GCSE results and applications are made a year or so before term of entry. Check with the school.

Girls applying to Sixth Forms of boys' or co-ed schools can expect tough competition and generally need to apply 18 months before date of entry and may well have to sit an exam.

TIPS

* Don't panic.
* Try the back door (get a list of governors, you may know one).
* Be prepared to wait.
* Chat up the Head. Make the right noises (weeping in the Head's office has been known to work).
* Always have a go at the school you really want, however late in the day it may seem; bear in mind shifting population, places suddenly falling vacant through expulsion, recession and demographic trends.
* Define for yourself what you want for your child: boarding or day is the biggest single factor to take into account.
* Even if you have done everything at the right time and in the right order there are still last-minute scrambles at all levels and it is all very testing, not only for parents and pupils, but for Heads and their secretaries too.
* Heads are only human – there are always exceptions and you may be one.
* Applying for more than one school keeps the options open, but it is expensive.
* Check what is meant by 'firm' or 'guaranteed' place or 'waiting list'. Schools have been known to wriggle out of their obligations should someone brighter and bushier come along.
* Overseas students' parents are often asked to pay a term's fees (or more) well in advance as they have a wobbly reputation for turning up in the first place.
* It has to be said: your cleverest move to get into a very good, very popular school is to have a bright child in the first place. It is quite amazing how doors open if a potential Oxbridge winner hoves into sight.

STATE SCHOOLS

Since the 1980 Education Act you, the parent, have been able to express a preference for the school at which you wish to have your child educated, and the

local authority or school in question has a *duty* to comply with any preference expressed *unless*:
a) compliance with the preference would prejudice the provision of efficient education or the efficient use of resources or
b) the school is an aided or special agreement school, or has 'opted out' and compliance with the preference would be incompatible with any arrangements between the governors and the local education authority in respect of the admission of pupils to the school or
c) the arrangements for admission to the preferred school are based 'wholly or partly on selection by reference to ability or partly on selection by reference to ablility or aptitude and compliance with the preference would be incompatible with selection under the arrangements'.
We think this is talking about competitive entry. . .

If you get what appears to be a 'No' on any count you have the right of appeal, stating to an Appeal Committee why you think little Johnny should go to x and not y. The most successful reason tends to be health: if you can get a doctor's letter stating that your ewe lamb gets asthma in Islington but flourishes in the pure air of Camden, then you are three-quarters of the way to getting into that Camden school you have your eye on. Like any other appeal you need to lobby like mad – the Head, the governors, the doctor, the local authority, your MP, the lollipop man – whoever seems good to you.

It is always worth appealing if you feel strongly about the school in question, but bear in mind that the state has no special incentive to be flexible. For a private school, one more desk squeezed in means one more fat fee, but for a successful state school it usually means straining an already bulging class to bursting point for no other reason than to please you.

SUSSING OUT A SCHOOL and HORSES FOR COURSES

Every single reference book on schools indulges in advice on this. Lists of questions tend to make Heads bristle – 'It's a question of attitude,' said one Head – but going in as a parent can be daunting. The following is a list of guidelines we drew up as we went round. Obviously, not all are applicable to every school: ask even half these questions and you will probably never be invited back again, but it does no harm to take them along for prompting.

ACTION
1. Send for the prospectus, last two editions of the school magazine, list of governors, fixture list, and ask for the last two years' results and any other bumph – and read it. This saves time on crucial but pedestrian matters such as size of dorms, exeats, getting in etc.
2. Make an appointment to see the Head and to see round the school. You may find you are fobbed off with open days, registrars etc, and for big schools with large numbers of applicants this is an understandable way to start. It is, however, time-consuming for you: you have to meet the Head (and/or Housemistress/master) some time – no amount of wonderful buildings make up for a rotten Head.
3. On the day of your visit, get to the school early in order to sniff around. Approach children/staff and ask them anything (eg Where is the main school notice board?) – it's amazing how telling their replies can be.

WHAT TO LOOK OUT FOR
Bearing of pupils – politeness, neatness etc. Bearing of staff, ditto. Do they look clean, bright-eyed and enthusiastic (or whatever you like)? Attitude of pupils to staff and vice versa. Does the Head know who they all are (you'd be surprised)? Do pupils flatten themselves against the wall as Head passes? Do they flatten him/her against the wall as *they* pass? Is the atmosphere happy? Fraught? Coerced or co-opted? Do you fall over pupils canoodling in corners? How many are slumped in front of the television? Do the drains smell? What is the state of the paintwork, etc – a glance at the ceiling will usually tell (not that it matters per se). Grab an exercise book or three in passing and look at the standard of work and standard of marking – this can tell you an enormous amount. Check the size of teaching groups – it's amazing how often numbers do not tally with the official version. What is the average age of staff? All old can mean not enough dynamic new ideas; all young can mean too inexperienced and also, possibly too transitory. Observe the state of the library: rows of dusty tomes look impressive, but bright new dog-eared is healthier. Look at noticeboards for signs of plenty going on.

QUESTIONS TO HAVE UP YOUR SLEEVE

1. What is the size of Sixth Form? This is a dead giveaway to the academic strength of the school.
2. What are results like? This is one for the Head. NB It is best to work your way up to this as it tends to stir them up. Monitor the speed of producing the results and/or not producing them. Schools of 'mixed ability' often feel, with reason, that the school will be unfairly judged by apparent weakness of results. However, you need to know a) how 'mixed' the school is, and b) which are the weak departments. Beware of statistics: 100% in Russian could mean they have one keen pupil whose father happens to be professor of Modern Languages at the nearby university. You need a) number of candidates sitting the exams, b) number of subjects taken altogether, c) numbers of passes split into A B C etc.
3. How do they monitor progress? School reports? Points systems? Incentives?
4. What is the size of classes – biggest and smallest?
5. What is the ratio of full-time teaching staff to pupils? How many part-timers are there?
6. What is the turnover of staff – do too many stay too long? NB You are unlikely to get a straight answer on this.
7. Which exam boards are taken?
8. What is the size of the library budget? What arrangements are there for getting new books/ papers?
9. What emphasis is there on religious teaching?
10. How are pupils selected? What are they looking for in pupils?
11. What special projects are currently on the go?
12. Does the school have special help on tap for learning difficulties?
13. How many pupils leave after GCSE? How many are imported into the Sixth Form from outside? (This probably will affect the school's results, and needs to be looked at with a cynical eye, ie they may be reaping the benefits of another school's hard work.)
14. What is the pressure of work? Amount of work? Homework? Setting? Streaming?
15. Who are the pupils and where do they come from? (Both geographically and socially.) How many ex patriot children are there? How many non-Brits and, in particular, how many non-Brits whose first language is not English? Too many of the latter can grind teaching to a halt – very few schools can afford to cater for them separately. How many are the children of old boys, old girls?
16. Where do pupils go on to?
17. What is the careers advice like?
18. What scholarships are available and won? What bursaries and provisions available when finances come adrift?
19. The cost: fees, plus real cost, ie size of bill? 'Extras' are usually listed on a separate sheet of paper (because they constantly rise), and tucked into the back of the prospectus.
20. Are games compulsory?
21. What extras are on offer? Can they really deliver? A small school offering dozens of extras is probably doing none of them very well. Ask pupils how difficult it is to get a go at the most popular options. How many learn a musical instrument, and for how long?
22. Who owns the school? If privately owned – and about 10% of the ISIS schools are – are there any checks and balances (eg governors, PTA)? And who is going to take over?
23. What is the Head's attitude to discipline? Drugs? Sex? Bullying? Alcohol? Homosexuality? Stealing? Breaking the more petty school rules? What form do punishments take? Are prefects allowed to mete it out? Ask for a copy of the school rules – this can be illuminating. How many people have been expelled/asked to leave/suspended in the last two years? (This could pinpoint specific major problems.)
24. What are the present numbers in the school and capacity? Acreage?
25. What is the structure of school houses, if any? What is the school's hierarchy?
26. Is there any privacy for boarders? Is there a shadowing system for new pupils, particularly at boarding schools?
27. Does the school feel responsible for pupils once they are accepted – or will it fire misfits/slow learners if they don't shape up quickly?
28. How much pocket money is suggested? A vital question, this.
29. How accessible are pupils by telephone in boarding schools?
30. What is the temperature in the school in winter? (A question particularly for Scottish schools.)
31. Who would not be happy at the school?
32. What is the pastoral care like and how does it work? Who is responsible to whom, and can problems be spotted early?
33. How good is the health care? Do they notice if the pupils skip meals? Is there a cafeteria system or table laid and 'table talk'? How much fresh, raw food is there?
34. Is there a second-hand shop?
35. Is this a *Neighbours*-watching school and what is the school's attitude to television?
36. Are there holiday reading lists and is there holiday homework ever? Never?

37. What are the strengths of this school and weaknesses? (Always interesting to hear the answer to this.)
38. What is the Head trying to achieve in the school? What is his/her history? What does he/she regard as most important?
39. Until when is the Head 'contracted' (ie is he/she about to leave). Is he/she married? With children (ie hands on experience)?
40. What does the Head really want for his/her pupils in the long term? This is your key question.

QUESTIONS FOR PUPILS
1. What is the food like?
2. What is the matron like? Which members of staff do they like best?
3. Which subjects do they like best?
4. What don't they like about the school?
5. What do they like best about the school?

QUESTION FOR NEAREST LOCAL SHOP
What is the school like from the locals' point of view?

THOUGHTS FOR PARENTS
What are you really looking for in a school? Before you start on your hunt, make an honest list for yourself of everything that occurs to you, however ambitious, frivolous or peripheral it may seem. Your list may include, for example: happiness, safety, beauty of architecture, Daddy's old school, stepping stone to university, very local, very convenient, exeats that fit in with your career, offers Japanese. What do you feel about punishment? Are you looking for a traditional approach, or something new and exciting? What do you really feel about co-education? Single sex? Day or boarding? Town or country?

Beware the danger of judging a school exclusively by the bottom end because your child is young – look at the end product. Is there a member of staff at the school who is on the same wave length as yourself? There must be someone you can turn to.

See several schools – it's a process of elimination and comparisons are vital to make. Go by your gut reaction. How did you get on with the Head? Did he/she appear in control of the situation? The Head really does make or break a school.

Finally and most importantly, what is your child really like? This is your starting point for finding the school to suit him/her rather than you. Never lose sight of this, even though it may involve change at inconvenient stages.

A HEAD'S VIEW
A Head has very kindly sent us the following comments on the view from the other side of the study door. The comments obviously won't apply to every school, but it is a good idea to pause and consider what he/she may be thinking.

'Many parents are apologetic when they visit. The old fear of the Head comes out at times like this – sometimes with cause! I remain convinced that this is some of the most usefully spent time in my day. For me it is an opportunity to learn a good deal about the parents, and about the child.

'Some thoughts on what parents might do to help themselves: Do read the prospectus carefully immediately before you visit – don't waste time on covering old ground. Be prepared to talk about hopes and realities, difficulties and concerns. Be willing to accept that, hard as we try, we are not perfect. Don't try to box us into corners which make us claim to be omnipotent and omniscient. Only fools or charlatans would claim to be either, and I doubt whether such a person would be a good Head! As you tour the school, remember that we are not a Trade Exhibition or a production line – we are a community of people, living and working together, warts and all.

'Don't be frightened to ask "silly" questions. If they matter to you, then ask them. Don't despair if your child interviews badly – however relaxed we try to make it, this is a very daunting experience for him/her. We do make allowances. As you build up a picture of us from different sources, so we too build our view, based on what we talk about and from our contacts with junior schools. Do be honest about your visits to other schools; and ultimately do be honest about which school is your first choice.

'Don't be bemused by facilities and exam results. Facilities are only as good as the use to which they are put by all members of the community. Exam results reflect both the ability of pupils and staff, and issues such as entry policy. Judicious withdrawal of weak candidates may not do much for the candidate but can do wonders for percentage pass rates! Most parents are concerned for the whole child – this is the most difficult thing to assess on a visit; but it is surely the most important. Make sure that you meet current pupils if at all possible.'

PAYING UP

Schools in this country are mostly state funded, ie paid for by the government from taxes. A small proportion are private, funded mostly from fees paid by parents, but also indirectly by the state, given that most private schools enjoy charitable status. (Approximately eight per cent of children in education are at fee paying schools.) Fees range from about £700-£2,300 per term for a day pupil – with wide variations depending on the age of the child, the staff/pupil ratio and so on – and £1,700-£3,500 or more per term for boarding. Given these astronomic sums, most people turn, sooner or later, to one or more of the following:

i) **Granny or Grandaddy** They may be able to make money over to your children by Deed of Covenant, which is tax-efficient, or they may be able to raise a mortgage on their house, to be repaid out of the sale of their house on their death (for example). Grandparents are the number one source of school fees.

ii) **Lloyd's** Though members are currently looking very jaundiced about the state of this institution.

iii) **Extra mortgage on parents' house.**

iv) **'Composition' fees and other schemes offered by the schools themselves, or by an insurance broker** A typical composition scheme quoted for a six-month old starting boarding school in September 2004 showed the grandfather stumping up £10,000 in a lump sum given to the Bursar of the school in question today to produce a guaranteed £32,000 by the age of 13. An independent broker quoted a better return of £37,000 by shopping around, and commented that you should do even better – about £44,000. The danger of composition schemes is that they are politically vulnerable (the Labour Party are planning to 'withdraw' the charitable status of schools as soon as they come to power 'except centres of Excellence'), and, of course, vulnerable to your child not going to the school in question (though you would get something back) or being expelled half way through.

v) **Scholarships** These are to attract the academically bright or specifically talented child (art, music etc) and they vary in amount. There is currently a move afoot (spearheaded by HMC schools) to spread scholarship funds more widely, on the principle that parents of scholarship awards can often afford fees, and that schools must be mindful of their charity status. Thus the largest scholarship award at age 13 is now 50% of the full fees, except for schools whose statutes do not allow change of this sort. The remaining funds now go directly into bursaries, the idea being that, come the Labour Party, the schools can point to *large* numbers of pupils being helped, in a charitable sort of way.

Beware, if you are skint, of the supermarket approach: £200 off may seem good news, but you still have to find a great deal more.

vi) **Bursaries** Usually for helping out the impoverished but deserving, and those fallen on hard times. We have listed them as far as possible under each school, but a more complete collection will be found in the *Public and Preparatory Schools Yearbook*, which is published annually and can be found in libraries.

vii) **Assisted Places** These are offered by HMCG for children of deserving poor who might 'benefit' from private education. The scheme is means-tested, and getting into a school on an Assisted Place depends entirely on the say-so of the Head. Not surprisingly, the scheme is controversial and is another wheeze Labour means to do away with.

PLAYING THE SYSTEM

It helps, when planning your child's journey through the maze of state and private schools, to know the main stages of jumping from one to the other. Advantages of state education are: usually close by, part of community, school bus operates in country areas, avoiding need to become full-time driver, broad social mix, avoidance of school fees, possibly greater understanding at the end of it. Advantages of private system are: greater chance of doing well in public exams, wider range of extras, opportunity to study elite subjects such as Latin, opportunity to board and all that that implies.

Eight Prep School starts in the private sector. If you have a boy headed for the private system, you may need to take him out of the state system at this stage in order to fit in with the changeover at 13 and to get in enough coaching to pass the entry exam (see below).

Eleven Move to grammar school, both state and private. These are by definition selective, and a wheeze used by some parents is to put children into private schools until age of 11 in order to train them up for getting into the state grammar of their choice – thus avoiding fees thereafter.

Girls may move from the state system to the private one at this stage, which can work well as there is a 'break' in both state and private systems here. Extra tuition may be needed in English and Maths – coaching after school is the answer.

Thirteen (or thereabouts) Move to most private secondary schools for boys (public schools) and to private co-educational establishments.

Move to secondary state schools. The important thing here is to be in the right *geographical* place at the right time to qualify for entry to good/popular ones, which are increasingly oversubscribed.

NB One or two public schools have arrangement to take state school children at 11 in order to coach them up for entry proper at 13.

Sixteen Once GCSE is over, all change is possible: girls may move from state schools to private ones to gain access to a proper Sixth form. Both boys and girls may move to state Sixth Form colleges as petty restrictions begin to irk (and parents heave a sigh of relief at saving of school fees).

NB If it looks as though A-level may be a struggle for your child, and he/she has set heart on university, it is possible (though the logistics may defeat you!) to change from the English exam system to the Scottish one of 'Highers'. This is much more broadly based – more subjects at a slightly lower level – and is now accepted by many English as well as all Scottish universities.

ADDRESSES AND BOOKS

The Department of Education and Science, Elizabeth House, York Road, London SE1 7PH Tel: (071) 934 9000. This has a helpful information division which will give you the names of schools, pressure groups and leaflets on eg how to apply for Assisted Places. Tel: (071) 934 9140 or 934 9007.

The Good Schools Guide Advisory Service (GSGAS), 59A Cadogan Street, London SW3 2QJ Tel: (071) 821 8140 run by the authors of the Good Schools Guide, to advise parents on various aspects of their children's education, including choosing the right school.

The Independent Schools Information Service (ISIS), 56 Buckingham Gate, London SW1E 6AG Tel: (071) 630 8790. This is the information and propaganda arm of the private sector.

For information on specific state schools, either telephone the county or borough concerned (eg Westminster City Council, Suffolk Education Authority) or the school direct.

The Educational Grants Advisory Service, Brockhill Lodge, The Wyche, West Malvern Road, West Malvern, Worcestershire WR14 4EJ (no telephone number given) will provide information on charities for parents who wish to send their children to fee-paying schools but cannot afford the fees. This service is part of ISIS.

For help on educational problems, eg dyslexia, misfits, behaviour, local authorities are usually excellent. Also worth knowing about are:

The Tavistock Clinic, 120 Belsize Lane, London NW3 5BA Tel: (071) 435 7111.

The Learning Centre, 89 Parkway, London NW1 7PP Tel: (071) 482 5854. Small, privately-owned, expensive, but good.

Helen Arkell Dyslexia Centre, Frensham, Farnham, Surrey GU10 3BW Tel: Frensham (025125) 2400.

McLure House Education Centre, 103 Pierrefondes Avenue, Farnborough, Hampshire Tel: Farnborough (0252) 370330.

The National Association for Gifted Children, Park Compass, Boughton Green Road, Northhampton NN2 7AL Tel: (0604) 792 300. Gives advice for parents with exceptionally bright children.

The private schools' 'bible' is *The Independent Schools' Yearbook* (A & C Black) published in two vols, one for boys, co-ed and preparatory schools, the other for girls. This is like a huge collection of prospectuses. Beware of books with entries written by the schools themselves. *Choosing Your Independent School* (published by ISIS) is useful for getting names and addresses and general information.

SPECIALIST SCHOOLS FOR CHILDREN WITH LEARNING DIFFICULTIES

Edington School, Mark Road, Burtle, Bridgwater, Somerset TA7 9NJ Tel: Bridgwater (0278) 722012 (Boys ages 8-13).

Fairley House School, 44 Bark Place, London W2 4AT Tel: (071) 229 0977 (Boys and girls ages 5-11).

Hornsby House School, Kyrle Road, London SW11 6JX Tel: (071) 924 3521 (Boys and girls, ages 4-11).

Kinloss School, Martley, Worcestershire WR6 6QB Tel: (0886) 888 223 (Boys ages 11-18).

Stanbridge Earls School, Romsey, Hampshire S051 9ZS Tel: (0794) 512323 (Boys and girls ages 13-18).

CRAMMERS AND TUTORIAL COLLEGES

The following offer high standards of teaching to very small groups, and most teach both GCSE and A-level; also Easter revision courses. Useful for re-takes (one term or one year), or full two-year courses. Phenomenally expensive, they usually charge per subject, and do not offer extra curricular activities. Much used by pupils who have fallen foul of school rules, others who have 'grown out' of school, have been ill, moved house, dropped out etc, and popular with English speaking foreigners who do not want a traditional English school. Beware the underworld of the rebellious and the super rich.

Abbey Tutorial College, 6-12 Fountain Street, Manchester M1 7DS Tel: (061) 273 4446 (A-level Maths and Sciences only).

Collingham's, 23 Collingham Gardens, London SW5 OHL Tel: (071) 244 7414.

Davies, Laing & Dick, 10 Pembridge Square, London W2 4ED Tel: (071) 727 2797.

d'Overbroeks, 15 St Giles, Oxford OX1 3JS Tel: (0865) 310000.

Mander Portman Woodward, 5 Wetherby Place, London SW7 4NX Tel: (071) 835 1355. Also branches in Birmingham, Bristol and Cambridge.

The Edinburgh Tutorial College, 29 Chester Street, Edinburgh 3 Tel: (031) 225 9888.

ABBREVIATIONS

A-level   General Certificate of Education, Advanced (Secondary) level

AS   Advanced Supplementary (equivalent to half an A-level)

BA   Bachelor of Arts

BD   Bachelor of Divinity

BSc   Bachelor of Science

CSYS   Certificate of Sixth Year Studies (used occasionally in Scotland)

CCF   Combined Cadet Force

CDT   Craft, Design and Technology

C of E   Church of England

C of S   Church of Scotland

D of E   Duke of Edinburgh award scheme

DES   Department of Education and Science

DPhil   Doctor of Philosophy

DT   Design Technology

FP   Former Pupil (Scot)

FRS   Fellow of the Royal Society

GAP   Work experience projects in year between school and university. Also name of organization specializing in this.

GCSE   General Certificate of Secondary Education

GPDST   Girls' Public Day School Trust, a foundation of private schools consisting of 24 members, almost all at secondary level

GSA   Girls' Schools' Association – female equivalent of HMC (see below)

HMC   Headmasters' Conference – a sort of Headmasters' trades union, with 230ish public schools whose Heads belong, and considered 'top' by those in it

IAPS   Incorporated Association of Preparatory Schools, which includes Heads of some 550 prep schools

IQ   Intelligence Quotient

ISCO   Independent Schools Careers Organisation

ISIS   Independent Schools Information Service

IT   Information Technology

JET   Joint Educational Trust

JMB   Joint Matriculation Board

MA   Master of Arts

MSc   Master of Science

Non-denom   Non-denominational

OB   Old Boy

OG   Old Girl

OTT   Over The Top

PE   Physical Education

PGCE   Postgraduate Certificate of Education

PhD   Doctor of Philosophy

PT   Physical Training

RC   Roman Catholic

RE   Religious Education

RI   Religious Instruction

SHMIS   Society of Headmasters of Independent Schools – another sort of Heads' union

TLC   Tender Loving Care

VR   Verbal reasoning

YE   Young Enterprise (hands-on business studies course)

PREPARATORY SCHOOLS

ABBERLEY HALL
Worcester WR6 6DD
TEL Great Witley (0299) 896275

Pupils: 209 boys • 188 board, 21 day • Ages: 8-13 • Pre-prep 41 boys, 26 girls, all day, ages 4—8 • C of E • Fee-paying.

HEAD Since 1974 Mr Michael V D Haggard MA Cantab (fifties). Educated at Winchester and Magdalene College, Cambridge. Previously Head at Eagle House, Camberley. Charming and humorous, works closely with Assistant Head David Birt.

Entrance No exam, but very definitely on (friendly) interview, ie suitable for bright boys. Book well ahead. A handful of scholarships and awards offered.

Exit Shrewsbury the number one choice, always a handful to Eton, Winchester, Harrow, Radley and lesser schools. NB Very careful advice given by Head.

Remarks Numbers will be down, by intent, to 195 in 1992 in order to take pressure off slightly over-crowded dorms, and chapel, despite obvious financial advantages of larger numbers and big demand for places. 'It's easier to increase than decrease' observes Mr Haggard. Exceptionally good teaching with very high teacher/boy ratio. Head (married with children) keen collector of single staff, who are notably lively, and not averse to occasional acrimonious disputes/discussions in the common room. Common room is a misnomer: breaks are taken around covered snooker tables, overlooked by antlers and oil paintings, in the hall of remarkable Victorian country house.

All children do two years at one level (four levels spread over five years), usually at the top end, occasionally at bottom. There may be a two-year age span in any one class. Three or four sets. Surprisingly small library. Peculiar and interesting timetable, endlessly being tinkered with. Six periods in the morning (30 minutes each), two lessons directly after lunch *every* term, then out for games at 3pm. Fairly strong emphasis on games, boys put in for local and regional championships (even ping pong). All manner of activities mostly going full blast. CDT strong, run by Peter Huxtable, recent winner of Duke of Edinburgh Designers Prize. Astro-turf sports hall and three new classrooms recently built in marked contrast to peeling wallpaper and fine crumbling stucco work of main house.

Interesting mix of liberal and formal—no uniform leads to occasional criticisms of 'scruffiness' from parents, but discipline is most certainly there and high standards evident in everything. Head banned staff from smoking except in own rooms and outdoors three years ago, and simultaneously banned tuck, though boys may buy two items on Saturdays, 'It's fairer.' Own pre-prep, (with girls too). Boys kept busy, noticeably confident and happy atmosphere. Tangible enthusiasm. School set in 90 acres of stunning country, overlooked by bizarre clocktower. No prospectus, school mag speaks for the place instead. Anthony Quayle and Sir Geoffrey Howe old boys.

ABERLOUR HOUSE
Aberlour, Banffshire, Scotland AB3 9LJ
TEL Aberlour (0340) 871267

Pupils: 138 pupils, approx two-thirds boys, one-third girls • All board except about a dozen • Ages: 7-13 • Non-denom • Fee-paying.

HEAD Interregnum, Mr David Hanson. New Head appointed and takes over in January 1992. He is Mr

John Caithness MA (forties), educated at Merchiston and St Andrew's, where he read General Arts. Currently head of Catteral—the prep school for Giggleswick.

Remarks School started 1936 as junior school to Gordonstoun, in converted stately home, with Kurt Hahn philosophy. Complete social mix of pupils. Fees on a sliding scale. Large numbers from overseas, mostly ex pats. Scholarships for string players. Most go straight on to Gordonstoun, one or two to Rannoch and elsewhere. Life is outward bound—fresh and healthy. Impossible to comment, as school in a state of flux at time of writing.

ALL HALLOWS
Cranmore Hall, Shepton Mallet, Somerset
BA4 4SF
TEL Cranmore (074 988) 227

Pupils: 161 boys, 104 girls ● Own pre-prep with 40, ages 4-6
● 123 board, 142 day ● Ages: 7-13 ● RC (though half the
pupils are not) ● Fee-paying.

HEAD Since 1971, Mr Paul Ketterer BA, PhL educated St Edmund's Ware, London University, and Univ Gregoriana, Rome. Previously housemaster at the Oratory. Four children (mostly grown up), jolly wife; avuncular, deeply committed. Nicknamed 'the Pimpernel' by his secretary, 'Because she never knows where I'll be.' Well known for turning up unexpectedly. Sees his main job as 'oiling the wheels'.

Entrance Interview and test, report from previous school once accepted, and via own pre-prep.

Exit 44 schools over last 10 years: boys mainly to Downside, also Worth, the Oratory; girls (mostly at 13) to Mayfield, St Mary's Shaftesbury, Leweston. Boys and girls to Millfield, Bryanston, Prior Park.

Remarks Explosion of day pupils in last three years. Was once the prep school for Downside (old boys include Auberon Waugh), school went co-ed in 1972. Head keenly aware that market forces will dictate, but does not want the boarding element to drop. Wide ability range, and good record of scholarships. At the top end, brightest pupils do Greek for last three years.

Setting in paired subjects (Maths and Science, History and Geography, English and French) on the principle that a child may be specially good in some, but not all, fields. Probably better for brighter children (though a few parents think the really bright could be further stretched), and there is an exceptionally good special needs department, run by Mrs Ann Crowcombe, with plenty of help fed in regularly and early.

Three-weekly orders; computers in every main classroom, linked to central system. Good music; sports could be better, according to keenly sporting pupils. Better art facilities badly needed (and next in line, along with new labs). Very strong on pastoral care (especially for boarders)—HWC (Handle With Care) note in staff room referring to pupil/s currently in need. Very pleasant house (originally the Paget family home) with stone balustrade, hanging flower baskets, log burning fires in library and music room; stables well converted to classrooms, new chapel doubles as theatre hall, has large windows overlooking games fields.

Saturday morning school, no fixed exeats, children may return Sunday evening or early Monday morning, and parents encouraged to come in any time for meals. Weakness: with such a fluid system, and so many day children, weekends are a source of complaint for some fully fledged boarders. Like other preps with their own pre-preps *in situ*, there is also a likelihood of pupils being too long in one place. That said, this is traditional prep school education of the best kind, and happy sunny faces abound. Sincerely Christian values matter here: school definitely not suited to materialistic or atheist parents.

ARDVRECK SCHOOL
Crieff, Perthshire, Scotland PH7 4EX
TEL Crieff (0764) 3112

Pupils: 89 boys, 50 girls ● 120 board, 19 day ● Ages: 7-13
● Interdenom ● Fee-paying

HEAD Since September 1990, Mr Jeremy Bridgeland MA Oxon (forties). Comes from Gordonstoun, where he was considered one of the best Housemasters—though it is early days to judge him as Headmaster. Before that, Mr Bridgeland was Master at

Shrewsbury—strange progression. Teaches science and his wife, Yvonne B Ed Oxon, also works in the school and helps with some tuition.

Remarks Serves a local need for boys' prep boarding school in this area. Gamesy—strong rugby and netball teams. Indoor shooting range, and shooting is 'par excellence in Britain'. Outdoor swimming pool. Good on country dancing, cubs, scouts, and shinning up the local mountain on a good day—'doing a Barvick'. Good keen teaching staff with splendid director of music and new music building. Considered locally to be the 'thinking Scot's Scottish prep school'.

Housed in purpose built Gothic in 1883 with new blocks dotted about the garden, including two 'half way' houses for older children. School founded by W E Frost, who was sub-warden of Glenalmond 'to foster patience, obedience and unselfishness in boys'— and we believe it still does that. Very strong links still with Glanalmond and boys go on principally to Glenalmond, Gordonstoun and Strathallan. Pupils the children of local businessmen, professionals and gent farmers—smart little list.

Dormitories for younger boys freezing and conspicuous lack of Jeyes' fluid in loos when we visited, and children white and stick-like as result of recent bug. Walls plastered with fishing posters and snapshots of the big one which didn't get away.

ASHDELL PREPARATORY SCHOOL

226 Fulwood Road, Sheffield S10 3BL
TEL Sheffield (0742) 663835

Pupils: Approx 125 girls • All day • Ages: 4-13 (formerly 3-11) • C of E • Fee-paying.

HEAD Since 1984, Mrs Jane Upton (forties), brought up in Cumbria, further education in France, teacher training in Sheffield. Married, husband is Deputy Head of Silverdale School in Sheffield—a powerful couple in Sheffield educational circles. Gentle, inspiring, tireless, forthright, sense of humour. Ambitious that the school should be 'excellent in what it does best', and for this reason has policy not to

increase numbers radically. Runs the school by the seat of her pants—at her post or round about all hours, has no Deputy. Comments that when she took on the job she had 'no idea how all-consuming and thrilling it would be'.

Entrance Parents are interviewed 'to see how much they are doing and what they want', and if their aim is the local comprehensive then she advises them *not* to come here, as being unfair on the child. Then child is interviewed and tested for ability. Register any time.

Exit Girls' boarding schools, Oakham, half to Sheffield High.

Remarks Rare commodity in this area—a 'proper' girls' prep school with the feel of a boarding school—doors open at 7.30am and gym club was still going on when we left at 5pm. Standard of handwriting unsurpassed—five-year olds turning in performances which would not discredit someone twice that age—and school regularly wins competitions. Mrs Upton reckons to achieve 'very high standards', academically speaking. School currently packed to the seams, but acquisition of new mid-Victorian building behind the current site on Fulwood Road (nice views over Sheffield, and near 'brother' school of Westbourne Prep) will ease the situation as well as providing extra classrooms to accommodate the 11-13 year olds. Coaching given not only to those falling behind in the race, but also to the extra bright ('it is unfair not to'). Parents are doctors (local hospitals very handy), lawyers, landed and builders etc. Children well behaved and good mannered, perhaps a bit subdued and lacking in zip, laden with briefcases and musical instruments. All children get chance to experience a week's boarding while in the school—ostensibly abseiling or whatever but the 'hidden curriculum' being to introduce them gently to life away from home.

School founded in 1949 as a dame school by coal and steel baronet Roberts, now charitable trust. Cheery cherry red jackets and boaters with snowdrop crest—' a humble flower, and the first sign of spring'.

ASHDOWN HOUSE
Forest Row, East Sussex RH18 5JY
TEL Forest Row (034 282) 2574

Pupils: 120 boys, 40 girls • All board except for 11 pupils • Ages: 7-13 • C of E • Fee-paying.

HEAD   Since 1976, Mr Clive Williams MA Cantab (forties) educated at Eton and Cambridge. Taught at Elstree before joining Ashdown (he is an Old Boy), contracted until 2004. Charming and diffident, he teaches 22 periods a week (more than most)—Classics, 'Greek for the bright', English and Scripture. His wife Rowena runs the domestic side and does some teaching too. Head thinks 'Maths perhaps the most important subject of all.' Very excited about latest purchase—a fab chateau in Normandy where pupils will spend regular two week periods, attending local school in Calvados.

Entrance   Interviews one year ahead, names put down three years in advance of entry. 50% from London, 20% overseas, 'handful of foreigners', 20% local, rest scattered. Quite a number of Head's friends' children.

Exit   The usual smart places. Girls ditto.

Remarks   Trad prep school (baths in rows), mixture of bunks and beds, duvets, girls in separate part of house, with some chez les Williams with Hubert the dog and Pybus the black pig who was anticipating motherhood when we visited. Gorgeous Grade II country house overlooking the Downs, with decent extensions round the back (including staff houses). Classes average 15, streamed after two years, scholarship class at top (regular scholarships), can cope with mild dyslexia (good unit). Hot on French (lots of one to one conversations), strong drama and music, good art, CDT, IT, new classroom block and centenary building with vast theatre and comfy chairs (used for assemblies too). Huge dining hall (super food), and new extension to tiny-wee chapel under construction—a most unusual departure from normal building programmes. Unbeaten soccer team at time of writing, outdoor swimming pool, and mega gym.

AYSGARTH SCHOOL
Bedale, North Yorkshire DL8 1TF
TEL Bedale (0677) 50240

Pupils: 118 boys • Almost all board • Ages: 8-13 • C of E • Fee-paying.

HEAD   Since 1988, Mr John Hodgkinson MA Cantab (forties), married to Hilary, with three daughters. Previously housemaster at Uppingham and taught at Horris Hill. Teaches Modern Languages and Classics.

Entrance   By registration. Local Yorkshire landed families; strong Scottish contingent.

Exit   With the departure of the previous Head, the school has lost its strong Eton link, but still sends boys there (12 in two years). The majority to a variety of widely spread schools, including Radley, Gordonstoun, St David's and Bootham.

Remarks   Traditional building, purpose-built in 1877 and many modern extensions, not always in harmony. Lovely grounds—40 acres—with walled gardens and splendid views. There are now carpets in the dormitory passages and the bleak image is softening gradually. Quite a lot of new classrooms for computers, physics, technology. 24 basins in each of two bathrooms. Good remedial teaching. Usual games, including COW (Cricket On Wall). Music: five scholarships in last three years (Stowe and Bootham). Organ, two choirs, listed chapel.

   Once the unquestioned choice for northerners, but there was a serious wobble in the latter days of the previous Headship. Now firming up and parents are sounding more confident about the place.

BEAUDESERT PARK SCHOOL

*Minchinhampton, Stroud, Gloucestershire
GL6 9AF*

TEL Nailsworth (045383) 2072

Pupils: 180, 60 in pre-prep • Ratio of boys to girls 2:1 • 90 board, 90 day • Ages: 4-13 • Mostly C of E • Fee-paying.

HEAD Since 1970, Mr J C P Keyte (pronounced Keet) MA, (fifties), educated Radley, Trinity College, Dublin; teaches Maths (half time), two sons and married to Josephine (Frobel Cert) who teaches History and Scripture. Mr Keyte is the third generation to teach at the school, which was founded by his grandfather A H Richardson and became an Educational Trust in 1968. Urbane and modestly exuding confidence, Mr Keyte admits that 'the school is seriously over-subscribed at the moment' and he has no intention of expanding. Good parent rapport and 'terribly lucky with staff'.

Entrance The earlier the better. Very stiff competition, particularly tough on girls: only 15 admitted each year and 'Gloucestershire breeds more girls than boys'. Those who do not come up through the pre-prep visit in February.

Exit Lots to Malvern, Marlborough (local, you see), Eton, Radley, and Bloxham's. Girls go to Wycombe Abbey, Downe House, Cheltenham Ladies College, the local grammar school. The Berkshire/Wiltshire set. Good scholarship record.

Remarks School is perched at the top of a hideous wiggly drive up a ditto hill on the edge of the common (with golf course). Splendid Victorian Gothic with many additions (sympathetic Cotsworld stone at the front). New CDT last year, lots of computers, mega-gym with swimming pool in the making (tiled like Roman bath house). Deservedly popular, pupils are streamed, 'utterly happy' and well disciplined. Good art, lots of options, fabulous drama. Lots of weekly boarders—the Gloucestershire set: pupils spend the summer weekends playing polo. Most board for the last two years. Boarders locked in at night, but panic buttons everywhere. Can deal with dyslexia. Vegetarian meals available and salad on every table every day.

BELHAVEN HILL

Dunbar, East Lothian, Scotland EH42 1NN

TEL Dunbar (0368) 62785

Pupils: 85 boys • 80 board, 5 day • Ages: 8-13 (can take earlier if home conditions critical) • Non-denom • Fee-paying.

HEAD Since 1987, Mr Michael Osborne MA (forties), educated at Radley, read Economics at Cambridge (a qualified accountant), and considered by many to be 'the best teacher in Scotland'. Lives in grounds with his wife Laura, a landscape architect, and their two young sons. Popular Head — a Pied Piper, the boys love him (he knows his 32 times table and 57 times table, too!)

Entrance As early as possible. Boys spend a day at Belhaven the term before they come.

Exit In the last two years pupils have gone to the following: six to Glenalmond, including top scholarship and two exhibitions, five to Harrow, four to Merchiston, three each to Eton and Gordonstoun; one each to Ampleforth, Fettes, Loretto, Milton Abbey, Radley and Winchester.

Remarks School based in friendly late eighteenth-century sandstone house flanked by familiar hotchpotch of extra classrooms. Streamed at top end. Remedial help on hand. Dormitories under one roof, teddy bears, bunks, duvets and old tartan rugs. Magnificent sports hall which adapts to .22 range. Central heating at last installed. Well-kept grounds with two cricket pitches, new artificial slips, a putting course, and a nine-hole golf course. Pianos everywhere. Piping lessons by Mr McCreadie and Housemaster David Conran-Smith, whose wife Rosie is an outstanding Matron. Archery and carpentry are bothpopular. Regular trips to Hillend Ski Slope, shooting in winter, boys encouraged to have their own bit of garden.

A friendly school. Parents are encouraged to take a large part. Mostly upper-middle class.

BOUSFIELD PRIMARY SCHOOL

South Bolton Gardens, London SW5 0DJ

TEL London (071) 373 6544

Pupils: 200 boys, 200 girls ● *All day* ● *Ages: 5-11* ● *Non denom* ● *State.*

HEAD Mrs Vicky Plotkin, BSc (thirties), previously Head of a north London infants' school. Delightful, both gentle and firm.

Entrance First come, first served. Until recently, 20 per term, now a two-term entry.

Exit One-third go on to independent schools—Latymer, Putney High, Godolphin and Latymer, Queen's College, Queen's Gate, Westminster Under, Oratory head the list; state favourites are Holland Park and Sheen.

Remarks Deservedly popular and highly sought after primary school. English is not the first language of about one third of pupils: 29 languages spoken here (Arabic and French chief among them). Well run, fun strong on parental involvement. Bousfield busily fosters the creative arts—music is exceptional, so is art; theatrical productions are constantly on the go. No musical specialists within the school, but they buy them in, and several teachers, attracted by the school's ethos and good practice, are musicians and teach guitar, recorder etc. New Head has influenced discipline (though it was never seriously loose here)—very keen on good manners. She has also introduced homework policy, now obligatory for third and fourth years once a week, and children throughout the school take notebooks home regularly. Mrs Plotkin is busy improving Maths. Library books well used, well displayed, 'but there aren't enough' says Head. Children heading for private schools hereafter typically get outside boost on English and Maths. Classrooms bursting with colourful, creative project work.

School is on the site of Beatrix Potter's childhood home; built in 1956 (and won architectural prizes), with light airy classrooms (too small, sighs Head), and grass playing area, plus very large playground, the envy of local private schools. Central body of school consists of two large halls mirroring each other (for juniors and seniors), used for dance, productions, gym, assemblies etc. From 1992 Kensington & Chelsea will put Bousfield in full charge of budget; meanwhile, it works on a delegated budget system, whereby the Head, secretary and doorkeeper work out all payments, 'from staff to loo paper—so there's not much time for me to teach!' Nursery section to be built on in near future to everyone's excitement (and consternation of locals?).

BRAMBLETYE SCHOOL

East Grinstead, West Sussex RH19 3PD

TEL East Grinstead (0342) 321004

Pupils: about 215 boys ● *185 board, remaining day* ● *Ages: 7-13* ● *Pre-prep: 40 boys and girls, ages 4-8* ● *C of E* ● *Fee-paying*

HEAD Since 1969, Mr Donald Fowler-Watt MA Cantab (fifties). Educated Harrow and Cambridge. Teaches English. A pukka, jolly figure and good egg who aims to create 'a bastion of manners and courtesy and decent, high-principled boys'. Organizes a lot of societies and extra-curricular activities so boys have 'many things to hang their hats on'. Mrs F-W is in charge of the social and pastoral side.

Entrance Enter child's name at three (or earlier), very booked up, waiting lists till 1996. Child's academic standard checked by a 'comprehensive form filled in by the previous school earlier in the year'.

Exit Wide mix—36 boys to 17 different schools at the last count, Charterhouse heads the list, Harrow and King's Canterbury popular too.

Remarks A school other prep school Heads compliment. Set in lovely countryside, glorious views, buildings look a bit bleak and baronial even though just outside East Grinstead. Recently built arts centre comprising theatre and music school—looks like Starship Enterprise. Inside the school is cosy—lots of panelling and even, said one small boy 'Good Lord, they've lit the fire'. Until the 1930s was home of Abergavennys. Small dormitories and younger boys have their own block.

Serious games, dozens of matches, win more than

they lose on the whole, highly competitive. Heated pool all year round. Shooting, golf and fishing popular and boys are taught to tie their own flies by Mr Muggleton, who is a keen fisherman. Enthusiastic music—three-quarters play an instrument—including bagpipes. Art is *very strong*. Good facilities, mostly recently built and school does not appeal to parents for money: 'We use our own resources. It's a matter of pride'. Happy little stockbrokers in the making; parents drive Porsches and Volvos. Good reports.

BRAMCOTE SCHOOL
Filey Road, Scarborough, North Yorkshire YO11 2TU
TEL Scarborough (0273) 3773086

Pupils: 91 boys • *All board* • *Ages: 8-13* • *Inter-denom* • *Fee-paying.*

HEAD Since 1990, Mr John R Gerrard, BA Cert Ed (early fifties), educated RGS Lancaster, Christ's, Cambridge. Classicist. Has taught here since 1973. Wife teaches in the school too.

Entrance No entrance test.

Exit Most to Uppingham (including two music scholarships in 1990), also to Sedbergh and Repton.

Remarks A prep school that serves local needs. Keen music, with over 60 pupils playing for local 'over 60s' clubs, puppy shows, and the choir sings for weddings. Eight forms with average of 11 pupils each. One part-time teacher comes in three times a week to help with dyslexics. Keen games—Scarborough beach five minutes away. The school is housed in basically sprawling Victorian villas and looks like a seaside hotel.

BUTTERSTONE HOUSE SCHOOL
Meigle, Perthshire, Scotland PH12 8QY
TEL Meigle (08284) 528

Pupils: 61 girls • *All board except one or two girls in exceptional circumstances* • *Ages: 7-13* • *Interdenom* • *Fee-paying.*

HEAD Since 1986, Mr Christopher Syers-Gibson MA Cantab (fifties) via Wellesley House, St Michael's Choir School and Horris Hill. Teaches Latin and History. There 'til retirement', ably assisted by his wife, Anita (Cert Ed) who teaches general studies. Aims to produce 'well-rounded children' capable of tackling their next school with confidence.

Remarks The only all girls' boarding prep school in Scotland. Has had shadow over its future owing to housing problems, but has now raised money and hopes to move to above address in Autumn 1991.

CALDICOTT
Crown Lane, Farnham Royal, Buckinghamshire SL2 3SL
TEL Farnham Common (0753) 646214

Pupils: 250 boys • *160 board, 90 day* • *Ages: 7-13* • *C of E* • *Fee-paying*

HEAD Since 1968, Mr R P Wright, Dip Institut du Pantheon Paris (fifties). A 'man and boy' Head—OB of school, returned to teach French and, in time, to acquire the school, which is now a charitable trust. Head very keen on 'appearance, manners, showing appreciation and all sorts of old-fashioned things that seem to be thrown out of the window'.

Entrance By exam and half-hour interview.

Exit Has recently won scholarships to Wellington, Stowe, Bryanston, Bloxham, Radley, Winchester,

Eton, St Edward's and Pangbourne, and this is a good indication of where they go on.

Remarks   English prep school at which numbers have doubled since the prospectus was written. Feels traditional apart from the large numbers of day boys. Very convenient for Home County parents. School may not be a great intellectual power house, but lots of personal attention is given and classes are kept small. Setting beautiful. No wild spaces for boys to explore, Head regrets, but school adjoins acres and acres of open space.

Dormitories light and bright with mother-appeal, library inviting and comfortable, common rooms with pastel sofas. Proliferation of specialist buildings including most recently separate teaching blocks and assembly hall. In Head's study is a photograph of every new boy and Head does not envisage further enlargements to numbers, 'It's still a family school—I don't want it to become impersonal' (NB a very large family). Very strong on main stream games, in particular rugby and hockey. Music enthusiastic, good Head of Department and regularly wins around three music scholarships a year. Ritzy magazine with colour repro of rather good grown-up looking paintings. Drama also strong—sons of Tom and Miriam Stoppard, Nicol Williamson, Hayley Mills and Ben Cross were here in the last few years.

comments he 'approves of interesting ideas, knowing the parents and having the children around'. Frowns upon thoughtlessness, grumpiness and unkind comments.

Entrance   No longer guaranteed through Nursery and Pre-prep (v successful). Preference given to boarders: pupils encouraged to spend a day (and night) beforehand to 'get the feel of the place'.

Exit   Strong links with Glenalmond (first and second scholarships recently), Strathallan, St Leonard's (scholarship in 1990) and other Scottish schools. About five a year go south — 'but a significant five!' Last two years — Eton, Winchester, Oundle, Sedbergh.

Remarks   Pupils move round staff: computer studies, CDT unit, Latin and Greek as well as Art and Music (good). Remedial and scholarship classes. All pupils play games daily, huge choice. Continuing passion: hockey on newly floodlit all-weather court (gift from parents). Girls play netball (not brilliantly). Ski-ing at Hillend and regular trips to Aviemore. Bath/shower arrangements almost American. Airy dormitories with teddy bears and jazzy posters. Founded in 1873, though not on present site. Cargilfield is purpose built, with magnificent War Memorial chapel/theatre. Esentially a boarding prep school—day children can board when parents are away if space allows. Dynamic board of Governors. Bursaries available for older children.

CARGILFIELD SCHOOL
37 Barnton Avenue West, Edinburgh
EH4 6HU
TEL Edinburgh (031) 336 2207

Pupils: 70 boys, 30 girls   •   70 board, 30 day   •   Ages: 3-13+   •   Junior School: Pre-prep 43, Nursery 27   •   Non-denom   •   Fee-paying.

HEAD   Since 1991, Mr Alan Bateman MA (forties). Educated at Trinity College, Dublin. Came via Colet Court, Canadian Secondary Boarding Schools (Housemaster and Director of Admissions etc), and then on the staff at Cargilfield for five years. He teaches History and Religious Education. 'Balanced' by his wife Suzanne: the recent appointment was seen as very much a joint one by the Governors. Mr Bateman

CHEAM SCHOOL
Headley, Newbury, Berkshire RG15 8LD
TEL (0635) 268242

Pupils: Approx 140 boys   •   All board   •   Ages: 8-13   •   C of E   •   Fee-paying.

HEAD   Since 1985, Mr Chris Evers BA (forties), head boy of both the Dragon School and Rugby in his day. Affable and cosy, pipe smoking; 'perhaps lacking in energy' said a parent. Wife a driving force, two young children (at local pre-prep and girls' prep). Mrs Evers currently setting up Old boy network, hoping to net sons of OBs.

Entrance   By registration.

Exit   Not a feed, but regular batches to major public schools.

Remarks Traditional. Rudimentary secondary games. Tendency to concentrate on the bright and gamesy, at the expense of weaker brethren. CE kept firmly in sight all along the line. Day recently restructured to have six lessons every morning ('because the brain is better then'). Prep finished by 6.30, so the evenings can be for fun. 'Digest' three times a week, when boys go and read a book straight after lunch. Well designed boy sized library, with low shelves—boys often take out books and read them lying on the floor.

30% boys from London, 60% from within 50 mins, 10% ex pats. Fathers typically City men—and sons look like mini City lads, with attache brief cases. Dark blue naval jumpers. Boys unafraid of staff and have nice manners. Dorms now quite cosy with posters and teddies. Two new houses being built for staff.

School built as country house by Edwardian architect Detmar Blow, pleasantly faded cosy atmosphere, set in 85 acres with lovely woods, but one side very close by road gives somewhat suburban commuter-y feel.

Not the school it was.

CHRIST CHURCH SCHOOL
1 Robinson Street, London SW3 4AR

TEL London (071) 352 5708

Pupils: 210 boys and girls • All day • Ages: 5-11 • C of E • Voluntary aided, state.

HEAD Since 1985, Mr W N B Richardson DL (early forties), educated King Edward's Birmingham and Goldsmith's, University of London, where he did English and Education. Gentle and unassuming, fond of travel (Fellow of Royal Geographical Society) comments that he aims to produce children who are, 'as literate and numerate as they possibly can be, also equipped to cope with the multicultural and multi-faceted society we live in'.

Entrance Come and see the school and put your name down, then in the March before your child is to start, the school will send an application form. Complicated pecking order for places, starting with brothers or sisters of children in the school (top priority) and ending with 'children of parents who in sympathy with the aims of the school'—read the very comprehensive prospectus.

Exit Westminster City, Greycoats, St Margaret's Fulham and about 30% to private schools—JAGS, Francis Holland, Dulwich, Emanuel etc.

Remarks Founded 1840, now tucked away in a corner of Chelsea in the shadow of Christ Church, one of the churches with which the school is affiliated (the Rev Simon Acland is a foundation governor) and which it uses for services. Generous patron of school is Lord Cadogan, who recently gave the verger's house to the school to increase their space, though by inner London standards the school is not badly off—not only has reasonable sized playground but has also acquired a piece of land which the ILEA left empty for 25 years and has converted it in to courts and a grass area with benches. Cherry coloured uniform. Bright classes—top heavy with girls (boys still given private treatment in Chelsea). Approximately 40% of pupils from Chelsea, 24% from Battersea, 7% Pimlico—'less than 10% go to the country every weekend' (= a Chelsea definition of middle class)—very mixed intake. School is on partially delegated budget (ie, it takes responsibility for some expenditure) until April 1992, at which point it takes over entire financial control, in accordance with Mrs T's policies. School's particular strengths are Maths, English and Science—good Science and Technology departments. Everyone goes swimming in Chelsea baths. Music budget increased from April 1991. PE activities in the much-used school hall.

COLET COURT
Lonsdale Road, London SW13 9JT

TEL London (081) 748 3461

Pupils: 400 boys • 30 board, 370 day • Ages: 8-13 • C of E • Fee-paying.

HEAD Since 1973, Mr Billy Howard (fifties) MA Oxon. Educated at Winchester and New College, Oxford; previously Head at Northaw School. Teaches

Scripture and fills in. Has strong views on scholarship exams (he's against them). Self-assured and warmly spoken of. Better with children than adults. Retires 1992.

Entrance Lists close early, and names should be registered soon after birth. At 8, 150-200 boys sit probably the toughest exam of all preps for 72 places. Top 50 get places straight away, others are short-listed and come back for more tests, lessons, games: 'It's not unlike selection for the Foreign Office' says Head cheerfully. No longer has entrance at 10, but assisted places still available for up to 10 boys. Also music scholarships, including three choral ones.

Exit St Paul's the first choice—and a condition of entry to Colet Court. Boys tend to win substantial amount of St Paul's own scholarships. Teaching geared to carry boys straight into senior school, though a few go elsewhere.

Remarks Incredibly high academic standards, with some extremely good teaching and marvellous facilities, notably the science labs. Classes of 22 max, streamed in their third year (Greek for the scholars in the fifth year). Most boys self-starters, and sons of motivated achievers ('One's task is to restrain them')—the parents—says Head. Masses of media parents. School very tough on non-workers. Much sharing of facilities (and some staff) with St Paul's and acres of games fields. Excellent games and sports (the best of any London prep), *very* strong on music. DT for prep schools pioneered here; new facilities, and well-used. Public speaking and debating both very strong. Cut in boarding capacity, from Sept 1988, despite pressure on places, and subject to availability boys can board at any age. Choir schools apart, the only London prep to offer boarding. Extremely good about taking boys in even for a few nights during a crisis. Rare to hear criticism: one of London's strongest preps. Disadvantage is that boys who go on to St Paul's will be on the same premises for 10 years, from eight to 18.

COTHILL HOUSE
nr Abingdon, Oxfordshire OX13 6JL
TEL Frilford Heath (0865) 390800

Pupils: 220 boys • All board • Ages: 8-14 • C of E • Fee-paying.

HEAD Since 1975, Mr Adrian Richardson, Cert Ed Oxon (forties). Much respected by other Heads, very popular with parents and boys. Lovely wife who refers to 'our ghastly mad system of sending children away to board—so it must be as like home as possible', and three young children.

Entrance Early registration (aged four) advised. Interview and assessment, 'to encourage and reassure, not to eliminate'.

Exit Mainly to Radley, also Eton, Stowe ('for support'). Head pushes Oundle.

Remarks The most family feel of any prep school we visited—main building is large, white and uninstitutional, the way in is through the Richardson's part of the house, where new little boys are allowed through to play Lego, help cook etc. Cosy—and traditional too. Huge teddy count. Skate boards currently very popular, lots of clubs, library looks somewhat bookless (though every boy's bed has his reading book by it). Handsome modern teaching blocks; lots of female staff (grannies and young). Three streams, with Maths workshops to sort problems. Good CDT and Art, also good choir. Rifle range and golf course. Boys divided into Greeks, Romans etc, and competitively seek good markings, generously given (for everything from being tidy to good maths work). Every boy writes personal report at the end of term answering questions on books he's read, food, staff he likes etc.

Brilliant new acquisition (and the envy of many other schools) is the Château de Sauveterre near Toulouse, (set in 25 acres, Alps not far off), where all Cothill boys spend one term in their penultimate year. Girls getting in on the act too, sisters etc—the word is fast getting round among parents whose daughters take CE in January and consider a French term more worthwhile than another English one. Teaching at Sauveterre starts in English, and by the end everything is in French (staff are all French). This is a success story:

Head bought the house lock stock and barrel, chandeliers to table napkins. 'The boys come home with smiley faces—and better French', say delighted parents.

CROFTINLOAN SCHOOL
Pitlochry, Perthshire PH16 5JR
TEL Pitlochry (0796) 2057

Pupils: 61 boys, 38 girls ● *79 board, 20 day* ● *Ages: 7-13+* ● *Interdenom* ● *Fee-paying.*

HEAD Since 1978, Sir John (Ian) Maclure IAPS Diploma (fifties), assisted by his wife Jane. He is contracted till 60 and was previously at Horris Hill. The Maclures prefer to be known as Mr and Mrs Mac.

Remarks School has improved enormously under current regime. Not many OBs' pupils. Most parents from N Scotland. Baronial splendour and magical floodlit games pitch (the nights are long in winter). New music centre, art room, superb kiln, stage. Annual camps are run, in which activities include climbing, abseiling, rafting and outdoor cooking. Computer room is a recent addition. Keen drama and the pupils do everything including stage manage, operating lighting etc. Annual poetry recitation competition. Small dyslexic unit. Some assisted places. Smart tough little feed for Gordonstoun.

DRAGON SCHOOL
Bardwell Road, Oxford, OX2 6SS
TEL Oxford (0865) 311660

Pupils: 560 boys, 100 girls ● *260 boys board, 340 day boys* ● *Girls are all day* ● *Ages: 7-13+* ● *60 babies in Junior School (6-7 year olds)* ● *C of E* ● *Fee-paying*

HEAD Since September 1989, Mr Nigel Richardson (forties), educated at Highgate and Trinity Hall, Cambridge, where he read History. Married with young family. Previously Deputy Head of Uppingham and comments that he appears to be the only prep school Head who has run a senior school. Also comments that running a prep school is a great deal more complicated... First 'outside' Head for the Dragon—previous appointments were dynastic. Described as 'survivor of the year' by visiting Headmaster. Quiet, and has an entirely different style from the flamboyant previous Head.

Entrance By early registration—embryos OK—though immediate places often available at the last moment, owing to floating population of Oxford. Head in the process of rationalising the admission system—trying to make it fair, and to be seen to be fair, with assessment days, but not a competitive exam. 9-15 months ahead of term of entry, potential pupils come to the school. Oversubscribed. Easier to get in to board than day. Lots of pupils from abroad, particularly Hong Kong.

Exit To 95 different schools, including over 100 at Eton, large numbers to Magdalen College School, and to Abingdon and St Edward's Oxford, also a fair number to Marlborough, Radley and Winchester etc.

Remarks Despite terrific upheavals in wake of departure of previous Heads, Mr Ingram (Inky) and Mr Gover (Guv) as well as other senior members of staff taking early retirement to give him a clean slate, and the remainder having to get used to the shock horror of Head from 'outside' after Inky's 24-year reign, school maintains its position as number one in the Oxford area.

Projects image of informality—scruffy cords, the scruffier the better (jackets only worn by day boys) masters all called by Christian names and matrons known as 'Ma Wilson' etc. Wonderfully laissez-faire attitude to outward appearances, which charms the children, who feel that somebody somewhere is on their side. Underneath, however, the school is very disciplined with rigorous academic timetable and absolutely no messing about allowed in class. 6/7 streamed forms in each year after the first one, in which pupils have extra TLC in new (1989) baby house (day pupils only), new boarders (up to 24 in house) live with Housemaster and wife, cook, matron etc. 'Fast stream' approach frowned on, but school is still quite capable of moving a child up three forms at a jump if found to be below his/her ability level.

40-50 do Greek in each of the top two years, a little German on individual basis, French uses computers a lot (everyone uses computers quite a lot). Strong water sports—canoeing as well as sculling and punting. The day goes on for ever, even for day pupils, with options at 4.30pm and 'teaching preps' till 6-6.30pm.

Houses clustered round Bardwell Road in N Oxford down by Cherwell boathouse with 12 acres of playing fields and children are allowed to play by the river once they have demonstrated they can swim several lengths in their clothes. Lots of Dragon traditions, including distinguished magazine, fairs, 'Stooges dinner'—the list goes on for ever. Genuine co-ed—note the size of school, though each house is manageable size. A very exciting school to be at.

DULWICH COLLEGE PREPARATORY SCHOOL
42 Alleyn Park, London SE21 7AA
TEL London (081) 670 3217

Pupils: 737 boys, 11 day girls (ages: 3-4 only) • *40 board weekly, 681 day* • *Ages: 3-13* • *C of E* • *Fee-paying* • *(Once 'largest prep school in the Empire' but NB it is not the prep school of Dulwich College—Cranbrook is.)*

HEAD From September 1991, Mr George Marsh MA (forties), previously much loved head of Millfield Junior School, before that in the senior school and before that taught for eight years at the Dragon School, Oxford. Tactful, beady-eyed and built Millfield Junior School into one of the best prep schools in the country.

Entrance Through own (excellent and hard-to-get-into) nursery school, otherwise normally at five or seven, into cosy, lively infants' school on first come, first served basis (some assessment).

Exit Around one-third to Dulwich College, fair numbers to Westminster, Winchester, Tonbridge and other leading schools.

Remarks Parent involvement essential: they sign homework nightly, state duration of work, 'an invaluable means of communication,' noted one parent, 'you can tell them that Tom's struggling with his long division …' Instructions and orders from school to parents come thick and fast: 'take Tom to the airport/

museum etc'—another project under way. But: 'parents should note it has no mercy on the working couple'. Also, 'It's hopeless for week-enders, because Saturday mornings are often busy.' Four streamed forms in each year of main school, average size 22. Drama (lots of it) amazing. Music also excellent with 140 instrumentalists mustered for one bumper orchestral feast (normally two orchestras), with a plethora of choirs (including one for the parents) and, regularly, several music scholars. Lively, attractive art department produces dazzling props for drama productions—impressive technical mastery of drawing. School bookshop super—one of the best-stocked in country with boys given plenty of encouragement to read widely—run mainly by older boys.

This continues to be one of the strongest prep schools in the country: bracing, intellectually stimulating junior power-house. In spite of size, the scale is domestic, the atmosphere very friendly. Most controversy revolves around the vexed question of heavy streaming; no fun at 10 to be relegated to the 'D' stream and boys have been known to be affected by being down-graded and/or left behind (a criticism voiced by a high-flying Old Etonian as well as by a low-flying anxious single parent). Also, we have received a few murmurs that such strong pressure is not always healthy and leaves the boys precious little time to socialise and play. Very mixed bag, both socially and ethnically.

EDGARLEY HALL
(Millfield Junior School), Glastonbury, Somerset BA6 8LD
TEL Glastonbury (0458)32446

Pupils: Approx 280 boys, 220 girls • *Ages: 8-13 (junior school) and 4-8 (pre prep)* • *Interdenom* • *Fee-paying.*

HEAD From September 1991, Mr Richard Smyth MA (early forties), educated at Sherborne and St John's College, Oxford, where he read Theology, and PGCE from University College of North Wales. Previously Head of Terra Nova School in Cheshire. Keen on music and drama. Jovial. Takes over from Mr George Marsh, much lamented, and a very hard act to follow.

Entrance More than one-third of pupils receive bursaries ranging from 5-75% of the fees, depending on need and/or ability. Most awards are carried on to main school and exams for them (held late Feb early March for September entry) are always crammed. Standard fee payers accepted on interview and report from previous Head.

Exit 90% to Millfield. One or two to Bedales.

Remarks Aims for 20% bright pupils, 20% in need of remedial attention, three per cent 'highly talented sportsmen' and the rest 'normal'. One of three prep schools used by the National Association for Gifted Children in its survey on how the gifted are stimulated and developed. Pupils from all backgrounds—genuine comprehensive intake, everything from miners' sons to Maharajahs, one or two Henrys, lots of new money, lots of foreigners.

Atmosphere dynamic, and, commented a parent 'the pupils breathe the confidence of the place'. Informal, pleasant houses, charming grounds, pre-fabricated classrooms grouped around main building. Slightly scruffy. Navy uniform. Girls' boarding houses half a mile or so down the road (minibus ferries them back and forth), boys on campus. Children use facilities of senior school where necessary, including the indoor riding school.

Embarrassment of extras—over 40 possible activities a week, and constant stream of expeditions, excursions etc. Staff:pupil ratio (1:7/8) allows for heavy streaming and very small classes, which produce very high standards, even from the less able and those entering the school from state schools and from abroad. Five star resources, also many very competent teachers. Sport outstanding—regularly beats other schools in all major games, also in trampolining, swimming, riding etc. Music department has been built up by current director, Brian Armfield and is now outstanding. Note: large size of school by prep standards, but this is counteracted by small size of houses and some outstanding Housemasters/mistresses, excellent pastoral care and popular chaplain.

One of the best all-round prep schools in the country at time of writing.

EDGE GROVE
Aldenham, Hertfordshire WD2 8BL
TEL Radlett (09276) 5724

Pupils: 160 boys ● *100 board, 60 day* ● *Ages: 8-13* ● *C of E* ● *Fee-paying.*

HEAD Since 1985, Mr Jolyon Waterfield Cert Ed (fifties), who 'ran away to sea' at the age of 13 (actually, was in the navy for 27 years—submarine commander), then came to teach at Edge Grove, which was started by his father and by the father of the previous Head, Mr Jimmy Pratt, who lives just down the road and still teaches part time. Head avuncular and sensible. Nice wife, who works full time in school.

Entrance Registration and testette two terms before pupil is due to come into school—'but not an exam' comments Head, 'ie it is not competitive. It is quite wrong to examine at seven—and wicked that children should fail at that age.' Most pupils come from within one-hour radius of school. Over 10% of parents living abroad.

Exit A rich mix. Lots to Harrow (30 pupils at Harrow at time of writing), and to nearby Aldenham, some to Haileybury, one or two to Eton and then all over the place—Rannoch, Torquay Grammar, Bradfield etc.

Remarks Fine seventeenth-century building and grounds in apple pie order. Formerly the property of J P Morgan. Whole atmosphere of the place is more like a country house party than a prep school. Largest dormitory an elegance of wood panelling—and hence no posters. Wood floors, bags of spit and polish and flowers, no carpets. Head and family live 'over the shop', five star gardener has cottage in grounds. Back of buildings less prepossessing than front. Good modern Science block. Horizontal streaming—11 forms = As and Bs, and children are moved in middle of year, or earlier if up to it (the forced rhubarb approach). An open family school, which, said a parent, 'unlike some of them, gives some awareness of the real world'. Firm on discipline. Some cosy, extremely long- and loyal-serving staff. Good support team—parents bustle about. Strong music—three-quarters of pupils play what Mr Waterfield calls a 'proper' instrument'. Games played with enthusiasm but 'should not be taken too seriously', said Head, 'and the less able ones should be catered for as well'. School privately owned until 1988; now a charitable trust. Keen ski club.

Pupils have exquisite manners and *a propos* these Head comments that, though they have some jolly good academic successes, the important thing is 'being part of a team and getting on with other people'. And it is as important to say thank you for lunch as to say thank you for anything else. 'It is also important', he adds, 'that social barriers are chipped away at...'

ELSTREE SCHOOL
Woolhampton, Reading, Berkshire
RG7 5TD
TEL (0734) 713302

Pupils: 169 boys, and 3 staff daughters (only) • *124 board, 49 day* • *Ages: 7-13* • *C of E* • *Fee-paying.*

HEAD   Since 1969, Mr T B McMullen TD Cantab, (fifties), says he will stay 'at least another five years' (Jan 1991), previously Housemaster at Tonbridge and Assistant Master at Bramcote. A gentle, kind, good man with a quiet sense of humour who has just married his super school secretary, Margaret.

Entrance   Locals come daily (waiting list), though many end up boarding and there is usually 'a bed or two available for emergencies', 25% from London, and most of the rest from the Thames Valley (M25 a boon), a 'sprinkling from abroad'. No test.

Exit   About two-thirds to Radley, Bradfield, Eton and Harrow, (when Elstree was in Hertfordshire it was Harrow's own junior school); the rest to Winchester, Sherborne, Stowe, Milton Abbey and Pangbourne.

Remarks   Traditional public school owned and run by the Sanderson family since foundation in 1848, became an Educational Trust in 1961 since when four mega building programmes. Lots and lots of play space, marvellous new classrooms, dorms, dining room, etc. All very stylish (Basil Spence) and fits beautifully into glorious Queen Anne building (though Bernard Sunley-inspired ceiling in Nelson room seriously suspect in colour).

Streaming, setting for senior classes and good teaching for dyslexics. Scholarship class at top, and seriously good French still via the traditional Mr Thomas. Design and Technology, and computer room (IT) as well as computers 'dotted around everywhere', the 21st Century is not a problem here. Marks for effort first, but lots of flexibility, boys happy and charming ('hoped I'd enjoyed my afternoon'). Lots of games, rugby, football and hockey throughout the two winter terms as well as squash, shooting and golf on own course. Strong tennis. Good art and music (boys do a musical every year, designing the stage sets themselves).

Lines given for naughtiness, but really wicked boys are 'talked to and made to see the error of their ways'.

Bi-annual 17-mile walk in aid of charity raises £10,000 plus (even the tinies do it) and lots and lots of extra-curricular activities — astronomy (with real 8" reflecting telescope) as well as archery, estate work and cooking. No tuck-boxes, but daily sweet ration. Pets in science block. Sports hall doubles as Assembly for morning prayers, and quiet period observed nightly for reading and — particularly — Bible reading, (more than a third of the boys ask for Scripture Union notes).

FALKNER HOUSE GIRLS' SCHOOL
19 Brechin Place, London SW7 4QB
TEL London (071) 373 4501

Pupils: 130 girls • *All day* • *Ages: 4-11* • *'Christian non-denom.'* • *Fee-paying.*

PRINCIPAL   (and founder, in 1954) Mrs Flavia Nunes. Famously talkative.

HEAD   Since September 1988, Mrs Jacina Bird BA Hons (forties). Mrs Nunes' daughter, a good egg, mother of three, practical, strong on admin but not a trained teacher, which worries a minority.

Entrance   Mainly at four, later only if/when places fall vacant. Early registration advised: school has a waiting list. Girls tested at 3, many turned away, 'Often for not answering the questions, though no doubt they are capable', according to Mrs Nunes.

Exit Nothing but the smart schools, boarding and day. Trend just started here for girls to leave after CE (ie, at the end of the Easter term) and spend a glorious and useful summer term boarding at Cothill's French Château de Sauveterre near Toulouse.

Remarks Traditionally very thorough, with much emphasis on the three Rs. Maximum of 20 per class, no streaming. French for all at eight, introduction to Latin for two terms after CE. Girls definitely well grounded in their subjects, comment senior schools. Homework is steady, Falkner House mothers and fathers very keen on the work ethic, table chanting and spelling tests popular on school runs from early on. Big emphasis on reading and thorough understanding of mathematics. Testing of three year olds means *all* girls are bright, so CE syllabus covered faster than it would otherwise be, and possibly making teaching less inspired/inspiring and stimulating than it used to be when intake was more mixed, according to long-term parents. However, on the plus side, there is more time for extra-curricular activities, to the envy of some other schools. Very lively music department, good gymnastics, keenly attended clubs (drama, French oral) on Friday afternoons. Small playground backs on to Old Brompton Road. School prettily decorated. Proprietary owned and run, which works well here.

FARLEIGH SCHOOL
Red Rice, Andover, Hampshire SP11 7PW
TEL: Andover (0264) 710766

Pupils: Main School 170 boys and (a very few) girls • 73 boarders, 17 board weekly, 79 day • Pre-prep: 60 • Kindergarten: 24 • Ages: 3-13 • RC • Fee paying.

HEAD Since 1983, Mr Francis Floyd Cert Ed St Mary's London (forties). Quiet but in control. Teaches Maths. Very keen on fostering happy family atmosphere underpinned by Christian values.

Entrance Early registration essential. Requires fluency in reading and writing and knowledge of elementary arithmetic at prep level.

Exit Primarily to Catholic public schools such as Downside, Ampleforth, and Worth, also to Lord

Wandsworth and Wellington—the list differs each year.

Remarks Basically a boys prep school with one or two girls in it, plus its own prep-prep and kindergarten. Clever boys encouraged, less clever not harried, those needing remedial or dyslexic helped by trained teacher from Winchester Dyslexic Centre.

Boarders are encouraged to bring back their own pets. Two-thirds of pupils are RC and there is a chapel, chaplain, and mid-weekly voluntary Mass as well as annual retreats. Parents a wide mix from landed Catholics to locals, ex-pats as well as a regular small intake of Spaniards.

Handsome Georgian country house with over 40 acres of grounds and outstanding specimens of trees. School founded in 1953. Keen games, has done very well in the past in both rugby and cricket. Floodlit outdoor play area. Happy children; warm atmosphere; very full weekend programme.

FINTON HOUSE SCHOOL
171 Trinity Road, London SW17 7HL
TEL London (081) 682 0921

Pupils: 78 boys, 108 girls • All day • Ages: 4-11 • Non-denom. • Fee-paying.

CO-PRINCIPALS Miss Terry O'Neill (forties) and Miss Finola Stack (thirties), who together founded the school in September 1987. Miss Terry is Head, and was previously Head of the Vale School, London, and before that taught at Eaton House for years. Much respected by one and all, with a real belief in what her school is about and a very thorough working knowledge of the London school system—and the pressures thereof.

Entrance Tests abhorred here, first come, first served—*but* this means entering child's name at birth. 36 children come in aged four, half in autumn term, half in January term, in order to stagger birth dates.

Exit Boys leave at eight (for London or country preps), 10 and 11 for London schools with junior intake, eg Dulwich, City of London, Emanuel, Latymer etc. Girls head for Roedean, St Swithun's, Benenden, Woldingham, Calne, the Ascot Schools, or stay in London for JAGS, Putney, Streatham, Wimbledon High, Francis Holland, More House etc.

Remarks   Remarkable new school, hugely popular—and so it should be. After many years teaching north of the river where children regularly arrived after traffic-jammy school run twitchy and nervous (mothers sometimes in tears), Miss Terry now finds it a huge relief to see school used by locals arriving by roller skates, bicycles, and walking—though increasing numbers drive over the river north from Fulham and Chelsea. A charitable trust (all money ploughed back into the school) with 10% places offered to children with special needs (eg epilepsy, partially sighted). Own team of therapists (speech, occupational) and educational psychologist mean than specific learning difficulties can also be helped on site.

Two parallel classes per age group, all of mixed ability, within which children are taught on a highly individual basis. Traditional—but not stultifying—with houses, Latin motto, uniform, homework notebooks, termly exams; much emphasis on reading. Strong on art, music, drama, and very lively extra-curricular activities including, swimming, tennis, judo. Generously proportioned house (previously dentists'/doctors' rooms plus flats, obtained after fierce battles with local residents and council), well-designed and efficiently run, with light rooms, exceptionally delicious food, good library, big playground—and notably happy, lively children. Co-principals yearning for larger building so girls can stay until 13.

GARDEN HOUSE SCHOOL
53 Sloane Gardens, London SW1W 8ED
TEL London (071) 730 1652

Pupils: 268 girls, 40 boys   •   All day   •   Ages: girls 3-11; boys 3-8   •   Non denom.   •   Fee-paying.

PRINCIPAL   Since 1973, Mrs Jill Oddy BA Hons (owner/administrator).

HEAD   of Senior School since January 1988, Mrs Carolyn Pringle (thirties), Cert Ed Cantab; Mrs Wendy Challon is head of Junior School (at 28 Sloane Gardens; boys are in Holy Trinity, Sedding Street, SW1).

Entrance   At three, four and five (also later when places arise), via entry test one year before entry (£40 application fee). Names need to be put down early.

Exit   To a wide variety of day and boarding schools.

Remarks   A good smart school which has grown rapidly recently, and now takes boys from kindergarten up to pre-prep. Parallel classes for girls all the way up the school. Covers the ground soundly and effectively with thorough teaching to get pupils into their next schools. Strong on visits, good art and ballet, drama, music and computer throughout. Plenty of outdoor activities despite lack of playground. Very non-institutional, bright colours and flowers. Teachers are glamorous (so are parents), and children wear the prettiest uniform in London. Complaints from some parents that there is no board of governors, no PTA, and, compared to many other schools, lack of possibility of talking at length to teachers. That said, it is a happy and gentle school.

GILLING CASTLE
Gilling East, York YO6 4HP
TEL Ampleforth (043 93) 238

Pupils: 95 boys   •   85 board, 10 day   •   Ages: 8-13   •   RC   •   Fee-paying.

HEAD   Since 1987, Mr Graham Sasse (pronounced Sass) MA Oxon, teaches Classics (fifties, open-ended commitment), previously Senior Tutor at Ampleforth College (he joined staff there in 1962 from industry). His wife Patricia, MA Oxon, was head of Mod Langs at Ryedale, now teaches at Gilling and helps with pastoral side.

Entrance   By interview. Boys come from far and wide.

Exit   All boys leave at CE and go to Ampleforth.

Remarks   Prep school for Ampleforth, two and a half miles away cross-country. Fabulous 'boy proof' castle with mini-Thompson chairs and panelling everywhere. Dungeons have sword marks on archways, dining hall panelling rescued (complete) from Liverpool Docks on way to Hearst Castle. Dormitories vary between austerity and boy-inspired hangings round bunks. Pianos everywhere, computer club, deliciously warm pool, new sports are fencing and judo, pottery room, aero-modelling club. Very happy, teasing school (lunch companions assured us straight-faced that the current passion was cards but the gin kept running out!). Lived-in chapel which attracts between eight and 35 boys to daily Mass. Charming home-made imaginative school mag with such wonderful record-breaking details as 'first boy to faint in carpentry this term', and French anagrams.

GLENDOWER PREPARATORY SCHOOL
87 Queen's Gate, London SW7 5JX
TEL London (071) 370 1927

Pupils: 185 girls ● All day ● Ages: 4-12 ● Interdenom ● Fee-paying.

HEAD Since 1986, Mrs Barbara Humber BSc (forties). Previously at Colet Court where she was Head of Science for seven years. Very keen that girls should be taught Science and provided with the same facilities as boys.

Entrance At four and a half, and 10 places for eight-year olds. All potential pupils are interviewed (though not IQ tested). Essential to put girls' names down early.

Exit Mostly at 11, some stay for 12+; three-quarters favour day currently (evenly divided between Godolphin and Latymer, St Paul's and More House, followed by City of London and Wimbledon High); boarders to Wycombe Abbey, Cheltenham Ladies, Sherborne Girls, Millfield and others.

Remarks Strong girls' school which operates very much along the lines of a boys' prep school, with unusual emphasis on Science, a lot of good sound teaching, and starts things at an early age (French at three). Setting at nine, combined Science for all at eight. Girls do electronics and soldering (in spare time as well as class); Latin at 10 for brighter girls, computers used from five onwards. Tuition room for slower children to catch up (included in fees). Parents keen on school because it 'stretches my child'.
Somewhat cramped space, but well used. Strong on

projects, very good music. Lots of visits and lectures, clubs after school four days a week. Teams win most netball matches, use Imperial College swimming pool. Active Parents' Association. Startling purple uniform. Glendower progressed from a dame school (founded in 1899) to a well-established jumping-off place to high-powered senior education.
All school lunches are now vegetarian.

GODSTOWE PREPARATORY SCHOOL
High Wycombe, Buckinghamshire
HP13 6PR
TEL High Wycombe (0494) 29273

Pupils: 262 girls ● 136 board, 126 day girls; 100 boys and girls in pre-prep ● Ages: girls 3-13, boys 4-7 ● C of E, but all faiths welcome ● Fee-paying.

HEAD New Head just appointed at time of writing. Mrs Frances Henderson MA, previously Deputy Head of Thornton College. Arrives after a patch of turmoil following the retirement of Miss Fitzmaurice-Kelly, who reigned for nearly 20 years.

Entrance By registration.

Exit The posh girls' schools—Wycombe Abbey, Downe House Cheltenham Ladies, Queen Anne's Caversham etc, and local grammar schools.

Remarks Founded in 1900, first boarding prep school for girls in England. Pupils with potential learning problems are taught in small classes 'for a year or so' until they find their feet, and school has formidable scholarship reputation. Lots of extra activities, Brownies, Guides, ballet, tapestry, needle-work and music, and seriously popular skiing trips (two a year). Very strong on the games front. Boarders have their own garden plots.

THE HALL SCHOOL
Crossfield Road, Hampstead, London
NW3 4NU
TEL London (071) 722 1700

Pupils: 375 boys • *All day* • *Ages: 3-13* • *C of E.* •
Fee-paying.

HEAD   From September 1991, Mr Nicholas Coates (forties), educated at Culford and Edinburgh University and previously Head of the Wallop School, Weybridge. Rumoured to be an impressive fellow. Takes over from Mr Heazell, who was in charge at time of writing, a man of understanding who reiterates that the aim of the school is to prepare children for the next stage, not to get 'strings of scholarships' or 'turn out little pothunters'.

Entrance   By registration before the age of three. 'We are in a seller's market,' comments the outgoing Head. Most come via The Hall's own junior school. Head selects 'the stable, not the colt'—parents given a stiff interview. In the children, school is looking for 'learnability', and at time of writing is utterly against exams for three-year olds.

Exit   UCS, St Paul's, Harrow, Highgate, Bryanston and King's Canterbury—and subsequently 90% go on to university.

Remarks   *The* school for NW media and intelligentsia. Pupils are articulate and bushy-tailed. Has been patronized by the offspring of the late Peggy Ashcroft, Colin Davis, Epstein, Alec Guinness, the Sinden family, H G Wells, George Robey, neurotic Hampstead psychiatrists. The Lord Mayor of London, at time of writing, is an OB and a governor. And that puts you in the picture. Highly competitive parents—it is not unknown for a father 'to come back from a day's work, get out the Livy and do an hour's parsing with his son at the kitchen table'. Mothers face school runs of up to six hours—the traffic here is horrific and feelings run at boiling point not only among parents but also among nearby residents.
   No streaming—but extensive setting. New hall built with funds raised by appeal—school's pride and joy and gives at least somewhere for the children to let off steam. Dynamic computer department—one of the early pioneering ones, with first micro computer acquired in 1976. Very popular drama option in the lunch hour. Endless patience taken with those who for whatever reason, fall by the wayside. Annual competitions in public speaking, reciting etc. School now finishes at 3.50pm and most of homework is done at home, but school is open until 5 for extras.

HANFORD SCHOOL
Childe Okeford, Blandford, Dorset
DT11 8HL
TEL Childe Okeford (0258) 860219

Pupils: 150 girls • *All board* • *Ages: 7-13* • *C of E.* •
Fee-paying.

JOINT HEADS   Since 1950, Mr M E Sharp, TD, BSc, and Mrs Sharp (sixties), and Miss Sarah Canning MA (fifties). Sarah (never Miss Canning) is the daughter of Clifford Canning, the distinguished Head of Canford, who, with his wife Enid, founded Hanford.

Entrance   Waiting lists. Locals, girls from the south and west, Londoners in need of real country life, and numerous families posted abroad.

Exit   Over half the girls go to Sherborne; others to Bryanston, Croft House, St Mary's Wantage, St Mary's Calne, Downe House, Tudor Hall, Wycombe Abbey, Cheltenham Ladies', North Foreland, West Heath, Roedean, St Antonys–Leweston, Millfield and Godolphin. Plenty of scholarships gained.

Remarks   Still takes the prize for happiest girls' prep in the country—and no significant changes from entry in the first edition. Very much a family atmosphere, (most of the staff are married family people), school is a glorious manor house of 1623 (instantly seductive to parents and children), in rolling Dorset country, with stunning stables (where Sarah is usually to be found). Inside, the old manor house is pleasantly shabby in places; five star in jolly dorms. Children cleverly guided through problems before they arise. In the garden, there is an enchanting chapel.
   Three or four streams in each year, average class size is 13, upper groups have four to eight girls, and they claim at least one scholarship per year to one of the big

girls' schools. No cramming. 'A' stream does Latin at 9 or 10, the rest follow next year. Assistant matrons are a succession of young Old Girls. Good art, memorable drama—with a wonderful wardrobe room—and Hanford is very proud of its music tradition (they use Bryanston music teachers). The veg garden supports the school, except for potatoes. (NB Food on plates must be finished.) Around the grounds are logs for playing 'villages'. Gym club at weekends is immensely popular, outdoors in the summer (visitors arrive to find girls in gym knickers standing on their heads). Thelwellian ponies are Hanford owned, and foolproof.

This is a privately owned, privately-run school: in a few years' time, the Sharps will retire, and hand over to LtCol and Mrs McKenzie-Johnston—both graduates (he is a Mathematician, she is a Musician), who currently have two daughters in the school. Mrs McKenzie-Johnston is an Old Girl.

HAWTREYS

Savernake Forest, Marlborough, Wiltshire
SN8 3BA
TEL Marlborough (0672) 870331

Pupils: 125 boys • *All board* • *Ages: 8-13* • *C of E* • *Fee-paying.*

HEAD Since September 1990, Mr Christopher Pyemont, educated Marlborough and Cambridge, then army, followed by the City as a stockbroker for five years. Then he grew tomatoes commercially for five years with three-quarters of an acre of greenhouse, then to St Bede's School in Sussex, of which his brother is Head. Last job before appointment to Hawtreys was as a Housemaster at St Bede's School. Has two full blues (cricket and hockey), and a half blue at skiing, also racquets player. Live wire, as will be seen from above CV, has come into Hawtreys absolutely fresh and undimmed by any previous experience of prep school life. Could be just what the school needs. Friendly, married with two children— wife comments, *a propos* of an earlier remark in the guide about bullying, that 'wobbly lips *are* terribly well looked after'.

Entrance Non-competitive, books full until 1998.

Boys come for a test two terms before entry.

Exit Most to Eton and Marlborough. Also to Milton Abbey, Harrow and one or two others.

Remarks Architecturally the most glorious prep school in the country, housed in the Marquess of Aylesbury's Grade 1 stately home in Savernake Forest. Prospectus reads like an estate agent's handout - 'The House is situated in the most beautiful country, well away from public high roads and stands, 550 feet up, in 50 acres of grounds with 200-acre Deer Park adjoining.' Much of upkeep is undertaken by the Estate, however, and so this is not quite the financial millstone it might seem—though large appeals are a familiar part of life and the fees are high. New bursar appointed 1990. School founded in 1869 by a Housemaster at Eton. Pupils mostly upper end of the social scale and consequently unfazed by the inevitably bleak and often freezing interior of an ex stately home. Untreated wooden floors. No bells between lessons.

New Head very keen on hobbies—craft, art, shooting is good with indoor and outdoor ranges, drama, riding at Pewsey Vale Riding School, tennis pro comes in four days a week—everyone must do something—more matches to be encouraged—'It is important for boys to play in third and fourth 11—almost more important than the first 11', he feels. There are two houses, though the school is not stunningly sportif. All-weather tennis courts. New points system 'for *everything* '—matrons included'.

Boys in divisions of about 12, and streamed in second third and fourth year. German and Greek offered for bright final year pupils (good Classics teachers). Good full time remedial teacher. Assessments for achievements and effort sent home every three weeks.

Difficult to comment at time of going to press owing to what may turn out to be new style of management, though Head comments that he doesn't intend to change things ...

HIGHFIELD SCHOOL
Liphook, Hampshire GU30 7LQ
TEL Liphook (0428) 722228

Pupils: 120 boys, 55 girls ● Boarders 140, 35 day pupils (all pupils must board by 10) ● Ages: 8-13 ● C of E ● Fee-paying.

HEAD   Since 1979, Mr Robin M Orr MA Cantab, (fifties), educated at Winchester and Clare College, where he read History. Cert Ed in English at Cambridge. Went to Highfield as a boy and taught here for 10 years before spending nine years in State system, the last seven at Langley Park, Beckenham. Teaches 10 periods a week, mostly English, but some Religious Knowledge, his wife Mary (Froebel trained) also teaches RK.

Entrance   By registration. Children must have chronological reading age, otherwise visit school for informal test. Most from within A3 corridor from London. Two or three foreigners, some expats. Good naval links. Waiting list for day pupils to 1997.

Exit   Lots to Bryanston, otherwise Charterhouse, Winchester, Eton, Harrow, St Swithun's (quite a lot), Marlborough, Sherborne Girls, Downe House etc. Good collection of scholarships including Art and Music.

REMARKS   Purpose-built red-brick conglomerate with masses of wooden additions, in 170-acre grounds. Lots of woods, cows, pets. Traditional chapel, good games hall, a theatre (hideous hard benches), music room. Girls dorms jollier (and warmer) than boys, but posters and own duvets everywhere. Older boys/girls have to 'supervise' younger dorms. Superb art, very hot on music (Mr Orr into the organ in his earlier days), Greek only as a hobby, but games 'no prob' on the computers in free time. Outdoor tennis courts good and floodlit hockey in winter, outdoor swimming pool. Daily reports are popular for slacking, and suspensions for boys invading girls dorms—the girls have to go past the boys to go to bed which causes envy and—minor—dissent. Serious naughtiness equals no sweets on Wednesday. Relaxed family atmosphere. Nice school, works well.

HILL HOUSE INTERNATIONAL JUNIOR SCHOOL
17 Hans Place, London SW1X 0EP
TEL London (071) 584 1331

Pupils: 700 boys, 400 girls ● All day ● Ages: 3-13 ● Non-denom ● Fee-paying.

HEAD   and founder, in 1951, Col H S Townend OBE, MA, (seventies), educated at St Edmund's Canterbury, and Oxford. An educational institution: when he retires (no signs of this at time of writing) his son, Mr Richard Townend, at present musical director, will take over.

Remarks   A unique school: people love it or loathe it. Colonel Townend *is* Hill House. terrific emphasis on challenge, sport, international pupils, with at least 50% foreigners (NB briefly HRH Prince Charles' first school). Bottom of school in good order, but reports of alarm bells from parents of children of six plus. Privately owned, entrance at any age, and any time during the year. Toughies and extroverts thrive here, but shy sensitive types won't feel at home, good at integrating foreigners.

HORRIS HILL
Newtown, Newbury, Berkshire RG15 9DJ
TEL Newbury (0635) 40594

Pupils: 172 boys ● 162 boarders, 10 day boys ● Ages: 8-13 ● C of E ● Fee-paying.

HEAD   Since 1978, Mr M J Innes MA (fifties) educated at Haileybury and Cambridge, read English. Unmarried, but has splendid 'dame', Mrs Charmaine Curtis, to help. Teaches English at top end, Maths at bottom. Has been in school 29 years. A dedicated and experienced Headmaster. A little reserved, but well worth the effort of getting to know. Keen gardener.

Entrance   By registration. No entrance examination, but little test and it is sometimes gently suggested, but not insisted, that a boy might do better at a school more geared to remedial teaching.

Exit   12-year breakdown of where boys go on to shows Eton top of list with 86, Winchester second (73 out of 74 sitting the exam)—some record, Radley third (36) and Marlborough fourth (31) though results for last two years would not look quite like this. OB: Richard Adams.

Remarks   A famous home county prep school which has managed to hang on to its traditional feel while softening the edges of discipline, environment etc. One of few successful boys' prep schools at which boys have time to play with model airplanes etc, have regular pit stops for 'cocoa' and generally behave like little boys rather than potential Derby winners.

That said—the school works and plays hard. No horizontal streaming but school adopts the 'filtering' approach and boys are constantly on the move upwards which, says Head, 'keeps teachers on their toes'. Average rate of movement is once every two terms. Good remedial help.

Outstanding art department under new (at time of writing) master—Ian Keen. Over 100 boys learn one musical instrument, 23 learn two and one learns three. New Head of Music needs watching. Whole room dedicated to wonderful model train set—pride and joy. Floodlit fives courts, squash courts, very keen footie and cricket. Classrooms a bit bleak and desks battered. Sports hall doubles as theatre—keen thespians here. No prefects—masters fulfil this role—no speech day, no motto—'no humbug', to quote the founder, who was an (ex) master of Winchester aiming to train up boys for entry to that school (date of foundation, 1888). Both boys' and masters' houses are dotted around the grounds which are pleasant and spacious, though main school building is of such hideous Victorian red brick that the prospectus features it heavily camouflaged with snow.

KENSINGTON PREPARATORY SCHOOL FOR GIRLS
(formerly known as 'Ken High'),
17 Upper Phillimore Gardens, London
W8 7HF
TEL London (071) 937 0108

Pupils: Approx 200 girls ● All day ● Ages: 5-12 ● Non-denom ● Fee-paying.

HEAD   For ages, Miss J Nelson Cert Ed (age not given), a confident and competent lady, with sense of humour. Has effortless air of silly-me totally at odds with the reality of the sharp end of administration. The epitome of girls' prep school Head, with a picture of a teddy bear elegantly executed on her study wall. Firm, but fair.

Entrance   By aptitude test, much competition at the bottom end of the school, though places come up later as families move away. First test is one to one—real duds don't even get this far. Second test—'group activity', eg, do they hide under the table when they see another child? Doesn't make much difference when name is put down, and Head doesn't look at nursery school and doesn't interview parents. Some priority given to sisters—16 pairs in the school at time of writing.

Exit   Most girls leave in Lower III having taken 11+, some stay to Upper III to take 11+ late or a few for 12+ (a harder exam and not as many places available). Go on to Godolphin and Latymer, More House, Putney High and other London day schools. Regularly gets large numbers in St Paul's Girls', including awards, and is probably still best bet for getting candidate under starter's orders for this. Boarders go on to Wycombe Abbey, Roedean, Downe House, Sherborne Girls etc.

Remarks   Atmosphere decorous in large Kensington house with super big garden at the back—much larger than most London preps, and one side is taken up with garden plots for budding gardeners. Slightly cramped (though less so than other similar schools) with rooms at top of house minuscule but rather sweet and homely. Teaching fairly traditional with some stars—particularly in English, also Maths and Science. Computers. Standard of work high, literacy and numeracy often exceeding that of girls two years older. Handwriting and spelling without exception good.

Summer carnival, Christmas carols, French plays, summer sports are in Holland Park.

Emphasis still on old-fashioned tenets of discipline and order—hair to be tied back if longer than collar length, berets worn at all times with coats, never with blazers, no tights. Each girl shakes hands with the mistress on duty as she goes. Pupils seem very happy and well adjusted, much more so than some of the mothers who, said one of them, are still 'monsters'—and pushy and ambitious with it, double parking their huge Mercedes etc, squawking at each other and generally disturbing the peace of the street.

GPDST school—the 'odd one out' as the rest are senior schools. Has for many years enjoyed the reputation of being *the* academic London prep school for girls, and deservedly so. Rumours of school moving to another, cheaper site.

KING'S COLLEGE SCHOOL
West Road, Cambridge CB3 9DN
TEL Cambridge (0223) 65814

Pupils: Approx 165 boys, 65 girls • Approx 60 board (including 24 choristers and probationers), the rest day (including all girls) • Ages: 7-13 • C of E, but all denominations acceptable • Fee-paying.

HEAD Since 1977, Mr Gerald Peacocke MA Oxford, Italian and German (fifties). Appointed via King's Canterbury. 'Stumbled' into teaching having been in industry and British Council. An approachable (yes) kindly man, popular within the profession and one who appears to put the pupils first and everything else miles down the list. Comments that King's (ie King's College Cambridge, with which school is connected) 'is a liberal kind of college, very flexible and kindly and I like to think the school reflects this atmosphere'.

Entrance Register early for ordinary place—list bursting, and in any case shortage of prep school places in Cambridge. They do not have a policy of taking the top 20, so registration date vital. School has own 'assessment' of English, Maths, intelligence. Chorister trials are usually in early October and you can enter your son for these up to a few days beforehand. Catchment area mainly within one and a half hours drive of Cambridge—dons' children.

Exit Some brilliant results, especially music scholarships -nearly 200 within space of 13 years—also lots of academic schools. Pupils go on to strong music schools such as Eton, Uppingham etc, to co-eds such as Oakham, Bryanston etc, also to King's Ely, St Mary's Cambridge and The Perse, The Leys, Westminster etc, and some to the maintained sector, in particular the Chesterton Community School, Cambridge.

Pupils leave at 11 and 13. Lots of famous OBs: Orlando Gibbons the most distinguished; this century though—Michael Ramsey, Christopher Tugendhat, John Pardoe.

Remarks Strong, strong strong—one of the two best preps in Cambridgeshire, if not in the country. Owing to ties with King's College, Cambridge, for which it provides the boy choristers, school is exceptionally strong in music, though it would like us to point out it is jolly strong academically too. Since 1981 there has been a dyslexic unit, which can now cater for around 20 children—one full-time specialist teacher, two part-time (NB this department is growing slightly, to the great gratitude of parents). Main sports—'everything'. Rugby (not so hot at the moment), football, cricket, hockey (including mixed girls' and boys' teams), tennis, squash, swimming, netball, and collects a good array of awards for athletics and gymnastics too, etc.

Ordinary, friendly slightly battered-looking and very busy, purposeful school. Only sign of choristers is their garments hanging in open wardrobes in largish dormitories (some bunks), unless you walk across to the Chapel and see them in action. Slightly casual atmosphere has been known to deter parents in search of highly-disciplined and formal behaviour.

PS: Now that St John's College has the superior choir, it could be that popularity of King's College School has fallen slightly in reflection, however, all is relative.

KNIGHTON HOUSE SCHOOL

Blandford, Dorset DT11 0PY

TEL (0258) 452065

Pupils: 145 girls • *115 board, 30 day* • *Ages: 7-13* • *Pre-prep: about 30, including 10 boys* • *C of E* • *Fee-paying.*

HEAD Since September 1986, Mr R P Weatherly BA, (early forties), previously Head of Geography at Bryanston. Popular with parents and children. Very caring and energetic about visiting senior schools.

Entrance Via pre-prep or at seven (report from previous school plus informal interview).

Exit At 12/13 mainly to Sherborne, also Bryanston, St Antonys-Leweston, Croft, St Mary's Calne.

Remarks Happy, cosy country school for girls—a place where they can stay relatively ('mercifully' from a parent) unsophisticated until they are 13. Very friendly and natural children who enjoy tree climbing and talking ponies as well as looking glamorous for the school disco. Much store set by initiative and honesty. Set in marvellous Dorset country; founded in 1950 by author Christopher Booker's parents. Gales of 1989 wrenched several roofs off school. New buildings include purpose-built music school, and all-purpose hall and gym, four new dorms, kitchens and fine large new dining-room with small tables 'so we can't shout across to each other'. Food is described by pupils as 'wholemeal, but good'. Lots of home-grown vegetables and fruit. NB building programme paid for out of fees, Head is his own bursar.

Teaching very sound all round; school volunteered to take part in national Key Stage I for seven-year olds. Small classes, heaps of individual attention, use of nearby Bryanston's facilities (some shared staff). Not a horsey school despite the fact that ponies are welcome (some lent by Old Girls). Miss Margaret Handy firmly in charge of riding, also Senior Housemistress, and has been with the school for 30 years. Fewer posh girls than nearby Hanford; Knighton children are exceptionally *nice* to each other. Uniform: red dungarees (girls love them), which fade to pink, currently the smartest are worn shortish. Head is determined for the school not to get bigger, despite demands. Book well ahead.

LADY EDEN'S SCHOOL

39/41 Victoria Road, London W8 5RJ

TEL London (071) 937 0583

Pupils: 170 girls • *All day* • *Ages: 3-11* • *Non-denom* • *Fee-paying.*

HEAD Since 1988, Mrs G A Wayne (early forties). Educated Moreton Hall in Shropshire, Florence and B Ed from Cambridge. Previously Head of History at Francis Holland, Clarence Gate for 15 years. Married with two young children. Teaches History of Art and Current Affairs in top forms and takes younger forms for Verbal Reasoning, General Knowledge and general lessons. Believes in a broad education; intent on extending sports and extra-curricular activities like debating and clubs. Sensible and well thought of.

Entrance Early registration essential. Main entry at 3 years. Some vacancies thereafter, for which entrants are tested. Book in at birth for kindergarten.

Exit Recently to Cheltenham Ladies, Sevenoaks, Godolphin and Latymer, St Mary's Ascot, Heathfield.

Remarks Smart but academically hard-edged school—keeps pupils stretched and reaches very high standards. This is a shock to some, who imagine that it is a nice school for Young Ladies. Extremely serious about education. Solid grounding in core subjects, with increasing stress on Science— fully-equipped Science room. National curriculum adopted 'but not enslavement by it'—courses for staff, design and technology timetabled, computers in every class etc. All take Latin at nine, French earlier; leavers put on a French play each year. Remedial help for slow learners. Excellent art work. Very strong on visits and going out, and after-school activities. Swimming, tennis, netball, bridge, calligraphy etc, annual skiing trip and a physical activity holiday offered. Good fresh food prepared in own kitchens. Nice and near Kensington Gardens. Traditional uniform—straw boaters but no longer white gloves. Privately owned by Lord and Lady Eden who take an active personal interest. More parental contact now than under previous regime.

LAMBROOK

Winkfield Row, Bracknell, Berkshire
RG12 6LU
TEL *Winkfield Row (0344) 882717*

Pupils: 135 boys • All board • Ages: 8-13 • C of E •
Fee-paying.

HEAD Since 1989, Mr M C Bickersteth MA (forties) educated at Lambrook and Rugby; read Geography at Dundee. Married with two young boys.

Entrance By registration. No exam, but a reading and writing test a year before entry. Boys accepted any term at any age.

Exit At last count 15 different schools in the first division.

Remarks A lot of London and local parents. Still popular with the army (Sandhurst just up the road) and with the Foreign Office. Well organized spare time. Magic Circle still 'very enjoyable'. Sadly, no longer fishing in the stream (it's drying up), but bird watching, a lot of camp fires and senior can camp out in the grounds on summer weekends. Boys polite and keen on shaking hands and opening doors.

LATHALLAN SCHOOL

Johnshaven by Montrose, Angus
DD10 0HN
TEL *Inverbervie (0561) 62220*

Pupils: 56 boys, 19 girls • 58 board, 17 day • Ages: 5-13
• Interdenom • Fee-paying.

HEAD Since 1975, Mr Peter de Iongh MA Oxon (fifties), till 1993, educated at Rendcomb College, and Exeter College, Oxford, previously housemaster at Dover College.

Entrance Locally and mid to North-East Scotland. International and rather more sophisticated children

than might be expected from the numbers. Pre-prep dept re-opening in summer term in association with Gateside Farm Nursery, St Cyrus, Montrose.

Exit Most Scottish schools, especially Strathallan and Glenalmond. Tiny dribble further south: Sherborne, Sedburgh, Eton, Winchester, Radley.

Remarks Tiny school, tiny classes, good teaching staff, good CDT dept, marvellous computers. Children sleep in Victorian castle (girls in servants' quarters) and work in nearby stable block. Set in 60 acres with 13 acres of playing fields. Pupils keen on team games and have own pipe band. Went to Salzburg last year and went to Vienna at Easter 1991. Community minded, swimming and church in Montrose, only 30 minutes south of Aberdeen. Discipline can be a bit heavy handed. Picture of dog in prospectus may well sell the school.

LATYMER UPPER SCHOOL

The Prep Department, King Street, London
W6 9LR
TEL *London (081) 741 1851*

Pupils: 4 forms of day boys of approx 22 each • Ages: 9-11
Non-denom • Fee-paying.

HEAD Since September 1986, Mrs Joan Chandler BA Hons London—English. Formerly assistant mistress here. Came to teaching late with grown-up family. Husband is Old Latymerian, sons ditto, daughters and self Old Godolphin and Latymerians— what Bingo Little might have called an Old Latmyerian Production. Head comments that she 'loves the ethos of the place'—that deserving children ought to be given a chance in life.

Entrance Hard-nosed competitive academic exam. No fear or favour. Registration up to a few weeks before the exam (usually held February or March).

Exit All to Latymer Upper at the age of 11 (NB not the usual 13). No exam to move to senior school—a good reason for choosing Latymer in the first place.

Remarks A sane and wonderful place on the banks

of the Thames, away from the fumes of the Great West Road. Dignified old building. Cosy relaxed atmosphere quite unlike other London day schools, possibly owing to lack of pressure to go on to next stage—school can concentrate on learning instead. New full-time art teacher with inspired work. Strong music. Classes vary in size—as few as 17, as many as 23—owing to standard of applicants. Enormous advantage of being able to use the senior school facilities, through the garden wall. Outdoor chess set, like Salzburg (well). Every Friday afternoon the Rivercourt Society puts on a play—'encourages them to be confident', said Mrs Chandler. 'Centre path'—leading up to school door—for VIPs only to walk on, though 'naughties' are made to stand there through break, which makes strong impression on them.

pro. Good drama, Christmas Show and Shakespeare midst the roses (with rabbit netting round them).

Lists of all boys in dining hall; older boys eat in the conservatory amongst 'the camellias'. Geriatric swimming pool now refurbished. Cosy dormitories (teddies and posters), duvets, own covers, and can choose to share with friends. Press shocked by homeliness, scruffiness and battered desks when shown round HRH's new school.

Posh friendly school which has always been one of the top 10. Lots of OBs' children from aristocratic list—the Duke of Kent, the Duke of Wellington, and currently the eldest son of the heir to the throne. And it says much for the school that it hasn't changed a jot for all this—apart from a £2 million nuclear bunker.

LUDGROVE
Wokingham, Berkshire RG11 3AB
TEL Wokingham (0734) 789881

Pupils: 185 boys ● *All board* ● *Ages: 8-13* ● *C of E* ● *Fee-paying.*

HEAD Since 1972, Mr Gerald Barber MA (forties) along with Mr Nichol Marston MA (fifties). Both educated Eton and Oxford and both friendly and popular with parents and boys, Mr Barber is the third generation to run the school (which is now a charitable trust), and previously taught at Mowden.

Entrance No exam, but expects a reasonable standard. Very, very popular, so register at birth—though there are occasional late places available.

Exit A feed school for Eton—over half go there—also Harrow, Radley, Wellington, Marlborough.

Remarks Red brick Victorian with masses of additions set in fabulous 130 acres of rolling countryside 45 mins from London. Smashing sports hall-theatre complex with two squash courts is rather at odds with trad fives courts and clapboard chapel. Old farm buildings have been converted into craft and technology centre. Computers and computer club, carpentry (they mend the gates when the boys aren't using the shop), cricket, riding, fencing, own golf-course and lessons from

MAIDWELL HALL
Northampton NN6 9JG
TEL Maidwell (060 128) 234

Pupils: Approx 80-85 boys ● *All board except two or three* ● *Ages 7+-13* ● *C of E, though other faiths welcome* ● *Fee-paying.*

HEAD Since 1978, Mr J H Paul MA (forties). Taught Classics at Papplewick before coming here. Wife is trained teacher and unofficial co-Head and teaches the youngest children. Both are gentle and approachable—not your whizzo public relations team.

Entrance By 'informal test'. Most pupils 1-1 hours' drive away, a lot from East Anglia and, increasingly, London. Very few non-nationals. Several sons of OBs at present in school.

Exit Traditionally it is Eton, though increasing numbers to Harrow, also to Stowe, Uppingham, etc.

Remarks Posh—socially speaking—cosy little prep school in a country house with nice lived-in feel, in 40 acres of lovely grounds. Head reckons school too small for streaming and no great feeling of competition, though careful points system charts progress of each boy, and parents get report every fortnight. Remedial teachers come in when needed—school can cope with 'a few' with 'learning problems'. Rab Butler's sons were here.

Cricket unbeaten for four years, rugger and football without the option, games keen, but school too small for startling results. TV allowed only at specific times at weekends. Good and much used library. Small lake for punting and fishing. All boys sleep under the same roof in dormitories with matrons in the middle of them—teddies looked a bit daunted. Atmosphere informal. Boys charming, outgoing and kind.

THE MALL SCHOOL
Hampton Road, Twickenham, Middlesex
TW2 5NQ
TEL London (081) 977 2523

Pupils: 250 boys ● All day ● Ages: 4-13 ● C of E ●
Fee-paying.

HEAD Since 1989, Mr T P A MacDonogh, MA (forties). Educated at Winchester and Cambridge, previously Deputy Head of Berkhamsted Junior School. Keen musician, he teaches IT and Maths, strongly emphasizes school as a community.

Entrance An unselective school: first come, first served and long waiting list.

Exit To a wide number of schools, mostly day. Hampton is a popular choice.

Remarks Traditional academic prep but with exceptionally friendly and informal atmosphere. Classes of 20 to 24 but final year broken down into three or four smaller sets, including scholarship class, the smallest group those needing most attention. Little ones 'mothered' for first three years and the six-year-olds have their own computer programmed for them by their teacher. This class also bakes, sews and learns to do joined-up writing. Good all round, mixing the cosy with sound traditional teaching. Remedial help for minor cases. CDT recently introduced. Strong on sport. Good music (three choirs). Lots of plays, annual Gilbert & Sullivan has given way to a broader diet.

Strong on clubs and projects. Boys queue up at the gates before eight o'clock each morning to get stuck into their activities—mainly table tennis at that hour—later they're into judo (especially popular and not expensive), fencing, chess, computing, and carpentry.

Weaknesses: the original Mall House burned to the ground in 1960 and was replaced by hotchpotch of pre-fabs giving overall scruffy appearance, despite new classroom block and another new block on the way. Still, there is a painful shortage of space, although they have managed to squeeze in an inviting-looking indoor pool. Large tarmac playground used for football and playing euphemistically known as 'the field'. Very strong rapport between parents and staff. Intimacy and warmth the keynote of the school.

MALTMAN'S GREEN
Gerrards Cross, Buckinghamshire SL9 8RR
TEL Gerrards Cross (0753) 883022

Pupils: 296 girls in all ● 80 board ● 16-18 in kindergarten
● Ages: 4-13 ● Non-denom ● Fee-paying.

HEAD Since summer 1988, Mrs M Evans BA (early fifties) History, Royal Holloway. Formerly Head of Roedean's junior house. Kind, understanding and very firm all at the same time. Has dear Cavalier given to her by pupils from previous school. Bursar has fat sausage dog and together the two animals appear to have the place sewn up. Head pays great attention to the sort of little detail which *you* might not notice but could make *all* the difference to your ewe lamb. Head could easily run public school if she so chose. Husband teaches CDT at Drayton Manor, Ealing, and is 'understanding' about his wife living in during term time, not to mention part of the hols. They also have a house in Twickenham which in spare moments is being 'lovingly restored'.

Entrance Register as soon as you know you will be in the area. Prospective pupils spend a whole day in school in the spring term before entry, they have a 'little test—standardised NFER also our own' and a meal and games 'to see how they are all round'.

Exit To major girls' boarding schools—Downe House, Queenswood, Queen Anne's Caversham, Wycombe Abbey, Roedean (of course) etc, also to local day schools—Beaconsfield High School, Dr Challoner's particularly popular. A complete record of who goes where is written out lovingly in copperplate every year and hung in the front hall.

Remarks   School is flexible so that, should you be in the Services, for example, (approx 25% of parents are), your child can board while you are posted abroad, and revert to day when in this country. Housed in what looks like just another grand stockbroker's pile in ritzy suburban belt of Gerrards Cross. New wing contains all things bright and beautiful for the national curriculum (gas taps etc). Lots of room behind the house, however, and pretty playing fields all on site, large gym with well-designed stacking hanging chairs (used for watching plays etc), heated outdoor swimming pool, an animal house (small caged animals only, please). Excellent music department. Children friendly, outgoing and confident. School has some ladies who will come in and do coaching. No specialist remedial department, but Mrs Evans has done course in teaching dyslexics and so is at the enormous advantage of being able to spot 'specific learning problems'. Homework rises from half an hour to one and a half hours at 13+. Weekends very relaxed compared with comparable boys' school—breakfast at 9am, small chores, lunch, a trip or two, parents may come and take out child any weekend.

THE MANOR HOUSE SCHOOL
*Great Durnford, Salisbury, Wiltshire
SP4 6BB*
TEL Amesbury (0980) 22163

Pupils: 56 girls • All board • Ages: 8-12 • C of E but transport for RCs to attend local services • Fee-paying.

HEAD   Since 1961, Miss M E Holder (fifties), contracted till 60, educated Charlotte Mason College, Ambleside with Cert of Ed from Manchester University, teaches English, Maths, Geography and verbal reasoning to the middles. Shy and somewhat formidable to meet, Miss Holder firmly believes that a 'happy child is a hardworking child'.

Entrance   Registration asap. Six down for 1998, by word of mouth and personal recommendation.

Exit   At 11 and 12. Mainly nearby. St Mary's Calne

and St Mary's Wantage, Tudor Hall, Godolphin, Sherborne, Down House.

Remarks   Ducky little school founded by Dreda, Lady Tryon, in the old family home (Wren House etc) in 1945. School became charitable trust in 1963, the present Lady Tryon—of Kanga frock fame—still keeps a (very) watchful eye on the place and top treat is to have tea with her and the goats. Pianos everywhere. No tuck. Children charming, open and pretty. School strong on 3 Rs. One or two pupils from abroad. Most board weekly. Seriously posh. No gym, but tennis, netball, swimming pool, ballet and ponies, rabbits and guinea pigs, games, science lab.

MILBOURNE LODGE
Arbrook Lane, Esher, Surrey KT10 9EG
TEL Esher (0372) 62737

Pupils: 180 boys, 18 girls • All day • Ages: 8-13 • C of E • Fee-paying.

HEAD   Since 1949, Mr Norman Hale (sixties, 'I'm still at the helm, and planning on another decade here'), educated at Shrewsbury and Oxford. Ebullient and brilliant, with a youthful manner. Wife does buns, bursar and bogs. Head knows his pupils far better than most. Some parents are allergic to him. However, ex-Milbourne's at Oxford give him an annual party.

Entrance   Stiff test; early registration advised. Some come in from Milbourne's own junior school but around two-thirds to three-quarters of entry come from a multiplicity of establishments. All children must take a test and no favours for ML's Juniors.

Exit   Outstandingly high percentage of scholarships, recently to Eton, Harrow, Charterhouse, Epsom, King's School Wimbledon etc.

Remarks   Hugely competitive and exciting school, on both academic and sporting fronts—everything done on points and the pupils thrive on it. Compared with a lot of prep schools this has relatively modest facilities (though the environment/decor is agreeable), which makes the results more astonishing. Very inspiring Head. Teaching is superb—most teachers have been here for years, though there is new young blood too. English teaching is brilliant. Latin still the subject in which scholars shine most regularly; Maths results often outstanding, and alphas go right across the board. But this is not a sweat shop: pupils work a very great deal on their own; A and B stream; old fashioned markings, regular form orders, with 10 forms of between 15 and 23. Greek for the A stream in their last three years (Gwen Stephen is a star teacher). Oldest scholars' lesson ends at 6pm or later.

Boys arrive dead keen at crack of dawn for judo and music (two orchestras) pre-morning lessons (five before lunch); games every afternoon. Bright, noisy, enthusiastically hard working. The scampi/BMW belt, with a constant stream of ambitious achieving parents moving in to 20-mile radius specifically for this school. Lots drive in daily from Wimbledon. Original school was founded by Woodrow Wyatt's father. High number of clever pupils of Indian and Asian origin.

MILBROOK HOUSE
Milton, Abingdon, Oxfordshire OX14 4EL
TEL Abingdon (0235) 831237

Pupils: 70 boys • All board • Ages: 10-13 • C of E • Fee-paying.

HEAD Since 1963, Mr H M Glazebrook MA, educated at King's School Bruton, and St Andrew's. Previously at Clayesmore Prep, before buying this school. His son, currently Second Master, will succeed. The transition is reported to be proceeding smoothly.

Entrance By registration.

Exit To a very wide cross-section of boarding schools.

Remarks A useful coaching school to know about for boys who need special tuition for CE because they are weak in a particular subject, Maths and French commonly—they have been living abroad, missed schooling through illness, etc. Very mixed ability therefore. Boys come for as little as one term. Remedial teaching on hand; staff:pupil ratio is one to eight. Saturday lessons until 2.30, last weekday lessons finish 7.20pm, children come home every third week.

Work only occasionally marked or graded; plenty of internal exams and practice papers; boosting of confidence very much part of the ethos. Regular reports by telephone to parents. 'Children come home noticeably good company, and not frustrated wiith themselves or with life,' said a parent.

Strongly family atmosphere, non-institutional comfortable homely farmhouse with outhouses, orchards and grounds to let off steam in; Mrs Glazebrook 'grannies' everyone, including streams of cleaning ladies and cooks who come in from the village. Good food. Well run and happy. Expensive (£2,800 per term from September 1991).

MOOR PARK SCHOOL
Ludlow, Shropshire SY8 4EA
TEL Ludlow (0584) 872342

Pupils: 104 boys, 69 girls • 110 board, 57 day • Ages: 8-13 • Also 35 boys and 35 girls in adjoining junior school, ages: 4-7 • RC (NB Half of school non-Catholics) • Fee-paying.

HEAD From September 1988, Mr J R Badham, B Ed Oxon, BA OU (forties), educated White Friars Grammar School, Cheltenham, previously Head of St Alban's prep school in north London. Lives with his family (three young sons—one a pupil here before his father took over—and a baby daughter) in the school.

Entrance Increasingly used by locals (including lots of first-time buyers), others from south-east, some from overseas. Test for children entering after age of eight.

Exit Boys go mainly to Downside, Ampleforth, Worth, Eton, Shrewsbury—and elsewhere. Good scholarship record though numbers declining. Girls to St Leonard's Mayfield, Woldingham, St Mary's Ascot, Moreton Hall.

Remarks Founded in 1964 in large country house and enjoyed rapid growth. Though the place ran down toward end of last Head's reign, girls' numbers are now increasing (NB their brothers are more likely to be at Abberley), and, contrary to national trends, day numbers are declining, boarding numbers rising. New girls' boarding house (once the old coach house), plush and appealing, with delightful French housemother, keen on crafts. New science block and new classrooms part of much needed refurbishment programme, including the conversion of the old dairy into a new English centre. Good language teaching. Head's declared aim is to stretch children, not drive them. Boys' dorms currently fairly grim. Strong pastoral care, on the extended family basis; all Houseparents are married. Keen drama, music and games. Shooting especially good (boys and girls), school third in St David's Shield. Religion not at all thrust down throats. Chapel in the old ballroom. Homey atmosphere—a log fire burns in the hall, home-made cakes for tea; the school fosters its reputation for entertaining (parents and teams), and lays much emphasis on encouragement.

MOUNT HOUSE SCHOOL
Mount Tavy, Tavistock, Devon PL19 9LJ
TEL (0822) 612244

Pupils: approx 192 boys • *162 board, 30 day* • *Ages: 7-13* • *C of E* • *Fee-paying.*

HEAD Since 1984, Mr C D Price BA (forties), educated Claysemore and Open University. Was assistant Headmaster at Cheam. An enthusiast who carries all before him. Boys appear to regard him as a human being—a rare state of affairs, in our observation. Tireless in promoting the school to the outside world. Steady back up from wife Sue.

Entrance From roundabout and far flung corners of the West Country. Interview, assessment and test. Healthy waiting list.

Exit Average of six scholarships a year—to King's Taunton, Blundells, Canford, Sherborne, Stowe and Radley in last three years. Majority go on to West Country public schools. OBs: David Owen and the Cashier of the Bank of England (the one who signs the notes).

Remarks School billed as 'best in the west' by one of the schools it feeds (ie, not a totally dispassionate source). Has one outstanding strength in particular, which is the bearing and behaviour of the pupils, who

are polite without being ingratiating, confident without being cocky, and cheerful with it.

School's main building is glorious old manor house overlooking Tavistock with view, on a good day, to Cornwall, and the river running at the bottom of the playing fields (has riparian rights) and surrounded by Dartmoor. Enthusiastic music—music scholarships to Radley just won at time of writing. Keen games players and will travel miles for a match (Caldicott, the Dragon—no distance too great) and were just off to Twickenham when we visited. Keen natural history (not surprising, with so much on the doorstep). Pupils streamed but not setted. New and rather smart sports hall, with a full size tennis court and two squash courts in it, also the requisite CDT centre. Sunday chapel a bit of a feature here—much attended by parents, and at time of writing 55 public school Headmasters have been lured down over the years to give of their best. School has bags of mother appeal and lots of lyrical reviews.

MOWDEN HALL SCHOOL
Newton, Stocksfield, Northumberland
NE43 7TP
TEL Stocksfield (0661) 842147

Pupils: 105 boys, 33 girls • *All board, except for 24* • *Ages: 8-14* • *C of E* • *Fee-paying.*

HEAD From September 1991, Mr Andrew Lewis (forties), previously Housemaster at Repton. Married, with four children (youngest daughter in school). Last Head, the much loved Andrew Morrison, left to become Master of the Underschool at Charterhouse, having built Mowden up to present strength. A hard act to follow.

Entrance By exam. Largely local children (ie Northumbrian, which could mean many miles/hours from home). Three-term entry, preferably nearest to eighth birthday. All required to board at 11.

Exit A quarter to the south—Eton, Winchester, occasionally Harrow; the rest to Oundle, Uppingham, Rugby, Sedburgh, Loretto and other Scottish schools. Girls to Queen Margaret's York, Wycombe Abbey, St

Leonard's, Oundle, Oakham, Giggleswick. Respectable scholarship record.

Remarks Traditional country prep school with initiative, where parents can feel confident their children are being really well taught by generous numbers of caring staff. Flexible streaming system (three-tier) from the start. Scholarship class given a week in the Lake District before summer term starts to top up tuition. More periods devoted to Maths, English, French, Science and Latin than anything else. Very good library, where the suggestions book is actively used and a well-developed system operates for children to remark on books they like/dislike/get stuck on. 'Quiet time' after lunch usually means reading. Computing is popular; gym teacher described by one and all as 'brilliant'. Keenly sporty (girls unbeaten at hockey), matches usually held on weekdays so that weekends are available for everyone to take part in activities—which are legion—camp fire cooking, beagling, expeditions, though many cite 'playing in the woods' their favourite pastime. Good food and sensible table clearing arrangements. Good facilities on a modest scale, and well used. New tennis courts, theatre and music school. Attics recently transformed into girls' dorms. All dorms are extremely simple: this is not a rich school, but it is much loved, efficiently run, and the best for miles around, set in pleasant country house with lovely parkland. Lots of enthusiasm, good atmosphere with discipline neatly balanced with free-range.

NEWCASTLE PREPARATORY SCHOOL

6 Eslington Road, Newcastle-upon-Tyne
NE2 4RH
TEL Newcastle (091) 281 1769

Pupils: 204 boys and girls ● *All day* ● *Ages: 2-13* ● *C of E* ● *Fee-paying.*

HEAD Since 1988, Mr G Clayton MA, Cert Ed (forties).

Remarks A small, very well thought of prep which

has been going for over 100 years (Kindergarten started 1988), with much individual attention, and a deserved reputation for giving children a keen sense of enjoyment in learning. In the thick of Newcastle's highest flying senior schools, with the RGS opposite, and Central High down the road. Cardinal Hume is an Old Boy. Alternatives for Newcastle families are Ascham House School (North Avenue, Gosforth), and Newlands Preparatory School (34 the Grove, Gosforth), both far larger.

NORLAND PLACE SCHOOL

162-166 Holland Park Avenue, London
W11 4UH
TEL London (071) 603 9103

Pupils: 158 girls, 90 boys (to age 8 only) ● *All day Ages: 4-11* ● *Non-denom.* ● *Fee-paying.*

PRINCIPAL Since 1955, Mrs S J Garnsey (fifties), who owns and runs the school with the aid of live-in bursar Patrick Richardson (he also takes the boys for games). Mrs G is not academically qualified herself, originally came in as a class assistant, and took over the school in 1966, from two old ladies; blessed with a soothingly gravelly voice and a fount of knowledge on senior schools (especially the 'fashionable' ones). Gives good advice in this direction. Well aware of London parental neurosis.

Entrance A rat race: babies put down at birth, literally, but embryos not accepted (parents still try). Special cases for children of Old Boys, Old Girls, grannies (NB school founded in 1876), siblings.

Exit London day schools, and boarding schools (eg Heathfield, Wycombe Abbey)—no pattern. All girls sit three schools 'as a safety net'.

Remarks Perennially popular prep and pre-prep that marches happily and successfully on in three houses joined together, rabbit warrens of twisty stairs and half-landings, every inch of space in use. Dinky, much-used playground, long narrow gym/dining hall, splendid head of gym Stephanie Price (swam for England). High teaching standards, and everything going full-blast. After school hours clubs now popular, science ('Very 'in' says the Head), art and netball. Art attic department due to be converted to CDT. Boys and girls split at seven, bright as buttons. More mixed staff currently, still a mixture of cosy and traditional. 'Things can get a bit twee with too many women,' thinks Mrs Garnsey.

Assessments recently introduced and carried out at the end of the spring term after child's entry to school, not overly popular with parents: usually at the age of four ('We've got four years to bring the boys to the boil'). Parents must pay for these assessments (block testing, carried out by two female ed psychs), not absolutely compulsory—but 'much encouraged'. Mrs G and staff are pro this, because it throws up the very bright—and also any learning difficulties. Remedial help is on hand.

THE OLD MALTHOUSE
Langton Matravers, Swanage, Dorset
BH19 3HB
TEL Swanage (0929) 422302

Pupils: 95 boys • 70 board, 25 day + pre prep 25 (inc 8 girls) • Ages: boys 4-13, girls 4-8 • C of E • Fee-paying.

HEAD Since September 1988, Mr Jonathan (Jon) Phillips BA (early forties), previously Senior Master at the Downs, Wraxall. Educated at St Luke's College, Exeter. Form master, teaches English and Geography and 'fills in' Senior Divinity. Very proud of school, enthusiastic and fun. Married with two children, James (10) and Georgina (7).

Entrance At seven or eight, register early, own Entrance Test. No places for three years for day boys, best route through pre-prep ('Littlies'). Pupils 'mainly Dorset', eight via London train and eight 'from abroad'.

Exit Mainly Winchester, Sherborne, Canford, Bryanston, Blundell's (top scholar last year), Eton, Harrow, Charterhouse etc.

Remarks Slightly surprising entrance off main street, but delightful converted Old Malthouse— dorms still called 'The Granary', splendid new multi-purpose hall with music rooms below and adjacent,

(music very strong, boys serenaded inception of new village loo with *Raindrops Keep Falling on My Head* and adaptation of *Daddy's Taking us to the Loo Tomorrow*). Latin, Greek, strong scholarship stream (Winchester etc), and school is sharing Sauveterre, South West of Toulouse, with Cothill, where five boys each term in penultimate year will follow CE Syllabus in French. Very structured, discipline includes cleaning silver, mucking out mini-buses and extra work. Boys say Sir, stand up etc, table napkins. Dining Hall (lovely old benches) doubles for assembly and chapel on Sundays when the dining hatch to kitchen converts to altar.

No longer the spartan place it used to be; outdoor swimming pool has replaced Dancing Ledge, but lots of boyish activities abound—target shooting in old gym at break, lots of clay shooting, gardens in old walled garden, and boys are fully immersed in local farming and village community. Good games pitches in school's 25-acre grounds including one all-weather area. Senior boys and Captains have own room with 'toyes' (curtained off private work areas) where they do their assignments as preparation for public school. Good strong school. Works well.

ORWELL PARK
Ipswich, Suffolk IPIO OER
TEL Nacton (0473) 659225

Pupils: 215 boys • 135 full boarders, 50 weekly boarders, 30 day • Ages: 8-13 • Non-denom—all are welcome • Fee-paying (actual bill approx £2,400 a term in 1991).

HEAD Since 1979, Mr I H Angus MA, HDipEd (forties). Educated Harrow and Trinity College, Dublin (Economics, English, History). Has been at the school for 23 years and is, 'wondering when someone will say I am over the top' (no one has yet). Two sons; widower at time of writing, but about to marry the Head of nearby girls' school, St Felix (*qv*) Miss Claydon, who joins the Orwell staff. Head is short, voluble, outspoken and can get on the wrong side of people, but very professional, energetic, outward-looking and speaks much good sense. Counts the main part of his job as 'getting good staff—I will go to any lengths to find them—and getting pupils to walk in the door. If I can do that, my job is a doddle.'

Entrance On registration. Occasionally a pupil is turned away when he reaches prep school age if he needs specialist help, though Mr Angus was hard put to say where the line was drawn in such cases. Otherwise, non-selective: 'I simply cannot tell at the ages of seven or eight what they are going to turn out like.'

Exit To an amazing 62 different schools over a period of 10 years, eg one to Bloxham, one to Wells Cathedral, one to Seaford College, but the majority to Uppingham, Felsted and Harrow.

Remarks Excellent. This is no place for little Lord Fauntleroy,' said the Head. 'We aim to produce practical, problem-solving human-beings.' To which end boys have to clean school every morning from 10.15-10.30am with brooms and mops etc, and can be seen toiling over the dirty plates at lunch. This is deliberate policy, but also helps with cost-cutting in a school which needs an enormous amount of upkeep and is not heavily endowed.

School in glorious setting—no adjectives too enthusiastic—overlooking the River Orwell with boats bobbing in distance (keen sailing school). Large 'Georgian-style' house with turn of century additions including brick skin. Beautifully proportioned rooms, an observatory with telescope (manned by local astronomy club), bell tower, dozens of music practice rooms in old cellars of house. Immense, ritzy—possibly *too* ritzy—facilities, and some boys are in for a shock when they get to their secondary school and find it can't compete. School believes in putting every possible opportunity before pupils and as far as we can judge, nothing is denied them—you might even find them building spare *beds*, not to mention surf boards, and making plastic moulds—Head's philosophy is, 'If we do it at all, we believe in doing it well'.

Emphatically *not* a swot shop; *don't* send him here to be crammed for anywhere and Head is against the 'narrowing of horizons required by Common Entrance exams'. School is stuffed with sons of East Anglian farmers (OK, 15%, to be precise). The Rt Hon Lord James Prior is Chairman of Governors and his sons were at the school, which sets the tone exactly.

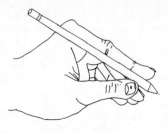

PACKWOOD HAUGH
Ruyton XI Towns, Shrewsbury, Shropshire
SY4 1HX
TEL Baschurch (0939) 260217

Pupils: 312 boys, 80 girls • *328 board, 64 day* • *Ages: 8-13* • *C of E* • *Fee-paying.*

HEAD Since September 1988, Mr P J F Jordan, MA Cantab (forties), considerate and thoughtful, a keen games-player and musician, who is busy developing the school and 'softening the edges', while maintaining the high academic and sporting traditions handed on by very long serving predecessor who ran the place as a one-man show. Previously Head of the Old Malthouse.

Entrance Short informal assessment on Maths and English; academic scholarships sometimes awarded. Children from Shropshire, Cheshire, Wales, London and abroad. Help for the needy.

Exit Shrewsbury, Rugby, Malvern, Eton, Rugby and many to local schools; girls to Malvern Girls, Cheltenham, Sherborne, Tudor Hall, Wycombe Abbey, Moreton Hall, Downe House, Wrekin and Oundle etc.

Remarks Academic country prep-school, surviving well after a tricky patch. Boys and girls work very hard—but there is far more emphasis on relaxation than under previous Head. At the time of his appointment, pupils were definitely over-pressurised and wound up, though also in need of discipline in all areas excepting academic, which was rigorous. Parents now report their children are happier, with more free time and more choice on options and activities. Broad range of activities, reflecting school's outlook—something for everyone, not just catering for the brightest. Remedial help on hand. That said, even the third stream boys are heading for Shrewsbury. Keenly sporting. Music, Art, CDT and Drama all play major roles. Children chirpy, polite and friendly. Full sized floodlit Astro-turf pitch much used. Handsome new spacious boarding house has been built for the girls, run by charming Head of Science and his wife. Boys dorms have dazzlingly action packed wallpapers. Famous topiary—of the Apostles—in the garden.

PAPPLEWICK

Ascot, Berkshire SL5 7LH

TEL Ascot (0344) 21488

Pupils: 200 boys • 151 board, 49 day • All must board by 11 • Ages: 7-13 • C of E • Fee-paying.

HEAD   Since 1979, Mr J S M Morris MA (late forties)—read Geography at Cambridge; born and bred in prep schools, was a Housemaster at Stowe for many years before returning to 'the real world'.

Remarks   Traditional and cosy, well-manicured little school, with 15 acres—every inch of them used. Stockbrokeresque architecture; boys carry brief cases. Assessments of progress are sent home to parents once every three weeks. House system with pluses and minuses clocked up for good work, effort etc. Boys go on to wide range of schools, Charterhouse and Wellington particularly popular. New teaching blocks and new Art, Design and Technology centre. Own chapel, cheerful Christianity a hallmark of the school. Good choral groups. Lots of children from overseas. Caring staff, some of whom live on the premises. Tuck twice a week and Mars bars sometimes dished out for a treat. Breeding ground for future Headmasters. Very Home Counties.

THE PILGRIMS' SCHOOL

The Close, Winchester, Hampshire SO23 9LT

TEL Winchester (0962) 854189

Pupils: 170 boys • Approx half board • 38 choral scholars (at half fees) • Ages: 8+-13+ • C of E • Fee-paying.

HEAD   Since 1983, Mr Michael Kefford MA Cantab Dip Ed (fifties), educated Lancing, and St John's College, Cambridge. Previously Head of Colston's Preparatory School, Bristol. Dynamic Scottish wife, two teenage children. Slightly reserved manner conceals a kind and caring man.

Entrance   By test at seven-plus. Substantial waiting list (especially on day boy side). Voice trials (for choristers—ie boys who sing in Winchester Cathedral—and quiristers—ie boys who sing in Winchester College Chapel choir) each November and by appointment.

Exit   A third to Winchester; and to Charterhouse, Canford, Marlborough, Sherborne, Cranleigh and other schools round about. Good record of academic scholarships and also bumper numbers of music scholarships—nine this year to Bradfield, Charterhouse, Frensham Heights, Bedales etc.

Remarks   Choir school for Winchester Cathedral. Effective team of teachers, (25% Oxbridge graduates); boys are hard working but not over pressurized. Gentle streaming from the start, scholarship class for two last years. Bright boys never limited by syllabus. Classes of 10-17. Computer studies now part of the syllabus. New building gives more subject class rooms and drama—often with musical involvement—a popular new development. Previous Director of Music has gone to Hawtrey's, new Director, Miss Hilary Brooks, long time Deputy Director here. Freelance professional players come down every week, most boys learn at least one instrument; choristers necessarily become self-disciplined in study time as they must fit so much in—and can only become choristers if they are musical *and* bright.

School a higgledy-piggledy mixture of old and new buildings, situated in beautiful Cathedral Close. Own good playing fields, though immediate grounds are somewhat cramped. High standard of sport, especially cricket. Use of Winchester College facilities—Olympic-size swimming pool (also their own small open air pool). Snooker, table tennis, cosy library and TV to fill boarders' free time.

School founded in 1931 by enlarging Cathedral Choir School. The magnificent choral music in the Cathedral and College Chapel has a great influence on the character of the school and is a big attraction to many parents. Good social mix. Happy, busy school.

PORT REGIS

Motcombe Park, Shaftesbury, Dorset
SP7 9QA
TEL Shaftesbury (0747) 52566

Pupils: 182 boys, 100 girls • 230 board, 52 day • Ages: 7-13 • C of E • Fee-paying.

HEAD Since 1969, Mr David Prichard MA Oxon (fifties), educated Radley and Oxford. Workaholic, forward-looking, a brilliant businessman—with critics and fans in equal numbers. Does not teach (his role is managing director), much liked by children, from whom earns heaps of Brownie points for endless repartee and jokes. 1990-91 chairman of IAPS (main concerns: to teach Heads to be better managers, to encourage 'good people to go into education rather than industry, and teach the seedcorn of the nation').

Entrance Overbooked (for girls especially): early application essential (but there's always a chance). Chemistry between parents and Head ('It must flow') essential at interview. NB Clientele shifting—now more county, fewer Hampstead intelligentsia offspring. One-third of pupils come from within 70-mile radius. Scholarships include one for gymnastics, one for music.

Exit Bryanston, Sherborne, Canford, Marlborough—and other schools.

Remarks As per last entry in the GSG, this still rates as probably the most go-ahead prep in Britain (and one of the most expensive). Head delighted with parental comment that, 'It's like an upmarket holiday camp'—because he fears many children have dull lives during the holidays in concrete jungles watching telly.

Amazing facilities include purpose-built specialist classrooms (each with own teaching office), county standard sports hall, plus the new national centre for junior gymnastics with quite incredible equipment from France by Gymnova. This was opened by HM The Queen (called The Queen's Hall, which should pack them in), simultaneously wearing her crown and her granny hat, and is regularly let out to the public. Staff encouraged to do their own thing, but when the Head of Sports informed the Head that he was now running a department with 12 full-time staff, 'I said,

"Hang on, can we afford this?"' and it seems they can. Also new is the 25m indoor pool (air temperature = 82 degrees, water 80 degrees), used by QE2 crew for sea rescue practice.

Very high standard of teaching, staff mostly young (some refugees from state system), all keenly committed and immensely energetic (necessarily so, to stand the pace)—and highly paid. Nine of them on duty every weekend. Tutorial system (children choose their own tutor) works well: mutual respect apparent between staff and children. Still some grousing from day parents that the day is too long: children are definitely stretched—often sideways—and most thrive. Praise is liberally heaped, self-confidence noticeable. At least 20% of the time-table is not geared towards exams which are taken on the wing. 50 different hobbies on offer, 15 different sports—they win most things, more because of facilities, plus their own in-board motors than because they are fiercely competetive. Big theatre, and two major productions per term which involve 60 pupils each. Set in rolling Dorset parkland, main block built for Duke of Westminster. Port Regis hums with energy, happiness—and hard work—and relaxed faces (children and staff). Head often tells parents they underestimate their children—he is constantly amazed by pupils. After a short hiccup, apparently unspoilt by presence of the Princess Royal's children.

RIDDLESWORTH HALL

Diss, Norfolk IP22 2TA
TEL Garboldisham (095 381) 246

Pupils: 135 girls • 95 board, 15-20 weekly boarders, 15-20 day • All girls • Pre-prep: 28 boys and girls • Ages: 4-13 • Fee-paying.

HEAD Since January 1991, Miss Susan Smith, BA (early forties). Studied music at Bristol University, PGCE at St John's, York. Previously Director of Music at St James's and the Abbey, Malvern. Lots of hobbies—theatre, opera, cookery and entertaining, walking, archaeology, reading, travel.

Entrance Registration and interview.

Exit Everywhere, from Gordonstoun in the north to

Roedean in the south, Felixstowe in the east, Malvern in the west and all stations in between. Riddlesworth is one of the 'Allied Schools'.

Remarks Charming posh country school in beautiful listed stately home (look at plaster mouldings). Gorgeous grounds, with lovely old trees, in one of the most unspoilt areas in the country. A bit isolated. Wood-panelled baths and even thunder-boxes, lots of room and time for (small) pets. General approach at time of writing is old fashioned virtues with a modern approach, that is, doing modern things but expecting good manners. Spelling, tables, detention, streaming, marks,—the *lot*. This may change under new Head. Dear little children—sometimes thickissima.

Indoor swimming pool with palms, big picture windows. Extras such as fly-tying, clay pigeon shooting. Pre-prep opened September 1986 for 'dwarves' (but new Head tells us that Snow White has now left). Fees 'stepped' to cushion shock of escalation as pupils get older. 30/40 ex pat families—banking, forces etc, eight Spaniards at time of writing. Princess of Wales' prep school.

SALISBURY CATHEDRAL SCHOOL

1 The Close, Salisbury, Wiltshire SP1 2EQ

TEL Salisbury (0722) 322652

Pupils: 125 boys, 30 girls • 93 day, 45 board (including all choristers and probationers) • Ages: 8-13 • Also own pre-prep, with 75 boys and 102 girls, ages 4-8; and second prep school, Holmwood, with 75 boys and girls, ages 4-8 • C of E • Fee-paying.

HEAD From September 1991, Mr C J A Helyer ACP (forties), previously Head of Exeter Cathedral Choir School.

Entrance Increasingly via schools' own pre-preps (hence the girls, 'I wish we'd taken girls ages ago'). At eight, tested after entry (severely dyslexic children not accepted). Choristers (all on half fees) come in by public voice trial—girls as well as boys, which has caused criticism from other choir schools.

Exit Wide variety of public schools (no more than two to each per year), regularly to the locals, ie Winchester, Marlborough, Sherborne, Canford, Bryanston; also Blundell's, Cheltenham, Lancing, King's Canterbury. Also to strong local grammar school (the only one left in Wiltshire), Bishop Wordsworth. Choristers regularly get music scholarships.

Remarks Set in shadow of the Cathedral (SE corner) in old Bishop's Palace, has existed elsewhere since the eleventh century. Surrounded by 27 acres of grounds, including lake (rainbow trout), outdoor pool, six hole golf course, playing fields. Modern block classrooms, science labs etc, plus fascinating old parts, including fine eighteenth-century drawing room (used for Assembly and Prep), tiny Jacobean chapel, history room in fifteenth-century Bishop's Gatehouse (NB immortalised in Trollope's *Barchester Towers*). Pleasantly down-at-heel and old fashioned—lots of worn lino, staff eat with children in splendid ancient vaulted dining hall; musical instruments parked everywhere, sounds of music lessons all over the place (all choristers must learn two instruments), and music generally of high standard: all children have music appreciation classes from the beginning. Classes are small (15, sometimes only seven), and maximum flexibility—pupils move up when they are ready, not by ages. (Parents can drop day pupils off at 8am.) Help on hand for slow coaches.

Head and his wife run the place as extended family at all times, though discipline is firmish, community spirit high. Stars and stripes system on pink/green paper slips, when five of either have been awarded the child goes to see the Head. City facilities—library, squash courts, indoor pool etc used by Cathedral School to supplement. The pre-preps use some of main school's facilities, including dining hall. Some mutterings from parents that school has 'run down' somewhat as outgoing Head 'appeared to lose interest'.

ST ANSELM'S

Bakewell, Derbyshire DE4 1DP

TEL Bakewell (062 981) 2734

Pupils: 115 boys, 36 girls • About 111 board, including 9 girls • Ages: 8-13 • Also pre-prep of about 30 boys and girls, ages 4-8 • C of E • Fee-paying.

HEAD Since 1967, Mr Tim Piper MA (fifties), classicist from Pembroke College Cambridge. Succeeded his father, who ran the school as a limited company, with family shareholders taking out dividends. School changed to charitable trust—not without a struggle—in 1974. Mrs Piper runs the school with her husband, doing 'everything—reading stories, bottlewasher, housekeeper, caretaker, matron, drain unblocker'. Four children. All but one of governors have (had) children in the school. The Pipers, according to parents, deserve to be described by that much abused adjective, 'caring, with a reputation for listening to both children and parents'.

Entrance Early registration advisable.

Exit Impressive scholarship and exhibition list—nine scholarships won in most recent year—to Repton, Cheltenham Ladies, Rugby, Oakham, Queen Margaret's Escrick—and this is fair representation of where the pupils go on to, plus Oundle and Uppingham.

Remarks You need to truffle out the virtues of this school, as it is not a place much given to worrying about appearances—distinctly scruffy, in fact, apart from girls' boarding house, which is immaculate and home-like, in a separate building across the road. Site tucked up behind Bakewell church, overlooking fields of sheep and cows. Well designed purpose-built blocks. School has had four Heads since it started in 1888—gives the place a totally family feel, and the Pipers live in a house practically in the middle of the school, with toys and treasured possessions scattered about.

The school's quite outstanding record of academic success (given mixed intake) is attributed by Mr Piper to the staff:pupil ratio - 'classes of a maximum of 10, and I challenge you to find a prep school which does better'—and to that precious commodity which boarding schools have in abundance—time. The heavy schedule is, Mr Piper, admits, much harder on the day boys. Pupils are children of doctors, lawyers, very nice farmers and seven expats.

Dedicated and gentle staff, including two Classicists and two and a half linguists, not to mention the Head of Maths who is an England rugby cap (got it while at the school). Terrifically keen computer room. Pottery outstanding, with wife of one of the masters coming in to inspire and direct. School newspaper contributors were off to interview Edwina Currie when we visited. School streamed after the first shake down, but Mr Piper says St Anselm's is definitely *not* a force feed. '...what I like is bringing up children and that, I like to think, is our greatest contribution'. Also, he says, he likes them to 'learn what trying is—when you are 40 down in a match...' Sport on 'only' four afternoons a week, options otherwise. Main games rugby, football, hockey, and 'mad keen' cricketing school.

ST ANTHONY'S

90 Fitzjohn's Avenue, London NW3 6NP

TEL London (071) 435 0316

Pupils: 290 boys • All day • Ages: 6-13 • RC • Fee-paying.

HEAD Since 1962, Mr T Winsloe Patton MA (fifties), educated at the Oratory and Trinity College, Dublin. Previously taught in New York. Grandson of the founder (school is a limited company), a hangover hippy from the Sixties, called Tim by one and all, enormously friendly, prowls aobut the school, puts head in classrooms and says 'Hi!'. Mad about mime, an enthusiast. Believes that, 'Home is the real influence, the input by families cannot be over-emphasised.' Due to retire in 1996, when his nephew, Mr Nigel Pitel (currently teaching in the school, and a more conventional figure) will take over.

Entrance Mostly at six and seven, must know the basics.

Exit Westminster, UCS, City of London, Highgate etc, a few to country RC boarding schools, also Bryanston, Malvern, Marlborough, Tonbridge.

Remarks Apparently very free range, but plenty of

hard work underneath—bright and busy, popular with media parents. Children much encouraged to ask questions and develop highly articulate oral skills. 'The silent child is the one that worries us.' Art every-where—you can hardly move for autumn leaves, skeletons, robots. Mostly male staff (some have been here 18 years), though school day finishes officially at 4.30 (3.30 for littles), the place still hums with energy far later. Pupils run lunch time clubs, including (currently) stilt walking and acrobatics, 'It's surprising what talent is uncovered'. Drama, especially drama workshops, hugely popular. Excellent mime, and groups take part in London and Paris mime festivals, also Glastonbury. 'Mime is terrifically confidence making and brings out some very good creative writing,' explains the Head. School buildings badly in need of lick of paint; large playgrounds, outdoor pool. Blazer and tie the only essential uniform—boys may wear jeans and trainers.

ST AUBYNS

Rottingdean, Brighton, Sussex BN2 7JN
TEL Brighton (0273) 302170

Pupils: 115 boys • *85 board, 30 day* • *Ages: 7-14* • *C of E/Non-denom* • *Fee-paying.*

HEAD Since 1974, Mr Julian James IAPS diploma, Cert Ed (fifties) educated at Charterhouse. A benign, fatherly figure, he has been at the school man and boy; he was a pupil and came back to teach when he left school. Runs a happy but disciplined ship (boys say 'Sir', stand up, open doors). 'Unless a child is happy he cannot fulfil all his potential.' The boys know exactly where they stand with him.

Entrance By assessment, interview and report from previous school.

Exit A wide variety to fairly local schools, eg Eastbourne, Brighton College, Seaford, St Bede's, Lancing. Also 11 in two years to Eton and Harrow.

Remarks Set in the middle of Rottingdean's main street, school has about 11 acres, with five acres of playing fields on a devilish slope. Fabulous pavilion. Successful appeal has paid for new Science and Technology complex. Sports hall with squash court, heated

swimming pool, standard games (only one tennis court). Good on fencing; school provides bugles and drums for local activities. Very integrated locally. Slightly morbid memorial Chapel has photos of Old Boys who died during the two wars displayed at back.

Senior boys have study bedrooms; posters and teddies everywhere. Bible reading is mandatory each night. Boys charming, articulate and self-confident. Food is good and Mrs James is magic, particularly with new boys, Mars Bars equal currency.

No longer up-market only. A jolly and very cosy school where the school's golden retriever, Perkins, (to whom we apologise for spelling his name wrong in the previous edition) helps to tuck the boys up at night. If the Head is away on business, Perkins carries on regardless.

ST JOHN'S COLLEGE SCHOOL

Grange Road, Cambridge CB3 9AB
TEL Cambridge (0223) 353532

Pupils: 290 boys, 120 girls • *55 board, 355 day (including all girls)* • *Ages: 4-13* • *C of E* • *Fee-paying.*

HEAD Since 1990, Mr Kevin Jones (early thirties), MA plus unfinished thesis on how best to acquire knowledge and preserve creativity. Educated Wool-vaston Hall (state boarding) and Caius Cambridge. Previous post—Deputy Head in the school and before that Head of Drama and Art at the Yehudi Menuhin School. Married with one son—the youngest pupil in the school. A thinker, good with children. Shows all the signs of being a worthy successor to previous Head, Mr Mould—no mean thing—if he does not move on to other things.

Entrance Embryo on. Big, big pressure to get in, though Mr Jones says modestly that Cambridge has terrific shortage of prep places. No testing at three-plus 'ridiculous'—but test at seven. Yearly scholarships for up to five boy choristers a year.

Exit Every year gets clutch of scholarships to strong music schools — Eton, King's Canterbury, Uppingham. Feeds The Perse School in Cambridge, also sends pupils to Oakham, Westminster, Winchester, Oundle (head of Oundle a governor) and a number of East Anglian schools.

Remarks Utterly wonderful prep school — well worth bustling about to get in. Feels like a honeycomb of schools—nursery department in separate house, 'so it feels like home'; five to six-year olds are in a wing of the smart tailor-made Byron House which was refurbished and reopened in 1990 to replace a multitude of Portakabins and provides not only classrooms, but smart hall/gym for tinies; older pupils in a house (and Portakabins) next door; boarders live above the shop with own private rather institutional-looking quarters. Computer for National Curriculum Council pilot scheme to look into the teaching of information technology is housed at the end of boarders' corridor. This is causing a certain protest.

New Head's aim is to 'meet the individual needs of each child, so the most (and least) able children get what they need,' and with that in mind he is conducting a long term review. School can cope with bright child who has learning difficulties—specialist teacher—but academically weak would struggle with the hot shot children of dons, government ministers etc. Jolly red uniform. High calibre of teachers who draw all that is best and most original from the pupils. Choristers under tutellage of organist George Guest (sadly retiring) now form part of one of the best choirs in the world. Terms fit in with university terms and hence do not fit in with anything else. Most helpful flexible school day/week includes weekly boarding, 'day' boarding (ie, until 8.15pm) and 'staying on' (until 6pm)—a miracle for working parents.

ST PAUL'S GIRLS' PREPARATORY SCHOOL

Bute House, Luxemburg Gardens, London W6 7EA

TEL London (071) 603 7381

Pupils: Approx 238 girls • All day • Ages: 5-11 • Non denom, predominantly Christian • Fee-paying.

HEAD Since 1972, Miss J E Lee, educated at St Paul's Girls' School and Froebel College (continues to keep her age a secret). Has worked in maintained schools as well as independent, and with maladjusted children. Delightfully old-fashioned and unbossy, which has more child than parent appeal.

Entrance Non selective ('It's a lottery' says Miss Lee), names chosen from huge pile *à la* tombola—children must be registered by January 1st of the year they will be three. Head firmly against testing this young, 'unfair on children and parents.' 25 girls come in at seven—150 try out, seen in groups of 10, selected via tests, and some teaching.

Exit All the London day schools, depending on geography, and usually several gain awards. (NB The prep school is no relation to the senior school.) Head advises that all girls sit entrance to three schools. On average 10 leavers out of 50-60 board.

Remarks Excellent on all the basics. The system apears informal—but this is deceptive. Work comes back with remarks not marks, there is no streaming, no positioning, no weekly or termly tests. Timed tests are given in the last year only—and marks may be kept secret. Classes are changed every year, mixing brightest and dimmest, though girls can write a list of two others they want to be with, and they are sure of being with at least one. Children with August to December birthdays often made to repeat a year (however bright) in the middle forms, 'Tiresome' say parents. However, parents are full of praise of the staff, and find the school very efficiently run. Specialist teachers for eight and nine years upwards (unusual feature in girls' prep); lovely science lab, lots of hands-on work. Extremely good art, visible everywhere. Strongly musical, with all instruments (including trombone and all the stringed instruments) all taught in school hours (other day preps please note); two general music lessons per class each week.

Lots and lots of space, and purpose-built premises altogether well used and well thought out—signs of a beady bursar at work. Large assembly hall acts as gym, dining and drama hall, and looks out over senior St Paul's playing fields, which junior school has allotted times to use, 'and the beech tree is ours,' says Head proudly. Unusually large library and own class libraries too; CDT in the art room. Fortnightly meetings for community discussions, children involved at every level, helping to run things, organising table-setters, litter pick-up teams etc. Mild moans from some parents who would like more after-school clubs. Like most independent girls' prep schools, no social mix to be found.

ST PETER'S EATON SQUARE

Lower Belgrave Street, London
SW1W ONL.
TEL *London (071) 730 8855*

Pupils: Intake 38 in each year • *Co-ed* • *All day* • *Ages: 5-11* • *C of E* • *Voluntary aided state school.*

HEAD Since 1980, Mr R W Cayliss (sixty), Licentiate of Trinity College, London, organ diploma. Hon Fellow and Treasurer of Guild of Church Musicians. Teaches piano but not in school, and sings. Hyperactive, works in the eye of the storm, charismatic, dynamic and a man of presence. Articulate and good at lobbying in high places. Comments 'the problem with this country is class'.

Entrance Visit school and put child's name down at third birthday. Admission according to governors' criteria, in strict order of qualifying, starting with 'children who attend St Peter's Church' and live in the Parish.

Exit Majority to Westminster City, Greycoat and Pimlico; in recent times, 30% to private sector—JAGS, St Paul's Girls, Christ's Hospital, Dulwich. Head comments that the school 'does not see itself as a pre-prep school'—and woe betide anyone who takes their child out before the appointed time to move into the private sector.

Remarks Outstanding state primary working wonders in the relatively cramped quarters of Gothic building in the shadow of Victoria station. If you are lucky enough to qualify, and can stand the cut and thrust at breaktime, look no further. Pupils mainly middle class 'well-motivated, dustmen to duchesses— excellent social mix 'like a good cake'. Some MPs' children and diplomats. Good community feeling, lots of parental support. Usually number one swimming school in Westminster area—consistently high standard throughout the school. Twice weekly hands-on music lessons for juniors—recorders, strings, wood-wind, percussion, brass, string orchestra, woodwind and brass groups: music in general good though tendency to over-ambition. Strong links with St Peter's Church (the one which was burned down), which provides 15% of the funding, weekly mass and most confirmed into C of E. Has suffered from difficulty of keeping staff in central London owing to low pay, but since the demise of ILEA and school's opting for a 'delegated budget' (ie St Peter's holds the purse strings), all are confident that this is a thing of the past. Ghastly food.

ST PHILIP'S

6 Wetherby Place, London SW7 4NE
TEL *London (071) 373 3944*

Pupils: Approx 95 boys • *All day* • *Ages: 7/8-13* • *RC.* • *Fee-paying.*

HEAD Since January 1990, H Biggs-Davison MA (thirties), educated St Philip's, Downside, Fitzwilliam College Cambridge, where he read Geography—and came straight back to St Philip's to teach in 1978. Ran school jointly for a time with Colin Atkinson, who is now happy to be back in the classroom teaching History. Aims to run an 'even more excellent little prep school and develop it, not in terms of expansion but as a place.' Seriously good-looking. Good at recruiting and good with children. Open. Wife is the ideas woman.

Entrance Several tests, but priority is given to Catholics, so intake is more comprehensive than the majority of London preps.

Exit A variety of private schools, both day and boarding, including St Benedict's, Ealing, Westminster and St Paul's, Downside, Worth, Haileybury etc.

Remarks One of central London's only Catholic private prep schools and has powerful Catholic patrons (Hume and assorted abbots). Housed in large red brick Kensington building which has been ruined by having to comply with fire regulations. Cramped class-rooms—though no more so than many other London schools—but saving grace is a wonderful leafy and muddy playground which runs the whole length of the block, with room for everyone to let off steam. Top two forms streamed. Pupils a riot of different nationalities—Italians, Portuguese, restaurateurs, diplomats, MPs, a Kuwaiti, a Japanese—some of whom do not speak English as first language. Mr B-D is confident though, that the school has the resources to train these up into the main stream of teaching—'we have small classes at the bottom of the school and can give them a lot of individual attention—and they catch up very fast'. Excellent art—art teacher does picture framing in spare time. A school to watch.

ST RONAN'S SCHOOL
Hawkhurst, Kent TN18 5DJ
TEL Hawkhurst (058 05) 2271

Pupils: Approx 100 boys • Majority full boarders, some weekly boarders and approx 27 day • Ages: 8-14 • Pre-prep: 14 boys, ages 5-7 • C of E • Fee-paying.

HEAD Since 1970, Mr John Vassar-Smith MA (fifties) educated at Eton. Charming. Johnny, as he is known, took over from his father Sir Richard, and his wife and sister both teach—sister-in-law and father-in-law also in school, which is a complete family production. Also promises, without worrying too much about hubris 'You choose the school, and we'll get him there'.

Entrance By interview. No exam, but boys have to be of fairly good standard (if only because of that rash promise). A small pre-prep, 'the puppies', 'because of local demand' but prefers boys to start at seven or eight.

Exit Pupils go on to local public schools.

Remarks An extremely happy, relaxed school, about which we get a constant stream of positive noises. Head's door is always open and boys constantly pour in and out to look at the computers. Day boys are included in everything and most demand to board sooner or later.
   Old Boys include painter Piers de Laszlo and cartoonist Sir Osbert Lancaster, whose Latin master used to tear up his sketches and demand prep instead. Popular with the Services and the professions. 'Volvos, not Rolls-Royces.' Combines wonderful family atmosphere with good results and yet not above 'sending for Mum' if child ill and Mum near by.
   'Normal' on games. Shooting and golf—they have their own course—popular too.

SANDROYD
Rushmore, Tollard Royal, Salisbury,
Wiltshire SP5 RQD
TEL Tollard Royal (0725) 516 264

Pupils: • 150 boys • All board • Ages: 8-13 • C of E • Fee-paying.

HEAD Since 1982, Mr D J Cann MA Cantab (forties), educated at Merchant Taylors' School. Read History and teaches French (a house in France). 'Came to education via three years in industry', previously at Kings Choir School, Cambridge and Joint Head of Copthorne, Sussex. Confident and charming, he giggles a lot. Mrs Cann efficiently in charge of boys' welfare.

Entrance Waiting list. Register early: requires fluency in reading, writing and 'rithmetic, assessment nine months before entry. Good social mix. Strong army links (8am news monitored at 7am before breakfast broadcast during Gulf Crisis); most from Wessex, 10% OB's children. OBs include the Lords Avon, Carrington, Snowdon, plus Sir Ranulph Fiennes, and Sir Terence Rattigan.

Exit Regularly to Sherborne, Eton, Radley, Milton Abbey, Wellington, Charterhouse, Harrow, Bryanston and others. 'The odd Wykhamist'.

Remarks Traditional prep school run on family lines in Pitt-Rivers family house, open fires (well guarded) and marvellous long hall focus of school with benches for all and super oak furniture everywhere and grounds (70 acres in middle of Rushmore estate) *beautifully* kept. Cann kitchen on ground floor (full of dogs), smallest Cann (Ben, at Knighton) wanders in and out (so do dogs up to a point), and Cann family sleep on first floor. Boys terribly polite, say Sir, and stand up as soon as you appear, table napkins, strong discipline. Punishments include 'sweeping out bootroom', standing outside Mr Cann's study, or being deprived of free time. All boys board, many with ponies (stables being rebuilt), pets, bikes and gardens. Whole school under same—somewhat sprawling—roof, with super swimming pool built to celebrate school's centenary in 1988. Computers all over (working Lego interface), strong art, very good music (three choirs, orchestra), and drama booming. No telly or sweets. God important, boys kneel nightly to say prayers, and chapel (gift of Ozanne family) being revamped. Delicious food.

Remedial teaching (about 10%), two teachers, but otherwise classes streamed after two years, 14/15 per class. Scholarship stream with mezzanine floor for senior boys to work in on own. A happy school.

STANCLIFFE HALL
Darley Dale, Matlock, Derbyshire DE4 2HJ
TEL Matlock (0629) 732310

Pupils: approx 170 boys, 30 girls • About 80 board, 110 day • Ages: 3-13 • Interdenom • Fee-paying.

HEAD Since 1985, and still going strong, Mr A R R Wareham BSc (thirties). Believes that the school should be run with a family atmosphere, with the children working hard and playing keenly. The Warehams own the school.

Entrance Older entrants are assessed by English and Maths staff.

Exit Feeds children to public schools all over the country.

Remarks Founded in 1899, housed in country house in glorious setting with 36 acres of woodland and park on the edge of the Peak District National Park. Tremendously active, 'It's all on our doorstep though the children go to Wales and the Lake District too'. Cubs, mountaineering, golf etc.

Traditionally strong rugby school, also strong at cricket and hockey.

SUMMER FIELDS
Oxford OX2 7EN
TEL Oxford (0865) 54433

Pupils: 242 boys • Approx 15 day, the rest board • Ages: 8-13 • C of E foundation with strong RC contingent • Fee-paying.

HEAD Mr Nigel Talbot-Rice ('Small but Nice' or 'Talby'), MA Oxon in History (fifties). Taught for three years at Papplewick, then at Summer Fields for 10 years before being appointed Headmaster. A building Head, keen on 'the plant'. Runs place as efficient business. Lively, accessible and tireless. Good at getting and keeping good and interesting staff. Currently pushing the day element.

Entrance Put down your son's name any time, 'the sooner the better'. Test set to check for reasonable intelligence. Three academic scholarships of up to half fees available. Day boys discouraged unless utterly brilliant dons' sons.

Exit Feed for Eton (50%). Gets four to five (last year eight) scholarships to major schools, including Radley, Winchester etc. Also sends boys to Ampleforth. Old Boys include Supermac, Wavell, James Pitman.

Remarks Sound institution which specialises in getting upper class boys of average intelligence into Eton by dint of sheer hard work and heavy streaming in final three years. Very structured timetable produces comment from master at one public school that Summer Field boys are, 'bewildered at the thought of free periods'. 'Leagues' system for all areas of school activity. 70 acres of north Oxford, boys constantly on the games fields and have scored an amazing recent string of victories, including beating the Dragon's five year run of victories in cricket and beating the hell out of Horris Hill. Smart indoor swimming pool. Pupils upper and upper-middle class and school also very class-conscious—Sid would be weeded out from list of hopefuls down for the school in an instant. Discipline on the lines of making boys stand in a corner throughout lunch most effective. If 'Talby' accepts you, what a relief, say parents, because you know little Edward is well on his way to Eton or Radley. The Summer Fields record of leavers gives an interesting insight into which top traditional public schools are most fashionable—

and probably the best. NB Only twice this century has a Summer Fields boy not won a scholarship to Eton.

SUNNINGDALE SCHOOL

Dry Arch Road, Sunningdale, Berkshire
SL5 9PY

TEL Ascot (0344) 20159

Pupils: 120 boys • All board • C of E • Fee-paying.

HEADS Since 1967, the famous Dawson twins (fifties)—a national institution. Nick Dawson is Head, Tim Dawson is Deputy Head—looks after plant, financial affairs etc—and Mrs Tim Dawson looks after flowers, and domestic side. Twins educated at Eton, no degree but two years in the Green Jackets. Energetic and enthusiastic—'this is home to us'—but school is owned by them (private limited company) and hence suffers from lack of checks and balances. All three keen on fishing.

Remarks School is run almost entirely by the Dawson triumvirate, with minimum of outside help. Very fierce matron. Keen sports school and only truly sporting types will flourish in this environment. 'It's in a time warp,' said a public school Head.

SUSSEX HOUSE PREPARATORY SCHOOL

68 Cadogan Square, London SW1X 0EA

TEL London (071) 584 1741

Pupils: 170 boys • All day • Ages: 8-13 • C of E •
Fee-paying.

HEAD Since 1969 Mr J H E Whittaker IAPS Diploma (fifties), educated at Wellington. Short, brisk, dapper, slightly military. Stands on the doorstep each morning to shake every boy by the hand, and is at the ready to have a word with/give an ear to parents. Elegant office. Contract renewed until 1994.

Entrance Taken at seven or eight, with their own paper at Sussex House, plus interview.

Exit This is the only boys central London prep that is not a feed. Boys go on to a *very* wide selection of all main London and country public schools. Boys regularly win one or three awards from the scholarship class.

Remarks Nice bit of real estate in central London, lease currently being renegotiated. Possible ownership changes. Some of staff, including Head, tucked into mini flats over the shop. Straight up and down academic approach, CE never out of sight for long. Initial intake (of 35) each September divided into two classes. First two years with a form mistress, then they are ready for the men. Head starts boys off on Latin (at nine), and they love it. Emphasis on learning to work on their own. Stars and stripes system of praise and condemnation.

Very strong on music. Also boys regularly take non-singing part in operas at Covent Garden, and art is good. Computer plays minor role. Games twice weekly, plus voluntary football/cricket on Saturdays, and at least two gym periods per week in school's own gymnasium, in adjacent annexe. No playground means discipline within the school is essential. Own dilapidated minibus, rarely free of crisps and cartons. Eleven clubs. Gymnastics team do well in national competitions; outstanding fencing, under controversial Mark Nelson-Griffiths (Welsh International, Commonwealth Campionships Team Medallist): still the National Prep Schools' champions, and London Schools champions (ie ahead of senior schools as well). Visiting speakers talk on religious themes; annual prize awarded for ambitious travel plans. Much inspiration at top end of school from outstanding young Deputy Head, Nicholas Kaye.

Pupils wear tweedy jackets and take lunch boxes. Efficient, strong links between school and parents (endless notes taken home), this is still a popular choice of many central London families who like the approach: sound and traditional but gentler than Colet Court and Westminster Under. A fair number of Middle Eastern pupils etc.

THOMAS'S
28–40 Battersea High St, London SW11 3JB
TEL London (071) 978 4224
and
17–19 Cottesmore Gardens, London
W8 5PR
TEL London (071) 938 1931

Pupils: 240 in Battersea, (115 boys, 125 girls), ages:4-13 • 218 in Cottesmore (113 boys, 105 girls), ages: 4-11 • Privately owned by Mr and Mrs Thomas, Principals of both schools • C of E • Fee-paying.

HEAD Since 1977, Mr Paul Moss MA (forties), with previous experience in state system; considered by parents to be 'remarkable—very caring, intelligent, approachable'. Head at Cottesmore: Miss Jill Kelham, Cert Ed (thirties).

Entrance Test at four, exam at eight (including for those already in school); some boys leave at seven or eight to go to all boys' preps. Children can transfer automatically from Cottesmore to Battersea at 11, in order to take CE at 12+ or 13+. Increasingly children's names put down at birth: registration fee to main list, which guarantees interview, (NB Approx twice as many seen as get in), currently £35.

Exit Girls to all top London schools or boarding to St Mary's Calne, Benenden, Roedean, North Foreland, Tudor Hall. (NB Can leave at 11, 12 or 13.) Boys widely spread to top schools.

Remarks Both schools expanded rapidly (founded 1977) and haven't finished yet. Fairly gentle approach, with very imaginative teaching and high expectations. Children streamed from eight onwards, 20 per class. Non-institutional, but also highly structured. Powerfully enthusiastic. Children are bright, happy and well-mannered.
French and Science only subject-taught classes at eight (French starts at five), Latin for all at nine. Good food. Unusual emphasis on non-exam. work and lots of projects (beginning at eight), history of art ('madly popular'). Lots of extra-curricular activities fitted into (long) school day—ice-skating, computing, ballet, fencing, swimming, lots and lots of clubs and far more exercise and sport than at some London schools. Flourishing and extremely keen drama. Heavy on homework. Since the last edition, Cottesmore have built lovely light conservatory art room, and re-jigged to have music room. The Cadogan Gardens branch moved to Battersea (at half term 1989) into large one-time grammar school. Heaps of room (currently rattling and under-using blocks, but numbers planned to increase to 330 in September 1991, and 460 by 1994). Three-quarters of an acre playground, pitches marked out everywhere, own gym, assembly hall/theatre, masses of labs etc. Lick of paint has brightened place up, and Sloane parents' gloom at depositing offspring in ugly Battersea totally dispelled over delight at space. This branch runs three school buses and a Hoppa. Unusually strong PTA.

TREVOR-ROBERTS TUTORIAL COLLEGE LTD
57 Eton Avenue, London NW3 3ET
TEL London (071) 586 1444

Pupils: 55 boys, 35 girls • All day • Ages: 9-14 • Non-denom • Fee-paying.

PRINCIPAL Mr Christopher Trevor-Roberts LVO (fifties) educated Bromesgrove; taught at prep schools in Malvern area, before setting up on his own in London in the late Fifties. Trained as a singer, has huge enthusiasm (for music especially) and energy. Known as 'the Barbara Wodehouse of the educational world' in some circles.

Remarks Still considered by many to be the best tutorial establishment of all, though run along the lines of a day prep school (but children are accepted—and released—at any age). Head notes increasing numbers of girls leaving now at 13. Very confident-building atmosphere. 'Confidence is 80% of learning—perhaps more—it's easily destroyed' asserts Mr Trevor-Roberts. He revels in getting children to study, ditto his staff (who include his own son), notably patient and enthusiastic. Good science lab and library. PT every day, swimming at least once a week, basketball (no football, no cricket). Well-designed large light rooms, fold-up Italian chairs and desks, good food. Paved playground used for outdoor teaching, games, theatre; pleasantly leafy space between neighbouring houses.

Piped classical music throughout the school every morning, and pupils encouraged to listen to opera over weekends. Good on getting lecturers, RSC workshops etc in. Structured system, but non-competititve. Half term reports. Head tries hard to help children to be self-reliant ('It's better for them not to borrow, good for them to know their own prep') and he adds that at this age, 'They're square children who will take advice.' Parents encouraged not to harass their offspring (sometimes easier said than done). High fees for so much individual attention, worth every penny according to parents delighted to find their work-shy/blocked children coping, and usually enjoying doing so; good results to a wide variety of public schools particularly Westminster, St Paul's, Bryanston, King's School Canterbury, Highgate.

WALHAMPTON SCHOOL
Lymington, Hampshire SO41 5ZG
TEL Lymington (0590) 672013

Pupils: Approx 123 boys, 82 girls • *130 board, 75 day* • *Ages: 7-13* • *C of E* • *Fee-paying.*

HEAD Since 1983, Mr A W S Robinson MA (fifties), educated at Repton and Oxford. Very involved with pupils and all school's activities. Previously Head of Brocksford Hall, co-ed prep in Derbyshire.

Entrance Registration three years in advance of entry (two years at pre-prep). Assessment one term before entry; children come from overseas, London (especially south-west eg Richmond), and Hampshire/Wiltshire and further west; increasing numbers of day children. Own pre-prep (started 1985 on the premises, comprising approx 45 pupils, run by Headmaster's wife).

Exit Overwhelmingly to Bryanston, Canford and Sherborne Girls. After that, absolutely everywhere you can think of, from the Highlands to the Isle of Wight, with the exception of Eton.

Remarks 'Vibrantly happy describes it exactly,' said a parent, commenting on our last edition. Breadth is emphasised—and makes some of the 'academic' preps look and feel narrow by comparison. A and B streams, 20 per class, remedial help on hand (though severe cases not accepted). Vivacious and devoted staff, all of whom (including matrons) spend much time outside their own subjects. Assessments are fortnightly. All boys wear shorts except in winter. Hobbies an outstanding strength—some say OTT and 'parents would be advised to keep a weather eye on the academic side,' commented a parent. They include bee-keeping, cookery (especially popular with boys), photography, needlework (boys and girls making samplers at time of our visit), stone polishing, fencing, archery. Clever encouragement by staff to get children going, and make sure they experiment with variety over the years. Woodwork of an extremely high standard and CDT better than some senior schools can offer. Lots of sports (including sailing), about 15 children keep ponies at school. Strong music, with visiting staff from Bournemouth Symphony Orchestra.

Emphasis on responsibility—four Houses, subdivided into Patrols, 12 per group, mixed ages. Leader acts more or less as Prefect, and undertake (by rota) organising different aspects of running the school, eg tidying/cleaning, sorting post etc, all under aegis of member of staff (professional dailies come in, too). School (fine old large redbrick manor) set in lovely gardens on the edge of the New Forest, with views of Solent and Isle of Wight. A week before summer term ends, school splits off into different directions (Mull, Devon) for field studies, expeditions, adventures, followed by three days back at school writing it up. Scholarly types might fare better elsewhere, but for average bright children this is education in the round.

WELLESLEY HOUSE
Broadstairs, Kent CT10 2DG
TEL Thanet (0843) 62991

Pupils: 137 boys, 54 girls • *175 board, 16 day* • *Ages: 7-14* • *Interdenom* • *Fee-paying.*

HEAD Since 1990, Mr Richard Steel BSc (forties), previously Headmaster of York House School,

Hertfordshire. Educated Bradfield College and London University.

Entrance Names should be entered as soon as possible.

Exit Very widespread, Eton, Harrow, Stowe, King's Canterbury and plenty of other establishments as well. Girls to Benenden, West Heath, Roedean, Cobham etc.

Remarks Charming school, which manages to get good results without pushing the children too hard (fairly rare). Good facilities including impressive music, art and pottery complex and indoor heated swimming pool. Children very friendly and chatty. Start in junior house with married Housemaster and matron for two years, then move out to senior house. Girls have their own house across the games fields, cramped but cheerful, sewing everywhere and teddy bears—much more feminine than mixed-school dorms often are.

Lots of hobbies, computers (more club than classroom), wonderful carpentry. Excellent games: Deputy Head Richard Boddington, who teaches French, is former Captain of England squash team; golf (Sandwich pro visits weekly), masses of cricket (famous cricketers' sons here, eg Colin Cowdrey).

Small school atmosphere, popular with establishment in the City. Selection of sunny red brick buildings set in 15 acres of manicured games pitches surrounded by suburban sprawl of Broadstairs.

WESTBOURNE PREPARATORY SCHOOL
50-54 Westbourne Road, Sheffield S10 2QQ
TEL Sheffield (0742) 660374

Pupils: 165 boys • All day • Ages: 4-13 • Non-denom • Fee-paying.

HEAD Since 1984, Mr Colin Wilmshurst BA from Open University (forties), promoted from Assistant Headship; formerly at Crawfordton House. Studied educational pyschology and the Arts. Jolly, gutsy, much liked by the boys and locals. Fun but firm.

Entrance No entrance or test—first come, first served; interview with Head and class teacher thereafter.

Exit To over 40 schools in the last eight years. In the last two years to Birkdale, Bootham, Gordonstoun, Malvern, Millfield, Mount St Mary's, Oakham etc, etc, also to local LEA secondary schools, eg King Edward VII, Birkdale, also to Oakham, Rugby, scholarships in 1988 to Stowe, Trent College, one to Millfield etc.

Remarks Small but pleasant site overlooking Sheffield, near hospitals and university. School has been totally tarted up over past five years with new classrooms, new reference and fiction libraries with computer, video and music centre facilities (opened by the 'Master Cutler'). Watch out for tinies' toy trains as you walk through the door. Home involvement encouraged. Intake is mixed—from local landed to doctors and tradespeople—school is unofficial 'brother' school for nearby Ashdell (*qv*). Snobbery is ironed out early on. Enthusiasm for computers greater than ever—computer room now contains 17 computers, plus another five dotted round the school. Playing fields not on site, but games not bad at all—rugby, football, cricket. Excellent down to earth day prep school which deserves its good reputation.

WESTMINSTER CATHEDRAL CHOIR SCHOOL
Ambrosden Avenue, London SW1P 1QH
TEL London (071) 834 9247

Pupils: 90 boys • 30 board (all choristers), 60 day • Ages: 8-13 • RC • Fee-paying.

HEAD Mr Peter Hannigan MA Oxon since 1977, when death sentence hung over Choir School—his contract is now extended to 1998. Educated Jesuit College, Wimbledon before reading English at Oxford (he teaches the final year). He is a bluff, kindly, efficient man, white haired, effective publicist and good speaker, and, incidentally, now employs a

Public Relations person to boost waning chorister applications. Gentle wife—very much a partnership.

Entrance   Exam and interview at eight-plus, voice trials for potential choristers in March, June and November. Academically now tough for day boys to get into, with only about one in four applicants awarded places. Criteria includes good manners. Choral scholarships awarded after tough screening. Head spells out commitment of entire family for the choral scholars for the five years of chorister life, which includes boarding through Christmas and Easter, regular 15 hours singing weekly, plus concerts etc.

Exit   To major public schools—Westminster, St Paul's, Eton, Harrow, Ampleforth, Stonyhurst, Oratory, Worth. Most impressive list of music awards in London and recent academic awards include Westminster, St Paul's, Eton, Ampleforth etc.

Remarks   A tight ship, cosy, happy, well-mannered. Outstanding opportunities for the musical boy here under an admired Head of Music with both a first and a training orchestra made up of diminutive budding professionals on half- and quarter-size instruments. Strong first year, good French under formidable French Madame, stimulating English and Geography. Uneven Maths; ditto Greek. Scholarship stream currently disbanded. Endlessly kind young Housemasters. Huge playground recently under threat (and may yet still be—currently 'called in' by Secretary of State for the Environment) of having a four storey 'office' built on it. Parents white with horror at the thought of it. Use twice weekly of nearby Vincent Square and five minute walk to Queen Mother's (public) Sports Centre for swimming and badminton. Parent-organized Saturday Rugby. A drawback of shorter than usual terms for day boys (ostensibly due to choristers' commitments) is in part offset by the convenience of after school prep facilities, club activities and supper for day boys who want it, as well as the chance for the latter to act as altar servers for Cathedral services. First class food (which boys must finish). Healthy social and religious mix, by no means all are RCs.

Interesting example of how a gentle also-ran inner London choir-only school can progress to division one.

WESTMINSTER UNDER SCHOOL

Adrian House, 27 Vincent Square, London SW1P 2NN

TEL London (071) 821 5788

Pupils: 260 boys ● All day ● Ages: 8-13 ● C of E ● Fee-paying.

HEAD   Since 1977, the Master, Mr R W W Dawe MA (fifties), educated at Denstone College, and Cambridge, previously Housemaster at Christ's Hospital. Leaving 1992. Incoming Head already appointed: Mr Gerry Ashton, previously registrar at Westminster, and before that a Housemaster there. Popular, efficient and cheerful and 'could be more very good news,' said a parent.

Entrance   Tough and probing entrance exam at the Under School, followed by interview. 120 boys for 40 places: lists open until one month before tests. Eight-year old entrants called 'petties'. Entrance at 10 (20 places) for state educated—in come very bright sharp boys who catch up with the rest remarkably fast.

Exit   Around two-thirds to Westminster School (formerly three-quarters), the rest to Winchester, Marlborough, Eton etc.

Remarks   Very high standard of teaching—English outstanding, Classics a great strength, and Sciences. Growing boys' developing intellectual curiosity satisfied and fed; boys streamed (normal and fast) at 11, for potential scholars. In the third year, prep is piled on. Prep may no longer be done at school—bad news for the working parent. Sample holiday prep during four-week Easter break for 10/11 year olds: read eight books (list provided). Minor criticism from parents is that staff are not always accessible, though Head comments that he hopes this is now less of a problem. Staff are immensely committed—and put in a lot of time outside school hours with, for example, trips to Italy and extra games on Saturdays.

Strong extra curricular activities all round—very good art and pottery, plays, across the road from the school building (large and light, once a hospital) is Vincent Square, the envy of all central London preps used daily for break, (letting off steam and mini games practices), and twice-weekly games. Good fencing. Hot on outings, eg Scotland, Lake District, safari in Kenya, half term in Egypt (though of course, you pay for it all). Scruffy anoraks etc a deliberate policy instead of pink blazer, to blend into London transport more safely. Being bright is not enough at this school: you need to be robust. Fair number of foreign folk.

WINCHESTER HOUSE SCHOOL

Brackley, Northamptonshire NN23 5AZ
TEL Brackley (0280) 702 483

Pupils: 250 boys, 50 girls • 140 boys and 30 girls board, the rest day • Pre-prep: 85 • Ages: 3-13 • C of E • Fee-paying.

HEAD Since 1975, Mr D R Speight (pronounced Spate) MA Oxon (fifties, contracted till 2002), educated at Stowe, then Christchurch. Came to the school (he was a pupil here) from Oxford and was previously Assistant Headmaster. Teaches History, eight lessons a week, all at the top of the school. Fun, not married (his sitting room is filled with comics and tapestries done by his 92-year old mother who lives on site), 'reckons to know the boys well'. His flat-coated retriever Satchmo accompanies him everywhere and tucks pupils up at night. His predecessor, Mike Llewllyn is still doing individual classics tuition and is enormously popular.

Entrance Day pupils through pre-prep, children come 'for an informal test, we walk round the school and do a spot of reading and 'rithmetic'. Most come from within 100-mile radius with an increasing number of enquiries from London following the opening of the M40. Less than a dozen ex pats and others from abroad.

Exit Again to public schools within 100-mile radius, Uppingham, Oundle, Rugby, Marlborough (usually OBs' sons), Harrow, Winchester, two or three to Eton each year. Five major scholarships in 1990 to Winchester, Wycombe Abbey, St Edwards, Sherborne and Ampleforth.

Remarks A comfortable school. Converted Victorian Hunting Lodge with chapel and (mini) billiard

room in earlier Tudor building. School founded in 1876, moved to present site in 1923, glorious ceilings, good conversion of stables to day rooms etc. New girls' boarding house under Thelma Jones, and complimentary science block next on building agenda. Classes set till 11, then streamed. Tutors appointed on an annual basis. Strong Classics (including Greek), also French (regular correspondence with French school as penfriends, writing in each other's language and the result is sent back to writer with corrections—great fun). Maths good, also English. Strong on games, athletics meetings here a great favourite (best teas for miles), playing fields over the road include tennis courts and pre-prep. Pets are encouraged, and Wednesday afternoons are devoted to extra curricular activities—boating, outdoor cooking (Scout-type) orienteering etc. Exceptional art, with CDT and art available after prep and over the weekend for boarders. Keen music, 65% learn at least one instrument, two choirs, orchestra; impressive drama.

Can cope with mild dyslexia, two trained part-time teachers available. God important, prayers each morning followed by 15 minutes Religious Instruction for everyone in their classroom.

WINDLESHAM HOUSE SCHOOL

Washington, Pulborough, West Sussex
RH20 4AY
TEL Findon (0903) 873207

Pupils: Approx 227 boys, 128 girls • Almost all board • Ages: 7-13 • C of E • Fee-paying.

HEADS Mr and Mrs Charles Malden, both MA Cantab (fifties), he was educated at Stowe and King's, she (Elizabeth-Anne) at Cheltenham Ladies College and Girton. Both Classicists, both teach. Known as Mr & Mrs Charles, (aka The Wonder Heads), *very* glamorous (she was wearing knee high black boots with black velvet jeans and a low cut black jersey when we visited), charming and *totally* accessible (Mrs Malden found one pupil in her bed) they run the school as a team with enormous emphasis on 'pupils as people first'. Lots of cuddles and *all* the pupils are called 'Darling'.

Entrance Name down asap and interview. Waiting list, but occasional last minute vacancies do occur, particularly in an emergency. 50% Diplomatic Corps, 25% ex London, 'not enough real foreigners'.

Exit Mainly to co-eds, Bryanston, Bedales, Stowe, Marlborough, but also Eton, Harrow, Wycombe Abbey and West Heath. Regular scholarships.

Remarks Seriously strong prep school, strongly co-ed on *everything* and pupils set for almost everything, 40 learn Greek, and work hard, athough the less able are catered for. Lots of extras—extra teaching for dyslexics (children recommended by Great Ormond Street) but also extra swimming and tennis so no one feels at a disadvantage. IT and CDT, computers everywhere—and used for teaching verbs to tinies. Very strong links with Europe, pupils learn French *and* Spanish. Magical art and drama, and everybody learns cooking and needlework (where they make cushions and the like from the fabric they have screen printed in art). Everything is timetabled, but lots of extra-curricular activities as well, though once a choice is made pupils must stick to it for at least a term.

Thoroughly naughty children (they are rare) are 'spoken to at length, a naughty child is an unhappy child'.

School was founded in 1837 by Mr Malden's great, great grandfather, has been in the family ever since and became an Educational Trust in 1963. The magnificent theatre cum sports hall (The Malden Hall) was built to celebrate the school's 150th birthday, and the school moved to its present site in 1934 (complete with wonderful chapel, and organ which has now moved house for times). Sixty acres of well-used grounds with lots of staff houses and games pitches, hard tennis courts etc, but games only compulsory twice a week. A cuddly school, tho' bed-time stories are broadcast to every dormitory at night. A gang of 10 night matrons put all the children to bed every night, the same children, the same matron. Great continuity.

School has an on-going policy of training their staff to go on to 'other things' (ie Headmasterships of other prep schools').

Good follow up on all pupils, regularly up to university level. Parents 'can't speak too highly of the school'; never an adverse comment; staff like it too.

WOODCOTE HOUSE
Windlesham, Surrey GU20 6PF
TEL Bagshot (0276) 72115

Pupils: Approx 110 • All board, though school will allow day boys in for a term or two 'to get used to things before parents go abroad' • Ages: 8-13 • Non-denom • Fee-paying.

HEAD Since 1990, Mr Nick Paterson BA (thirties), educated at Westminster and Exeter University. Runs the school with the help of Mrs Nick and his parents, Mr and Mrs Mark, who themselves ran the school for 30 years before him. Mr Nick's grandfather bought the school in 1931 when it was going 'but only just'.

Entrance Send for what is still the smallest prospectus in the country, small 'because it is vital they (the parents) come and see us and the boy, and really we must get on pretty well'. School also sends 'little test' to make sure boy is not completely dyslexic. Always prepared to talk to parents right up to the last moment.

Exit 'Everywhere'—to Wellington as it is close by, also Sherborne, Eton, Milton Abbey, Charterhouse etc.

Remarks Each boy is carefully cocooned so that the shock of leaving 'nursery environment' will not be too much. Main problem might be the shock of leaving Woodcote for public school. Exeats every third week, though ex-pupil commented it was more fun staying at school during an exeat than going home, because they did all sorts of nice things like playing golf with the Paterson family. Buildings and classrooms elegant but delightfully worn at the edges. Lots of golf played, and cricket, squash (uses courts up the road), rugger. Head concentrates on placing boys in the school of their parents' choice rather than on getting scholarships. Some remedial help—school considered 'very good' by educational psychologist.

New block with 'three very smart classrooms'. New small CDT centre. Pupils: third to half are sons of ex pats (Foreign Office, Gulf etc), third local and a third from 'far afield', by which they mean eg Dover. One or two Thais (long standing tie with Thailand), two Americans, otherwise no non-nationals.

One of a dying breed—the family-owned school—and, unlike the majority, it is successful, if short on ritzy facilities. Our consumer testers here—both parents and boys—pronounce themselves very happy.

SENIOR SCHOOLS

ABINGDON SCHOOL
Park Road, Abingdon OX14 1DE
TEL Abingdon (0235) 531755

Pupils: 740 boys ● 590 day, 150 board (more than half of these are weekly boarders) ● Ages: 11-18 ● Size of Sixth Form: 225 ● C of E ● Fee-paying.

HEAD Since 1975, Mr Michael St John Parker MA Cantab, 50 this year, formerly Head of History at Winchester. Combines conscientiousness and a rather weighty approach with charm, says things here are delightfully unexpected after the past decade, such as that he wishes his pupils were (in the philosophic sense) 'more sceptical'. Works hard, systematic in organising structures to keep school hard at it, bit of a stickler for discipline. Married, four children.

Academic Matters 'Completely competent,' says one parent, implying highly satisfactory all round, rather than outstanding. Strong across the board: Classics, Modern Languages, English and economics-politics-business type subjects having grown to match Science, itself now the recipient of brand new block plonk in the centre of school. Biggish chunk of Sixth Form timetable given to general studies.

Games, Options, the Arts Plenty of sport (compulsory twice a week right through to Sixth Form), rowing especially strong (and lately badminton), new sports hall, but school doesn't live or die by it. Music is strong (perhaps the reason a Lloyd-Webber child is coming), concerts and plays often in conjunction with local girls' school. Art good. Well organised computing, new technology centre. Hobbies much encouraged even at Sixth Form—parents not always delighted by this aim of avoiding academic tunnel vision.

Background and Atmosphere Ex-direct grant school, original foundation very ancient. 'A sweatshop,' said one observer, 'which will really get them on. Better if they haven't gone to a truly splendid prep school first, then they'll be more grateful.' Sprawling undistinguished red brick, pscyhologically separated from Abingdon centre by parkland. Houserooms—rather battered—are the centre of social life, featuring lockers, toasters, pool tables.

Discipline Pastoral system thorough-going: boys have tutor to watch over work progress (lists of boys in detention for poor work pinned on main notice boards), and report into tutor group sessions first thing in the morning. Housemasters for the personal side, system far more than just nominal.

THE PUPILS Plenty of first-time private school parents; favoured by Oxford gown, professionals, farming families. 'Relatively unpretentious,' says Head firmly. Clever, industrious and pretty well-groomed. Recent ruling whereby boys more than 45 minutes bus time away must board.

Entrance Complicated. Entry at 11 via own competitive exam, and at 13 via CE, but must also take 11-year old exam at appropriate time (and register at least one year ahead of that). Lots from the Dragon.

Exit 85% to degree courses, 15-20 pupils to Oxbridge, big batches to Bristol and Durham, to read traditional subjects, also to music, architecture, film.

Bottom Line Fees per annum less than some schools' fees per term. 15 Assisted Places per year, plus five at Sixth Form. Several major and minor scholarships at 13, plus one for art and design, one for music; bursaries.

Remarks Very thorough day school with some boarding, a sort of St Paul's without the polish: steady fund-raising and building under present Head reflects confidence and vigour as well as plenty of hard graft.

ALLEYN'S SCHOOL

Townley Road, London SE22 8SU

TEL London (081) 693 3422

Pupils: 470 boys 400 girls • All day • Ages: 11-18 • Size of Sixth Form: 240-260 • C of E • Fee-paying.

HEAD Since 1976, Mr D A Fenner MA (fifties). Tall, pleasant mathematician, cricket buff.

Academic Matters The school believes in supporting and stimulating pupils—'we are pupil centred'—who are from many different backgrounds, to produce worthwhile exam results which offer options to a wide range of careers. Staff work very much as a team to uphold the school's traditions of solid teaching (if a child is struggling in a subject, extra help is given at break, at no extra charge). GCSE courses have injected new life into teaching of some subjects (there have been mutterings in the past of too much 'chalk and talk'. Electronics taught to all pupils. Much enthusiasm for Craft and Design Technology—'as design becomes increasingly technological and more mathematical, more high fliers are opting for design courses than would ever have done so before.' Everybody does two years compulsory Latin (more Classics than any other school in the Trinity Group) and in terms of Modern Languages, German is being introduced in first year (previously only available in the Third) and pupils with other languages as first language—Japanese, Urdu, Swedish etc—are encouraged to take them at exam level, at Alleyns, though usually tutored outside the school.

Games, Options, the Arts One afternoon a week is devoted to sport (in the first and second years girls and boys have combined games) in the 20 acres of grounds surrounding the school. There's a new Field Centre and Sports Hall. Badminton, hockey, cricket, basketball, netball and fencing are popular. Strong swimming tradition; girls take on JAGS and St Paul's GS and beat them regularly. Voluntary CCF—liberal parents not crazy about this but their children always among the keenest. Drama popular.

Lots of lunchtime and after school options: railway society, music, table tennis, Russian etc. Staff are very committed to pastoral care where necessary and see it as a forte, attending counselling courses etc. They also attend Institute of Education refresher courses in their subjects (school keeps a fund for such training). Strong awareness of social needs of those less fortunate; community service is taken very seriously here.

Background and Atmosphere Part of the South of the Thames Trinity group of schools, connected to Dulwich College and James Allen's School via the Elizabethan actor-manager Edward Alleyn, under Royal Charter of 1619, but no close links between the three schools. Was very much in the shadow of nearby Dulwich College until it created a new identity for itself by going fully co-ed in September 1979. Large Victorian building of South London red-brick, flanked by purpose-built blocks. Still retains atmosphere of direct grant school; committed staff, intelligent children from a wide variety of backgrounds and nationalities but strictly unsmart. Awful girls' uniform of prison warder grey.

THE PUPILS A very wide cross-section. 300 primary schools (the majority state) submit pupils for entrance. Pupils have been known to come from as far away as Sevenoaks and Knockholt.

Entrance Approx 600 candidates sit for 130 places at 11. Each child is asked to read a passage and questioned on it. Later there are tests in Maths and English ('What we're looking for is an enquiring mind and potential. We see all parents too and what we're looking for there is support.') Around 10 children are also accepted at the age of 13.

Exit Majority to university, rest to polytechnics.

Bottom Line Around 30 Assisted Places and about 12 scholarships worth half fees. One scholarship for music. Head's instinct is to cut down on scholarship so as to keep an 'emergency' fund for parents *in extremis*.

Remarks A very caring school popular with pupils and parents—particularly if the latter don't want any hint of the conventional public school image. Thoughtful, enlightened staff.

AMPLEFORTH COLLEGE
York YO6 4ER
TEL Ampleforth (043 93) 224

Pupils: 700 boys (Upper School: 600, Junior House: 100) ●
Ages: 10-18 ● *Size of Sixth Form: 250* ● *RC.* ● *Fee-paying.*

HEAD Since 1980, Father Dominic Milroy, OSB MA (fifties), educated at Ampleforth and St Benet's Hall, Oxford (Modern Languages). Joined the monastery at Ampleforth as Benedictine monk, taught languages in the school, thence to Benedictine College in Rome, returned as Head (NB chosen by Abbot). Thoughtful, intelligent, a figure of dignity and calm, president elect of HMC (for 1992). School talk of managing directors, end products and clients is anathema to him: Father Dominic has a clear policy, demographic trends notwithstanding, of not compromising, 'But to continue to offer what we do—and if people don't want it, so be it.' Firmly believes in holistic education—'going far further than bits of paper, the merely vocational, the merely academic: we are preparing pupils for life—and death.' NB not everyone would go along with his credo.

Academic Matters Variable, some teaching excellent, especially arts subjects. English, Classics and History probably strongest departments. (Exercise book comments from some staff tend to be minimal). Head has strong views on education of 16-19 year olds, well aware that not all are suited to A-levels.

Games, Options, the Arts Strong games school (games are compulsory); Don Wilson and Martin Robinson, head coach and assistant respectively at Lords, have both returned home to Yorkshire to run the Ampleforth sports centre (used by locals as well as school). Famous beagle pack. Good art department; CDT appears underused. 'On the face of it there seem to be plenty of activities on offer—but boys are not really encouraged, let alone coerced, into taking part,' is a familiar parental comment.

Background and Atmosphere Founded 1802. Fine setting in lovely Yorkshire valley—very isolated. Vast amount of new building work, sympathetically done with good use of materials, 'the Benedictines have joined forces with Holiday Inn,' commented an architect. Interesting roofscapes. Huge central hall, 'rather like a liner,' according to a pupil. Quite a contrast with some of older areas; after tuck shop cola cartons lurk in corners; unlively notice boards. Huge study hall with carrels (individual study desks), even boys' books are padlocked into lockers. Houses are autonomous (10 senior, four inner, six outer), boys eat by House (most have their own dining rooms; screw-pull in place before the Housemaster, not often used—though the day before our visit, boys had persuaded staff to allow senior pupils beer at lunch 'to celebrate Thatcher's resignation'. Sixth Form bar vetoed, senior boys may go to pub (maximum two pints with a meal) once a week. Sense of community (dear to the Benedictine principle, dear to the Head) carefully nurtured. Though isolated and very much a country school, Ampleforth has strong links with the outside world via excellent and regular lecturers, and far away projects, eg Chile and Eastern Europe. Dress code rather than uniform. Delicious Abbey Yogurt recently started.

Discipline Ampleforth has a 'long standing bias towards a liberal education,' in the words of the Head: much ('too much,' from many parents) is left up to the individual. Recent sex scandal hit the tabloids and stung the Head into complaining of inaccuracies to the Press Council. Head the author of a masterpiece to parents on the subject of trust, sparked by police drug raid on school in 1990. Thirsk and York both out of bounds at the time of our visit.

THE PUPILS Scions of good Roman Catholic families from all over the country, and some from abroad.

Entrance Registration for Junior House at age 10, and upper school at 13 following CE. Lots from Gilling Castle (qv), the Ampleforth prep school. Quality of intake is variable, bearing in mind less able brothers and generations.

Exit 70-80% to further education, approximately 20% to Oxbridge.

Bottom Line Generous scholarships and bursaries, no Assisted Places (in order not to cream off from RC maintained schools). Reports of staff being laid off, to keep prices down.

Remarks A monastic boarding school for boys, where the Head firmly refuses to 'rescue the numbers situation by making concessions'. Deep spiritual reserves—a truly rare thing. Also gamesy, gaunt, hardly a female in sight, cut off—and liberal: works best for the highly motivated; some might need a firmer hand.

AYLESBURY GRAMMAR SCHOOL

Aylesbury, Buckinghamshire HP21 7RP

TEL Aylesbury (0296) 84545

Pupils: 1100 boys ● All day ● Ages: 12-18 ● Size of Sixth Form: approx 400 ● Non-denom ● State.

HEAD Since 1967, Mr K D Smith MA Cantab (fifties), recently elected to HMC (a rare accolade for a state school Head from this essentially public school mafia), chairs and serves on many county and national advisory committees. Much respected and popular. Long serving Head who, among other amazing feats, has helped save Buckinghamshire's grammar schools (the envy of all) and expanded this school from 450 to 1,150.

Academic Matters Formidable academic record over a long period. Outstanding particularly in Physics, Mathematics, Information Technology, but strong in virtually all departments. Computers brilliant and used in many subject departments—including Latin. Pupils gain heady distinctions, eg gaining a gold medal in the UK Physics Olympiad—the only pupil from a state school to do so. Another pupil gained maximum marks for a physics investigation in the Nuffield Advanced Level exam—one of only eight out of 7,000 candidates. In 1990 there were an average of 8.9 A–C passes at GCSE (previous year it was 9.1). 33 boys passed French AS level two years before the normal time of entry etc, etc.

Games, Options, the Arts Not madly sporty but have an extremely positive approach, eg 'the under 15 tennis team won the South of England championship before losing eventually to a very strong Millfield side' (1990). Numerous clubs thrive, with much community work. Good public speaking. School quiz team were runners up in the Schools Challenge competition—1990—won it the year before. Rugby school—some would say *too* ruggy buggy—and keen on squash. Plays the girls' high school at drama and concerts.

Background and Atmosphere Sturdy 1907 low lying buildings and purpose-built centres for Science, Computing, Geography, Geology and Sixth Form. Parent support strong, and lots of fund raising events.

Excellent pastoral system—six housemasters and six heads of year give immediate extra help to anyone struggling with class or homework, freeing class teachers for job of teaching. This is a key factor in the school's phenomenal success.

THE PUPILS Half from Aylesbury, half from surrounding areas. Around 95% from state schools, rest from prep. 20-30 boys in Sixth Form from public schools and roughly the same from secondary moderns. Beady middle class parents without capital behind them move here in droves.

Entrance Via school reports and examination. Roughly top 30% of ability range. At 16+ one of few schools that does not lay down minimum requirements for entry into Sixth Form.

Exit One of leading state schools in gaining Oxbridge places. Huge numbers to university, some to polytechnics and some straight into employment.

Remarks One of the few, rare, old fashioned 'free' grammar schools. Run on the lines of a traditional public school. Outstanding.

BATH HIGH SCHOOL

Hope House, Lansdown, Bath BA1 5ES

TEL Bath (0225) 422931

Pupils: 615 girls ● All day ● Ages: 4-18 ● Size of Sixth Form: 85 ● Non-denom ● Fee-paying.

HEAD Since 1985, Miss Margaret Anne Winfield, BA (forties). Ex-grammar school girl; read History at Leicester University. Previously Head of Hulme Grammar School, Oldham. Lively, enthusiastic, slightly difficult manner, well thought of, neat and precise. Miss Winfield is a firm believer in discipline. 'There should be rules, a structure and framework carried out with consistency—benevolent dictatorship is one way of looking at it...' Dealt well and firmly with recent batch of disruptive pupils.

Academic Matters Highly academic. Gets excellent results, very high A-level pass rate, with 52% A and B grades latterly. Hot on Sciences—three Sciences taught separately to all pupils, 'Desperately time-consuming,' comment parents who would like more breadth. Greek and Latin. All Sixth Formers take General Studies course. Only two male members of staff. Very heavy indeed on prep. Regular fall out after GCSE, usually to boys' schools. Some complaints from parents of difficulty in discussions with staff, 'other than at the annual session—which is just not enough.'

Games, Options, the Arts Sport plays minor role, though wide range of activities on offer and Bath High girls are the county netball champions. Plans to improve sports facilities hampered by Bath District Council. Thriving music department; enthusiastic and productive Art, Textiles and Home Economics departments. Grumbles from parents who would like after school life/hobbies etc, 'though of course it's impossible because of the vast radius from which children come'.

Background and Atmosphere Has some lovely Georgian buildings with views over the City of Bath, and beautiful grounds. Businesslike and efficient, but friendly, atmosphere. Girls appear neat, tidy and cheerful.

THE PUPILS Approximately half from Bath, half from surrounding counties, many arriving by coach or train. Predominantly middle class with reflective attitudes in girls. Even the cleverest are academically challenged.

Entrance At 11+, and 14+ by test and interview, also at 16+ (dependent on GCSE results plus interview). Cramming for entrance is common: Head is aware of it and considers it 'most unwise'.

Exit Practically all go on to higher education, and later take up professions.

Bottom Line GPDST scholarship awarded on entrance for excellence; Sixth Form scholarships on examination and interview (open to girls within and without the school). 18 Assisted Places at 11+, and five at Sixth Form.

Remarks Academic hot house where achievement is much valued. Parents may need to provide the frills.

BEDALES SCHOOL
Petersfield, Hampshire GU32 2DG
TEL Petersfield (0730) 63286

Pupils: 190 boys, 210 girls ● The majority board ● Ages: 13-18 ● Size of Sixth Form: 154 ● Non-denom ● Fee-paying

HEAD Since 1981, Mr Euan MacAlpine (forties), educated Cranleigh and Edinburgh University. Mathematician and 'occasionally' teaches Maths. Former posts: Housemaster at Winchester, and Pure Maths lecturer at Liverpool University. Sits in office in middle of school like spider in web, twitching a thread from time to time. Articulate, and good at public/parent relations. Farms a croft near Aviemore in the holidays and says it is perfectly possible to run both school and croft in the time available. Comments that the school is a 'one off—you either like it or loathe it'. Wife teaches maths at Highfield School nearby.

Deputy Head is Mrs Willcocks, daughter-in-law of Sir David, whose son was formerly director of music here.

Academic Matters School's traditional bias towards the Arts shows signs of swinging to Science, though English still strong. Overall results good, given mercurial nature of some of pupils. Exotic subjects (such as Dutch) catered for if required. There is the strong impression that academic results are not the be all and end all here: '13 got three grade As at A-level last year but equally there are one or two struggling...' Good school library (over 30,000 books). Classes of about 20 pupils, streaming for French and Maths only—the rest 'set at random'.

Games, Options, the Arts Brilliant Art and Design Centre, and deservedly famous for this. (Viscount Linley was here.) Strong tradition of crafts, as indeed there is in the surrounding villages—in particular woodwork, pottery, jewellery, metalwork. Strong music—new head of music at time of writing was ex director of music at Durham School—four resident musicians and 32 visiting music staff. Drama popular also. Games recently 'beefed up' so they 'even beat Winchester at football in 1989'—but not a school well known for games. Keen green following. Lively societies, outward bound and first aid training. Steamy sex stories (slithering satin sheets, hot breath etc) in alternative school magazine. Everyone is asked to help on the school estate and gardens for one year.

Background and Atmosphere School started by J H Badley in 1883 in an attempt to retain the best features of the traditional public school while reforming the narrow bias towards Classics, muscular Christianity and ruggybuggy. One of earliest genuine co-educational schools; intensely bouncy, almost cocky atmosphere.

Informality—all on Christian names, and no rules on dress *at all*—formerly gave this school an avant garde reputation. Recent ISJC inspectors found they had 'never been in a school where staff-pupil relationships were so well developed,' and that 'pupils were not inhibited by authority' ('an understatement, that,' said a parent, 'if ever there was one'). School a mish mash of old and new, with masters' houses squatting on the outskirts. New 30-50 year 'master plan' for development of new classrooms etc, though school plans to remain the same size. Some double glazing to insulate against bypass. Some pretty bleak looking boys' dormitories, though girls much cosier. All dorms mixed ages.

Not noted for religious fervour—spokesboy looked totally bewildered when asked about this and pointed to a place which looked like a dungeon.

THE PUPILS Media brats, children of diplomats, musicians, Pink Floyd etc. OBs are Daniel Day Lewis, Malcolm MacDonald, Roger Powell. Watchout for 'Bedale droop' (a fashionable posture) and, at time of writing, the fashion for sticking bits into the hair. Uniformly scruffy appearance.

Entrance Popular. Lots from Danhurst, the school's own prep school, and this is the safest way to get in. Entry at 11, 13 and a few to the Sixth Form. Potential pupils come down for three days of tests while staff assess talent over a wide range, and categorize applicants as 'acceptance', 'reserve place' and 'reject'.

Exit All go on to further/higher education, mainly university but also to polytechnics, art and music colleges. Around 10 places to Oxbridge a year.

Bottom Line Five Assisted Places in each year of Sixth Form. Academic, art and music scholarships sometimes awarded at 13+ and 16+.

Remarks An inspiration. *The* place for your bright but difficult child, particularly your bright arty one. Give the school a miss however if you are looking for a neat, tidy, straightforward public school performance.

BEDFORD SCHOOL
Burnaby Road, Beford MK40 2TU
TEL Bedford (0234) 353436

Pupils: 1,115 boys • Approx 271 board, 844 day • Ages: 7-18 • Size of Sixth Form: approx 300 • C of E • Fee paying.

HEAD Since 1990, Dr I P Evans MA Cantab, PhD (Chem), MRSC. Previously at St Paul's. Cricket enthusiast, organist, fond of poetry, a Welsh-speaking Celt, Mr Evans is keen on pastoral care: 'too much was taken for the granted in the past'. Comments on himself, 'rather puritanical in some ways, but a keen sense of humour'.

Academic Matters Many staff Oxbridge, good staff-pupil ratio in upper school, fair number sporty, strong structure throughout the school, strong on Science (impressive Science block), History and English. Results appear to be reasonably steady, though difficult to comment from breakdown as presented. Not the place for intellectual sparks—although they would disagree with this comment.

Games, Options, the Arts Traditionally powerful games school, a rugby school, currently under-18 National Indoor Hockey Champions; first VIII are national junior rowers. Magnificent sports centre, three afternoons a week of sport. Huge swimming pool (used by various clubs in locality) and lots of lesser sports, with shooting well to the fore. Cadet Force surprisingly only has 150 out of posssible 600 opting to join. Community Service Unit. Most boys now enjoy the march past. Keen on music with good facilities— Chamber ensembles played in the Purcell Room in 1990. Purpose-built theatre.

Background and Atmosphere Robust, hearty school with strong service connections (mostly RAF now) which has been at centre of Bedford community for over 400 years. Part of the Harpur Trust together with Bedford Modern School, Dame Alice Harpur School for Girls, Bedford High School for Girls. Has unusual day/boarder mix—roughly one-third boarders—with school striving hard to minimize the differences. They like the mix—it keeps the boys in touch with the outside world and friendships do develop across the divide, they say. Also plenty of contact with sister schools for joint drama, debating and choral society activities. In 1979, after an arsonist caused £3,000,000 of damage, school was magnificently rebuilt, retaining its Victorian facade. Fortunately its pleasing chapel (G F Bodley) was not destroyed. Six boarding houses all recently refurbished, six day houses—usually comfortable Victorian houses, with pleasant gardens.

THE PUPILS There is much loyalty to the school and most UK boarders have strong Bedford connections or live within a 50/60-mile radius. Around 50 boarders have service connections (mostly RAF). Twenty Malaysian and Hong Kong Chinese pupils at present. Paddy Ashdown is an OB, also Peter Parker.

Entrance From Prep and Lower Schools (400 boys) by exam at ages seven to 10 (main intake at eight). CE at 13 (special arrangements for boys entering from maintained schools).

Exit 10% to Oxbridge, majority of rest to universities and polytechnics (more interest now, than formerly, in polytechnics with good vocational courses—eg surveying, accountancy), 10% services, 10% city and professions.

Bottom Line Several scholarships, and bursaries large and small.

Remarks Unpretentious, conventional and sporting school with strong services links, a good sense of proportion and a pleasing sense of realism about the outside world.

BENENDEN SCHOOL

Cranbrook, Kent TN17 4AA

TEL Cranbrook (0580) 240592

Pupils: 407 girls • All board • Ages: 11-18 • Size of Sixth Form: 126 • C of E • Fee-paying.

HEAD Since 1985, Mrs Gillian duCharme (pronounced Dewsharm) MA Cantab (forties), formerly Head of independent co-ed day school in Manhattan. Read modern languages at Girton, tennis blue, worked for British Council. Tall and chic, brings a strong

whiff of the outside real world to school (rare indeed, particularly among female Heads). Has made several staff changes since we last went to press ('I hire the best available'). Sees her job as 'training adults, as well as educating children'. Wants girls to 'make something of themselves, whatever they're good at: if they can achieve home land work, I think that's lovely—but it's really hard: we're not pushing anyone out to do careers.' Hot on subject of self confidence (Head clearly has oodles), 'Girls must feel good about themselves.'

Academic Matters Pleasing according to parents—though not startling. Stronger on Arts subjects; Maths are good; Nicholas van der Vliet (a Dutch Welshman) is 'inspiring', to quote several pupils (also glamorous) new Head of English. Head not at all keen on girls taking GCSEs early, 'Because then what do you do with them?', *but* they are taught beyond the syllabus so that (in principle) GCSEs are taken on the wing—and they are more prepared for A-levels.

Games, Options, the Arts Still hot on these: lacrosse, 14 tennis courts (including all-weather), squash etc. Strong tradition of riding at the excellent nearby stables (see Old Girls). Also judo, ballet, sailing, clay pigeon shooting—wide choice of extras/options. Splendid new indoor swimming pool (25 metres), plus dance studio, and area well thought out for seminars. New Technical Centre (opened January 1991). Good music, good drama—and lots of opportunity to take part.

Background and Atmosphere Founded in 1923 by three mistresses from Wycombe Abbey. Huge, elegant and slightly gloomy Victorian mansion built by Gathorne Hardy, first Earl of Cranbrook, set in 244 acres, with lots of rhodendrons, suffered bad hurricane damage. Mixed age dormies; new boarding House and new Sixth Form House, re-vamped interiors all over the place. Also change of caterers, and food is much better say staff and girls. Girls may wear trousers or skirts, not overly smart despite tie and darkest of navy blues. Rogues gallery close to staff room with named photograph of every pupil, ditto staff. New policy on television a source of angst to some parents: now television watching is unlimited (providing this is free time)—the thinking behind this is that they will watch less, and 'must learn to budget their time'. Hmmm. Some reports of sloppy pastoral care, despite cutting sizes of Houses and installing more married Housemistresses, ('I wouldn't want to be a single parent with 50 or 60 kids, would you?' asks the Head). Atmosphere described now as 'more normal' with more family life, and more men around. Another girls' school that claims to have worked hard recently on their weekend programme to occupy/interest pupils—but still complaints.

THE PUPILS Interesting and rich geographical and social mix, predominantly upper crust. Most famous Old Girl: HRH Princess Royal. Virginia Leng, Charlotte Brew (the first lady to ride in the national).

Entrance By CE and interview—from 50 different preps at 11+, 12+ and 13+. A few at Sixth Form—and keen to have fresh blood at this stage though NB post-GCSE leavers have, says Head, 'flattened out'.

Exit 93% on to degree courses, including around eight to Oxbridge.

Bottom Line Scholarships sat at school in Jan/Feb; four major scholarships (up to 70% of fees) two of 20%, four of 10%, also music and art scholarships. Limited bursaries.

Remarks Certainly rates high among top girls' schools, firing on all cylinders. Conflicting reports, however: some girls feel free and happy, others cannot wait to leave after GCSE.

BIRKDALE SCHOOL
4 Oakholme Road, Sheffield S10 3DH
TEL *Sheffield (0742) 668408*

Pupils: 670 boys • All day • Ages: 4-18 • Size of Sixth Form: 70 • Interdenom but 'Christian ethics pervade the school' • Fee-paying.

HEAD Since 1983, the Rev M D A Hepworth MA (early fifties). Educated at Birkdale and Cambridge—read theology. Comments 'It's an exciting school to be in'—given the increase in numbers from 450 to 700 within the year as school acquires a senior department, this is hardly surprising. Very nice. Hobbies are sailing, rowing, hillwalking and relaxing with his family.

Entrance Pre prep: four-plus admission following interview. Prep: entrance by examination (English and Mathematics plus verbal reasoning) and interview. Also via CE and scholarships (up to two-thirds the tuition fees) at 13+.

Exit Complicated, owing to ex-prep school status. Some go on to public school, with 1990 scholarships to Ampleforth, Malvern, Trent College, Oundle (six awards out of six sitting). Sixth Form scholarship to Gordonstoun. Others now staying in the school until 18 go on to university—'including Oxbridge'— or polytechnic. Pupils end up as businessmen, doctors and chartered accountants etc.

Remarks A lively school which has been gradually climbing up the age ladder so that it now provides private schooling, for the first time in Sheffield, for boys up to the age of 18. Early days to judge the result of this metamorphosis, as the school still feels in a state of transition and, whereas it was an excellent prep school, it cannot yet be described as firing on all cylinders throughout. School still has the feel of a prep school, operating with a senior department. Fulfilling a very much needed educational gap in the area, however, and pupils come from as far as Barnsley and Worksop. Sixth Form launched in 1988 in partnership with very nearby Sheffield High School for Girls, offers a good (though not great) range of subjects, including Classic, Politics, Design and Technology (large new Art Design Technology Centre and music school, which now dominate the site), Geology, Art etc. Some good results—first ever A-levels in 1990 produced a 40% A or B grade, with an average of 2.9 subjects per pupil (some doing four subjects, some doing one).

Founded at the turn of the century and moved to current site in 1915—near the university and other private schools in Sheffield—a little huddle of privilege in a sea of local authority socialist principles. Main buildings Victorian, with box-like Sixth Form block. Good outward bound-type activities with a hillwalking and rock climbing club and expeditions in the Peak District and to eg Iceland. Music active, and link with Sheffield Cathedral (some of the choristers are Birkdalians). Firm Christian bedrock, and every school day starts with prayers. Sixth Form scholarships available up to half the tuition fees, or more in case of need. Prep School is now in a Grade II listed building near the Botanical Gardens and a short plod from the main campus.

BLOXHAM SCHOOL
Banbury, Oxfordshire OX15 4PE
TEL Banbury (0295) 720206

Pupils: Approx 300 boys, 60 girls (all in the Sixth Form) • *298 board, 62 day* • *Ages: 13-18* • *Size of Sixth Form: 170* • *C of E* • *Fee-paying.*

HEAD Since 1981, Mr Michael Vallance MA Cantab (mid fifties), formerly Head of Durham School.

Remarks Good music—Sam Kahn Music School opened 1988 in centre of school in what was the old gym. Good facilities in general for a school of this size. Well-known for work with dyslexic children, although school anxious not to be known as school for dyslexics—very small department, and they are 'constantly turning people away' and also not interested in dyslexics with IQs of less than 120. Deputy Head is distinguished chemist. Entrance by CE, or, for pupils from state schools, a series of tests set by the school. Entry in to the Sixth Form by interview. Good scholarships at 13+ and 16+. 80% of Sixth Form go on to higher education; 55% of them to university. One of the Woodard group of schools; has professional public relations consultant working for them.

Large increase in size of Sixth Form, and this is reflected in the results. Well regarded by educationalists and well run.

BLUNDELL'S SCHOOL
Tiverton, Devon EX16 4DN
TEL Tiverton (0884) 252543

Pupils: • *432 boys; 42 girls (in Sixth Form)* • *324 boys board, 108 day boys; 29 girls board, 13 day girls* • *Ages: 13-18* • *Size of Sixth Form: 200* • *C of E* • *Fee-paying.*

HEAD Since 1980, Mr A J D Rees MA (forties), educated at Royal Grammar School, Newcastle, and Cambridge. Previously Head of Economics at Harrow. 'Popular with the mums,' commented another Head enviously, though one or two mums disagree with this—provokes strong reactions. Runs the school very much on prep school lines—power resides in the Head rather than the Housemasters, Head knows every pupil well, and 'manages by walkabout'. Comments on his current post: 'I love children, and running a bigger school would miss them terribly.'

Academic Matters Academic work continuously monitored and Head sees all good (and bad) work with author after regular Mark Orders. Maximum class size 20; five ability bands and some setted subjects. Good Physics and Electronics teaching and plant, also Modern Languages stronger than average, and some interesting General Studies courses. Exam results not published, owing to mixed intake of pupils.

Games, Options, the Arts CCF compulsory for one year. Ondaatje Hall (named after OB benefactor) contains concert hall, theatre, art studios, Sixth Form bar etc and much prized. Keen on community work and at time of writing building a garden for the mentally handicapped. Lively music—has taken the Purcell Room for concerts, arranged visit to school of Allegri Quartet—full programme of concerts and, as we visited, a budding pop singer was knocking them in the aisles in the lunch hour. Good workshops—including textile design, silver-smithing, cabinet-making, engine repairs.

Background and Atmosphere School founded in 1604 through the will of a local clothier—one Peter Blundell—whose 'great vision' was to found a school in his home town of Tiverton. School has long association with the Amory family, whose endowments have been generous. 100-acre site on outskirts of town, school moved to present site in 1882—red brick building with well-designed glass doors in cloisters. Original school block has high ceilings and chalk-ridden feel. School mentioned in *Lorna Doone*.

Uniform country brown bristly tweed and atmosphere gentle and unpressured. New arrivals are given a guide written by their elders, and at some stage have lunch or breakfast with the Head (an early riser) and are invited to keep a diary for the Head of their impressions of the school—which makes fascinating reading.

'Old-fashioned discipline'—ie lines drawn and pupils kept to them.

THE PUPILS Mostly within a two hour radius, some Londoners and numbers of ex-pats (often with Torbay grannies). Gentle middle class. OBs: Donald Stokes, Michael Mates (MP), Anthony Smith.

Entrance CE and school's own test for boys unprepared for CE. Competitive exam for girls.

Exit About 85% to higher education, a handful to medical school, some to agricultural college and to armed forces—broad range.

Bottom Line Consolidated fees mean few extras. At least 10 scholarships and exhibitions. Foundation places for some day boys. Six music and art awards. Two military bursaries, a CDT award or two, and one for 'all rounders', and Draper's Company awards for the hard up.

Remarks A small public school with a prep school feel which is popular with mothers seeking reassurance that little Johnny will not be toughed up, and with fathers seeking 'traditional' disciplines and values.

BOLTON SCHOOL (GIRLS' DIVISION)

Chorley New Road, Bolton, Lancashire BL1 4PB

TEL Bolton (0204) 40201

Pupils: 940 girls • All day • Ages: 11-18 • Size of Sixth Form: 240 • Also own Junior School, 175 girls, ages: 8-11 • In the grounds, Beech House: • 200 pupils (100 boys/100 girls), ages: 4-8 • Non-denom • Fee-paying.

HEAD Since 1979, Mrs M A Spurr BA (fifties), grammar school educated, and Keele University. GSA President in 1986, Chairman of Governing Council of ISIS 1987. Recently resigned 'to do other things', but Governors persuaded her to stay put, and here she is dynamic, articulate, powerful presence as ever, with northern directness. Her number one priority is 'to try to encourage girls to think for themselves—and to be flexible.' Very keen on service to the community, hot on girls in industry. Head's key words 'response' and 'confidence'.

Academic Matters Strongly academic school. Practically all Sixth Formers take four A-levels, including General Studies. Physics and Pure Maths the main strengths, followed by English. Classics is small but strong. Some classes at top end of school are shared

with the boys' division (which is next door, on the same premises). 'We get better results than the boys,' declare the girls gleefully—and truthfully. Too much homework, thinks the Head, though she sees it as inevitable. Good careers department, strong links forged with local industries and also with Europe. School now runs language bureau teaching local businessmen at 8am, considerably enhancing Modern Language teaching for the pupils. Several Old Girls on the staff. Over 50% A grades at A-level in Physics, Maths, English and Geography is typical.

Games, Options, the Arts Lacrosse, netball, swimming all very strong. Head of PE played lacrosse and netball for England. Much used fine Sports Hall; 18 hard tennis courts, indoor swimming pool and girls can also take up golf, sailing, squash etc. Joint literary society and debating with boys ('We wish the boys would take it more seriously'), also drama and some music with the boys. Flourishing clubs and societies. In-house desk-top publishing company strongly commended by recent HM Inspectorate.

Background and Atmosphere Founded in 1877, took present form as separate but equal partner in single foundation under generous endowment and vision of first Viscount Leverhulme, and links with the family remain firm and unbroken. School set in 32 acres of playing fields to the west of Bolton, close to motorway network, huge neat collegiate red sandstone buildings. All well-proportioned and well laid-out, updated when need arises and money available. Structure of the place firmly reflected in pupils—the ambience breathes hard work, strong discipline, firm purpose. Very efficiently run, with strong parental use. Grounds and facilities well used for sporting purposes over weekends and holidays.

THE PUPILS Come from far and wide, and include lots of merchants' and local businessmen's daughters. Chatty, bright, friendly girls, unsophisticated by London standards. Old Girls include Judith Judd, Ann Taylor; Harriet Steele MP; currently nine Old Girls are Headmistresses.

Entrance Highly competitive, own exam at 11+ (lots via own Junior School), some 57 feeder preps and primaries; some at Sixth Form (slight expansion and filling in). 43 Assisted Places (mostly at 11+, some at 16).

Exit Almost all go on to further education, l2-15 to Oxbridge. Eventually to a wide variety of careers.

Remarks Very strong academic urban day school, where traditional values count for much, well endowed and worthy.

BRADFIELD COLLEGE

Reading, Berkshire RG7 6AR

TEL Bradfield (0734) 744203

Pupils: 510 boys, 80 girls (all in Sixth Form) • 480 board, 30 day boys; 70 girls board, 10 day girls • Ages: 13-18 • Size of Sixth Form: 280 • C of E • Fee-paying.

HEAD Since 1985, Mr Peter Smith MA (forties), educated at Magdalen College School and Lincoln College Oxford. Previously Housemaster at Rugby. Energetic and open-minded.

Academic Matters More turnover of staff—the majority of whom are under 40—and Head has appointed first class honours graduates in Maths, Biology, History, Religious Studies, Physics and Classics Departments (though, of course, a first class degree does not necessarily make a first class teacher). GCSE results improving. A-levels show steady numbers in all grades, and a slight improvement from the last edition of this book. Size of Sixth Form has grown (the girl factor). Classics Department still going well, though smaller than ever. Surprisingly, the most popular A-level subject in 1990 was Economics. Sciences also popular. Streamed into five sets. NB Bradfield one of few boys' schools honest enough to state that their girls achieve 'above average academic results'.

Games, Options, the Arts Has the wonderful distinction of being the British National Junior Hovercraft Racing Champions at time of writing. More seriously, still famed for performing Greek play in Greek every three years in outdoor theatre, a tradition started in 1890. Drama strong in general, and Greek play is normally performed by non-specialist pupils who happen to be keen on drama. Serious games school. Cricket and soccer both strong, and The Pit is possibly the most beautiful school cricket pitch in the country (though there are other contenders). Very good record of winning shooting competitions. CCF, D of E, etc etc. Lively music.

Background and Atmosphere Founded in 1850, housed in mellow red brick down the M4 corridor. Rugged macho atmosphere tempered by arrival of girl boarders in 1989. Now there are two purpose-built girls' houses and numbers of female staff are creeping up. Some of boys' houses cramped. Rural setting. Compulsory chapel three times a week, boys still wear gowns (contrary to our previous report, we are told they prefer to). Beer available in Blundell's, the school's own bar.

THE PUPILS 60% from London and the Home Counties, 15% from overseas (mainly expats in services, banks etc), 15% sons of OBs. Few from rural backgrounds—mostly from business and high tech industries. OBs: David Owen, Richard Adams, Leslie Glass.

Entrance By CE or Bradfield scholarship. Doubtful candidates can be tested and weeded out before CE. Potential pupils drawn from over 120 prep schools.

Exit 66% to university, 90% to higher education, including a number to Oxbridge. Thereafter, large numbers to electronic engineering, business and management, the arts, and about five per cent to the services.

Bottom Line Up to 15 scholarships from 50% to 10% of the full fees. Sixth Form scholarships, plus music, art and design ones.

Remarks Very male public school which turns out charming and steady chaps but doesn't set the world alight.

BRADFORD GRAMMAR SCHOOL

Bradford, West Yorkshire BD9 4JP

TEL Bradford (0274) 542492

Pupils: 1,150; of which 150 in 'Clock House', the junior school • 60 girls in Sixth Form • All day • Size of Sixth Form: 350 Non-denom • Fee-paying.

HEAD Since 1974, Mr D A G Smith JP MA, Balliol Historian. Six feet four inches in height and shrewd with it, and said that when he was young his school reports always used to say he 'opened his mouth and spoke without thinking and this would get him into trouble one day…' Wonderfully outspoken. Formerly Head of King's School, Peterborough. Has written two history books including *Left and Right in the*

Twentieth Century. 1987-88 chairman of HMC conference. Introduced girls to Sixth Form six years ago and is a 'total convert'.

Academic Matters   Good all round. Huge numbers of mathematicians—and a sprinkling of Ds, Es, Ns and even Us at A-level (1990) to go with them. Girls performed 'slightly better' than the average. Soft options not nurtured.

Games, Options, the Arts   Strong rugby. For this and other sporting prowess, all credit to Mr Wappett, who presides in scruffy office at back of the school. 'Really, Mr Wappett' said a pupil, 'you know, he could train *anybody*'. One in six or five learns an instrument, there's a brass band, v good choral singing, keen acting. Pupils use Yamaha synthesisers Cavalier attitude to CDT and all that—though assured this is not so. No sign of home economics or anything of that sort.

Background and Atmosphere   Get a copy of The Bradfordian—BGS' yearbook—it is all there, right down to quotes from recent productions. School dates back to sixteenth century at least. Formerly a Free Grammar, became Direct Grant then private, following abolition of Direct Grant. 20 acres of grounds and all classrooms, games etc actually on the site—present sandstone buildings planned with 'incredible foresight'. Pleasing feel of space to corridors and quads between buildings. Subjects grouped together in Classics 'row' Geography ditto. New library and info technology. Huge indoor swimming pool in the midst of the class blocks. No pre-fabs, though new Science block extraordinarily badly designed. Pupils courteous.

THE PUPILS   Sons of local businessmen, professionals. 15% Asian, who are either bright or hardworking, usually both. OBs: David Hockney, who comes back to the school; Denis Healey (who doesn't); Adrian Moorehouse; Fr Delius. Gorgeous-looking girls who comment 'it's wonderful to have men friends who aren't boyfriends'.

Entrance   Selective exam; entrance into junior school at eight, nine, 10; into senior school at 11 or 13; girls at 15/17. V modest registration fee.

Exit   'Half of all who leave Bradford Grammar School to read for degrees do so to follow studies in science, engineering or mathematics'—according to the yearbook. Exit lines of great interest. 90% go on to university or polytechnic. Used to get 40-50 into Oxbridge, now 20-30 maximum 'competition's greater'. Strong links with big civic universities eg Birmingham, Nottingham, Liverpool. Pupils go on to

be engineers, yuppies etc and although they 'do not seek their careers in Bradford', nevertheless, several scudding about the textile industry etc.

Bottom Line   Fees at (currently) £2,850 a year—a *bargain*. At that price 'I can look mothers in the face' said the Head, 'and say, yes, it is worth going out to work.' Ethos is still to provide opportunities for able children regardless of ability to pay, and to this end has 35 Assisted Places. Also assorted scholarships.

Remarks   As we said before, a first class outward-looking grammar school. Motto: *Hoc age*—which the Head translates as 'get on with it'.

BRYANSTON SCHOOL
Blandford Forum, Dorset DT11 0PX
TEL *Blandford (0258) 452411*

Pupils: 430 boys, 240 girls • 630 board, 40 day • Ages: 13-18 • Size of Sixth Form 273 • C of E • Fee-paying.

HEAD   Since 1983, Mr Tom Wheare MA Cantab (forties), educated at Magdalen College School, previously taught at Eton and was Housemaster at Shrewsbury. Fun, civilised, a good communicator ('an administrator' say the pupils), and 'on top of the situation'. Aims to 'instill a sense of value' and produce well-balanced and happy pupils. Lives on campus, married with two daughters, who are currently at local school.

Academic Matters   Teaching based on tutorial system, (the American Dalton system, akin to university regime) pupils are allotted a tutor on arrival but can change if syllabus warrants it, or for personal (or parental) reasons. Charts are filled in each week, with weekly assessments on individual standards, using Greek alphabet, but currently being modified so that parents—who are being sent copies of chart—can understand. Individual timetables are on the reverse of each pupil's chart, and each day has free periods in which weekly assignments 'must be done'. Prep school Heads insist that 'pupils who go to Bryanston have to be highly motivated', pupils there would dispute this. Latin, Greek, as well as standard Modern Languages, plus Russian, Japanese, Chinese and modern Greek,

Arabic by special arrangement. Strong Science and Biology dept. All subjects setted, and pupils learn to organise their own timetables. A-level choices left late (after GCSE if needed), and the essence is on flexibility and adaptability. Pupils maintain that 'Physics is the worst taught, too much turnover in staff' and that Economics 'well, it isn't a very difficult subject is it?' is taught mainly by the PE staff. 25% of Sixth Formers time is 'spent on humanities'. Dyslexia no problem.

Games, Options, the Arts Brilliant CDT centre (designed by Piers Gough) has masses of computers as well as good Design Technology. Pottery on ground floor, and art teaching still disappointing, despite consistent complaints. Strong music (regular collection of 40+ pupils at Grade VIII—the entry to music college—playing in orchestras, brass bands, choirs etc) and super drama, either in the Coade Hall (boring 1966 building but much used by locals, and good, even by today's standards) or Greek theatre (much improved midge-wise post 1989 gales). Lots of sports, water activities very popular and pupils must do *something* twice a week (but lots of excuses to opt out). Pioneering is compulsory: charity work, maintenance of the school and grounds, forestry etc. Driving lessons. Minimum lip service to God.

Background and Atmosphere Norman Shaw's house for Viscount Portman is 'more like a Town Hall that a private house' to quote John Betjeman. A centrally run school, with life revolving round vital 24-hour notice board outside recently extended dining room in basement (surprisingly uncrowded, pupils say 'it never is'). Self service meals, with recently installed omelette bar (150 omelettes in 40 minutes) highly popular, but go early for the best fillings. Hundred yard long Main Hall has groups of chairs where pupils congregate apparently at all times of day, and there is parquet flooring everywhere.

Minimal house system, bigger boys all accommodated in main block, graduating from dormitories and separate work rooms via 'elephants' (beds over desks) to individual study bedrooms for Sixth Formers. Younger boys and all girls live in purpose-built houses up the hill, (girls houses all have hair dryers). Huge sports complex with swimming pool and new multi-gym. No uniform, skirts must be no longer than calf length (but often are) and pupils look a lot tidier than many we have seen. Good career guidance and interview guidance courses. Prefects are called 'stripes'. Social Club with bar (beer and cider only) for Upper Sixth.

THE PUPILS Media parents. About 100 ex pats, wide selection of foreigners. Very self-confident. Vocal 'can talk their way out of a paper bag' said a parent, 'which can be dangerous'. Fair amount of mooching visible.

Entrance Serious waiting list, four years for boys, seven for girls), apply early but also worth applying at last minute. Currently pupils from over 70 different schools, lots from co-ed preps. Pass mark still 50% in every subject. Approx 12 places available for girls post GCSE.

Exit Progressively more to university, 81 at last count with 17 to Oxbridge, plus 18 to polytechnics. Slight preponderance towards social sciences (34%), with 27% maths & sciences, 29% arts courses and 10% languages. Three visiting Fellows, young graduates always on hand. Lots to music and drama. Old Boys include male Conrans, Quinlan Terry, Lucien Freud and the conductor John Eliot Gardiner.

Discipline Automatic expulsion for drugs or being caught in bed (five in Mr Wheare's regime at time of writing). Drinking, first time gated and dealt with in school, second time suspended, third time expelled. But if offences are spread over long period, pupils are not necessarily expelled. Smoking, fined, suspended, punishment will be more severe if caught smoking in a building. Mr Wheare thinks that drinking is potentially far more dangerous than drugs. Parents comment they wish he was firmer about (not) smoking.

Persistent 'night wandering' (boys particularly had a habit of climbing onto the roof and racing round the parapet—now less popular since the barricade went up), may result in expulsion, but the Head must consult the chairman of the governors for a pupil to be 'withdrawn out of time', there are perhaps 'one or two a year'. Many move voluntarily, and Mr Wheare will then do his utmost to 'find another school' for the child. Reputation for wildness lingers.

Bottom Line Eight academic, four music and one art scholarship.

Remarks Still one of the strongest co-ed schools in the country, but pupils say 'it doesn't work if you can't be bothered to work'. People love it or loathe it (particularly seductive to those in the London prep school system) and children very happy. A few grumbles.

BURFORD SCHOOL AND COMMUNITY COLLEGE

Cheltenham Road, Burford, Oxfordshire
OX8 4PL

TEL Burford (099382) 3303/4

Pupils: 600 boys, 500 girls • *Approx 85 board, 1,000+ day*
• *Ages: 11-18* • *Size of Sixth Form: 210* • *Interdenom*
• *State.*

HEAD Since January 1990, Mr Robert Back, BA DoB (early forties). English teacher, currently teaches Sixth Form English, General Studies and assists with Business Studies. Comments that he 'recognizes the need for Burford to maintain and protect traditional standards and values while adjusting to demands of 1990s'.

Academic Matters First year consists of mixed ability, thereafter setting in every subject. Roughly two hours' prep for fifth formers each day. Latin optional up to GCSE level plus the usual Spanish, German etc. Work exchanges (BMW) and France. Good Home Economics block and new Resources Centre.

Games, Options, the Arts School has its own orchestra—*Calamity Jane* and *Noah* are recent productions. Good rugby team sending boys into the Oxfordshire under-eighteens. Compulsory games until Sixth Form very much encouraged—'My daughter often stays late to play extra games, whatever the term, or plays tennis in the lunch hour with the staff.' Full fixture list with lots of Saturday matches. Large, attractive playing fields plus decidedly cold-looking swimming pool. Also cross-country running. New sports hall. School has its own farm which is excellent: it breeds Jersey cattle which win awards at shows, also goats, pigs, sheep, hens etc, whose produce can be bought by pupils 'and I think the farm helps some of the children sort some of their own problems out,' remarked one mother.

Background and Atmosphere Founded in 1571 and a grammar school until 1954. Has a large catchment area (as far as Lechlade). Reasonably attractive front buildings with instant access to Burford. Boarding houses are sited in the old grammar school. Smoking and drinking not allowed, no record of drugs problem. The navy uniform of blazers, ties, etc, makes children look presentable and strongly supported by all. The atmosphere is of not too much hanging around 'and a good relationship between staff and pupils'.

THE PUPILS A real social mix, from local working class to children of wealthy farmers and parents in professions. Boarders also come from various places and backgrounds.

Entrance This as stated is a comprehensive, and boarding places are offered for a variety of reasons, some times social, eg single parent families, or for those whose parents spend long periods overseas. Can be paid privately—£809 a term.

Exit Sends two or three regularly to Oxbridge each year, last year 35 went to other universities, six specifically to agricultural higher education. Others to banking, the services, local high technology. Build up over five years to a 'profile' on each pupil. Known as the Burford Certificate which has a high value locally. A-level tendency towards the technical sciences.

Remarks An excellent comprehensive offering many subjects and choices. Impression given that it is run along old grammar school lines with its house systems, prefects and ushers. Strong accent on agriculture, rural studies, crafts. Extremely structured, and discipline firmly in place.

CAMDEN SCHOOL FOR GIRLS

Sandall Road, London NW5 2DB
TEL London (071) 485 3414

Pupils: 725 girls • *All day* • *Ages: 11-19* • *Size of Sixth Form: 193* • *Interdenom* • *State.*

HEAD Since 1989, Mr Geoffrey Fallows MA (late forties), previously Deputy Head here. Classicist, very well thought of by parents, staff and pupils.

Academic Matters Voluntary Aided Grammar School until 1976, with large numbers entering Sixth Form from private sector. Mixed-ability teaching may account for very disappointing GCSE results, yet A-level results are very good. Because of high morale and high expectations, Camden Girls' attracts dedicated and clever teachers. Many staff are at work in school by 7.30am and still going strong at 5pm and are to be found giving extra tuition in odd corners of the school at odd moments, also at their own homes. 'Endlessly patient,' from a parent. Arts notably stronger than Science, particularly English and Art. Classics Department also considered good. Russian is sadly no longer an option but Technology options funded by MSC now on offer. School is bursting with musical talent. Many pupils in London Junior Symphony Orchestra. Careers advice a strong point. Angst among parents of unstudious types that at Sixth Form girls do not need to turn up except for lessons. Joins with other local schools for A-level subjects.

Games, Options, the Arts Definitely not sporty but has own football team, is achieving growing success in athletics, and possesses a good gym. Full-time dance teacher. Lively Art.

Background and Atmosphere A Voluntary School for Girls. Frances Mary Buss Foundation (together with North London Collegiate School, *qv*). Buildings are a hotchpotch: remains of Victorian main school (partly decimated during Blitz), and inconvenient Victorian houses (preservation order keeps them upright), linked to modern centre block. Fairly recent Sixth Form building gives pupils much autonomy—many miss the close link with main school. Dramatic collapse of assembly hall roof in 1973—first of the pre-stressed concrete disasters—brought bonus of music and drama workshop; latest addition is the workshop for design. Friendly, relaxed, informal, and no rules about clothes—counterbalanced by tight and caring pastoral system. Girls feel themselves to be known and valued individually.

THE PUPILS Very mixed-race school, although ethnic minority groups are small. Fairly equally divided between highly articulate offspring of Camden Square intelligentsia, and children from local council estates. An interesting mix of the very rich rubbing shoulders with the very poor. Highly aware of social issues.

Entrance Places much sought after. School admits only 25% of children classified as 'clever' within the official catchment area, ie living no more than 850 metres from the school (1988 measurement), measured door-to-door by Divisional Officer. Catchment area less confined for average/below average children. Parents (wealthy) move into the area for education.

(Much publicity in Seventies when John Pardoe's daughter failed to get in.) At 16+ entrance regulations are much more relaxed: lots from private schools and some from other comprehensives.

Exit Majority of those who stay for Sixth Form go on to universities, polytechnics or colleges of art. 10 to 15 Oxbridge places a year.

Remarks Exceptional and exciting school, happy and lively, which nevertheless still harbours significant areas of underachievement. Fairly left-wing image persists.

CANFORD SCHOOL
Wimborne, Dorset BH21 3AD
TEL Wimborne (0202) 882411

Pupils: 476 boys, 56 girls in Sixth Form ● *387 boys board, 89 day boys* ● *46 girls board, 10 day girls* ● *Ages: 13-18* ● *Size of Sixth Form: 236* ● *C of E* ● *Fee-paying.*

HEAD Since 1976, Mr Martin Marriott MA Oxon (fifties), contracted till 1992, educated Lancing followed by Oxford and RAF. Teaches Shell (ie First Year) History, and Responsible Living, mainly to Sixth Formers, 'Marriage and social relationships *always* on the agenda.' Very keen on discipline, and makes it quite clear to pupils, 'that if I find them in bed together *they are out*'. Encourages pupils to 'make their own decisions based on responsibility within certain parameters'. Much liked by staff, pupils and parents, his no-nonsense attitude inspires trust. Mr Marriott believes that 'the more stretched children are, the more stimulated they become'. His wife, Rowena, is greatly supportive.

Academic Matters Setted for Maths, French, Latin, 20 maximum per class, top movers streamed. Average 90% overall GCSE and mid-90s on As. Computers throughout, and computer room with former pupils (currently at Oxford) 'helping to devise new programmes'. Strong English and Geography (Field Trip to Paris to study Urban Geography).

Games, Options, the Arts Strong on games (Astro-turf hockey pitch) used by locals, ie Bournemouth Clubs, who also pay to use Royal tennis court, squash and golf course. 300 acres superbly sculpted grounds with pool, hard tennis courts and games fields enjoyed by pupils and staff alike (serious competition on the rugby field between masters staff v catering staff). Sailing on flooded quarry at Ringwood, racing at Poole Harbour, sculling on river Stour which runs through the estate. Girls keen and good coxes. Prominent music, also theatre (outdoor theatre). Art fun. CDT less important than IT. CCF, shooting option and strong charity work locally.

Background and Atmosphere Marvellous Gothic Barry design, built for the Guest family, on (not much visible) Norman design; ponderous nineteenth-century interiors, splendid dining-hall, (with twenty-first century facilities—vegetarian meals popular); desperately over-heated lodges (dormitories). Girls have own house (sewing machine) and common room in main school. Norman chapel in grounds is used for services in rotation (too small for the whole school) and by Canford Magna for funerals etc. Serious security problems (bikes the favourite theft), only one entrance in use, spy cameras, trench all round grounds, vicious anti-car spikes everywhere.

Discipline Smoking 'continuing problem which will always be so', fine of £10 and doubled if caught inside the building (danger zone). Will rusticate for persistent smoking. Drink, 'most common', usually gating, but those over 18 can go to local Chinese or Italian resturant in Wimborne, and there is a Union on Friday and Saturday nights at school with beer or wine available.
Nine expelled for cannabis in 1991.

THE PUPILS Huge car park for older day boys; boarders mainly within two hour drive. Few from abroad (11 currently), lots of naval children. Assisted Places not always taken up.

Entrance 50% pass-mark; interview. Prep school recommendation matters most. Girls and some boys after GCSE, girls chosen very selectively, 'though it takes some time to adjust and settle'.

Exit 80% tertiary education, 8-10 to Oxbridge annually. Strong on engineers, professions.

Bottom Line Eight open scholarships of 10-50%; one Royal Naval scholarship of 20%; up to four music scholarships.

Remarks Thriving school that does well for the middle-of-the-road, with a smashing Head and good vibes. Low profile.

CARDINAL VAUGHAN MEMORIAL SCHOOL
89 Addison Road, London W14 8BZ
TEL London (071) 603 8478

Pupils: 580 boys, 40 girls (all in Sixth Form) • All day • Ages: 11-18 • Size of Sixth Form: 160 • RC • State.

HEAD Since 1976, Mr A S J Pellegrini BA, FColl P (forties). Was teacher and Deputy Head at school, first lay Head.

Remarks Small west London comprehensive with the highest academic standards amongst London comprehensives. Great wodges of homework from day one—quite a shock for children coming from primary schools where little or no homework is set. Some mutterings about creaming off from lesser RC establishments, though Head says remark is 'old hat', but it is quite an exceptional school and stands head and shoulders above the rest.
Intake mainly drawn from Kensington, Chelsea, Hammersmith, Fulham and outer London boroughs to the west. Highly thought of, very caring community with impressive numbers into interesting selection of universities each year, including Leeds, Swansea, Southampton, Aston, Aberystwyth. School has two orchestras and two choirs which are reputed to be excellent. School acquired Grant Maintained status in 1990. Large numbers of children of foreign origin.

CASTERTON SCHOOL
Kirkby Lonsdale, Cumbria LA6 2SG
TEL Kirkby Lonsdale (05242) 71202

Pupils: 365 girls • 305 board, 60 day. • Ages: 8-18 • Size of Sixth Form: 92 • C of E • Fee paying.

HEAD Since 1990, Mr Tony Thomas MA Cantab (forties). Previously a Housemaster at Sedburgh.

Mathematician. Former England lacrosse international. Keen thespian. Also keen on shooting, caving, bellringing, ornithology and stage lighting. Norwegian wife. Two small sons. Took over from Gerald Vinestock. NB not many girls' schools have a tradition of male Heads.

Remarks The Brontes' school. OK GCSE results. A-levels less impressive. Averages 2.7 A-levels per candidate. No class is larger than 20, staff are stable. Computers everywhere. Standard games, keen drama, riding, ballet. Almost all girls do D of E. New Creative Arts centre.

Founded in 1823. Central house includes dining room and libraries, etc, surrounded by modern classroom blocks. Limestone conversions, including Brontë (junior) House, are scattered throughout the tiny village. Small dorms (own duvets) or study bedrooms for Sixth Form. Pupils are mainly local; 70 expats or forces. Approx 20 leave each year after GCSE. Of the rest 50% go to university, 25% polys, rest to professions, nursing, etc. Scholarships at 11+, 12+, 13+, Sixth Form. Bursaries throughout for clergy daughters, Assisted Places.

A friendly, happy school which encourages the less academic as well as the bright. Regular trips to London and good work experience and careers guidance. Lovely little country boarding school serving a local need.

CENTRAL NEWCASTLE HIGH SCHOOL
Eskdale Terrace, Newcastle-upon-Tyne NE2 4DS
TEL Newcastle (091) 2811768

Pupils: 565 girls • All day • Ages: 11-18 • Size of Sixth Form: 153 • Non-denom • Fee-paying.

HEAD Since 1984, Mrs A Chapman MA (forties), educated Teeside High School, Bristol University and the Sorbonne. Previously taught at Church High, a neighbouring girls' day school. A most charming and articulate woman, keen tennis player, and linguist (teaches French to Sixth Formers in small groups), extremely actively interested in careers. Tells the youngest, 'Always ask, why?'. Most of all wants girls to emerge with confidence, does not aim to produce feminists, but tells girls, 'If you know your value, then you will get ambition from that.' Urges them to stay calm: 'If you want something and are really determined (so few are), and remain quietly determined, you will get it.'

Remarks A school with very high academic standards, and regularly remarkably good results. Six to eight to Oxbridge annually ('It's often not the first choice'), Newcastle for medicine, Sheffield, Manchester and Leeds all popular. Hard to get into. Languages are especially strong (Head is proud of alterations she has made to language rooms); Sixth Formers can do Arabic, Italian, Japanese, (pupils even have Japanese pen friends). Sciences also very strong (better labs here than at RG—*qv*), especially among Asian community. General English course for non-English A-levellers, and good general interest programme for all Sixth Formers, some for full year, others in 10-week blocks. Girls often notch up another GCSE in their first year in Sixth, some AS, French and Maths refreshers. 28 per class, northern work ethic visible, though Head points out that such is the atmosphere that girls apply pressure to themselves ('I tell them they must have a good holiday during Christmas').

Strong tennis school (girls often in quarter finals of Midland Bank competition), Head is very pro tennis coaching, and convinced that playing tennis well has a good effect on concentration. School considers itself quite gamesy, though parents mutter that it there is not much for the also-rans, though it is more rounded than some of its sister GPDSTs. School (founded 1895) situated in quiet area of Jesmond (convenient for underground); Sixth have their own house, round the corner; the local (erstwhile) synagogue recently acquired: downstairs is the school's own canteen (local black cat a familiar figure here), manned by parents in the morning and used by Central High and RGS Sixth Formers; upstairs is a splendid Art Department, run by Mrs Rankin. Gym round yet another corner. Very committed staff, ditto parents. Daily assembly, 'to start the day on a calm note', tolerance inherent in ethos. Annual one-day conference on Relationships for Upper Sixth, recently led by Old Girl Miriam Stoppard. Rare to hear complaints about this strong school.

CHARTERHOUSE
Godalming, Surrey GU7 2DN
TEL Guildford (0483) 426222

Pupils: 611 boys, 90 girls (Sixth Form only) ● *673 board, 28 day* ● *Ages: 13-18* ● *Size of Sixth Form: 341* ● *C of E* ● *Fee paying.*

HEAD   Since 1982, Mr P J Attenborough MA (early fifties), educated at Christ's Hospital and Peterhouse, Cambridge—Classicist. Greek motto carved over fireplace which head translates as 'live as on a mountain top'. Quiet and tolerant. Wife Sandy full of zip. Houses some of the girl boarders at the moment.

New appointment: Andrew Morrison, previously Head of Mowden School, to be Second Head and responsible for the years below Sixth Form.

Academic Matters   Surprisingly good, given broad range of IQ on intake. GCSE passes for 1990 mostly in the 90% range for ABC combined; A-levels also consistently excellent—the very lowest percentage of ABCs combined is 67 (Physics), most are in the eighties and several of 100%. Previous years show similar form. Strong and keen following for Politics at A-level, with stunning resource library. Glorious main library which has recently had addition of central shelves to the greater glory of scholars but dismay of style purists. Recent £1.9 million refurbishment of Science block. A founder member of Schools Arabic Project.

Games, Options, the Arts   'There is,' said a pupil, 'so much to do it is staggering.' School has one of the best public schools' theatres in the country—named after OB Ben Travers. Good music—nearly 50% learn an instrument and NB Vaughan Williams was here. Nine-hole golf course—gift of another OB. First at Bisley in 1988. Sailing usually on offer though slight technical problem at time of writing. Scouts prominent (Baden Powell was here). Keen cricket. Trillions of societies—debating, photography, you name it.

Background and Atmosphere   A golden place ('though you should see it,' said a pupil, 'on a day when the mist rises up over the cricket pitch—very gloomy'). Strong feeling of fellowship—read *Fielding Gray* by Simon Gray (OB) for a nostalgic vision of this (though edit out the homosexual overtones). Idyllic cricket pitches surrounding the turreted and Gothic brickwork of the main building. Towering chapel by Sir Giles Scott has name upon name of OBs who fell in the world wars, and awe-inspiring organ.

Founded in 1611 in London by Thomas Sutton, moved to present site in 1872 and school now feels like a fully paid up member of the Victorian-railway-station family. Boarding houses all very different—oldest have cubicles and rooms for Sixth Formers of amazing, if shabby luxury,—head of one house even has a fridge. 'Cubes' for younger boys. New houses look like ocean liners rising out of the grounds and rather Sixties university campus in style. Girls' studies dotted about the houses, and girls are boarded hither and thither.

Discipline   'There are two clear rules,' said the Head, 'no drugs, and no bedroom scenes. I tell the boys this every year.' Interesting reaction from parents on school's acceptance of a 'rotten apple' from another school: 'we were all up in arms about it...That he should come here bringing all his nasty little ways...'

THE PUPILS   Surrey stockbroker, almost to a man. Charming and thoughtful and with a nice appreciation of what everything costs. OBs: the school has more distinguished old boys in more walks of life than any other school in the country, eg Joseph Addison, Max Beerbohm, Don Cupitt, John Alliot—to pick one or two out of the top of the alphabet. Many judges, statesmen, soldiers, scholars.

Entrance   No 'feeder' schools. Medium stiff common entrance exam. Also entry at Sixth Form. No set time for registration, but lists usually close two years ahead.

Exit   34 pupils to Oxbridge for 1990. 80% in all to university—the collegiate universities popular.

Bottom Line   Has maintained its position over the last five years as one of the most expensive schools in the country. Parents currently being asked to divi up *very* large sums for latest appeal. School run 'like a business' which the parents like—recently called in Coopers & Lybrand to report on the governors' role in running the school. Pots of money about. Generous index-linked scholarships at 13+ and 16+. Up to five Assisted Places a year (given what's on offer, these are the bargain of a lifetime).

Remarks   Division one public school about which consumer reports vary. One the one hand—pupils are charming, happy, get excellent academic results, and pastoral side is good; on the other hand school has been critised as being a bit 'cosy and dozy'—not enough turnover of staff—not enough action at the weekends, younger pupils not kicked into action, too much watching of tele etc. However, the appointment of four new Housemasters and creation of post of Second Head may shake things up a bit.

CHELTENHAM COLLEGE
Cheltenham GL53 7LD
TEL Cheltenham (0242) 513540

Pupils: Approx 521 boys, 51 girls in Sixth Form • 388 board (including some girls), 184 day • Ages: 13-18 • Size of Sixth: 230 • C of E • Fee-paying.

HEAD Since 1990, Peter Wilkes MA (late forties), educated at Radley and Trinity College, Oxford—Classicist. Previously Head of Ryde School. Takes over from Mr Richard Morgan, who will be a hard act to follow. New Head comments that his aims are, ' to maintain Richard Morgan's academic/technology emphasis, increase girls numbers up to 80, but *not* make Cheltenham co-educational'.

Academic Matters School at time of writing has a number of young teaching staff of very high calibre—higher than pupils. Has strong Physics department and Electronics teaching could be best in country: has won the Young Design Electronics Award for two years running (the Booker prize of school electronics). Under Head of Department school set up electronics trading company: Cheltenham College Enterprises Ltd, selling activity boards etc to eg Millfield Junior, Marlborough. Head of English Department is the poet Duncan Forbes. Operates a module system to allow for a 'very broad foundation and wide opportunities thereafter'.

Games, Options, the Arts One of the Lord's (ie Lord's Cricket Ground) schools and cricket strong. Busy-looking careers room and hi-tech careers centre, and school is keen to encourage links with business. Has industrial link, exchanges pupils with Houston and Tokyo.

Background and Atmosphere Victorian foundation with strong army links and rumoured to have more Old Boys eaten by tigers than any other school... During past 50 years has heartbreakingly and repeat-edly sold off land to keep going and has now retreated behind the fortress of impressive-looking buildings in the middle of Cheltenham, with through-traffic outside the windows. 'They even sold the running track,' commented a pupil wistfully. Definitely a town school. Short on mother appeal. Dining hall used to be chapel—in fact, school looks like one big chapel.

THE PUPILS Now has only about five per cent service families. Non-nationals, 'under four per cent'. Majority from local catchment area. Old Cheltonians include 14 VCs, largest per capita number of any school apart from Wellington (though NB Eton comments that it has more altogether), and distinguished soldiers such as Field Marshall Sir John Dill and Lt General Sir John Bagot, Glubb Pasha, also one or two OCs in Falklands Campaign. Also Edward Wilson, who died with Scott of the Antarctic.

Entrance By registration and CE.

Exit Several to Oxbridge. Other pupils to other universities, further education of some sort.

Bottom Line Six or more scholarships of 50% of fees. Others between 10% and 40% on academic merit, or can be supplemented in the case of parental need.

Remarks One of top public schools earlier in the century; did massive nose dive but climbed back under previous Head and is, at time of writing, a school to be recommended.

THE CHELTENHAM LADIES' COLLEGE
Cheltenham, Gloucestershire GL50 3EP
TEL Cheltenham (0242) 520 691
Fax (0242) 227882

Pupils: 852 girls • 684, board, 168 day • Ages: 11-16 • Sixth Form: 260 • C of E • Fee-paying.

HEAD Since 1987, Miss Enid Castle JP, BA London, (fifties) contracted till 60, teaches History to First Formers. Educated at Oldham Grammar School, previously Head of Kenya High School and Queens College Nassau; and came to CLC from Redmaids'

School in Bristol ('the rising star from Bristol'). President of GSA at time of writing. Political and ambitious. In great demand by prep schools for Brains Trusts and the like. An iron fist in a velvet glove, staff and pupils hold her in enormous esteem—'she swam 26 lengths in the sponsored swim'; 'if she makes up her mind, she rarely changes it'. Her visits to houses are to see the pupils and 'not,' said one Housemistress, 'to pass the time of day with us, though she is very accessible'. Firmly believes in single sex education 'and I have taught in both,' and hopes that 'girls will come out with self confidence, and with reasonably well-balanced outlook on life'. Maintains that CLC is 'not a hothouse, but we do push them'.

Academic Matters   Very strong, particularly in Maths, French, and Latin (classes up to 20), Greek a serious option, also Spanish, German, Russian, Mandarin Chinese, Japanese classes in town; Italian at Sixth Form. Modern lang labs contrast with old fashioned desks, pupils streamed after first two years. 25 labs, only one that we saw with overhead booms—*and* a shower in the lab area. New IT in 1989, CDT much encouraged by Dowty Engineering, (aeroplanes everywhere) we saw no evidence of computers in either; computer rooms. Huge staff, 95 full-time plus part-timers, and low turnover, not many come here for their first post. Tutors for Sixth Formers, otherwise class teachers who liaise with Housemistresses—there is a day girls' house. Can cope with 'mild dyslexia'.

Games, Options, the Arts   Superb careers dept, work shadowing in holidays and work experience during term. 600 music lessons weekly, masses of choirs, orchestra, all under John Sanders, organist at Gloucester Cathedral and, by tradition, Director of Music. Drama strong, cooking (super Christmas cakes), excellent fabric design and pottery, art appeared less popular, good History of Art. Huge gym in main building, new games hall, indoor tennis, swimming pool, great enthusiasm and spectacular results (well they would be, wouldn't they?), slight grouch from pupils that 'not allowed enough time for Field (ie games). Teams for everything, cross country. Debates, concerts and occasional drama with Cheltenham Boys College half a mile away and 'plenty of unofficial contact'. Strong on charity work, D of E.

Background and Atmosphere   Founded in 1853, granted Royal Charter in 1935, main school revolves round huge purpose built Victorian campus, with magnificent stained glass, marble corridor, Princess Hall, vast library etc in the middle of Cheltenham. Based on the concept of boys' public schools, pupils go home to their houses for lunch, tea and at night, (pets and table napkins!); most houses are about 10 mins walk away, and each girl has a 'walking partner' who must go with her *at all times* (you have a late music lesson, she does prep in the old hall). Serious and important pecking order for everything. Junior boarders mainly live in vast rooms converted into cubs (cubicles) though dormitories much preferred: 'Friendlier, you get to know each other better,' say the girls. Yet again 'there is a real terror of lesbianism, we are constantly on our guard' said one Housemistress. Sixth Formers retain strong attachment to their junior houses; sleep and work in individual room each with a panic button ('with 190 girls in the middle of town what else can we do,' said one Housemistress). House-mistresses in Junior Schools are non-teaching whilst Sixth Form Housemistresses also have academic responsibility. Tellies, videos, computers and sewing machines much in evidence, girls in Sixth Form houses can 'have dinner in town' (taxi there and back) and invite their boy friends back—'the boys often become house friends'.

Girls wear rather boring green skirts and jerseys (called 'greenflies' by townfolk) and magnificent loden coats. Staff have been known to accost total strangers wearing the school coat 'on the lawn' at the National Hunt Festival. Usual moans about food, Sunday evening supper is 'yuk', vegetarian meals available (letter from parents required) and 'few anorexics'. Girls carry books in 'sacks', send internal messages via 'slab' and have names for almost everything: Slodge (Sidney Lodge), St Mags (St Margarets), the bunny run. No bells, just clocks.

THE PUPILS   Academic, middle class, 20% from abroad—expats, the services, rather than foreigners, though sprinkling from Hong Kong. Very caring of one another. Outspoken and charming. Perhaps a trifle jolly hockeysticks. Old Girls: Rosie Boycott.

Entrance   Stiff competition. Entrance, at 11+, 12+, 13+, at Common Entrance and own exam post GCSE.

Exit   85% to universities, polys, 17 to Oxbridge last year. As you might expect 94%+ success at A-levels, 98% passes (A-C) at GCSE. Strong medical following. 'All the girls are destined to have careers.'

Discipline   Drugs—'not that I am aware of'—worst offence 'getting out at night and risking the security—otherwise depends on the offence'; gatings and house doors locked at dark. Smoking: fine £10 for first offence, then one week's suspension. Two sackings lately, mostly for going OTT.

Bottom Line Good value. Seven academic and seven music scholarships available annually, also four per cent of income available for bursaries, total £25,000. Benefactors' Award for daughters of Old Girls via Guild (Old Girls soc).

Remarks Strong, not over-imaginative, but the most marvellous facilities. Miss Castle totally in control of one of the best known traditional girls school in the country: not for the shrinking violet, however clever she may be.

THE CHERWELL SCHOOL
(Cherwell Upper),
Marston Ferry Road, Oxford OX2 7EE
TEL Oxford (0865) 58719

Pupils: Approx 830 in all, boys and girls • *All day* • *Ages: 13-18 (NB Cherwell also has middle and primary schools)* • *Size of Sixth Form: approx 245* • *Non-denom* • *State.*

HEAD Since 1981, Mr H M Roberts MA (forties), educated at Christ's Hospital and read History at Merton College, Oxford. Started teaching at Leeds Grammar School, then went into the state comprehensive system and has stayed in it. Married to Diana, who is a social worker, with son in Sixth Form at time of writing and daughter at Manchester University. Hobbies: squash, dog-walking and writing history books for schools.

Academic Matters Good, though not considered anything out of the way by locals, who live in the academic hot house of Oxford. Physics and Science in general strong. Languages—French, German and Spanish now on offer. Sixth Form greatly strengthened by intake from surrounding schools. Sets for Maths and Modern Languages. 'Block' subjects now on timetable, so departments can organise groups as they wish. Signs of academically strong being sacrificed for weaker brethren, but former flourishing none the less.

Games, Options, the Arts Under-19 county champions at football in 1988 and 1989. Netball and basket ball good local reputation. Strong and enthusiastic music department. Lots of extra curricular bands and concerts. Five star gifted music teacher Mrs Anna Haxworth.

Background and Atmosphere Modern brick and prefab buildings off the Banbury Road. Cramped and ugly and school assembly hall so overused that it was starting to look dirty by 9am. New music and drama block completed 1991. Whole school bursting with energy, and staff radiating interest in and concern for the wellbeing of their charges, like kindly shepherds. A feeling of safety and spiritual warmth. Interestingly, school started life as a secondary modern.

THE PUPILS Some middle class, some connected with the university, but also large numbers from nearby housing estates. Ability range a fair spread. Maureen O'Connor, ex-education correspondent of *The Guardian* is a governor. Six staff, including Head, have own children in the school.

Entrance Majority from the middle school. Oversubscribed now from years 9-11. A staggering 20+ pupils come at sixth form level from local private schools.

Exit Some at 16, some do two years in Sixth and on to university.

Bottom Line A local 'winner' under the new approach to school finance—the Head and governors have more to spend and much more discretion in that spending than formerly.

Remarks Brilliant state comprehensive. Locals need look no further, unless they are in search of frills.

CHRIST'S HOSPITAL
Horsham, Sussex RH13 7LS
TEL Horsham (0403) 211293

Pupils: Approx 562 boys, 275 girls • *All board* • *Ages: 11-18* • *Size of Sixth Form: approx 220* • *C of E* • *Fee-paying—but see paragraph on Bottom Line.*

HEAD Since January 1987, Mr R C Poulton (pronounced as in 'old') JP, MA (early fifties), who came from Wycliffe College. Read History. Before that ran third girls' house at Bryanston, where, according to pupils, he was 'excellent', 'likeable'. Describes himself as 'liberal' and aims to 'humanize' CH 'not that it was *in*human before'. Described by member of staff as 'kindly pipe smoker with lovely yellow labrador'—this last an animal of extremely strong character. Head is steelier than he appears. Has embarked on huge public relations campaign on behalf of the school, with tv programme, Harry Secombe etc.

Academic Matters Strong academic tradition, particularly Arts, good results all round, with very high exam success rate—solid wodges of As, Bs and Cs, girls doing slightly better than boys. Satellites sprouting up into Physics labs (weather signals feeding in) and Language Departments.

Games, Options, the Arts Very strong musical tradition. The school band leads the Lord Mayor's procession in London each year and hundreds of people turn up to hear the school beating the retreat—an old tradition. Band also plays while school marches in to lunch and it is considered status symbol to be in it (though it makes you late for rather good lunch). School has *five* organs—a record! Good Arts centre with a theatre seating 500, said to be inspiration for the Swan Theatre, Stratford. School now claims to have the 'best' sporting facility of any school in the country opened by their President, HRH the Duke of Gloucester, at a cost of £3 million, which includes a social centre, and even disabled facilities.

Background and Atmosphere Founded in 1552 by the boy King Edward VI for the education of London's sick and poor and still sticks by and large to the spirit of this aim. School moved from its five-acre site in the City (good grief!) to 1,200 Sussex acres in 1902. Large complex of avenues and quads designed by Victorian architect Sir Aston Webb, looks like a huge, smart, red brick barracks with gracious cloisters. Vast dormitories—think of Florence Nightingale and you've got the picture—currently in the process of being 'restructured into units of study-bedroom accomodation.

In September 1985 joined forces with the sister school which has moved down from Hertford.

Boys wear wonderful ancient uniform (and bring it home at half term to wash, stiff with dirt) of floor-length blue wool coats, black breeches and saffron coloured stockings, and tab and 'broadie' buckle on leather belt. Girls wear the same blue coats in winter, and picturesque navy suits with old-fashioned cuffs and buttons, and could all step straight into a Tudor play without changing a thing. Uniform provided free, worn seven days a week.

Discipline Swift turnover of Heads entailed period of disruption and disaffection. Things have tightened up considerably under present Head. Still occasional outbursts of trouble. NB largeish proportion of single parent families.

THE PUPILS Anybody poor and deserving from miners' sons to those of bankrupt bankers. Mostly from South East, though school is trying to rectify this. Both working class and distressed gentle toffs. A few pupils pay full fees (see Entrance below). Also one or two children whose daddies have their own businesses and so are able to hide their real income, except on Founder's Day when the Rolls Tells All. OBs: lots of distinguished ones, as you might expect, including bouncing bomb man Barnes Wallis; William Glock, Bernard Levin, Colin Davis, cricketer John Snow, Coleridge, Leigh Hunt.

Entrance Very complicated, owing to ancient charitable foundation. For majority of places will only consider children whose parents cannot afford boarding school fee and who have a definite 'need'. It helps to be in the Church, the RAF, or to be a single parent. Registration form asks: Do you think your child needs a reasonably academic education—and has the capacity to profit from it? Would education at CH meet a real family need? etc.

School sets its own exam. Places gained either by competition (for those who can afford full fees), or by 'presentation'—governors and certain Livery Companies have the right to sponsor a child. Get up to date governors' list from the school to see who may help.

Exit Most to university, though school gets some fall out from children whose family circumstances make it impossible for them to continue.

Bottom Line Fees assessed according to income. Current maximum for cheapo deal is £23,500 gross at time of writing, earning which, you would have to contribute approximately £3,813 a year. Get admissions leaflet and puzzle it out. Also get a good accountant.

Remarks If you can stand the humiliation of the entry process, this is the best value in public schools in the country. Should benefit from the current recession.

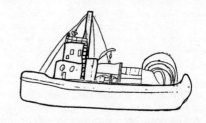

CITY OF LONDON SCHOOL

Queen Victoria Street, London EC4V 3AL

TEL London (071) 489 0291

Pupils: 850 boys ● *All day* ● *Ages: 10-18* ● *Size of Sixth Form: Approx 240* ● *Non-denom* ● *Fee-paying.*

HEAD Since 1990, Mr B G Bass MA (fifties), educated Wells Cathedral School, Christ Church, Oxford (read English), previously Headmaster of Hymers College, Hull, and before that Head of Arts at Manchester Grammar School. A delightful enthusiast, 'brilliant teacher' (teaches English to 13-year olds, according to pupils, and not afraid of being thought old fashioned in minding about good order and decent standards of behaviour). Emphasizes equipping pupils for the next stage as, 'identifying what they might be good at' and 'having their capacities extended' while at school—as well as leaving with exam results.

Academic Matters Very academic, wide use of 'setting'. No specialization below Sixth Form level. Considered outstanding in Mathematics (distinguish themselves in Mathematics Olympiad) and Sciences boys themselves (also parents) mention a string of other strong subject areas, from Electronics to English (English master Jonathan Keates, book reviewer and winner of James Tait Black Memorial Prize for *Allegro Postillions*, 'brilliant teacher'). Staff considered to be very supportive and friendly—'they'll invite us round to their houses'. Equal strength on Arts and Sciences sides (first school in country to teach Chemistry).

Games, Options, the Arts Extremely good Music Department (Sir Colin Davis a father). Probably more sporty than Westminster and St Paul's, lots of staff involved on games side. 17 acres of playing fields at their disposal 35 mins away, whence the under-14s are bused one afternoon a week, plus keen over-14s. Rowing, judo, fencing, squash (three courts), shooting (run by their Cadet Force) are amongst number of over-14 options, with the competitive edge going to swimming (there is an indoor 25-metre swimming pool) and water polo (national champions 1985 and 1986). New sports facilities on site are superb and well used and include a sauna. Large Design/Technology

Centre due to be opened September 1991. Pockets of energetic after-school activity: rehearsals (boys as young as 14 take up directing), a jazz group, 30-40 clubs operate at lunch break. Very lively political debates.

Background and Atmosphere Since autumn 1986, school moved to splendid new high-tech building right on the Thames just east of Blackfriars Bridge. Five-star facilities, quite stunning view of St Paul's, attractive terraces for the boys, constant hum of boats from the river. New school boasts an extremely attractive small theatre and a drama studio for use only by the English Department (drama is part of the curriculum up to Third Form), and a Great Hall with splendid Walker organ. Good library with annual £10,000 book allowance. High-pressured day. Well developed tutor system, all boys report to tutor first thing each morning. Head busy building up closer contacts with parents, including half termly reports.

THE PUPILS No defined catchment area—to some extent 'pig in the middle'—but most come from north London, 75-85%, in a great arc that reaches from north west London down to Essex—lesser numbers from South London. All hardened commuters (lots of homework done that way) and very mixed socially, economically and ethnically; fairly large Jewish contingent. No readily identifiable CLS type. Robust and unsnobby, meritocratic, very conscious of how the world outside works. Old Boys include H H Asquith, Mike Brierley, Kingsley Amis, Julian Barnes, Denis Norden.

Entrance Four boys sit exam for every available place. Exam is set at three different standards according to age group (entry at 10,11 and 13), 'all a bit of a bear garden, as almost all candidates trying for at least two and sometimes as many as five schools'. Interviews last 20 minutes. 75% come from maintained sector at 11, almost all from private sector at 13.

Exit 75% to university or medical school, including nearly 20% to Oxbridge—others to degree courses at polytechnics or to careers in business, commerce, banking.

Bottom Line 20 Assisted Places at 11+ stage, five for entry to Sixth. Six Corporation scholarships at 11+, four at 13+, two for Sixth Form entry, one music, (all two-thirds fees). Several Livery Company scholarships. Choristers of Temple Church and Chapel Royal, St James's, are bursaried pupils. Some bursaries available for hard-pressed parents.

Remarks Impressive school with fantastic facilities that realistically prepares boys for the future.

CITY OF LONDON SCHOOL FOR GIRLS

Barbican, London EC2Y 8BB

TEL London (071) 628 0841

Pupils: *660 girls* • All day • Ages: *7-19* • Size of Sixth Form: *80-120* • Non-denom • Fee paying.

HEAD Since 1986, Lady France MA, FRGS (fifties), educated East Ham Girls School and Oxford. Geographer and Mathematician; previously Deputy Head of Bromley High. Grown up son and daughter, husband is a civil servant. Extremely energetic, pioneer in setting up new London girls' schools consortium for entrance exams. 'She inspires confidence', from a parent.

Academic Matters Academically, school at top end of the league: impressive results achieved without too much hothouse pressure, (five-10 lost at Sixth Form, 15-20 new arrivals). It is not uncommon for girls here to take four A-levels. Probably stronger on Arts side than Science (though around a third do Maths and Chemistry A-levels). Unusual choice of Modern Language in first year—French or German, (most do French)—second Modern Language taken up (Russian is popular) in second year, also Latin; strong Classics Department (eight girls took Greek A-level 1990, all got A grades, 12 out of 17 achieved A grade Latin). Not much streaming lower down the school, 'Frankly, they're all bright,' commented one teacher. Good tutorial system with staff regularly monitoring on one-to-one basis enables girls not to panic and to know they can go at their own pace, or repeat wobbly areas. Sixth Form work far more closely monitored than at many schools.

Games, Options, the Arts For a city-bound school CLSG is surprisingly sporty—helped by spacious gymnasium and indoor swimming-pool. Tennis courts and small grass patch—this latter used by junior school only -(above subterranean car park) against roar of City traffic. 'Not enough drama,' according to some girls plus parents, but music is strong, (all manner of musical instruments taught during school hours, a rare occurrence among day schools, with much benefit from neighbouring Guildhall School of Music and Drama). Good paintings in evidence, also textiles (almost as sophisticated as you might see in art school). DT department in the pipe line. Public speaking taught by Head.

Background and Atmosphere Purpose-built block erected in early 1960s surrounded by water on all sides, in the midst of towering Barbican buildings, a concrete jungle amid remains of ancient historical monuments. Box building is set around well of main hall (used for assembly, dance, plays etc), corridors covered with rubbery lino off which classrooms lead gives drearily monotonous effect. But noticeboards are lively— evidence of girls' pricking consciences, and vending machines do good business (school let to London Poly etc). School is part of Corporation of City of London, and connections with Livery Halls etc are undoubtedly good for business and finance, all of which should, in principle, make the girls aware of the wider world, though some parents cast doubts. Fairly democratic use of school council and suggestions book; all Sixth act as prefects. Foyer with gladioli.

THE PUPILS Robust, articulate, unpretentious. Very similar intake to City of London (boys), *qv*, loads from Islington, but children descend from all points of compass on all commuter lines from as far afield as Buckinghamshire and Essex. Over one quarter Jewish, and peppered with ethnic minorities. Social mix is very wide—the odd Lords and Commons offspring, children of shopkeepers and shipbrokers.

Entrance Exam at 11: 300 for 50 places; seen by staff first and short listed, looking for 'flair, open minds and children who can respond'.

Exit About 10-15 a year to Oxbridge, 90% into higher education—most to university, and all manner of careers.

Bottom Line Assisted Places at 11 and at Sixth Form level. Three full scholarships a year and quaint-sounding lesser scholarships such as Pewterers' Company Scholarship, Baltic Exchange Scholarship.

Remarks Top end of league for London (girls)- and yet the school lacks glamour. 'It doesn't vibrate,' according to one disgruntled parent, another described the girls, including her own, as 'straight-laced'. Powerful but curiously unexciting and low-profile.

CLIFTON COLLEGE
Bristol BS8 3JH
TEL Bristol (0272) 735945

Pupils: 676 pupils, boys and girls ● 401 boarders, 213 day pupils, 62 'day boarders' (day pupils in boarding houses able to board short term if needed) ● Ages: 13-18 ● Size of Sixth Form: Approx 260 ● C of E and one Jewish house ● Fee-paying.

HEAD   Since September 1990, Mr Hugh Munro MA (early forties), educated at Rugby and Pembroke College Cambridge, where he read Economics and History. Rugby blue. Started teaching at Haileybury. Married with one son and one daughter.

Academic Matters   Traditionally strongest on mainstream subjects. Strong English Department. Successful research-scientist-in residence scheme and pupils have just been north of Canada to research on the Arctic Hare and its sense of smell.

Games, Options, the Arts   Has 86 acres of playing fields on the other side of the Clifton Suspension Bridge and pupils are ferried back and forth in former London Transport buses. Main games: rugger, soccer, cricket. All boys and girls join Terriers ('apprentice' CCF) in first year. CCF voluntary however. Bournemouth Sinfonietta in residence for five days to train up pupils. Some rather good artists among pupils at time of writing. Strong rackets team too.

Background and Atmosphere   Founded in 1862 to provide a 'thoroughly good and liberal education at moderate costs'. Location is in the middle of Bristol's smart residential area, next door to the zoo, which pupils can visit for 10p (useful for field studies). Imposing Victorian chapel (compulsory attendance four times a week plus alternate Sundays, apart from Jewish pupils, who have own services) and main school buildings. Boarding houses have nice view of the playing fields. Three girls' houses, including one which caters for day girls.
Lessons tend to grind to a halt on Saturdays as boys of the Jewish house, Polack's, celebrate the Sabbath, and Gentiles tread water, feeling slightly resentful.
Atmosphere in liberal tradition.

THE PUPILS   Locals, ex pats, and boys from 'wherever there is a motorway link'. Girls from wide range of schools. Also popular with Americans. Old Boys: Earl Haig, John Cleese, Henry Newbolt, Trevor Howard, Sir Michael Redgrave, Sir David Willcocks etc.

Entrance   CE or scholarship exam. Boys from Clifton Preparatory sit an exam before entry into the College. Girls pinched from nearby Clifton High, plus other girls' schools roundabout.

Exit   70% go on to a degree course in university or poly. Then into business, commerce, the law etc.

Bottom Line   Not well endowed, but one-sixth of school on some sort of bursary.

Remarks   Tradtional public school which appears to have benefited greatly from the introduction of girls—numbers and morale up, and a new sense of purpose in the air.

CLIFTON HIGH SCHOOL FOR GIRLS
College Road, Bristol BS8 3ID
TEL Bristol (0272) 730201

Pupils: Approx 775 girls, including nursery school ● 60 board, 715 day ● Ages: 3-18 ● Size of Sixth Form: 102 ● Non-denom ● Fee-paying.

HEAD   Since April 1985, Mrs Joyce Walters MA (age not given), Oxford Classicist. Previously Head of St Mary's Calne. Charming, brave, and, according to one pupil, 'knows all of us'. Has been tightening up on discipline and clamping down on scruffiness.

Academic Matters   Average to reasonably good academic standards. Head keen to promote Sciences. French, History, Classics, English still good. Biology traditionally strong (easier than Physics, Maths etc). Tutorial system. New library also computer resources centre. Leakage post GCSE.

Games, Options, the Arts   Sports consistently good—keen pupils—especially tennis—Jo Durie is OG. Head encouraging and 'goes out on to the hockey field in her high heels'. Disadvantage is that playing fields are quite a distance away, and is a slog to get to them. Yearly drama festival. Music as strong as at

Badminton, plenty of music rooms for individual instrument lessons and practice. Joint Choir with Clifton College and Badminton. Excellent Home Economics Department.

Background and Atmosphere   Site of school is a bit cramped, with hardly any grounds, but this is made up for by being part of Clifton 'village', the Georgian suburb of Bristol. Good social life (lots of scarf swapping, and meetings at the back gate) with Clifton College, now co-ed, and just down the road. Green guernseys and grey kilts for winter uniform.

THE PUPILS   Mostly local children of business-men, doctors, lawyers etc. Day girls mainly from Clifton and areas round about. Boarders often ex pats. Broad spectrum of ability. Old Girls: Sara Keays, Mary Renault.

Entrance   Exam for outsiders; test for those coming from own (very good) Junior School.

Exit   Five or six into Oxbridge each year; 75% going on to degree courses in all. Pupils go on to become doctors, lawyers, editors, home economists etc.

Bottom Line   Fees average. Six Assisted Places for 11-year olds, two at 13, five at Sixth Form. Also four John James scholarships and seven others.

Remarks   Continues to be a good, sound high school which would suit stable, middle class all rounders, though it appears to be feeling chill winds with neighbouring Clifton College recently becoming co-ed.

CRANLEIGH SCHOOL
Cranleigh, Surrey GU6 8QQ
TEL Cranleigh (0483) 273666

Pupils: 480 boys, 80 girls (all in Sixth Form) • *490 board, 70 day* • *Ages: 13-18* • *Size of Sixth Form: 265* • *C of E* • *Fee-paying.*

HEAD   Since 1984, Mr Anthony Hart MA (fifties), educated at City of Bath, and Oxford. Ex-Treasury and consequently keen on graphs and pie charts, the prospectus looks like a company's annual report. The glossiest prospectus and magazine in the business.

Academic Matters   Differences of ability recog-nised by careful streaming, some boys taking subjects early. French strongest subject, also steady Economics. School had an exceptionally bright A-level year in 1989, but appears to have slipped back. Teaching tends to be very thorough, sound rather than brilliant. Regular progress checks via Profiles. Good library.

Games, Options, the Arts   Drama good with excel-lent Head of Department. Keen games, with plenty of scope for the girls. Rugby, hockey, tennis the main sports (Fives popular), Charterhouse the main rivals. Keen debating, encouraged by inter-House debating competition. Very well used, and well equipped, engineering and metal workshops. New swimming pool and theatre opening 1991, at a cost of £1.4 million.

Background and Atmosphere   Redbrick building, founded in 1865, with central courtyard the centre of school life, plus neo Queen Anne block, 1928, (and newer additions), set in very pretty fold of Surrey country. Handsome new house, Loveday, built like the main school block around a central courtyard, a shining example to other schools of building in the vernacular. Girls belong to Houses, like the boys, but live in flats joined to staff apartments. Houses meet twice daily (once for prayers, once for notices), and are fiercely competitive. Boys very relaxed about girls and vice versa, 'So it really works well,' according to mother of one whose elder daughter suffered lack of integration elsewhere. Pastoral care is particularly good (without being overbearing); fortnightly exeats partly to ensure parental links and co-operation. Staff meet daily for pre-prandial drinks in new Common Room (cost of building = £½ million).

THE PUPILS   60% from Surrey and Sussex, 20% from further afield, 20% with parents overseas (of which eight per cent foreign). The school has strong links with multi-nationals, oil companies—Shell and BP—and airlines. Cranleigh was actually built to educate the sons of local gentlemen farmers. Friendly and well-mannered pupils, some definitely money oriented. Americans love it. Old boys include Euan MacAlpine.

Entrance   'Get in touch in good time.' 20% from Cranleigh's own prep. Pupil pie reveals ex-pats are all over the world, eg in Sri Lanka, Borneo, Venezuela— but still half the pupils are from Surrey.

Exit   All but a handful go on to university or polytechnics, 15-22 to Oxbridge, business or business allied fields, eg accountancy, overwhelmingly popular.

Bottom Line   Up to 13 scholarships (all scholars

grilled annually, and reminded their role is missionary, and to help others); up to five music scholarships. Assisted Places.

Remarks Rich and low-profile local Surrey traditional public school with good pastoral care.

DANIEL STEWART'S AND MELVILLE COLLEGE AND THE MARY ERSKINE SCHOOL
Queensferry Road, Edinburgh EH4 3EZ
TEL Edinburgh (031) 332 7925

THE MARY ERSKINE SCHOOL
Pupils: 551 girls ● 32 board, 519 day ● Ages: 11-18 ●
Size of Sixth Form: 220 ● Non-denom ● Fee-paying.

DANIEL STEWART'S AND MELVILLE COLLEGE
Pupils: 785 boys ● 43 board, 742 day ● Ages: 11-18 ●
Size of Sixth Form: 280 ● Non-denom ● Fee-paying ●
Also The Combined Junior School, with 1,122 boys and girls,
about 3 board, ages: 3-12 ● Non-denom ● Fee-paying.

HEAD Principal, since 1989, Patrick Tobin MA (late forties). Read history at Oxford. Previously at Prior Park College, Bath. Interests include reading and travel. Married with four children. Takes over from Robin Morgan, who took early retirement in 1989, saying that 'running a huge show is exhausting'. Mr Tobin 'divides the week 'between a rugby-proud boys' school and a cultivated girls' school'. In an attempt to avoid a 'split personality' has 'constant resort' to his 'balls in the air' file.

Academic Matters Classes of up to 25 setted, groups sub-divided in an attempt to extend the most able. Good remedial back-up. GCSE followed by Highers and Certificate of Sixth Year Studies. Computers everywhere (start at age four), schools are particularly strong in Mathematics and the Sciences. Children continue without CE right through the school. New technology centres, containing the 'latest in CAD/CAM', which opened at both schools in 1991.

Games, Options, the Arts Magnificent facilities. Girls are better at shooting than boys, and both join CCF. 27 rugby teams, masses of music, drama, orchestra, can learn to fly (girls too), skiing (Hillend and the real thing), brilliant debating teams (almost always win locally and were 1990 World Debating Champions). Superb Junior ceramics. Junior school has large scale musical productions twice a year.

Background and Atmosphere Two huge senior schools, and a huge combined junior school (called The Mary Erskine). The junior school is housed on the senior schools' premises. In other words, impossibly complicated. Large unwieldy blocks described by Head as 'imaginative' and 'create a surprising feeling of "belonging"'. Interlocking timetables, a regular bus service (every 20 minutes). Junior school raised an amazing £20,000 for charity in 1990.

THE PUPILS Many from Merchant background (discounts), but increasingly from non-Scots who have been sent to work in Edinburgh and the surrounding districts. Children living far out can spend the night when doing evening activities—as can their parents. Lot of 'New Town' children. Pupils 'relaxed and happy, friendly and responsible' to quote a recent school's Inspector.

Entrance At three, five, eight, 10 and 11; then again at 12 or Sixth Form— otherwise 'by default'. Entrance exam in Maths and English and report for Senior School. Waiting lists for some stages—but just go on trying.

Exit The majority of Sixth Year go on to university. Links with Cambridge. Some Juniors leave to board at (predominantly) Scottish public schools (Strathallan, Glenalmond, Loretto, St Leonards, etc).

Bottom Line Assisted Places, bursaries and scholarships. Merchant Schools tend to be heavily endowed. Governing council now administers the schools on behalf of the Merchant company.

Remarks Largest private conglomerate in Great Britain. Absolutely enormous, but works well.

DOLLAR ACADEMY
Dollar, Clackmannanshire, FK14 7DU
TEL Dollar (0259) 42511

Pupils: • *625 boys, 510 girls* • *230 board, 905 day* •
Ages: 5-18 • *Sixth Form: 220* • *Fee-paying.*

HEAD Rector since 1984, Mr Lloyd Harrison BA Oxon. Classicist. Educated Bradford Grammar School. Taught at Glenalmond and previously headmaster of Northallerton Grammar School. Wants to encourage enterprise and wide vision and committed to study with a wide curriculum.

Academic Matters Scottish system—using A-levels occasionally. Wide range of subjects and flexible timetable to fit pupils' options, rather than the other way round. Possibility of Japanese in future, with close ties with Japanese faculty at Stirling University. Classes, particularly in prep school, large for fee paying school 25—27 and in senior school 17—22. Mixed ability classes. New block will be built and will include special facilities for Modern Languages and Business Studies.

Games, Options, the Arts Successful teams based on extra-curricular games. New music block/lecture theatre has just been completed. Strong choral tradition and emphasis on this rather than orchestra. Enthusiastic Pipe Band wears MacNabb tartan. CCF, Drama, D of E, work experience in local hospitals etc. Good facilities, plenty of clubs.

Background and Atmosphere Established as co-ed boarding school in 1818 by Andrew Mylne, the local minister, with legacy from John McNabb. Formerly Direct Grant, but in 1974 became independent. Elegant Playfair facade, but following fire in Sixties, main building was rebuilt entirely. Firm discipline often involves cleaning up school. Boarders complain of not wearing own clothes enough—school uniform has to be worn to all meals at weekends.

THE PUPILS Pupils from all over Scotland and children of expat Scots, but vast majority from 20 mile radius. Some fourth generation pupils. Rector says pupils are perhaps 'too conservative' and an English master said 'they would have difficulty discussing the concept of rebellion'. An OB is Peter Maxwell-Davies, the Composer.

Entrance Five, 10 or 11, the latter two by examination which is very selective. Well over-subscribed. Four academic scholarships of 50% at 11, two at 15/16.

Exit 68-70% go to university and some each year to Oxbridge. Very few leave without a purpose.

Bottom Line 55 Assisted Places. Very reasonable and excellent value.

Remarks Very solid, traditional school with consistently successful academic results, but in many ways operates as a state comprehensive. Very popular locally.

DOWNE HOUSE
Cold Ash, Newbury, Berkshire RG16 9JJ
TEL Hermitage (0635) 200286

Pupils: 471 girls • *436 board, 35 day* • *Ages: 11-18.* •
Size of Sixth Form: 130 • *C of E* • *Fee-paying.*

HEAD Since 1989, Miss S R Cameron BA (forties), educated at Wycombe Abbey, London University (read History of Science), teaches 'a little' (History for First Formers, General Knowledge to Lower Sixth). Previously Head of Cobham Hall for a very short while, and before that Housemistress at Sherborne. Admits to having a fairly tough time at Downe at the moment, 'more is expected of you the second year. The staff found it difficult to have a different personality at the helm.' She hasn't changed a lot, but is looking for 'fresh blood', and describes herself as 'in the business of ecucating'. Has a 'very competent Deputy'.

Academic Matters Very flexible. Excellent Classics (Greek an option), strong Maths, English, Physics and Chemistry. Fabulous new Science block (where pets are kept via a waiting list), with computers—two rooms, but computers everywhere and more in the pipeline (library etc). IT and Science networked. Miss Cameron is 'reviewing the curriculum' (and so much else). Can cope with mild dyslexia.

Games, Options, the Arts Strong on lacrosse: team round Australia in 1989, girls in National Team, oodles of tennis courts (tennis coaching in December when we visited), marvellous swimming pool, girls in ghastly green swimsuits with hats in house colours playing water polo, no mega gym, voluntary CCF. New programme of weekend activities 'under review'. Music everywhere, and good choir (to USA in summer 1990), 90% of girls play one instrument (and practise in nuns' former cells). Marvellous adaptable Jubilee Hall, and drama on the up under Miss Ewing. Art is exciting and inspired, with textiles and screen painting to A-level. All do needlework (also available to A), and cookery, and can continue as an option.

Background and Atmosphere Whitewashed building in hispano-Surrey style, buildings disjointed and scattered (lots of walking—library well down the hill), set in 300 acres of top-of-the-hill grounds. School is markedly house orientated; rather splendid, dining hall (vegetarian option), where girls eat with other girls from their houses. Sixth Formers have their own single or double rooms, and log cabin with telly in which they can entertain boys (dinner parties are possible). New lower Sixth house should be ready shortly, which will mean extra responsibility for Fifth Formers—GCSE level, 'the rebellious ones'. Former Convent Chapel too small for whole school, but much used and popular with girls. Driving lessons can be arranged, and girls who have passed test can bring cars back. Miss Cameron has instituted change of uniform (cloaks still popular), pupils can wear green or red tights; Sixth Formers and a large number of staff when we visited opt for kilts with their own tops.

Discipline Serious breach in November 1990 when seven Fifth Formers were found 'drunk by local police' who 'were fairly tough'. Girls gated, all school privileges withdrawn, no trips to Newbury affected the entire school (culprits and their crime unpopular). Miss Cameron is re-thinking punishments and is 'not averse to expelling'. 'No drugs' but 'girls do bring vodka back in shampoo bottles'. Smokers fined £10, but Head reckons that 'lying, cheating and stealing are much worse than smoking and drinking,' and she will expel regular offenders. She likes to think that the girls operate 'on trust, if they abuse it, they lose it'.

THE PUPILS The Thames Valley. Also always some from Scotland, Ireland, Cornwall; some ex-pats, though hardly any foreigners (great excitement over the Russian Ambassador to Luxemburg's daughter, who has followed Miss Cameron from Cobham). Old Girls: Lady Plowden, Dame Rebecca Murray, Baroness Ewart-Biggs.

Entrance Mostly 11+, some 12+ and 13+. Some after GCSE.

Exit Some leakage after GCSE. 'Nearly all go on to university.' Extra coaching for Oxford and Cambridge.

Bottom Line Scholarships—two major, two minor, at 11+. Two for those under 14, plus two open music scholarships and two academic scholarships for Sixth Formers. Assisted Places not taken up ('too high a threshold?').

Remarks Good traditional school in a state of flux. Highly structured, with a good academic record, the current niggles should iron out.

DOWNSIDE SCHOOL
Stratton on the Fosse, near Bath, Somerset
BA3 4RJ
TEL Stratton on the Fosse (0761) 232206

Pupils: 444 boys • Approx 432 board, 12 day • Ages: 13-18 • Prep school 40 boys, ages: 11-13 • Size of Sixth Form: 178 • RC • Fee-paying.

HEAD From April 1991, Dom Aidan Bellenger MA PhD. Takes over from Dom Philip Jebb, who becomes Prior. Palace revolution: new Head chosen by new abbot. Father Bellenger is large and intellectual and a Historian. He has taught at the school for some time, but only been a monk for two years.

Academic Matters Results downsliding again. Impossible to comment on this at time of writing. Staff young and mainly male: 20 monks, the rest lay. Languages a strength (include Welsh, Hebrew, Russian, Latin etc). Arts stronger than Sciences. Boys are setted in subjects from the start: 'A' to 'F' grading and 'G Group' for less able boys who aim at fewer GCSEs. Some disquiet expressed by parents at scrapping of fast stream. General Studies at Sixth Form give way to Moral and Social Studies on such matters as Third World, nuclear war. Downside's effort for Europe: everyone is now studying one modern language alongside their A-levels.

Games, Options, the Arts Good theatre, and enthusiastic Head of Music has restarted the lapsed orchestra. All first-year boys must play an instrument. Jazz prominent. Annual visit to Lourdes and Community Service. Good Art. CCF, indoor rifle range, Duke of Edinburgh's Award, fencing and archery, and hockey in spring term etc, etc. Interesting visiting speakers include Lord Hailsham (a regular) and Shirley Williams. New space-age sports hall.

Background and Atmosphere   Part of the Benedictine Monastery (which still owns the 300-acre farm) transferred here from Flanders in 1814. True to Benedictine tradition as a seat of learning, Downside Review, a slim theological quarterly, is internationally known. Hexagonal monastery library (recently modernized) with 500,000 books—'We have some that aren't in the British Museum'—is used by scholars from all over the world. The Abbey Tower dominates the lush landscape for miles around. Architecture by Giles Gilbert Scott, plus many additions. All six houses of the school are under the same vast roof, linked by cloisters and corridors. 'This is our Colditz block,' say boys happily—and happy they are. Acres of brown lockers and panelling within. Highly polished floors generate careful walk known as the 'Downside Shuffle'. New CDT block etc. Computer link-up system for Maths, Science, Geography and History and flourishing computer club. Huge dorms with minimum privacy accepted as the norm without complaints. Study bedrooms for Sixth Formers. Prep late, ie after supper. RC atmosphere 'pervasive but not obstrusive' according to parents.

Discipline   Now definite though quiet, and the atmosphere settled and conducive for work to a purpose, though reputation for unruliness lingers. Sixth Form bar under supervision of members of staff. Drugs are met with instant expulsion—and there have been some over the years. Eccentricity is tolerated: 'It's expected and understood, accepted at a monastery,' according to one monk. 'By tolerant, they mean they're good at dealing with "individuals"—ie, pains in the neck.' The stability in a monastery cannot be overrated, say some: there exists the grandfatherly tradition—old monks observe problems, and pick them up early. Lid kept on drugs and alcohol. The school has been called a 'spiritual Butlins'.

THE PUPILS   More sons of Old Boys than most other public schools (over 40%) often three of four generations. 'How can you refuse a man whose father and grandfather were here?' said previous Head. Wear dark grey suits and they are charmers. Usual adolescent tendencies (graffiti writing, climbing on to roofs, etc) counterbalanced by well-developed instinct to help others in difficulty.

The school expands to take in Spaniards with English (Sherry) links, South Americans (from St George's in Buenos Aires), Portuguese, Americans, outposts of the old British Empire. Has over 50 foreigners—most of Catholic Western Europe is represented.

Entrance   Wide range of ability from the very bright to slow-stream entrants. Entrants at Sixth Form a 100-year tradition here.

Exit   Between 10 and 20 to Oxbridge; 40 and 60 to diverse universities, 20 to polytechnics, some to art school, music school, Cirencester Agricultural College. Regimental families provide strong links for many boys to join the Army. The rest to jobs.

Bottom Line   Top scholarship £4,000 and for Sixth Form (with special paper); several minor scholarships totalling £10,000; also art, choral and music awards. Bursaries available to help those unable to afford fees.

Remarks   School has suffered from lingering reputation of underachieving—unfairly, perhaps—and is being watched with interest. Outgoing Head undersung and undersang.

DULWICH COLLEGE
London SE21 7LD
TEL London (081) 693 3601

Pupils: 1,400 boys • 130 boarders, 1,270 day • Ages: Lower School 8-18 • Size of Sixth Form: 400 • C of E • Fee-paying.

HEAD   Since 1986, Mr Anthony Verity MA (fifties), formerly Head, Leeds Grammar School, read Classics and Oriental Languages at Cambridge. Pleasant, reserved, diplomatic.

Academic Matters   Distinguished academically, though not seen as in same league as Westminster and St Paul's. Nevertheless spectacular results considering school admits much wider ability range than the former two, with average of 10 GCSE passes in 1990. Increasing number of mixed Arts/Sciences courses. Energetic, able staff of 125 (20 women), with regular injections of new blood as established members leave to become Heads of Department—or Headmasters—

elsewhere. Very large number of A-level options, Sciences and Modern Languages strong.

Games, Options, the Arts Super new gym the size of an aircraft hangar, used daily for a wide number of indoor sports, including martial arts, weightlifting, fencing etc. Strong Army, Navy, Air Force corps. Many clubs: computing, biology (rocketry popular in Middle School); very strong generally in music, including a celebrated choir which has recently performed in Russia. Field Centre in Wales also used for Sixth Form studies. School trips are long haul; in 1990 the rugby team played in Austirlia and New Zealand. Strong tradition of drama; purpose built theatre is thoroughly used with over 30 plays produced annually.

Background and Atmosphere Founded by Elizabethan actor-manager, Edward Alleyn (1619). Stately 1870s pile (the original manuscript of *Moby Dick* is rumoured to be lost somewhere in the vastness), with spectacular frontage, standing in handsome grounds with trees, parks, woods—the sheer scale and mood of the building and its grounds automatically confers a sense of considerable privilege in otherwise mundane, red-brick South London.

Inside, corridors are wide and spacious, skirting boards unscuffed and rooms light and tidy, with no noise or suggestion of overcrowding, simply of an orderly flow. Exceptional facilities—The Wodehouse library is one of the most attractive libraries in the country; beautifully lit, inviting, comfortable. The school shares a careers officer with JAGS. Mood throughout school of understated affluence.

THE PUPILS Very wide but not conspicuous social and ethnic mix, including Asians, and Hong Kong Chinese ('strong on work ethic, totally committed'). Boarders come from Japan, Zambia, also Knightsbridge, Hammersmith etc. Catchment for day boys ranges far beyond Georgian Dulwich to Blackheath, and Greenwich, suburban Kent and urban Croydon. Boys pleasant, mannerly, cosmopolitan, good mixers. 'There is such a thing as a Dulwich atmosphere and there's a Dulwich boy at the end.'

Entrance At eight, nine, 11, 13 (by exam and interview); some into Sixth Form. Desperate lack of reasonable state schools in the area results in high number of boys subjecting themselves to the entrance exam and parental and offspring misery.

Exit More than 80% to universities, a slightly increasing number now go to polytechnics. Wide spread of universities, including 'northen university tour'. Regular flow to Oxbridge (39 in 1990) to read the traditional subjects, English, History, the Classics,

Languages. After that, Manchester second most popular university for its wide variety of choices, and Newcastle coming up fast.

Bottom Line Well endowed school, with a generous provision for scholarships (more than 40), bursaries and Assisted Places.

Remarks Strong day public school, with boarding element, with good neighbourhood links and loyalty and a good track record of race relations, a stone's throw from Railton Road, Brixton.

THE EDINBURGH ACADEMY
42 Henderson Row, Edinburgh EH3 5BL
TEL Edinburgh (031) 556 4603

Pupils: 565 boys, 31 girls (Sixth Form only) • 79 board, 517 day • Ages:10+-18 • Size of Sixth Form: 96 • Preparatory School: 355 boys (girls in nursery only); 3 board, 352 day; Nursery: 9 girls, 26 boys • Ages: 3+–11 • Nondenom • Fee paying.

HEAD Rector (since 1977), charming, ambitious Mr Laurence Ellis MA (fifties, contracted till 1992), Winchester scholar, read Maths at Trinity College Cambridge and came to Edinburgh Academy from Marlborough. Two grown-up sons; talks very fast, dry sense of humour, professes to be 'enthusiastic about everything' and believes children need the ultimate challenge whether in the field of sport, creative activity, or work achievement in order to 'find themselves'. 'Discipline has to come from inside you.' Keen (too keen? wonder some parents) on pupils making their own decisions. Sacks for OTT, talks to police re drugs 'but no known connection with the school'. Expulsion for repeated smoking. Impressed 'how well girls sort themselves out' but doesn't see the school going totally co-ed.

Academic Matters Edinburgh Academicals rate around 80% passes on all results, with more than 30% getting 'A' grades. After GCSE 40% move directly to A-levels, the rest take Highers in Lower Sixth and A-levels in following year. Russian, Greek (mainly myths) and French at 11—then they choose one. Four sets in every subject. Head of English and History recently devised excellent broad based Arts Civilization course.

Games, Options, the Arts 90% of games on Saturday mornings—to dismay of some. Famous for Rugby, slight feeling of gamesy-ness lingers, particularly amongst the yuppies of Edinburgh. Marvellous music, and superb art (department set up under protege of Robin Child of Marlborough)—pupils are designated an art subject per term and have to work round it—brilliant. Excellent ancillary teaching. Keen CCF and Pipe Band. Huge swimming pool. Field Centre in the hills (much used by boarders, 'who see themselves as the heart of the school' according to Head, but not according to majority ie day boys).

Background and Atmosphere School founded in 1824, distinguished though somewhat gloomy classical building with Greek inscription. Magnificent library and assembly hall. Lick of paint everywhere since our last visit, and new music school, so facilities now match the Department. Successful appeal for Seventh Centre (for Sixth Form), who now tend to stay on premises over lunchtime, especially since food much improved to ubiquitous self-service system. Preparatory and pre-prep housed in grim and bleak building—though children appear merry withal.

THE PUPILS Sons of Edinburgh and Lothian professionals, often with sisters at St George's School for Girls. Ethnic minority and farmers' sons board. Pupils wear tweedy jackets and cricket sweaters. Competitive lads (this is encouraged), fairly strong on sons of Old Boys. Sir Walter Scott among the Academy's founders, Robert Louis Stevenson among OBs.

Entrance On test at all levels, fairly competitive. Boys post Fifth as well as girls. Fairly strong on sons of Old Boys.

Exit Over 75% to university, 95% to higher education, increasing numbers go to art school in preference to university or other degree course.

Bottom Line Scholarships available for pupils not already attending Edinburgh Academy (always known to aficionados as *the* Academy), also available for music and art, and bursaries for sons of parents fallen on hard times.

Remarks Fine, toughish academic independent day school, though lapses of discipline still commented on by other local schools. Numbers down.

ELLESMERE COLLEGE
Ellesmere, Shropshire SY12 9AB
TEL Ellesmere (0691) 622321

Pupils: 350 boys, 50 girls in Sixth Form ● *280 board, 120 day* ● *Size of Sixth Form: 160* ● *Ages: 11-18* ● *C of E* ● *Fee-paying.*

HEAD Since 1988, Mr David Du Croz MA Cantab (forties) educated Winchester and Cambridge (captained First and Third Trinity Boat Club). Previously Head of Sixth Form Studies at Berkhamsted School. Keen sportsman, married with two children.

Remarks Minor, small and traditional public school, well thought of locally, set in lovely North Shropshire country (regularly used by boys who didn't make it into Shrewsbury, Wrekin College the other likely choice). Good music department (possesses two organs), international players regularly perform in the school's Arts Centre. Flourishing CDT, Engineering Drawing and Design taught in first year. Good and sympathetic remedial help for the dyslexic, 'very confidence building,' say parents. Well used tutorial system, and good pastoral care. Keenly sporty; school is well-placed for expeditions like rock climbing, fell walking. Sailing is popular (including canoeing on Ellesmere Canal). College has marked community atmosphere. One of the original Woodard schools, founded in 1884, architecture is grimly red-brick collegiate. Two academic, two music scholarships.

EMANUEL SCHOOL
Battersea Rise, London SW11 1HS
TEL London (081) 870 4171

Pupils: 750 boys ● *All day* ● *Ages: 10-18* ● *Size of Sixth Form: 160* ● *C of E* ● *Fee-paying.*

HEAD Since 1984, Mr P F Thomson MA (forties), accessible, unstuffy, much liked by pupils, parents and staff. Educated at Haileybury, Trinity College Cambridge, and Queen's College, Oxford; teaches History (top end) and Divinity (bottom end). Keen ambassador for his school. Knows all the boys—and cares. Previously Second Master at St Paul's. Numbers have surged under his Headship.

Academic Matters   Not a hothouse, does very well indeed for the average boy, though hopeful parents have been heard to say that it is getting 'too academic now'—though all is relative. Particularly strong on Maths and Science. CDT outstanding. Entrance at 10 came in with the present Head, in response to local demand, and 'what started as an experiment soon proved an undoubted success'. Long terms compared with many private schools, for less academic boys to pack in more studying.

Games, Options, the Arts   Exceptionally strong rowing, superbly equipped boathouse at Barnes. Some in the current first eight sometimes row for Britain; winners of Head of the River 11 times. Also strong Rugby and cricket—toured Australia in 1991. Parental support for sport is 'phenomenal' to quote the Head. More sports facilities at Raynes Park. Keenly attended voluntary CCF.

Background and Atmosphere   Actually founded in 1594 by Lady Dacre, a descendant of whom is now Chairman of the Governors, moved to present buildings (originally an orphanage) on edge of Wandsworth Common in 1883. Many additions to the Victorian block, handsomely set in 12 well-treed acres, an oasis in noisy Battersea, including, most recently, new classroom block for youngest boys. Workmanlike atmosphere with plenty going on, currently confident (the happy product of rising numbers). Dedicated staff willing to talk to parents and help pupils outside classrooms.

THE PUPILS   Catchment area goes way beyond Battersea, Wandsworth and Clapham, to western and south-western suburbs, via Clapham Junction. First choice for many, and second for increasing numbers of boys who fluff elsewhere. Lots of first timers in private education. Polite, fairly scruffy looking.

Entrance   At 10 and 11 via exam; by CE at 13 and also Sixth Form. Entrance at 10 came in with this Head, in response to local demand, and what started as experiment has proved undoubted success—putting greater pressure thereby on 13+ entry.

Exit   Half the boys go on to further education; business studies course at polys are popular. Medicine, engineering, law, commerce, architecture, the Services

are likely targets. Old boys include Dr J B Phillips, the Bible scholar, Michael Aspel, Stuart Surridge (cricketer and founder of sports outfitters).

Bottom Line   Offers 55 Assisted Places. Scholarships at 10.

Remarks   A successful alternative for Londoners, flexible with difficult boys, and answering a desperate need for places in the metropolis. Big social and ethnic mix. Very well thought of locally.

ETON COLLEGE
Windsor, Berkshire SL4 6DW
TEL Windsor (0753) 866439

Pupils: Approx 1,270 boys   ●   All boarding   ●   Ages: 13-18   ●   Size of post GCSE classes: approx 540   ●   C of E (other faiths 'excused' chapel). 160 RCs, who have resident chaplain   ●   Fee-paying.

HEAD   Since 1980, Dr Eric Anderson B Litt, D Litt, FRSE (fifties), educated George Watson's College, University of St Andrew's and Balliol. Previously at Shrewsbury. Projects simple Scottish scholarliness and laconic manner which totally belie steely qualities of discipline and ambition. Brilliant after dinner speaker. Gets together with former (Gordonstoun) pupil, HRH the Prince of Wales, on eductional matters. NB Eton is ruled by triumvirate: Head, Provost, Vice Provost.

Academic Matters   First class all round. Teaching outstanding—Eton can pick and choose whoever it wants. Very high overall standard of staff; few complaints. School aims to keep curriculum as broad as possible, as long as possible, recently slimmed from 'too heavy a load'. Pupils need a considerable amount of self-discipline to cope with the pressure and have been known to fall by the wayside, here more than elsewhere. Public exam results produce stunning numbers of A grades at both levels.

Games, Options, the Arts   Also excellent, with huge choice of things to do, but 'he never finds the opportunity to do all these wonderful things,' said a parent. Main games: soccer, rugby, the Wall Game, the Field Game (Eton football), cricket, boats (lots of this last). Also on offer: archery, beagling, fencing, golf, judo, sailing, CCF, car maintenance—to pick a few at random—and huge resources mean anything on offer is actually delivered. Other schools queue up for the privilege of playing against Eton, which does its best to oblige.

Background and Atmosphere Founded 1440 by Henry VI; sister college of King's Cambridge, which was founded a year later still prays for school. Buildings of mellow old red brick, grounds run down to the Thames; most elegant dining hall is for Collegers to eat in. Boys still wear traditional tailcoats and stiff white collars, which gradually impart stiff neck to wearer—a good way of telling OEs in later years. Dressing up also gets boys used to being singled out as different—the position of the 24 boarding houses strung out along the streets means boys goggled at by tourists. 'But,' refuted Head, 'we don't "flaunt" ourselves in front of tourists. We were there before they were and we carry on as normal.'

Atmosphere very much alive, *not* easy. All boys have own rooms from the start—this can make for a dauntingly lonely beginning—state of decor variable depending on TLC of parent or what the last occupant has flogged on. Minimal tradition of parental involvement can cause mummy angst.

Currently top of the Housemaster popularity list: i) NJTJ—Nigel Jaques ii) JNBC—James Cook.

Discipline Broad-minded and liberal in principle though in fact exercises a tight day-to-day academic structure and is quite capable of firing a pupil at a moment's notice, often to the consternation of unprepared parents. Drink a perennial problem, drugs from time to time.

THE PUPILS Around 45% sons of Old Etonians. Also largish element of new money to keep up academic standards and/or provide useful contacts.

Entrance Big change here. All children down on to a general list, then called up for inspection and exam at 11—large amount of fallout at this stage. Choose Housemaster at age of four or after 11-year old exam. Entries for scholarships accepted until beginning of May for exam in May for 12+ (or indeed 13+—Eton is increasingly looking for later, more mature candidates). NB beware of pushing your force fed son into this school: 'They need to be robust to cope' said a feed prep school Head.

State entry also for about four pupils a year at 10, at which point Eton pays for three years prep school education in traditional Eton feeders for successful candidates, as well as providing scholarships into the school, and for four pupils at 16.

Exit Large numbers to Oxbridge, though 'fashionable' choice is to popular redbricks, eg Manchester, plus 10/12 to America. Some parental distress and/or fury when pupils fail to make Oxbridge despite brilliant A-levels. Oxford in particular is very good at weeding out and rejecting what they consider overcooked and unsuitable material. Otherwise 'gap', travel and into the family business.

Bottom Line Fees roughly on a par with other major public schools. But beware—the uniform, for example, is amazingly expensive. Foundation income goes mainly on upkeep of historic buildings, building new facilities or on scholarships. These include 70 King's Scholars. Also large numbers of bursaries etc, for parents who fall on hard times. School well deserves charity status and with all on offer still has to be very good value.

Remarks This traditional—and many would say best—public school in the country is currently reaping the problems of a highly competitive entry exam, which only those rigorously trained for get through.

FELIXSTOWE COLLEGE
Felixstowe, Suffolk 1P11 7NQ
TEL Felixstowe (0394) 284269

Pupils: Approx 320 girls • All board, except for about 30 • Ages: 11-18 • Size of Sixth Form: approx 85 • C of E • Fee-paying.

HEAD Since January 1989, Mrs Ann Woodings MA London (forties), read History. The first married Headmistress in the College's history. Believes in both 'pure and applied learning'.

Academic Matters Not your hot shot academic school, but a girl will be refused entry if she is going to find GCSE a 'real struggle'. Some help for dyslexia laid on for girls who *are* struggling but making 'outstanding' contribution to the school. Sixth Form now split into Academic and 'the Creative and Practical Arts', so the genuinely artistic and practical girl can do courses which suit her and not necessarily A-levels, eg two girls at the time of writing are doing Dance as one of their three Sixth Form subjects. CDT now part of the timetable (with its own special building). Results bumped up by clever non-nationals.

Games, Options, the Arts Strong on the Performing Arts, which provide an oasis of civilization in a sea of oil seed rape. Vigorous music, new sports hall. Lots of Duke of Edinburgh awards being taken, popularity has led to Housemistress developing similar scheme for younger girls called FLEAS (Felixtowe Leadership and Educational Award Scheme). Some form of physical exercise compulsory, main games: tennis, hockey, rounders and swimming (girls do well in national life saving competitions). Speech and drama both strong, all Lower Sixth take course and exam in public speaking. Well thought out personal and social education programme spread over the years, stretches from road safety to interviews. Extras include riding, driving lessons, sailing etc, this last almost to finishing school level.

Background and Atmosphere One of the 'Allied Schools', which include Riddlesworth (former 'feed') and Stowe. Originally founded in Surrey in the early years of the century, moved to East Anglia, and in 1929 re-named Felixtowe College. Run on house system—Ridley and Cranmer are the Sloane houses, with glorious sea views, rather pleasant. Main buildings good example of Victorian Seaside—just up the Front from Mrs Simpson's old place.

THE PUPILS About two-thirds have 'roots' in East Anglia, often 'real' farmers' daughters and daughters of 'managing directors' and City. Bright girls from the far east.

Entrance CE or scholarship exam. Into Sixth by interview and school report.

Exit About 70% to university, others to art and dance colleges, hotel and catering, retail management, secretarial etc.

Bottom Line No endowment, but over four per cent of fee income set aside for scholarships—numbers depend on need.

Remarks Strong new sense of direction under the new Head, who is combining the academic and practical strands with imagination, while fostering traditional values of a boarding school for young ladies.

FELSTED SCHOOL
Dunmow, Essex CM6 3LL
TEL Great Dunmow (0371) 820 258

Pupils: 440 boys, 60 girls (all in Sixth Form) ● *420 boys board, 20 day boys; all girls board* ● *Ages: 13-18* ● *Size of Sixth Form: 240* ● *Also prep school of 150 pupils* ● *C of E foundation* ● *Fee-paying.*

HEAD Since 1983, Mr E J H Gould MA (forties). Looks like a large teddy bear and read Geography at Teddy Hall, also played 'one or two games', by which he means four rugby blues, swimming half-blue, rowed for Great Britain etc. Housemaster at Harrow before he came here. Comments that is concerned with 'the happiness of the school and the morale... When they (pupils) arrive at the age of 13 they are inevitably moving into a slightly bigger pool and there will be some failure. It is very important to create some success as soon as possible, so they get confidence. It is important to be able to say "well done"...'

Academic Matters Statistical average number of A-level 'passes' per candidate is 2.7, with 71% at grades A, B and C. Girls in particular tend to 'over-achieve' according to a master. Maths, CDT, Science traditionally strong here. English or Maths can be done with anything at A-level, and any other combination is organized, providing there is a viable set (ie 5-6 pupils). Modern Languages have 'experienced a revival'. Some excellent teaching staff.

Games, Options, the Arts A school well-known for prowess on the games field and competitive attitude of the 'professional' games players. Immensely strong hockey school (only Bedford competes)—even the girls, who only arrive at Sixth Form. Pupils unkeen on games now have a 'rolling programme of health related fitness'.

School currently in the grip of the official computer freak (Head of Computing) Chris Dawkins, who has more or less succeeded in his ambition to wire up the whole school into one huge network—one of the first and few to have done this— into which anyone can plug at any time and check on eg whether Smith mi is currently on a bicycle ride/ill/doing exams.

Messages are timed and dated and in this way, said Mr Dawkins, they get to learn about computers quite naturally. Like most hot shot computer people, he is not too keen on Computer Studies exams because they are soon obsolete, and in general not much use. But: 'Even the unkeenest boy will sooner or later want to use it, if only to look up the latest Test score on Prestel.'

The school also has wonderful old farmhouse next door (The Bury), left to the school by an OB in the Thirties, in which all manner of societies take place. Some distinctly good art.

Background and Atmosphere   Set in the heart of yuppie East Anglian commuter belt, surrounded by fat Ferraris, BMWs and flitches. School is on good terms with the local village in which boys flit to and fro, and a local commented that it was a 'lovely school' (unusual to get a compliment like this).

Founded in 1564 by Richard, Lord Riche, Lord Chancellor of England, who came and 'buried his conscience here' after his successful part in the decapitation of Sir Thomas More. For 300 years thereafter, the Riche heirs were patrons of the school, which still solemnly celebrates the existence of this arch-baddie on Founder's Day.

Peaceful, pleasing and quietly purposeful, almost civilized to look at, though some Dickensian horrors tucked away out of sight. Modern buildings in the grounds (diligent groundsmen), well planned and unobtrusive. Main buildings recently Grade 1 and 2 listed, which has necessitated reorganisation and refurbishment.

THE PUPILS   'Broad' spectrum of backgrounds, from round Felsted, Southend, also London and south of London. Local accents predominate. Most famous Old Felstedian is Richard Cromwell, son of Oliver (a letter from him hangs in the rather static looking library). Most famous present OB is probably Kenneth Kendall. Lots of engineers among OBs.

Entrance   By CE or exam. Special provision for pupils from state schools. School has own preparatory school over the road, pupils also come from local prep schools and eg Brambletye.

Bottom Line   An unspecified percentage of fee income goes towards bursaries and scholarships— Head aims to give out more than the school gets as a charitable trust—'otherwise it is not a charity'. A variety of scholarships including eight of 10-80% of total fees. Three boarding Assisted Places for 13-year olds; five day places for Sixth Form. School does not have heavy endowments.

Remarks   A good solid public school. Image has moved from very tough, ultra-sporty to one of wider interests.

FETTES COLLEGE
Carrington Road, Edinburgh EH4 1QX
TEL Edinburgh (031) 332 2281

Pupils: 200 boys, 175 girls • 300 board, 75 day • Ages: 13-18 • Size of Sixth Form: 195 • Non-denom • Fee-paying.

HEAD   Since 1988, Mr Malcolm Thyne MA (forties), previously Headmaster at St Bees School, before that at Oundle and Edinburgh Academy.

Academic Matters   Not a hot shot, but does well for the middle of the road; 40% take Highers (spread over two years), 60% take A-level. Sir Nicholas Somerville practises pupils' interview techniques; sensible careers advice.

Games, Options, the Arts   Usual games (girls wear bright pink kit, and do well); games keep pupils busy on Saturday afternoon. CCF for boys and girls, most continue after compulsory period, rest opt for DofE or community service. Very good new Head of Music school badly needs proper theatre, but drama is lively anyhow; splendid high tech department, sophisticated compact computers etc, university standard equipment, with keen following. Ski-ing, canoeing, mountaineering, sailing.

Background and Atmosphere   Vast Grimms' Fairy Tale turretted edifice, purpose built on the edge of the city in 1870 (by Bryce). Not bad on cultural outings Sixth Form Club with controlled drink, regular Saturday evening discos. Huge sums spent on refurbishing Houses comfortably; everyone given House chores Charming little chapel.

Discipline   Head very hostile towards smoking and illegal alcohol, still tightening up discipline and ha sacked wilder element.

THE PUPILS   Fairly cosmopolitan at the last count—52% with houses in Scotland, 20% from England, Wales, Ireland; 28% live abroad (more than half of these are ex-pats). Wide social mix. Happy and relaxed. Splendid striped bright pink blazer. Famous Old Fettesians include James Bond, Tony Benn, Iain MacLeod, Selwyn Lloyd. Breeds Headmasters.

Entrance   Full to capacity with girls—can pick and choose—but touting for boarding boys. Via CE, o own exam in English and Maths (if from abroad); approximately 30 places at Sixth Form.

Exit Around 70% to universities/polys. Edinburgh, Glasgow, Aberdeen, Durham, Bristol popular choices. Nine to Oxbridge in 1990.

Bottom Line Adequately endowed, school offers several scholarships (academic and musical), also Foundation Awards, Assisted Places and Bursaries.

Remarks Solid, firming up academically, well run—but lacking inspiration. Still treated with suspicion by locals following drugs problems.

FRAMLINGHAM COLLEGE

Framlingham, Near Woodbridge, Suffolk 1P13 9EY

TEL Framlingham (0728) 723789

Pupils: 291 boys, 132 girls • 295 board, 128 day • Ages: 3-19 • Size of Sixth Form: Approx 150 • C of E • Fee-paying.

HEAD Since September 1989, Mr James Miller MA (forties), previously Housemaster at Winchester. An economist who is 'keener on individuals than statistics'. Reported to be positive and friendly.

Remarks Mixed. School reckons to do well with 'middle range boy or girl' who, if he or she had gone to highly academic school might have sunk without trace. School sets but not streams. Head has introduced some new subjects eg engineering, and a 'pukka business admininstration/secretarial course' for 'the minority for whom unadulterated academic A-levels are not right'. He goes on, 'given the amount of pure lip service that is generally being paid to 1992, we are also encouraging all Sixth Formers to carry on with a language.' Results for 1990 'frankly disappointing' to quote Mr Miller, who adds, 'The easiest way of ensuring a high pass rate is to stop those likely to fail doing exams—a policy that we do not adopt.'

Games compulsory and good—one parent commented that it was 'a bit ruggy buggy'. Main games hockey, rugby, cricket. 50 acres of playing fields, sports hall, floodlit Astroturf type surface pitch. CCF voluntary but quite keen, including about 40 girls.

Fringe extras fluctuate 'depending on who is keen on what, when'.

College founded in 1864 as 'Albert Memorial College for Sons of the Middle Class' to commemorate the Prince Consort. Beautiful setting and well-tended grounds perched on one of the few hillocks in Suffolk. The pupils are healthy, happy, energetic and manners still not polished. Some local farmers' sons, many from 'humble homes making huge sacrifices'. Some *Independent* readers' children. Famous Old Boys: Alfred Munnings and Andy Hancock (famous for 'Hancock's Try' at Twickenham). Parents by and large satisfied.

FRANCIS HOLLAND SCHOOL

Clarence Gate, Regent's Park, London NW1 6XR

TEL London (071) 723 0176

Pupils: 360 girls • All day • Ages: 11-18 • Size of Sixth Form: 85 • C of E • Fee-paying.

HEAD Since April 1988, Mrs P H Parsonson MA (early fifties), educated at Casterton and St Hilda's College, Oxford. Mother of four, her husband has recently retired from running a house at Harrow. Head of Maths, and subsequently Director of Studies, at North London Collegiate. Has experience of teaching in state schools too. A most delightful woman. Breathing fresh life into the school. Thinks it vital girls leave 'versatile and flexible—and able to express themselves'. Open door attitude much appreciated throughout the school.

Academic Matters Steady and strong. Selective intake weeds out weaker candidates; more Arts than Sciences at A-levels. Strong Modern Languages. Big staff change-overs. Good General Studies course for Sixth Formers, English, Art Appreciation, Economics and the Environment, and Information Technology all compulsory subjects. Strong Careers Department.

Games, Options, the Arts Regent's Park five minutes' walk away, much used. Keen match players (Sixth Form PE optional, currently popular, as is the exercise bike in their Common Room). Art is strong; drama keen, with form plays taken passionately seriously. Music another strength, with choirs taking part in public arenas, and Madrigal Society. Flourishing debating includes a Junior Debating Society, 'They're *very* articulate, and it's hard to stop them sometimes.' Lots of clubs during the lunch break, many of them started and run by Sixth Formers.

Background and Atmosphere Sixth Formers lunch out of school, juniors allowed (in threes) into Park, or slightly further afield according to forms, a freedom that causes some parents anxiety, (heavy penalties for abusing privileges). Curious wedge-shaped building, pleasantly decorated, next door to Rudolph Steiner establishment.

THE PUPILS Interesting cross-section socially and ethnically, strong Jewish element, favoured by diplomats with bi-lingual daughters.

Entrance Own exam at 11, oversubscribed. Some at Sixth Form (up to 10) to fill leavers' gaps.

Exit 75% go on to degree course, (three or four to Oxford in a good year), four or five annually to good art schools. Wide variety of careers.

Bottom Line One scholarship at Sixth Form (internal or external); bursaries. Have applied for Assisted Places. Two scholarships at Sixth Form (half fees) internal and external. Two Exhibitions (one-twelfth fees) at 14+. One music scholarship at 11+. Generous bursaries for those in school. Five assisted places at 11+.

Remarks Low profile but steady. Academically stronger than the Sloane Square branch.

FRANCIS HOLLAND SCHOOL
39 Graham Terrace, London SW1 8JF.
TEL London (071) 730 2971

Pupils: 337 girls • *All day* • *Ages: 4-18* • *Size of Sixth Form: 45* • *C of E* • *Fee-paying.*

HEAD Since 1982, Mrs Jennifer Anderson (fifties) educated St Paul's and Cambridge. Was a civil servant.

Taught at Westminster Tutors and at FH's sister school at Clarence Gate. A mother. Divorced. Remarried to a poet. Approachable, sympatic and populat with parents and pupils.

Remarks Excellent junior school. Safe, straight good sound and fairly gentle inner London school. Does everything. Tidy grey uniform. Nice children. Maths and French streamed. Good languages. Good History of Art, with lots of visits to galleries. Competent at careers advice and work experience. OG: Joan Collins. Large playground by central London standards. Traditional Church school founded in 1881. One scholarship for an eleven-year old and two exhibitions for Sixth Formers.

FRENSHAM HEIGHTS
Rowledge, Nr Farnham, Surrey GU10 4EA
TEL Frensham (025 125) 2134

Pupils: 135 boys, 145 girls • *175 board, 105 day* • *Ages: 11-18* • *Size of Sixth Form: 75* • *Non-denom* • *Fee paying.*

HEAD Since 1973, Mr A L Pattinson MA Oxo (fifties). Very strong character, formerly Benedictin monk, subsequently read Philosophy at Balliol. Unusually for a Head of school of this size to belong t the HMC. Serious, dignified, with quiet sense o humour. 'I didn't want it to be a progressive school, wanted it to be a liberal school,' Head comments, and adds, 'If you're going to run a liberal school you hav to have a rigorous mind.'

Remarks Small co-ed pioneering (1925) school, wit generous one-to-seven staff/pupil ratio. Competitio is discouraged, but 'nobody looks down on you her because you work hard'. Much energy is devoted t art, CDT and drama. Karate has been good, but spor not much in evidence. Committed staff, and pupil walk in and out of staff quarters and share their lif Beautiful grounds, magnificent views, school nor mally an oasis of peace and calm, with large, imposin Edwardian house at its centre (built by brewer magnate), and former stable block used for class rooms. Younger girls have bright, welcoming room at top of main house. Children are unpretentious an very friendly. 'No two accents the same.' School has 35% ex pats. Noticeboards full of charity appeals, pleas for Third World. Interview plus exam at 11, 12, 13, academically middle brow. Few taken into Sixth Form. Generous provision of scholarships and bursaries and even occasional free places are offered. Alternative education favoured by the liberally minded.

GEORGE WATSON'S COLLEGE
Colinton Road, Edinburgh EH10 5EG
TEL Edinburgh (031) 447 7931

Pupils: Nursery 60, ages: 3-5, Junior School 790, ages: 5-12, Senior School 1,250, ages: 12-18 • Boy/girl ratio: 55/45 • 2,030 day, 70 board • Size of Sixth Form: 425 • Non-denom • Fee-paying.

HEAD Since 1985, Mr Frank Gerstenberg MA Cantab, PGCE London (forties), educated at Glenalmond and previously Head of Oswestry School. 'Not a Committee Man', he has 'tightened on discipline, removing the cobwebs and complacency', physically as well as metaphorically, and George Watson's now has a Headmaster worthy of the Merchant tradition. Very hot on industrial liaison and work-shadowing. Aims to produce the 'best parts of a comprehensive without the worst parts'. Mr Gerstenberg teaches History 'a little' during first and last year. Sackings for OTT.

Academic Matters Enormous range of subjects. Scottish system, pupils do O and Standard grades, followed by Highers and CSYS. Brilliant remedial (said to be best in Britain) with Dr Collins and the Cabin. George Watson's supports slower learners in the Junior School, and takes six children each year 'with specific learning difficulties'. Very strong on Maths and allied Sciences, but big enough to be good on almost everything. Rows of computers. Good library.

Games, Options, the Arts Best games tradition, rugger good, games fields on campus, quaint old-fashioned swimming pool and outdoor gym adjacent to new sports hall (with parquet flooring, but just too small to play tennis on). Art, pottery, and now one of

Scotland's leading schools in technology. Brilliant music school with exotic roof. Music everywhere. No CCF, but shooting, and full-blown pipe band.

Background and Atmosphere Magnificent hall. Purpose-built, long-corridored, totally symmetric building sporting the Merchant Company boat, with masses of modern conversions and additions. No class larger than 28. Pupils are positive, doing things, particularly extra-curricular. Timetable on seven-day cycle.

THE PUPILS Offspring of Edinburgh professionals and from outlying suburbs as far as Kirkaldy and Peebles. Some boarders are ex pats, Border farmers' children, OB's ditto. Malcolm Rifkind is an OB.

Entrance At age five by interview; 11 and 12 by interview, assessment and test. Occasional acceptance throughout, space permitting.

Exit Typically 120 pupils to university, with a further 40 to polys. Little leakage at CE (one or two every so often), 'about six' after Standard Grade.

Bottom Line The school can give some help with boarding fees, reductions for forces, various bursaries, music scholarships after performance within the school. Assisted Places.

Remarks Very (too?) large polyglot school forging strongly ahead to the 1990s, now under its own recently formed board of governors, as opposed to the Merchant Board.

GIGGLESWICK SCHOOL
Settle, North Yorkshire BD24 0DE
TEL Settle (0729) 823545

Pupils: Around 194 boys, 110 girls • 271 board, 33 day • Ages: 13-18 • Junior School: 132 boys and girls ages: 8-13 • Size of Sixth Form: 130 • C of E • Fee-paying.

HEAD Since 1986, Mr Peter Hobson MA (forties), educated at Rossall, The Queen's College, Oxford. Formerly Housemaster at Wellington College, where he was Industrial Liaison Officer and taught Classics. He still teaches Classics, and has forged links with local industries. An enthusiast who enjoys challenge.

Academic Matters Consistently under review. Good solid staff. Support system for dyslexia.

Games, Options, the Arts Beefy games, girls' tennis unbeaten at time of writing, and successful junior netball. Strong drama started by the late Russell Harty. Ballroom dancing now on the menu. Revamped swimming pool. Bar above games hall for Sixth Formers. Outward bound, CCF (including girls).

Background and Atmosphere Set in Yorkshire Dales, 60 minutes north of Manchester, Giggleswick was founded in 1512 and the cluster of limestone houses are spread throughout the tiny village beneath an incongruous-looking mini St Paul's (copper dome and all), gift of another benefactor. Much needed revamp of some living quarters completed, Sixth Form centre now being built. Happy atmosphere.

THE PUPILS Many local, large catchment area. Stalwart lads and lassies. Five per cent foreign, ditto ex pats. Parents in professions.

Entrance At eight via own test and reports. CE at 13. Entrance into Sixth Form is by five GCSEs at 'C' grade (about 20 a year). Steady input from local (Cheshire, Notts, Lincs) prep schools.

Exit 80% to further education. Some leakage after GCSE (daddy's firm).

Bottom Line Few extras. Applied for Assisted Places. Masses of scholarships including General Distinction, Art and Music.

Remarks Has gained confidence, and is well spoken of by educationalists and parents.

GLASGOW ACADEMY
Colbrooke Street, Glasgow G12 8HE
TEL Glasgow (041) 334 8558

Pupils: 1,000+, dropping to about 1,000 • Boy:girl ratio approx 3:1 • All day • Ages: 4-18 • C of S/Non denom • Fee-paying.

HEAD Rector (since 1983), Mr C W Turner BSc, King's College, London. Educated at Torquay Gram-

mar School, and previously taught for 25 years at Edinburgh Academy.

Remarks In a state of flux and impossible to comment at the moment: boys numbers considerably down since previous edition, school in process of amalgamating with nearby girls' Westbourne School. Chairman of the governors of the latter comments, 'Both schools share similar ideals and traditions'. Academy renowned for debating, and has produced a significant number of MPs eg Bob Maclennan. Many pupils leave to do Sixth Form studies elsewhere.

GLENALMOND COLLEGE
Perthshire, Scotland PH1 3RY
TEL Glenalmond (073 888) 205

Pupils: 340 boys, 60 girls • All board but day pupils from September 1991 • Ages: 12-18 • Size of Sixth Form: 148. • Episcopalian • Fee-paying.

HEAD Previous Warden left in a hurry. Interregnum at time of going to press.

Academic Matters Does GCSE at Fifth Form and then plays the system—offering both A-levels and Scottish Highers. Very good record of A/B grades at A-level. Traditionally an academic school, but has in the past had surprising amount of academic success with some of its less able pupils as well. Solid three Rs ethic and competent, if not always inspiring, staff.

Games, Options, the Arts Strong on rugby, with many international and university caps to its name. Excellent at skiing, with own artificial ski slope and regular trips to Glenshee. Own nine-hole golf course, canoeing, rock climbing, own pipe band—in fact, another school which could double up as an outward bound camp. CCF from second year, but pupils can opt out to do community work instead. Debates and dances with Kilgraston, St Leonard's and St George's. Superb gym, CDT centre (now reported to be getting into gear).

Background and Atmosphere Elegant cloisters, magnificent chapel and library rise startlingly to meet you out of the wild and wonderful grouse moors of Perthshire. Nearer inspection produces hotchpotch of modern buidlings, labs, theatre etc, and a Basil Spence-designed music block which looks like a public loo. Pupils wear kilts. Boys graduate from tie-dyed draped dormitories, via 'horseboxes', to separate study bedrooms. New purpose-built boarding house—Lothian House—for girls. Note that all pupils used to board (school too far from main road for easy commuting) but will be taking day pupils from September 1991. School founded in 1841 by W E Gladstone.

Discipline   Last Head suspended seven boys in second term for philandering in Perth. Lectures in Sixth Form on AIDS and drugs, fines for smoking. Distinct army overtones here - miscreants report to the (kilted) Manciple (Head porter) for punishment.

THE PUPILS   Scottish upper middle and middle class, army, Highland families and Paisley grocers. Foreigners are 'very welcome'—six at present and college advertises widely in UK and abroad. Rather high level of spottiness among boys.

Entrance   Either via own entrance exam at 12, or by CE ex-prep school (toughish). Early application advisable, though late places do occur.

Exit   Majority to university—steady stream to Oxbridge, Edinburgh and St Andrew's also popular. Army is an option.

Bottom Line   Various open scholarships, special exhibitions for under-14, music scholarships and exhibitions. Special bursaries for sons of clergy (NB bishops on the board of governors) and for 'outstanding personal qualities'. Fees on a par with top English public schools.

Remarks   All out advertising campaign in progress to restore numbers.

GODOLPHIN SCHOOL
Milford Hill, Salisbury SP1 2RA
TEL *Salisbury (0722) 333059*

Pupils: 337 girls   •   235 board, 102 day   •   Ages: 11-18   •   Size of Sixth Form: 75   •   C of E   •   Fee-paying.

HEAD   Since 1989, Mrs Hilary Fender BA Hons (forties), previously Deputy Head (since 1987); edu-

cated at The Marist Convent, Devon, and Exeter University, where she read History, followed by King's College London. Previously Director of Studies at St Gabriel's, Newbury, and the first married Head since school's inception. Teaches History at Second, Third and Sixth Form and reckons she was a 'powerful Deputy' to Miss Hannay, who left—somewhat abruptly—after nine years. An eminently likable Head. 'We know where we are with her' said one pupil. 'She trusts us.'

Academic Matters   Strong on traditional subjects, Greek an option (via computer), good Business Studies. Computers everywhere, good language lab, modern library, (encyclopaedia on computer), though house libraries more used for serious reading (*My Friend Flicka* very popular in junior houses). Two languages, German and French with Spanish an option. One essential to 18, otherwise must take Foreign Language at Work (FLAW). Super new CDT block—lots of safety buttons everywhere—marvellous photo lab. Modern Geography area with light boxes for maps and overhead projector. Tutors for girls in Sixth Form, otherwise combination of tutors and form teachers: forms 25 at first year, but small classes post-GCSE. Average six GCSEs. Pupils move round classes, all clutching blue book bags.

Games, Options, the Arts   Modern games hall, old gym used for drama. Lots of tennis courts and lax pitches. Games improving. Excellent art, (seriously good pottery), linked to textiles (though straight sewing still possible). Home Economics to A-level, with Cordon Bleu Cookery a popular extra. Good careers advice, work shadowing and CRAC. Music now very strong under charismatic Mrs Sharp in charming 1920s cottage. Singing in Salisbury Cathedral and parents' music workshop in February. Skiing, field trips, D of E award etc.

Background and Atmosphere   Cluster of purpose-built classrooms and houses atop chilly Milford Hill (fabulous view of Salisbury Plain), school divided by fast unpavemented road (footbridge for juniors mandatory). Moved to present site in 1890 under Miss Douglas, and founded under terms of Elizabeth Godolphin's will of 1726. All girls to Sixth wear blue pinnies, with nostalgic blue and red cloaks and straw boards (boaters). 25% school currently vegetarian, 'not many anorexics'. Mixed age Junior four-bedroomed dorms (teddies, make-up, plants everywhere) and married Housemistresses (small children and toys in Douglas, which has a prehistoric collection of much-loved steel baths!). Basins in rows are divided like stalls: 'the girls are going through a very prudish phase, they won't even *lie* on each other's beds,' said Mrs Loxton (HM of Douglas). Girls have use of house sewing machine. Sixth Form have own recently expanded House with double studies, personal televisions much in evidence, boys are allowed to visit. Access to Salisbury until 10pm for 'one night a week' and Fridays and Saturdays as well, there is a regular mini-bus service. Security guard with dog roams the grounds at night.

Discipline 'Not a huge amount of vice, just enough to be streetwise.' Two recent expulsions for regularly going OTT and being 'disruptive'.

THE PUPILS London and local girls who live nearby try and board in Sixth (possibly more freedom than at home?), 17/18% services, very few from abroad. Girls well-mannered, helpful and articulate.

Entrance 'Healthy waiting list'; by interview and exam at 11+, 12+, 13+; five or six to Sixth (if room).

Exit 'Girls serious about careers', 80% to university or poly for degree courses. Three or four leave post-GCSE—to go to boys' schools.

Bottom Line Open scholarships at 11 and 12, six foundation scholarships for one-parent children, day scholarships, and one Sixth Form scholarship.

Remarks Thriving broad-based small school which makes full use of the Cathedral city in its widest possible sense. Possibly too liberal at Sixth Form level?

GODOLPHIN AND LATYMER SCHOOL
Iffley Road, London W6 0PG

TEL London (081) 741 1936

Pupils: 700 girls • *All day* • *Ages: 11-18* • *Size of Sixth Form: 200* • *Non-denom* • *Fee-paying.*

HEAD Since 1986, Miss Margaret Rudland BA (forties), educated at a mixed grammar school in Essex, and Bedford College, London. Impressive—very fair, perceptive, approachable and an excellent administrator, she has gained the respect and liking of staff, pupils and parents.

Academic Matters Solid academic, with high expectations and good record of academic achievements. Excellent GCSE results, sound but not startling A-levels. 22 subjects taught at A-level, and a wide choice of General Studies. Strong Science teaching (a pioneer in the Nuffield Science scheme). Languages another strength, also English. Pupils expected to be self-motivated and self-disciplined, and from the start are taught to be academically self-reliant. Strong tradition of individual research. Patchy teaching, but good on individual attention and helping less able. Classes of 25 for first three years, far smaller thereafter. Non-competitive, no regular read-out markings. Staff often take courses, intellectual inquisitiveness a characteristic of the school—as school mag shows.

Games, Options, the Arts Extra-curricular activities busy over lunchtime. Out-of-hours and out-of-term travel, field trips, social work, regular exchanges with schools in Hamburg, Paris and Moscow. Compulsory gym twice a week, own playing fields adjacent, and swimming available four evenings a week between 4pm—6pm at Latymer Upper School. Good drama with weekly classes for all during first two years, with annual form play competitions and musicals (often written by pupils).

Background and Atmosphere Sister school to Latymer Upper. Stands in four-acre site, originally built (1861) as boys' boarding school, since when it has evolved through many stages (including LCC aided, voluntary aided status, and mid-seventies fought hard not to become comprehensive). School has recently completed a major building programme with new facilities for Sciences and Technology, also the Godolphin Library has been extended. Place is warm, friendly, fairly untidy. Lacking in glamour. Liberal progressive tradition. Good careers information and discussions. Old Dolphins and parents dedicated and helpful. Sixth Formers (uniform free) may lunch out of school. Christian values subtly emphasised now.

THE PUPILS Lively, questioning. Complete social mix from all over London and outskirts. Lots of foreigners (Indians, Middle Easterners and Americans etc). Not for social climbers.

Entrance Not as tough as it is cracked up to be, although large numbers sit for 100 places from 136 schools, half maintained, half private and are put through an enormous number of hoops. (NB This school interviews the girls, never the parents, as so many do.) Not only interested in high flyers. About 20 come in at Sixth Form to fill in from leavers.

Bottom Line Reasonable fees, with few extras.

One music scholarship, Assisted Places, some bursaries available at all levels for special needs.

Remarks Strong girls' day school but sadly in a grotty area of London.

GORDONSTOUN SCHOOL
Elgin, Moray 1V30 2RF
TEL Hopeman (0343) 830445

Pupils: Approx 210 girls, 260 boys ● 470 board, 30 day (mostly staff children) ● Ages: 13-18 ● Size of Sixth Form: Approx 200 ● Interdenom ● Fee-paying.

HEAD Since August 1990, Mark Pyper BA (early forties), educated at Winchester, did one year History at Oxford, got bored and left to finish his degree externally at London University. Won present post in teeth of strong competition, by dint of wearing tweed suit (all the other short-listed candidates wore City grey, but governors, of course, all in tweeds) and by telepathy. Fourth generation Headmaster and steeped in schoolmasterdom so he is unlikely to put a foot seriously wrong, though one or two complaints have gone up over two early expulsions 'because lines have to be drawn', though most parents in sympathy. Sees his general goal as 'doing for the pastoral side what Michael Mavor (the previous Head) did for the academic'. Previous post was Deputy Head of Sevenoaks. A thoughtful analyst, easy to talk to and pupils find him very approachable. Gorgeous wife.

Academic Matters School has earned the right to be judged on academic matters. Comprehensive intake makes for unstartling performance but results are remarkably solid, and school's policy of concentrating on untaxing options (classical civilisation rather than Latin for example) is a wise one. Some weeding of staff needed. School gets five to 10 into Oxbridge a year. A-levels rather than Scottish Highers.

Games, Options, the Arts The school takes part in services to the Community and in this it is outstanding—manning the local fire engine, doing rescue patrol in the mountains and at sea. Each pupil learns the basics of survival—kiss of life, first aid etc and all help at something. Famous for its 'expeds'—outward bound

expeditions—with seamanship v popular and 'the cruise' during which, says Captain Tanner who has run it for years, 'the pupils have to to take whatever weather is chucked at them'. Owns 66 ft yacht and charters another yacht, has own glider, does orienteering, birdwatching, tough indoor climbing wall (and good coach to oversee use of), new sub-aqua equipment, permanent obstacle course etc, etc. CDT good - work practical. Music keen and the Head is hoping to introduce drama to all, as part of the curriculum 'it is important in so many ways'. Problem with main stream games is finding nearby teams to play against.

Background and Atmosphere School founded in 1934 by the German educationalist Dr Kurt Hahn, founder of the famous Salem School in Germany, who believed, along with Plato, that youth 'should dwell in the land of health, amid fair sights and sounds; and beauty, and affluence of fair works...' There is now, we gather, a faction who believe that the values and beliefs of Hahn (compassion, *plus est en vous*, etc) no longer have relevance to the modern world, but the Headmaster sees his role as meshing the old fashioned virtues and the new technological age together. Excellent portrait of Hahn hanging in the hall of what used to be one of the Gordon-Cummings' residence (G-C of the famous card-cheating case)—worth a detour.

Grounds and setting glorious. Pupils still complain a bit of the cold. School houses spread out so pupils may walk as much as six miles a day getting from A to B (NB to mothers—do not wear stilettos when visiting this school). Wonderful old circular stable block converted half into cosy library and half into boys' house.

Deputy 'Guardian' (Head of school) at time of writing comments 'what this place has got is a fine line between concentrating on work and sport and "expeds" or whatever—they've got the balance about right.' Classes finish at 2ish, them there's outside activity, then an hour 'off' from 4-5—'brilliant,' said a pupil 'you can just talk to your friends or slob in front of the television'. Prep finishes by 8.30. By southern standards the academic day is short, but the school believes that any more hours spent working would be counter-productive.

School has beautiful walk for silent thought—for Sunday use only. Member of the Round Square Conference of 14 schools including Aiglon, Salem and Lakefield School in Canada, and has good overseas network.

Horrendous distances to be covered getting to Gordonstoun—even Scottish parents have problems. At time of writing, Apex return to Inverness is £69 per child and Jimmy the taxi will charge around £18 one way. A good idea to book accommodation for school's open day well in advance or take a tent.

Discipline Headmaster has abolished all physical punishment (ie press ups, running round the block etc: 'there was too much of it and too easy to apply'. Bullying rigorously and visibly stopped, by expulsion if needs be. 'Personal and social education is in its infancy here,' Head comments. 'Often girls are ignorant on the inside though sophisticated on the outside and when things go right, it's great, but when they fall apart, there is much more possibility of them falling apart *totally*.'

THE PUPILS Majority of parents are now professional or in industry, though crofterlanded gents still in evidence, not to mention media and a ducal child or three. Gradually becoming more local and larger portion living within an hour of the school. A small percentage of exotica from overseas, much appreciated as bringing a bit of the outside world to an otherwise isolated spot. Most famous OB: HRH the Prince of Wales (and his Pa), a credit to the school, even if he hated it. The Duke of York is a governor and it is a good bet that his children will come here.

Entrance CE, report, interview. Aberlour House is prep. Competitive Sixth Form entry.

Exit Agricultural colleges, St Andrews, Edinburgh, some to Oxbridge and American universities, with which school has ties. Pupils become social workers, media folk, farmers, go into the armed services etc.

Bottom Line About 170 pupils are paying less than the standard fee (and that itself is not as high as many), this in line with Dr Hahn's philosophy of taking in those who would benefit from his education, as well as those who could afford it. For school's fiftieth birthday appeal nearly £1 million was raised for a new scholarship fund—an unusual emphasis on education rather than ritzy extras. Also Assisted Places and *lots* of scholarships, including music scholarships, and a fees' assistance fund. Parents assess themselves on 'above standard' or 'below standard' fees. Summer school helps keep fees down.

Remarks A school pupils either adore or hate. Girls very much the dominant sex. Shy, retiring, swatting or unconventional flowers may find peer group pressure rough. Resulting product however can be charming, and your child is probably less at risk here from drugs than in comparable schools in the south. But boozing is still a regular activity. Slightly other worldly.

GRESHAM'S SCHOOL
Holt, Norfolk NR25 6EA
TEL Holt (026 371) 3271

Pupils: Approx 330 boys, 160 girls • Approx 350 board, 140 day • Ages: 13-18 • Size of Sixth: Approx 200 • C of E • Fee-paying.

HEAD Since 1991, J H R Arkell MA (fifties), read English at Selwyn College, Cambridge. Previously Head of Wrekin College and was founder Head of junior school at Fettes. Married with two sons and a daughter.

Academic Matters Lots of Assisted Places in Sixth Form—and girls—and lots of midnight oiling helps bump up results to not bad. Science and Maths strong.

Games, Options, the Arts Definitely a 'games' school. A boy not keen on the outdoor life might not be happy here—though he might turn into a famous poet—see below. Strong in Outward Bound activities. Keen shooting—better than ever—also plays rugger, cricket (lots of that), soccer and hockey. A bit starved of culture and intellectual pursuits and slight tendency to restlessness.

Background and Atmosphere Far from the madding crowd. Founded in 1555 by one Gresham, turned into public school at turn of century. Set in 170 acres of most beautiful North Norfolk landscape. Only three pubs in Holt (the village) and they can 'spot a Greshamite a mile off'. Fagging officially abolished 'I delivered the coup de grace on that' said previous Head. Feeding time takes place in central block aptly nicknamed 'the trough'. Atmosphere homely and friendly, rather family-like. Over 18s allowed beer in common rooms at specified hours.

Discipline Hot on this and all manner of penalties for disobedience. Recent expulsions for drugs.

THE PUPILS Charming. Nearly all sons/daughters of local farmers, accountants, lawyers etc. Percentage of non-national wavers between five to eight per cent. Famous for famous artistic Old Boys eg Sir Stephen Spender, W H Auden, Benjamin Britten, also Lord Reith, Tim Brooke-Taylor, Hugh Johnson, and Maclean (of Burgess and Maclean) whose name still graces the Oxbridge honours board.

Entrance By CE. School fed by own prep school, Beeston (good prep, this), Taverham Hall and Town Close, Norwich. Own exam for Sixth Form entry.

Exit Largest numbers tend to go on to engineering or medicine or veterinary medicine, accountancy, farming, the Services.

Bottom Line No endowments, but the Fishmongers' Company, with whom the school is associated and who form a majority of the board of governors, dole out a generous 10 scholarships a year. There are also approx 20 other assorted scholarships including one for Maths. 10 Assisted Places in the Sixth Form, for six of which the governors stump up 75% of boarding fees—not nothing. Exam held in Easter term before entry.

Remarks Unusual small country co-educational public school.

GREY COAT HOSPITAL
(Upper school) Grey Coat Place, London
SW1P 2DY
(Lower school) Graham Terrace, London
SW1W 8HL
TEL London (071) 828 0968

Pupils: Approx 900 girls • All day • Ages: 11-19 • Size of Sixth Form: 150 • C of E • Voluntary Aided School. State.

HEAD Since 1987, Mrs M Parsons, MA (forties), forwards looking, firm, co-operative.

Remarks Multi-racial top choice girls' comprehensive for central London and south of the river parents. Holds fast to many grammar school traditions, with some concern about lack of stimulus and boring lessons. Discipline good, firm line on uniform (grey with flowery shirts). Sixth Form can now study with pupils from Westminster City and Pimlico schools, which gives the Hospital access to a wide range of courses, and a little taste of freedom for girls. A disadvantage is the split site, with 11-14-year olds housed in ghastly Sixties ex secondary school building,

one mile distant from the 'serene and elegant' Hospital which is in the heart of Westminster, and consequently popular with politicians. Head divides her week between the two sites. New Technology block completed. Grey Coats is the sister school to Queen Anne's Caversham (*qv*). Huge domestic science room in the junior school. Produces curious little handbook for new pupils with diagrams apparently aimed at those not yet used to reading text. Keenly socially aware pupils, somewhat chippy.

THE HABERDASHERS' ASKE'S SCHOOL
Butterfly Lane, Elstree, Borehamwood,
Hertfordshire WD6 3AF
TEL London (081) 207 4323

Pupils: 1,300 boys (including 200 in prep) • All day • Ages: 7-18 • Size of Sixth Form: 300 • C of E • Fee-paying.

HEAD Since 1987, Mr Keith Dawson MA (fifties), educated at Nunthorpe Grammar, York, and read Modern History at The Queen's College Oxford. He teaches Third and Sixth Form level. He also teaches General Studies and Drama (his great love). Previously Head of King James School Henley (Sixth Form college), Scarborough (ditto)) and the John Mason School in Henley. History Master at The Haberdashers' 17 years before returning as Headmaster. An unassuming and diffident Head, he has obvious rapport with the boys and a quiet sense of humour. Admits he 'used to be not bad at teaching', and believes in treating boys as individuals which 'enables you to fulfill the potential you have'.

Academic Matters 'Good spread of ability among the bright range', says Mr Dawson. Excellent English, Maths, Sciences (modern overhead labs and others being converted), very computer literate, £100k worth of Nimbus—for whom they do product testing and 32 networked machines where each boy has his own space and can use in spare time), super computer linked CDT under enthusiastic Mr Angus Thomas (ISO programming). Serious computers in library—and more computers in Language lab. Good keen staff (100 with turnover of about 4%) with classes of 25/26 at bottom end to grouping of 10/12 at A-level. Greek is extra-curricular. Remedial assistance for mild dyslexia. Hot on careers advice, with work experience and work-shadowing both at home and abroad.

Games, Options, the Arts Good games record (Rugby trips to France and Scotland in 1990), hockey tour to New Delhi, and outstanding individual track records particularly in athletics, cricket and swimming in national teams. Swimming pool, games hall etc. Good games pitches. Magnificent pottery and art department, strong drama (usually in conjunction with the Haberdasher's Girls School next door—the girls pop over regularly at lunch time for combined music, clubs etc). Music itself outstanding under Mr Taylor, with boys currently providing the choir for Carmen at the Royal Opera House, apart from singing in the Festival Hall, Albert Hall, St Paul's and the Barbican. Hyperion Records use the acoustically perfect Seldon Hall for recording. CCF, Community work, masses of clubs.

Background and Atmosphere Founded 1690 in Hoxton by the Worshipful Company of Haber-dashers, who still play a powerful role in governing body; the school moved to its present site in 1961. The self contained prep school is in rather better shape than the random selection of Sixties flat-roofed classrooms which cluster awkwardly beside Lord Aldenham's pretty red-bricked former stately home, now used as the admin block. There is accommodation available upstairs for the younger teachers, to off-set high cost of local housing.

School shop stocks uniform as well as stationery and—other schools please note—brilliant Haber-dasher-designed school blazers that are totally *washable*. Contact Michael Hall for info!

THE PUPILS Polyglot. (Arabic part of core curric-ulum.) Lots with family links to the school, huge catchment area. Boys and girls are bussed in together (fare from Rickmansworth £196 per term). Parking permits for pupils currently limited to 12. Former OBs: Leon Brittan, Alan Whicker and 'one or two pop stars'. School uniform till Sixth Form.

Discipline Strong. Swearing 'disapproved of—must apologize'. Smoking means suspension. Drugs (one known offence two years ago), instant dismissal. Series of detentions and minor punishments (ie litter collecting), which can be handed out either by prefects or staff for minor demeanours (the latter an official detention).

Entrance At seven to prep school, main school entrance 11, occasional places at 13 via CE (none available this year) and progressively more after GCSE. Tough.

Exit Impressive. 3% leave after GCSE. In 1990, 129 pupils to university (44 to Oxbridge), out of 150.

Bottom Line 35 Assisted Places, governor's and music bursaries. 300 boys currently being assisted financially.

Remarks Boys fiercely loyal. Highly successful aca-demic day school.

HAILEYBURY
Hertford SG13 7NU
TEL Hoddesdon (0992) 463353

Pupils: 559 boys, 93 girls in Sixth Form only ● 500 board, 152 day ● Ages: 11-18 ● Size of Sixth: Approx 320 ● C of E ● Fee-paying.

HEAD The Master, since Easter 1987, Mr David Jewell MA MSc (fifties), educated Blundell's and St John's Oxford (Chemistry). Dynamic, efficient and good at projecting his school to the outside world. Sense of humour. A fighter and full of fire. Three daughters, one son. Taught at Winchester, was Head of Bristol Cathedral School. One of four national reps of Headmasters' Conference; co-founder of Assisted Places Scheme. Believes parents are looking for a good standard of teaching, the widest possible variety of extra-curricular activities, some indication that their children are being prepared for the outside world and 'training in some sort of moral and ethical code', probably in that order, and that is what he aims for. 1990 HMC chairman.

Academic Matters Results good, especially consid-ering intake. Well-deserved reputation in the Sciences, though 'large' number of girls is evening out the Arts side. Recent Geography results poor, and weak Maths. All 16 Art and Design candidates in 1990 gained grade A at A-level. Economics good.

Games, Options, the Arts Famous for producing successful sportsmen—Rugby internationals, Stirling

Moss an OB. Standard varies but outstanding fencing and shooting. Indoor Sports Hall, CCF popular—girls too go in for it. Old Gym converted into Technology Centre and a small theatre, named after OB Alan Ayckbourn. OBs look back and comment how philistine it was in their day, how amazingly civilized now.

Background and Atmosphere   Amalgamated with Imperial Service College, housed in defunct East India College, the training ground for generations of boys destined to govern India. Fine William Wilkins architecture, college-style, laid out around vast quad—sympathetic additions hidden among trees. Houses are small—48ish in each—and whole houses share one dormitory, which is a popular arrangement, though there are now smaller dorms and bed-sits in three of the 10 houses. Old iron bedsteads and curtained cupboards now sadly replaced by wooden furniture. Very strong sense of community, partly, say pupils, because the whole school meets together four times a day (morning chapel and at meals in the domed dining hall, which has an incredible echo). Cafeteria system—pupils eat at magnificent polished oak tables made by the Yorkshire carpenters who signed their work with a mouse. School shield is a crossed sword and anchor surmounting three flying hearts.

Discipline   Head cares passionately about pastoral care. His letter to *The Times* on discipline was a model of fairmindedness and common sense, and taken to heart by other schools. At time of writing, few major disciplinary problems.

THE PUPILS   About one-tenth children of OBs; some from overseas—mainly ex pats; lots of parents in the Services and one or two sons of the clergy on reduced fees. New boys are still called 'New Guv'nors'. Decent sorts, conventional on the whole. Old Boys: Clement Attlee, most of the founding fathers of the Royal Air Force including Sir John Slessor. Also Lord Oaksey, Nevill Coghill, Rex Whistler, Lord Allenby etc.

Entrance   Haileybury Junior, which is officially connected with the school, provides steady stream. Girls have harder time getting in than boys, as usual.

Exit   85% to further education, with approximately 20-25 going on to Oxbridge. Traditional careers now the Empire is no longer with us: banking, medicine, accountancy, estate management etc, or the Church.

Bottom Line   10 academic scholarships and exhibitions (two of half fees or more); three music scholarships and exhibitions; one art scholarship. School had wonderful windfall of £3 million recently, left in his

will by OB Russell Dore—good name for rich OB, this—who made his money in the City.

Remarks   Still a distinguished, conventional, traditional, low profile public school.

HARROGATE LADIES' COLLEGE

Clarence Drive, Harrogate, North Yorkshire HG1 2QG

TEL Harrogate (0423) 504543

Pupils: 400 girls, 335 board, 65 day   •   Ages: 10-18   •   Size of Sixth Form: 100   •   C of E   •   Fee-paying.

HEAD   Since 1973, Mrs J C Lawrence MA Oxon (fifties). Has taught in and out of state and private schools, previously Head of a state school. A Lancashire lady, husband a clergyman, direct, sensible and enormously committed. Teaches French to the youngest, ethics and comparative religion to eldest, and 'I pour oil on troubled waters.' Hopes fervently girls will leave 'having enthusiasm and stability, and will achieve something for themselves and others'. She is also keen for them to 'seize opportunities, be willing to take risks in their stride'.

Academic Matters   Thorough teaching and high standards. National Curriculum inserted; Maths increasingly popular A-level subject, Science strong. Good, though small, Classics contingent (Mastermind Classics winner on staff). Computers networked throughout school. Head notes staff are attracted and stimulated by facilities. Girls have a 10-period day.

Games, Options, the Arts   Keenly sporty—northern lacrosse champions, golf course nearby, lots of tennis courts, 25-metre pool, riding, six badminton courts—good facilities and much used. Keen D of E (member of staff is head of northern scheme). Ballet; strong music, especially choir, and no-one misses a class for music lesson, a masterpiece of ingenious timetabling. Sensible use of local theatre, cinema, concerts and opera (Leeds). Huge new Art room (for art and design), plus new Design Technology department. Amazing radio transmitting satellite station—

the only girls' school to have one—girls have contacts with USA, Japan etc, run by infectiously enthusastic master Mr Horton.

Background and Atmosphere School founded 1893 elsewhere. Present premises akin to seaside hotel with mock Tudor beams and gables. Houses neat but basic, common rooms focused round the telly with easy chairs. Formal feel, though ages mix freely, and Head (who moved schools nine times as a child), puts much emphasis on child's happiness, 'But you can't make them happy'. At 16+ girls are allowed out one night a week—10 minutes' walk to town centre.

THE PUPILS Mainly northerners; one third of boarders are from overseas, including 17 foreign nationals; Buddhists, Jews and Muslims in the school. Solidly middle class. Manners very strictly monitored.

Entrance Own entrance exam for the over-12s, Head's report, interview.

Exit Two-thirds to degree courses. Three to five to Oxbridge.

Bottom Line Eight Assisted Places, bursaries at 11 or 12 of up to half fees, two or three into Sixth Form. Not a rich school, but run by good housekeeping— 'Yorkshire people like value for money', notes the Head.

Remarks Solid, respectable, well run and very caring.

HARROW SCHOOL
Harrow on the Hill, Middlesex HA1 3HW
TEL London (081) 422 2196

Pupils: Approx 770 boys ● *All board* ● *Ages: 13-18* ●
Size of Sixth Form: Approx 320 (one or two girls) ● *C of E*
● *Fee-paying.*

HEAD Since September 1991, Mr Nicholas Bomford MA (early fifties), educated at Kelly College and Trinity Oxford, where he read History. Previously Head of Uppingham. Married, two children in their twenties, wife plays full-time Head's wife role. Keen on shooting; half blue at rifle shooting; gun dog (Tosca) in constant attendance, demanding regular 'walkies'. Enthusiastic fisherman, has a cottage in Herefordshire near the Usk. Acknowledged to be a first class teacher. Aims 'never to forget the individual' and to be 'quite deliberately accessible'. He is 'agin' co-education. At the time of writing he commented he had 'an entirely open mind' on the subject of Harrow. Succeeds Ian Beer—a considerable contrast in personalities.

Academic Matters Steady results, particularly good at GCSE, top heavy with As and Bs, and also outstanding French. A-levels show largest numbers and some strong results in a slightly surprising list of subjects—History, Geography, Economics and English. Outgoing Head reports a 'shift to Sciences has been been maintained', though the mainstream Sciences are still not that popular.

Games, Options, the Arts Still very keen games school: rugger tradition upheld, though boys now may be equally proud to be good at swimming (eight years ago it would not have counted). School has smart indoor sports complex with indoor 'ducker' (swimming pool), sports hall, changing rooms and a 'social' area. One of Lord's cricket schools. Also strong tradition of drama and debating (*cf* Old Boys' list) and the Speech Room, a huge amphitheatre on the Hill, is a focal point for this, also for the famous school songs which Old Harrovians return to listen to year after year (get a copy of the school song book).

Lots of extras, but most unusual one is the school farm, splendid institution for London suburb school, which has a piggery, beef cattle unit, oxygen baryatric unit for sufferers of MS, and provides the school's milk and cream.

Interesting innovation, to give a little balance to former ruggy bugginess, is the creation of The Guild—boys elected for their creative excellence *outside games*. They too are allowed to wear their special tie, along with the traditional Gods—the Philathletics— and the Monitors—the 'disciplinary chaps'. School also has 'way of life' course given by trained guidance counsellors—everything from birth to death and in between. Pioneers in this among public schools.

Background and Atmosphere Founded in 1572 by John Lyon. Clarendon Committee of nineteenth century found the school was not sticking to its charter of educating the people of Harrow, so started a whole new school for *them*, the John Lyon School, out of endowment funds—hence has as real right to call itself a charity. 11 houses, including modern undistinguished building housing the 'old' Knoll. All but two of boarding houses now modernized in giant and slow undertaking.

School's most magnificent uniform with 'bluers' (blue jackets), braid, straw hats etc has inspired generations of fashion designers (one of Coco Chanel's lovers was at Harrow). The school's location on the Hill produces an element of true grit in pupils, especially, as they point out, there is nothing between Harrow and Siberia.

THE PUPILS Map in Head's study pinpoints boys coming to school form all over the world, 28% are sons of Old Harrovians. Strong smart trade element with household names such as Sunley, Millett, also strong links with aristocratic and old landed families. Lots of keen Cresta runners. Famous Old Boys: scores of them. Lots of prime ministers, including Winston Churchill (Lady Soames is a governor of the school), Byron, Peel, Trollope (who hated it and left after a term or so), Palmerston, Galsworthy, Baldwin. Also the Earl of Lichfield, the acting Fox bros and King Hussein of Jordan. Formerly popular with maharajahs and other pukka foreigners.

Entrance Name down asap for a particular house: Elmfields is still the posh one. CE.

Exit 'Gap' year and university, which is now 'much more of a lottery', according to previous Head. 22 boys to Oxbridge in 1989.

Bottom Line 78 boys hold entrance scholarships or bursaries: 20 of them well over half the fees. Also 15 leaving scholarships. Appears well-endowed to us (land), but most frustratingly for the school is a trust for the upkeep of the road from Harrow to London, which has been going for yonks, is apparently unbreakable, but is no longer appplicable and rumoured to be worth about £200 million.

Remarks School is now up and running strongly, and the outgoing Head has achieved his aims, in particular helping 'an awful lot of boys be leaders of European management'. The new Head's aims may well be entirely different.

HEADINGTON SCHOOL
Oxford OX3 7DT
TEL Oxford (0865) 62711

Pupils: 570 girls • Approx 231 board, 339 day • Ages: 10-18 • Sizes of Sixth Form: 130 • Junior School: 140 girls and boys, ages 4-10 girls, 4-7 boys • C of E • Fee-paying.

HEAD Since 1982, Miss E M Tucker MA Cantab. Teaches Latin. Head could not speak to us for this edition as she was ill.

Academic Matters Great academic tradition, with emphasis on Sciences and Classics. Vast range of subjects, from Russian to Japanese. Small, old-fashioned classrooms with traditional ('old fashioned' according to some parents) teaching methods. Gets good results.

Games, Options, the Arts 20 tennis courts, good games reputation, fencing, hockey, netball. 'Not hot on music', said one pupil, but pianos and practice rooms everywhere. Art is conventional. Good Home Economics.

Background and Atmosphere Traditional school building: functional red brick with corridors, and modern extensions. Girls sleep 30/60 in four boarding houses, one across the busy Headington Road at the Junior School. Sleeping accommodation is functional, girls in Sixth Form have study/bedrooms. Air of purpose everywhere that is slightly at odds with Sixth Formers in mufti and tights with seams.

THE PUPILS Local professional and academic. Large number of weekly boarders, as well as ex pats and 'foreigners' learning English as much as benefiting from a British education. It is occasionally possible for day girls to board temporarily. Barbara Woodhouse was an old girl.

Entrance Apply early. No formal test for tinies, but thereafter test to see 'if up to standard'. Own exam at 10, otherwise CE at 11, 12, 13. Occasional incomer post-GCSE.

Exit The majority to further education, little leakage after GCSE.

Bottom Line Selection of scholarships at 11, 12, 13; music scholarship. Clergy bursary (day fees one pupil at a time), and internal scholarships and bursaries available.

Remarks In the shadow of Oxford High. Suffers from stuffy image.

HEATHFIELD SCHOOL
Ascot, Berkshire SL5 8BQ
TEL *Winkfield Row (0344) 882955*

Pupils: 220 girls • All board • Ages: 11-18 • Size of Sixth Form: 50 • C of E • Fee-paying.

HEAD Since 1982, Mrs Sarah Watkins (forties, here until 1993) educated at Queenswood, and London University (read Philosophy, later took a degree in Linguistics). Teaches German, French and Current Affairs. Direct, beady and realistic; strongly anti-snob. Ambitious, both for herself and for her girls. Her own career started in the Foreign Office; wide experience of teaching in a variety of schools. Husband at the head of the military police tree; the Watkins have four children.

Academic Matters Sound and thorough, and pace is less cosy than it looks. Very high (1:7) ratio of staff to pupils. Sciences building up well, with new Science block, and some very good Science teaching. Some good staff in several departments: team accrued by Head tend to stay put because they like it, 'though I feel they should be moving on'. Girls' morale boosted where needed, encouragement part of the ethos.

Games, Options, the Arts Very good art with two resident artists, also music, with three resident musicians. Not noted for games, but the Head of PE keen for girls to try *everything*. Even croquet matches are on the menu. Good drama, also needlework.

Background and Atmosphere Very uninstitutional, with 130 single bedrooms (privacy is what used to sell the school), a few rooms for sharing. Set in 34 acres of pine and rhodie country, near busy main road. Upper Sixth live in their own bungalow (without a uniform), partly cater for themselves, occasionally give dinner parties and are allowed to keep cars. Good food. Strongly Anglican. Some grumblings from girls about not being allowed out more (parents mostly

relieved), and some of the older girls still admit to being 'a bit bored' at weekends, despite good weekend programme.

THE PUPILS Well-mannered (the Head minds), from near and far, several whose parents are posted abroad; some bi-linguals (whose special problems interest Mrs Watkins). As ever, a nice place for making the right friends.

Entrance School's own 11+ assessment (done in the previous October/November), three or four girls seen for each place. Musicians get priority. Head consistently vetoes any potentially disruptive pupils. Aims for a mixed ability intake, but all capable of taking A-levels, and 'Lots of nice girls to provide middle background'.

Exit After GCSEs a few girls leave to learn typing or study languages but of the rest increasing numbers go on to higher education. Head firmly believes you enjoy what you are good at, and emphasises that Heathfield girls 'are good at jumping into the slot that's there'. Suspects (from her own experience) that career planning can be misleading.

Bottom Line 5% of fee income allocated to scholarships.

Remarks No longer simply a posh place, but safe haven for girls, good for building up confidence and getting steadily stronger, particularly on the academic side. Deserves to be taken more seriously.

HIGHGATE SCHOOL
Highgate, London N6 4AY
TEL *London (081) 340 1524*
Highgate Junior School
TEL *London (081) 340 7674*

Pupils: 580 boys (in Senior School) • 495 day, 85 weekly board • Ages: 13-18 • Size of Sixth Form: 200 • Junior School: 310, ages 7-13 • C of E • Fee-paying.

HEAD Since 1989 Mr Richard Kennedy MA (early forties), educated at Charterhouse and read Maths and Philosophy at New College, Oxford; taught at

Shrewsbury, Westminster and was Deputy Head of Bishop's Stortford. Very ambitious; talented musician (sings with the Academy of St Martin's), one of the few Head's whose wife (a high powered civil engineer) has her separate entry in *Who's Who*; two young sons.

Academic Matters Slightly out of London main academic stream, and all the more refreshing for that: good all round. Intentionally broad intake: can—and does—cope with the bright, (who flourish here), the average, the screwballs and the slower learners too. (There is a remedial department.) 'Maximize potential' is one of the Head's favourite phrases. Maths and Science traditionally the strongest departments, 'Economics getting good', commented several parents. Good General Studies at Sixth Form. New Deputy Head (190 applied for the post), Barnaby Lenon (young and ambitious), ex Eton, has taught Holland Park comp, in charge of academic studies.

Games, Options, the Arts Strong games reputation—national champions in Eton fives; splendid new sports centre. Also strong music: Channing girls collaborate sometimes, also on the drama front. Lunchtime activities include large number of societies (environmental, conjurors, Jewish Circle), also urban survival course for older boys (how to fill in tax forms, use a laundrette), CCF, D of E; Welsh outlet. Unusually impressive list of visiting speakers. Complaints from boys about lack of careers advice.

Background and Atmosphere Founded 1565, on hill, buildings spread over generous acreage and covering many architectural dates and hotch potch of styles—surprising and pleasing patches of greenery and space, main block on main thoroughfare and across the road (via subterranean passage) another teaching block with astonishing view over London. House system arranged by geography, eg West for boys whose families live west of school; Housemaster visits boys' homes before they come. Quite a caring school, and a popular one to work in with obvious perks—greenery, plus near enough to the centre -and some housing goes with the job. Weekly boarding decreasing (surprisingly, considering there is so little available), enabling prep school to increase in size.

THE PUPILS Very popular locally (though parents with *really* bright boys likely to opt for Westminster), strong on ethnic minorities. By and large, they develop all round more than most London pupils. Distinguished list of Old Boys includes, Anthony Crosland, John Rutter, Clive Sinclair, Patrick Proctor RA, Barry Norman. John Betjeman was taught by T S Eliot in the Junior School.

Entrance Via Junior School (which is on the point of expanding to take 380 boys), thereby virtually gaining a guaranteed place, or by CE—about 70 from each; the lowest hurdle at 13+ likely to rise.

Exit Most to higher education of some sort; approximately nine to Oxbridge annually.

Bottom Line Five Assisted Places at age 11, one in Sixth Form.

Remarks Has had chequered history, now in hands of very capable Head giving clear directions.

HOLLAND PARK SCHOOL
Airlie Gardens, Campden Hill Road, London W8 7AF
TEL London (071) 727 5631

*Pupils: 1,600 boys and girls ● All day ● Ages: 11-18 ●
Size of Sixth Form: 300 ● Non-denom ● State.*

HEAD Since 1986, Ms Maggie Pringle BA (forties), educated 'tiny grammar school in Oxfordshire', followed by first in English at Somerville, Oxford (and B Litt in Thackeray). Previous five years at George Green's School in Isle of Dogs (one year Acting Head, having been Deputy Head). Charming, fun, confident and hard-working (60/70 hours a week). Aims to turn Holland Park into 'the finest comprehensive in England'. Slightly daunted at prospect of 'taking on budget of £4 million next year'.

Academic Matters Difficult to assess under normal criteria with such a high proportion of non-English speakers, many of whom arrive with no English at all and stay but a short period. 17 staff (out of 108) teach English as a second language, often in tandem with a regular teacher. Newly arrived children are put in small groups for special tuition with one or more speakers of their native language. 57 different mother tongues at the school and options include Arabic and Bengali as well as French, German and Spanish; school had 100 GCSE passes last year in Modern Greek, Polish, Russian and Turkish and 66 in Persian, none of which are taught at the school.

Classes are not streamed or set. School divided into

three faculties—CDT, Maths and Science—very strong on DT (computers everywhere), but no physical link with C. Language and Humanities, including Media Studies, and CAPE (Creative Arts and Physical Education). Strong on Arts, brilliant drama and music (sitar on offer)—though supply teacher in drama class was happily chewing gum. Good results in English lang and lit. Science less well represented. 19th-century Thorpe Lodge has Sixth Form library and studies. Strong on careers and vocational guidance, with pupils doing two weeks work experience under the Compact scheme which gives them job priority with Compact employers.

Games, Options, the Arts Three games pitches on campus, bussed to football at Barn Elms (30 mins), Ms Pringle looking for 'somewhere nearer'. Tennis courts, multi-purpose gyms etc. Fabulous re-vamped swimming pool. First year pupils regularly spend week away with tutors, Royal Borough of Kensington and Chelsea have grant available so no one is disadvantaged for lack of funds.

Background and Atmosphere Uninspiring conglomerate of concrete blocks linked (when we were there) by leaky passages. Currently undergoing massive £1 million revamp to repair 1958 architectural problems. Fabulous garden within and overlooking Holland Park (children often go to the Cafe there for spaghetti lunch—less of a queue than eating at Munchies).

Discipline 'Children just go outside to smoke', no sign of drugs 'two cases in four years' said Ms Pringle, 'though children probably try them at weekends, but not the hard stuff', and absolutely no question of pushers said one pupil—'We'd tell the staff if someone was acting strange.' Child is reported to parent for swearing, and must apologize. Regular offenders are excluded for one day; perpetual offenders report to the governors for a final warning. Heavy sexist stuff a bit of a problem—'usually with chaps who've just found what it's all about'. (Girls have own photography and computer clubs, but Life Class is mixed.) Pupils who are late report to Ms Pringle for a week or more.

Each class has a tutor who remains with that class to post-GCSE. Each year has a Head of Year with a Deputy, and Ms Pringle has four Deputy Heads. Pupils have excellent rapport with staff: 'When one of my friends was having a hard time with his parents' divorce, his tutor gave him his phone number and said to ring him any time', said one.

THE PUPILS Holland Park locals whose parents range from indigent refugees and foreign diplomats to a hard core of media folk, often with siblings at Latymer, the French Lycee, or Godolphin and Latymer. No uniform, lots of national dress; trainers the current craze. A Rastafarian with dreadlocks to his waist showed us to the Deputy Head. There was no obvious pushing or shoving and very little bullying.

Entrance Complex. Local primary schools. Post ILEA, the *only* interdenominational County Secondary school in the Royal Borough of Kensington & Chelsea. Entrance not restricted to those living in the Borough. Pupils are admitted throughout the school. Rarely 'full at the beginning of term for the first year', the school fills up rapidly thereafter with waiting lists at every level, but with an annual turnover of 25%, pupils come and go on a weekly basis with about four or five comings and goings each week. Preference given first to siblings, then to those who live closest to the school (though pupils come from as far as Ealing and Hillingdon). Many, who come from the B&B area of Bayswater, stay only a few weeks, moving on when permanent accommodation is found elsewhere.

Masses of Bengalis. Current influx of East Europeans after 'the virtual collapse of the Russian School in London'. Popular with the diplomatic community and, recently, financially disadvantaged locals who find Holland Park a viable alternative to traditional private schools. Regular influx post-GCSE from private schools.

Exit 30-45 pupils a year go on to higher education.

Bottom Line Next year the Royal Borough will spend a further million pounds on the interior (red and darkened pine panelling). Cash not a problem.

Remarks A challenging school which appears to do its best in a very complicated set up. All children benefit from the truly international flavour—Ms Pringle discusses an issue of major importance at Assembly each each week, eg The Gulf Crisis, the Salman Rushdie affair—and the library stocks Arab and Bengali papers as well as *The New Statesman*. Impossible not to leave this school streetwise at the very least.

JAMES ALLEN'S GIRLS' SCHOOL (JAGS)

East Dulwich Grove, London SE22 8TE

TEL London (081) 693 1181

Pupils: 725 girls ● *All day* ● *Ages: 11-18* ● *Size of Sixth Form: 180* ● *Also prep school of 250 girls and boys, ages 3-11* ● *C of E* ● *Fee-paying.*

HEAD   Since 1984, Mrs Brigid Davies MA (forties), educated at Alice Ottley School and Cambridge, previously Head of History and Assistant Head here. Mother of three daughters. Gentle but firm, imaginative, admired and liked by parents and pupils as being straightforward and fair, and with a sense of proportion. Teaches both youngest and oldest. Thinks girls, including JAG's own Sixth Formers, have an inbuilt tendency to be too modest: 'I want them to feel free to explore, to try out new things, to be tough—and not *always* to aim to please.'

Academic Matters   Outstanding GCSE results at time of writing over a wide range of subjects, including German and Italian, lots of Biology, Computer Studies, Latin, Greek and pass rate a solid 90-100% in most subjects (though a slight blip in Chemistry). A-levels also excellent, and showing none of the signs of pupil burn out that was threatening the school three or four years ago.

   The Head reports that the school supports the aims of the National Curriculum 'in that it seeks to ensure that all children study a broadly based core curriculum covering all major subjects in reasonable depth', but adds that they are 'unhappy about the arrangemenets made for Key Stage 4 (the fourth and fifth years of secondary education)' because as it stands it is 'far too limited in subject options for bright children..'—an opinion voiced by other academic schools. They are watching the National Curriculum closely.

   In preparation for Europe, all Sixth Form girls are to continue with a Modern Language with a view to taking the Institute of Languages Proficiency Test. They are also reorganising their languages further down the school so that half their 11+ intake will do German and the other half French—annoying if you happen to be in the year of the language you don't want.

Games, Options, the Arts   Excellent art department, and popular with it—65% of girls currently doing art at GCSE—with 87% gaining an A grade—you can't call that nothing. Music under Rupert Bond, who is also conductor of the Docklands Sinfonietta—exciting and colourful, and, report the pupils, much easier now there is somewhere to play. Good drama—JAG's was the first London girls' school with a professional theatre, designed by architect of the Cottesloe. Good playing fields and sense of space (the plus of being south of the river), heated indoor pool, sports hall etc. Flourishing Design and Technology department.

Background and Atmosphere   Founded in 1741, one of the three schools of the 'Foundation of Alleyn's College of God's Gift at Dulwich', named after James Allen, warden in 1712 of Dulwich College and described as 'Six Feet High, Skilful as a Skaiter; a Jumper; Athletic and Humane'. School became girls-only and moved to present 20-acre site in 1886 following act of parliament passed to reorganize the Foundation. School currently developing 'warm relationship with Dulwich Boys'.

   The school vibrates with energy and life, and is in almost constant throes of new building. 1991 is JAG's quarter millenium anniversary and an appeal is going out for yet more facilities, OGs please note.

Discipline   Not without drugs.

THE PUPILS   From all over London, mostly from south of the river, but also from north, and many trek for miles. Wide social mix. Charming and unpretentious. Anita Brookner is an OG.

Entrance   A quarter from their own junior school (which is on the same site), though all must pass 11+. At least four girls sit for each place (and they will be pupils considered strong enough by their prep/primary school). Liveliness is an essential ingredient, as well as academic ability. Interview takes place before exam, in an attempt to weed out poor little over-cooked girls. Some intake from state sector.

Exit   75% go on to university on average, 12-15 to Oxbridge, and practically all go on to further education of some sort, including several to top art colleges. Medicine is a popular career, so is teaching.

Remarks   One of the two top London girls' academic schools. Goes from strength to strength, but still needs more work on bolstering up pupils' sense of self-worth. Slightly surburban feel.

KILGRASTON SCHOOL

Convent of the Sacred Heart, Bridge of Earn, Perthshire

TEL Bridge of Earn (0738) 812257

Pupils: 275 girls • 190 board, 85 day • Ages: 8-18, 30 under 11 • Size of Sixth Form: 60 • R C but inter-denom • Fee-paying.

HEAD   Since 1987, Sister Barbara Farquharson BD (Hons), (forties). Has been at Kilgraston 16 years teaching RE and involved in administration and loves the place. Kind and quiet, with good sense of humour. Since appointment has changed management structure. Believes school has tremendous potential and is committed to developing school in all areas and individuals as whole people.

Academic Matters   Mixed ability, but streaming for Maths. No remedial facilities but 'learning support' in English and Maths primarily for non-English speakers. Approx class size 20—two classes per year. French, German, Spanish, Italian, Latin for Standard Grade and Highers. Run on Scottish system—SCE and Highers with entrance to university (even English ones) decided on Highers' results—Sixth year studies or A-levels in one year to fill the gap to 'uni'. In the past has had reputation as soft academic option and many left for Sixth Form elsewhere.

Games, Options, the Arts   Only four PE periods per week, as school is run on day school timetable—extra activities after school hours. Magnificent new sports hall and nine Astroturf tennis courts being built. No swimming pool, but swimming at Perth is an option. Wide choice of other sports. Good art and drama. String and wind groups, but no full orchestra except at Carol Service. Strong D of E and debating.

Background and Atmosphere   Founded 1930 as part of Society of the Sacred Heart. Handsome red sandstone house after Adam, originally belonging to Grants of Strathspey. Feeling of lightness and brightness especially in new Barat Wing (named after founder of Society). Bedsits (from Third year) are comfortable and well appointed but a little cell-like—no posters are allowed on walls). Younger girls sleep in dormitories which are locked during the day and have little privacy or personal space. Uniform old-fashioned (girls have to wear ties and gabardine mackintoshes). Boyfriends allowed to visit in common rooms and weekend trysts in Perth with Strathallan and Glenalmond. Very little for boarders to do at weekend.

THE PUPILS   The only Catholic girls' boarding school in Scotland. Girls from all over Scotland, and faithful following of Old Girls send their daughters. A few European/Mexican etc, from other Society schools. Girls charming and well-mannered but could perhaps have more ambition.

Entrance   Automatic entry from junior school, but further entry 11+ (from primary schools) and 12+ (from prep schools). Own entrance exam, which serves as scholarship exam as well, but as mixed ability entry, by and large only those with learning problems do not make it.

Exit   Further education, occasional Oxbridge, Project Trust, ESU scholarship, art school etc.

Bottom Line   Fees reasonable and good value. Scholarships, including art and music, bursaries and a waiting list for Assisted Places. Aprox one-third receive fees in assistance.

Remarks   Possible fragmentation of *esprit de corps* owing to day girls/weekly boarders/full boarders, but terrific facilities and great labs mean that opportunities are there to be taken and academic standards are improving. Some rumbles of discontent.

KING EDWARD VI HIGH SCHOOL FOR GIRLS

Edgbaston Park Road, Birmingham B15 2UB

TEL Birmingham (021) 472 1834

Pupils: 550 girls • All day • Ages: 11-18 • Size of Sixth Form: 165 • Non-denom • Fee-paying.

HEAD   Since 1977, Miss E W Evans BSc (early fifties), educated at the Queen's School, Chester and London University. Cool, calm, careful, fair-minded and very competent. Hopes for pupils stand firm, that they will leave here 'Having acquired the taste of enjoyment of study for its own sake, and feel they are talented and achievers—and therefore responsible to serve the community.' Previously at Bolton School, Bath High, and Friends' School in Essex. As President of GSA 1987-88, noted for commitment to building bridges between maintained and state sector.

Academic Matters Very strongly academic school for achievers with high expectations. Very wide syllabus, breadth and depth the strength here. Girls encouraged to work conscientiously and enjoy it. 'Outsiders sometimes think teaching here must be a soft option', commented one member of staff, 'because all the girls are bright—but the fact is that a little *doesn't* go a long way—they lap it up and want more.' One-third of pupils take A-level Sciences, a third Arts, a third mix. Strong Maths, particularly at GCSE, all do at least one year of Maths in Sixth Form. General Studies as their fourth (rarely third) A-level. Blocks (options) undertaken on non-examined subjects (eg Politics, Communication Skills) and scientists required to do some work in English and vice versa. 26 per class throughout the school, down to groups of 15 or less in Sixth Form. Girls are adept arguers and verbalizers, class discussion encouraged from earliest forms.

Games, Options, the Arts New sports hall, computer network and performing arts suite. Music, sports and drama all strong. Some activities eg debating, undertaken with adjacent King Edward's School for boys. Some Sixth Form subjects are shared. Building new Design School. Emphasis on understanding Industry. Head very keen on girls being practical as well as academic—cooking, needlework, and lots of community service (girls expert at fund-raising). Pupils with initiative start clubs for juniors.

Background and Atmosphere Direct Grant school until 1976. Very marked discipline, with strong work ethic, and not much larking about. No prefect system, no head girl, no houses.

THE PUPILS From as far away as Lichfield, Bromsgrove, Wolverhampton, Solihull: there's not a school in this league for miles, and precious few anywhere.

Entrance School's own test ('Designed to test the children not their teachers'). Vast majority come in from state primaries. 10—12 places at Sixth Form (caused by early vacancies).

Exit A regular 12—20 to Oxbridge, 'though we don't regard Oxford and Cambridge of paramount importance—some of the most able girls go elsewhere'. Nearly all to higher education. Medical studies/careers very popular, also law, engineering, and teaching.

Bottom Line Three full-fee scholarships at 11, two half-fee scholarships at Sixth Form; 25 Assisted Places at 11, five at 16+.

Remarks One of the country's top academic girls schools. A place which does not breed intellectual arrogance, partly because of a conscious effort by staff to purge the girls of any feelings of superiority—whereby sometimes pupils yearn for the warmth of praise, and intelligent girls worry about not being academic: 'You tend to think you're hopeless if you're not outstanding.'

KING EDWARD VII
Glossop Road, Sheffield S10 2PW
TEL Sheffield (0742) 662518

Pupils: 1,350 boys and girls ● *All day* ● *Ages: 11-18* ●
Size of Sixth Form: 350 ● *Non-denom* ● *State.*

HEAD Since September 1988, Mr Michael Lewis BA Oxon (early forties), came from Icknield School Oxfordshire (comprehensive). Took over from Mr Russell Sharrock. School's aims as stated are, 'We value equally each individual within the school but recognize that personal needs will vary accordingly... We recognize that education is life-long and for life and that our students are entitled to an education which prepares them fully for adult life...'

Remarks Stunning classical pillared 1837 (Flockton) building overlooking Sheffield, which recently received an award from the Royal Society of British Architects—the most distinguished in the state sector. Unfortunately short of outdoor space and site is split.

Solid comprehensive co-educational state school with good reputation. Multi-racial, with more than 20 different mother tongues spoken. Large Sixth Form intake from surrounding schools, majority of pupils take three A-levels. Wide catchment area, with 30 contributory schools at 11/12+ and pupils from 12 other secondary schools joining at 16. Also some from private preps. 1990 A-levels excellent, with high proportion of A/B passes for school with mixed ability intake, and 12 pupils going on to Oxbridge. Strong Mathematics and Languages at time of writing—including Japanese studies in partnership with the University of Sheffield (which is nearby), and keen Geography. GCSE not so hot.

Good range of extras, with work experience programme and Duke of Edinburgh awards particularly keen.

Wonderfully open and objective attitude. Should and could be one of the strongest state schools in the country.

KING EDWARD'S SCHOOL
North Road, Bath BA2 6HU
TEL Bath (0225) 64313

Pupils: 640 boys, 45 girls in Sixth Form • *Ages: 11-18* •
Prep school, 185 boys, ages: 7-11 • *C of E* • *Fee-paying.*

HEAD   Since 1982, Mr J P Wroughton MA (fifties), educated at Ashby de la Zouch Grammar School and Oxford; taught at his own school, Dame Allen's, Newcastle, Head of History here before becoming Head. Unmarried, worthy, business like, and considerate. Thinks big; very keen on community aspect of school. Has expanded school at 13- and 16-year old levels, increasing intake by almost 100 pupils.

Remarks   Ancient grammar school (1552) with a distinguished history (Old Boys include Sir Sidney Smith; Arctic navigator and explorer Sir Edward Parry; Major General Le Marchant, founder of Sandhurst). The school moved from the centre of Bath in 1961 (selling up brought much needed funds), into large old country house on the edge of the city (cows in next door field) with a splendid view over Bath, also large and dreary Sixties purpose built block: 'Built at the worst period' moans the Head, who plans to turn it into the school theatre.

Sciences traditionally strong (true of many grammars), Maths the most popular A-level subject, and Modern Languages have taken upwsing recently. Results are solidly good but not outstanding. 75% go on to degree courses, approximately 10 to Oxbridge; thence local business, retailing, armed forces, finance and occasionally academia. Large catchment area and extremely popular locally—with high speed trains in from Swindon, even a few pupils from Bristol. Pupils come from all walks of life, polite and lively. 18 Assisted Places (mostly at 11) also 12 and 13, and two for Sixth Formers. Fees are kept purposely low.

Unlike some similar establishments, this is not just good for high flyers—art is distinctly good, so are pastoral care, out of school trips, sports (two English internationals are on the staff), school runs a hockey festival. Head holds a conference for staff each year (NB excellent area for part-timers) at local country house hotel: this year's theme is the underdog. The Junior School (away at the back) is handsome design (architects: Alec French of Bristol), with clever use of wood and stained glass, classrooms centred around open-plan library.

KING EDWARD'S SCHOOL
Edgbaston Park Road, Birmingham
B15 2UA
TEL Birmingham (021) 472 1672

Pupils: 800 boys • *All day* • *Ages: 11-18* • *Size of Sixth Form: 214* • *C of E* • *Fee-paying.*

HEAD   Chief Master since September 1991 is Mr Hugh Wright MA Oxon, (fifties) educated at Kingswood School, Bath, read Greats at the Queen's College, keen sportsman—played Rugby and rowed for his college. Formerly Head of Gresham's in Norfolk, before that Head of Stockport Grammar School. Wife Jillian is diocesan treasurer for the Mother's Union. Three grown-up sons. At time of writing, the high-powered Mr Martin Rogers, champion of young people getting out of academic tramlines and having a 'year off' before going on to university, is still at the helm.

Academic Matters   *All* departments strong. Excellent staff can cope with the brainiest of boys. One third of boys rumoured to have IQs of 140-plus. No streaming here: 'Why bother to create a bottom-stream mentality for clever children?' posed the outgoing Head. 25 to a class. Boys take heaps of GCSEs and usually average of four A-levels each. Outstanding academic results.

Games, Options, the Arts 'Music brilliant' according to parents. Usual sports are offered, ie Rugby, football, hockey and cricket, also two gymnasia and a multigym and a sports hall for badminton, indoor tennis and squash etc. Indoor swimming pool. 15 acres of playing fields, tennis courts dotted around the grounds. Golf, sailing, fives all on offer. The usual CCF, Scouts and community service to be done.

Background and Atmosphere Edwardian foundation. Large attractive brick buildings with lovely old chapel merging to some extent with the girls' counterpart (King Edward VI High School for Girls). Sited in Edgbaston, it opens out on to Birmingham University. Because of the wide, competitive intake, all religions are studied and catered for, though there is also a school chaplain. Very strong demand for places has led to ongoing expansion from 11-year old entry.

THE PUPILS Complete social mix, coming from various parts of Birmingham. Par for the course in appearance, some conservative-looking, others sporting the latest hairstyles.

Entrance At 11+ or 13+, via highly competitive exam, at least four for one place.

Exit Rare for a boy not to go on to university. In 1989, 49 boys had places at Oxford and Cambridge: as we said before, if you can get in you will probably get on. J R Tolkien, Bill Oddie, Kenneth Tynan among the Old Boys.

Bottom Line At 11 and 13 up to three full scholarships; up to 10 major scholarships and exhibitions between half fees and £300pa. Up to three music scholarships; up to three art scholarships. Also scholarships for new entrants at A-level. 40 Assisted Places at 11, two at 13, five at 16.

Remarks One the country's top academic boys' day schools with consistently strong results year after year, churning out dozens of high-fliers.

KING'S COLLEGE
Taunton, Somerset TA1 3DX
TEL Taunton (0823) 272708

Pupils: Approx 450 boys, 50 girls (in Sixth Form) • *370 boys board, 80 day boys* • *Ages: 13-18* • *Size of Sixth Form: Approx 200 (ie good and large)* • *C of E* • *Fee-paying.*

HEAD Since autumn 1988, Mr Simon Funnell MA (forties)—read English at Cambridge, formerly a Housemaster at Shrewsbury, keen on music.

Remarks School's success due to previous Head, James Batten, creating a happy school and gathering together a young good and enthusiastic staff, who are still in place. Very sound in mainstream subjects, also in Science. Two full-time Classics teachers. High A-level pass rate with lots of As and Bs.

Traditionally very strong rugby school. Also strong cricket and hockey. Games compulsory until aged 15 as a general policy. School history goes back to the thirteenth century, but present foundation dates back to 1880, at which point it was set up as one of the Woodard schools— to further the cause of Christianity. Huge Betjemanesque school chapel, on which thousands have recently been lavished for new roof. Good portrait of Bishop Fox in the Lady Chapel— worth a detour. Apart from Memorial Quad, school is not one of your architectural glories (though NB OBs disagree about this). View all round is of the outskirts of Taunton.

The pupils are largely local, also parents set out from Cornwall en route for Eton and run out of petrol when they get here. Strongish army and navy element, dozens of parents are GPs, lawyers and small businessmen. Approx 25 non-nationals in school, of which majority are Hong Kong Chinese. Famous Old Boy: Geoffrey Rippon. Generous percentage of fee income goes on scholarships and bursaries, including those to sons of clergy and schoolmasters. Scholarships in Sixth Form for music. One JET place plus two totally free prep scholarships for seven years for local boys.

Mostly middle class middle of the road public school with an unusually good common room.

KING'S COLLEGE SCHOOL

Wimbledon Common,
Southside, London SW19 4TT
TEL London (081) 947 9311
King's College Junior School
TEL London (081) 946 2503

Pupils: 660 boys • All day • Ages: 13-18 • Size of Sixth Form: 260 • Junior School: 380 boys, ages: 7-13 • C of E (but other faiths welcome). • Fee-paying.

HEAD Since 1980, Robin Reeve MA (fifties), educated Hampton and taught there, previously Head of History at Lancing, also Director of Studies. Tall, handsome, serious and unassuming, a vigorous campaigner for academic standards for high flyers.

Academic Matters Impressive—Head believes firmly in academic discipline and attainment—though well aware that narrow success is the besetting sin of London day schools, thus he is busy trying to enrich the diet, keen on subjects being studied 'because they are intrinsically interesting subjects to study rather than because they're going to lead to X'. English especially strong. Masses of labs.

Games, Options, the Arts Enthusiastic about sports—Rugby/hockey fields in situ, cross country on Wimbledon Common, rowing. Renaissance of extra-curricular activities since Saturday school was abolished. Societies fairly busy after lunch and after school hours (4.30 popular time to lure speakers in). Good Art. Strong music, very good drama, and excellent new theatre. Impressive school newspaper includes in one issue, for instance, interviews with Sir Keith Joseph *and* Teresa Gorman.

Background and Atmosphere Curious hotch potch of buildings, including fine collegiate hall, elegant eighteenth-century house and sundry modern additions with plenty of elbow room, nicely set on edge of Common, with pub opposite; new Sixth Form block with good common room much welcomed by boys. Strong tutor system, fairly firm discipline and no long hair. Founded in 1829 in the Strand, as junior department of King's College, University of London.

THE PUPILS Middle class, largely from south-west London, Kingston and Surrey, lots of ethnic minorities, mainly Asian. Most boys here are naturally hard workers. Some drive in. Old Boys include Dante Gabriel Rossetti, Profs Jimmy Edwards and Peter Moore, vast numbers of Oxbridge dons.

Entrance Two-thirds from school's own wonderful prep (terrific competition to get into this, NB entry at eight, nine and 11, and 90% come on to senior school). CE passmark is 65, 'but boys need spare capacity as well'.

Exit Practically all to university and a steady stream (around 25) to Oxbridge. The Law, the City, medicine, engineering are likely careers.

Bottom Line Scholarships at 11 to Junior School, then up to 12 scholarships at 13+ and one at Sixth Form level. All up to a maximum of 50% fees.

Remarks Very strong all round school, well worth considering for London bright sparks.

KING'S SCHOOL

Bruton, Somerset BA10 0ED
TEL Bruton (0749) 813326

Pupils: 337 boys, 26 girls (all in Sixth Form) • 299 board, 38 day (all boys) • Ages: 13-18 • Size of Sixth Form: 130 • C of E. • Fee-paying.

HEAD Since 1985, Mr A Beadles MA (forties), ex-Harrow Housemaster. Purposeful, direct, extremely competent.

Remarks A small, competent and efficient school, traditional, well-suited to the academically average who will be well-taught, and gain confidence in a compact and caring school—a good place to be a big fish in a small pond. Currently very full on the boys' side. 50% of new boys come in from King's own very good prep, Hazlegrove House at Sparkford, also from Mount House and south coast schools. Popular with sons of doctors and solicitors in rural areas. 70% of leavers go on to degree courses (two or three to Oxbridge), decreasing numbers (five or six) leave post-GCSEs.

Staff tend to stay put—this is a beautiful and ancient

place—average age probably higher than in many public schools. New Library, new History and English departments, and all boarding houses recently refurbished reflecting well deserved confidence in school. Stunning Design Centre opened by The Princess Royal in November 1989, incorporating Art, Technology and all Info Tech—producing some exciting work: pupil won BP 1990 engineering prize. Famously strong CCF (army only). Pupils kept busy, structured ethos, three-weekly reports, record of achievement, regular church services and assemblies, Saturday evening prep, games most days for everyone (including Saturdays). Major rugby tour every few years to New Zealand and Fiji. Sensible arrangements for Sixth Formers on pubs—the school is, after all, right in this charming little town. Close links with other local schools. Not smart, low profile, and doing a very good job. Morale is currently high here—and rightly so.

THE KING'S SCHOOL

Canterbury, Kent CTl 2ES

TEL Canterbury (0227) 475501

Pupils: 548 boys, 157 girls ● *574 board, 131 day* ● *Ages: 13-18* ● *Size of Sixth Form: 344* ● *C of E* ● *Fee-paying.*

HEAD Since 1986, Canon Anthony Phillips BA, AKC, PhD (fifties). Fellow and Chaplain of St John's College, Oxford since 1975, also Canon Theologian of Truro. Educated Kelly College, qualified as solicitor before taking degree in Theology at King's College, London and PhD at Cambridge. Married with three children. Canon Phillips (and his wife) play very active role in local Canterbury life. Modernist, innovator, sees himself as a father figure to everyone in the school, spear-headed highly successful integration of girls throughout the school, and is keen to emphasize the benefits of co-education to boys *and* girls. Combines strict approach with caring attitude, greatly supported by his wife Vicky, makes strenuous efforts to get to know individuals. Boys claim Canon Phillips 'is better with girls than with us'.

Academic Matters Strong all round, more of a shift towards Sciences now (1990 awarded several A-level Science prizes), Biology generating excitement (new Head of Department), though still predominantly Arts based. Broad based academic outlook, good teaching for the middle rank as well; pupils streamed and setted with 16 per class down the school, 13 in upper. Newly opened IT labs (all pupils proficient word processing at end of year one). Fortnightly reports, and strong tutor system covering academic and pastoral matters. Heavy on prep: even Lower Sixth prep periods are supervized, initial resentment by in-coming pupils who later look back with relief, 'because we really got our work done'. Some complaints from girls that there are not enough female staff.

Games, Options, the Arts Outstanding music,(new Director of Music) and also very fine drama. King's Week Festival (Drama and Music) the last week of the summer term is the annual highlight. Most promising musicians taught by visiting London professionals. Marvellous Art Centre (in converted thirteenth-century priory), includes textile design and carpentry, CDT centre with fantastic facilities. More emphasis on Arts than Games—though excellent new Recreation Centre with huge pool, Fitness Suite(!), six squash courts, blue sports hall etc (already let to public and paying for itself) proving highly popular. Girls now rowing too—girls' games fairly strong, though a minority of boys also take games seriously. Fine fencing. Vast amount of options—Head hot on subject of 'doesn't matter what it is, but everyone *must* do something well'.

Background and Atmosphere Network of ancient buildings in and around shadow of the Cathedral (and therefore right in the town), and most beautiful. Tradition has it this is the oldest school in the country, dating back to the sixth century and founded by St Augustine. Ancient buildings steeped in history, pretty gardens, flint walls, winding streets to other departments dotted round the town, constantly expanding into yet more cottages. Tourists a nuisance (with right of way through school's main archway), keep the Porter busy on his walkie-talkie. Good food here. Badly needed Junior Common Room now being built—Saturday nights have seen some noisy gatherings of Sixth Formers in the courtyard. Sixth Formers have own bar. Discipline firmish, though drink has been minor problem among younger boys. Sixth Formers have cosy study bedrooms (milk/newspaper orders outside) with individual kettles, toasters, even fridges. Girls' showpiece house, prettily and lushly decorated, (another girls' house to be built 1992). Some Sixth Form girls live in noisy town cottages. Daily assembly (NB fairly rare in public school); not overly religious establishment.

THE PUPILS Mostly well-motivated (because they are kept busy?), polite, look you in the eye, and neat in uniform (girls look like incipient barristers). Largely upper middle class—offspring of barristers, diplomats, wealthy farmers, and government ministers. Relatively small contingent of 'usual public school yobs', to quote a current pupil.

Entrance 55%-60% at CE. Lots of boys (and, from 1990) girls from Milner Court, King's own prep school. Books very full. Lots from Windlesham. Intake at Sixth for girls running down. Competitive entry (two-and-a-half per place) for girls at bottom end.

Exit Consistently good A-level results. About 90% go on to university/poly, average Oxbridge annual entry of 45 pupils. Old Boys include William Harvey, Somerset Maugham (who hated it, and is said to have based *Of Human Bondage* on it), Walpole, Marlowe, Patrick Leigh Fermor.

Bottom Line Up to 15 scholarships, including music.

Remarks Brilliantly orchestrated transition from boys' public school to fully-fledged co-educational, with well-taught, well-handled pupils—an impressive school that strikes a good balance between being traditional and forward-looking.

THE LADY ELEANOR HOLLES SCHOOL

Hanworth Road, Hampton, Middlesex
TW12 3HF
TEL London (081) 979 1601

Pupils: 612 girls in Senior School, 190 girls in Junior School •
All day • *Ages: 7-18* • *Size of Sixth Form: 150-170* •
C of E • *Fee-paying.*

HEAD Since 1981, Miss Elizabeth Candy BSc (late forties) dynamic, fit (she golfs, swims, cycles), perceptive, with a dry sense of humour. A Chemist by background, she has more of the air of a successful investment analyst or QC; study decorated accordingly ie not so much William Morris as Osborne & Little

executive (LEH is said to be just as sound but more relaxed under her Headship). Has strong feelings about career choice: 'Girls should be allowed to follow their own inclinations—with expert advice—rather than forced into law/medicine etc because that's the field their parents know about—it's their life.' Also deplores the increasing tendency to a Sixth Form brain drain from the girls' schools to the major public schools. Thinks it is often for the wrong reasons ie parents' social aspirations, and because it is believed to enhance a girl's chances of acceptance at the university of her choice.

Academic Matters Strong academic record and generally achieving, though unpressured, environment highly thought of by parents. Girls take on average nine subjects at GCSE and then often one extra subject the following year; the Head believes that the GCSE are a better form of exam in that they are 'a co-operative effort, but that they are not necessarily a good preparation for A-levels, in that the average girl does well and can then find A-level work a cold shower'.

Games, Options, the Arts Head regrets school's 'aggressively sporty image', and says that not all girls are sporty, nor do those who aren't feel out of place. Facilities are excellent though—15 tennis courts, two badminton courts, facilities for athletics, swimming pool, a fine gym (a member of staff trains the English Schools' Under-16 Netball Team). Rowing is important. Music is strong and parent commitment considerable—the choral society, which includes both parents and staff, meets regularly on Sunday afternoons. Lively drama. There are many clubs (chess, science, photography, modern languages and gardening etc), usually run by Sixth Formers in the lunch hour to accommodate smooth post-school coach departure. Sixth Form girls organized a bouncathon for this year's charity—the Christian Children's Fund—in which the Head herself took part, bouncing for 20 minutes. Super new art block under much respected newish Head of Art (impressive framed creative work from all levels of the school is hung on walls of main corridors). Good links with neighbouring Hampton School in areas of debating, drama, music, including a joint A-Level Theatre Studies course.

Background and Atmosphere Founded in the Cripplegate Ward of City of London 1711—two early eighteenth-century plaster figures from the original school bear rather incongruous witness to the transplant to the suburbs in 1936. The school (largely inaccessible by public transport) stands, a visually tranquillizing oasis among the suburban avenues. Main building is a cross between a Thirties factory and an American high school—all on one level, light and airy, with wide corridors and spacious grounds, in tremendous contrast to cramped central London schools. Uniform of grey and cherry red considered generally acceptable by girls; Sixth Formers wear no school uniform, but almost uniformly T-shirts, jeans, DMs.

THE PUPILS Fairly bouncy middle class girls—the sort who have their own pony, or access to one. Girls are mostly bussed in from all over Surrey in parent-organized buses and coaches. Lynn Barber is an OG.

Entrance Half the intake comes from the Junior School, though not as of right. Competition for remaining places keen (five sit for every place) though entrance not specially rigorous, allowing a good mix of promising pupils from both state and private sector. Large non-returnable deposit required on acceptance of place to stop later defection to St Paul's.

Exit 75% to university and polytechnics (Head is very open-minded about choice here, believing firmly in horses for courses), including 14 to Oxbridge in 1990. Law and psychology two particularly popular choices. Girls go on to be doctors, personnel officers, ophthalmic opticians and journalists, not to mention a BA airline pilot.

Bottom Line Around 20 Assisted Places or Governors' Bursaries (means tested), two or three other scholarships from funds at Head's discretion.

Remarks Sound and popular girls' day school with user-friendly Head; comfortably-off, middle class, co-operative parents and sensible, friendly staff. Happy, productive vibes.

LANCING COLLEGE
Lancing, Sussex, BN15 ORW
TEL Shoreham-by-Sea (0273) 452213

Pupils: 420 boys, 76 girls (all in Sixth Form) ● Ages: 8-13 ●
Size of Sixth Form: 270 ● C of E ● Fee-paying.

HEAD Since 1981, Mr Jim Woodhouse MA (fifties), educated at St Edward's, Oxford and Cambridge where he read English. Previously head of Rugby, before that Master of the Queen's Scholars at Westminster. Had term's sabbatical teaching English at Rollins College, Florida in 1990. Charming, dapper, slightly fierce, with a social conscience. Wonderful wife, Sarah.

Academic Matters Steady improvement in results over past 10 years. Head comments 'My experience at Westminster and Rugby suggested that there was some slack in the system here…The staff were encouraged to raise their expectations.' Classes in the Lower School do not now exceed 20 pupils. A-level sets 'normally' range between six and 12, with an upper limit of 15. No streaming, but setted for Maths, Sciences and Languages. European Liaison Adviser ('Mr 1992').

Games, Options, the Arts Keen drama. At time of writing, girls are Sussex Hockey Champions. Keen farming club 'swelling the number of budding vets'. Cricketing school. Also football and hockey played, but boys 'not very games-minded', said a parent. Strong debating and public speaking—has won the *Observer* Mace and the Oxford and Cambridge Unions Schools Competitions. Music traditionally a strength, choir toured Granada. Water polo, Eton fives and shooting popular. More expeditions and biennial Malawi trip a 'special feature'.

Background and Atmosphere Most attractive school in 550 acres of glorious south downland. Founded in 1848 by the educational philanthropist, Canon Nathaniel Woodard. Flint-faced buildings, set out in two quadrangles, rather like an Oxford college. Chapel one of the glories among public school places of worship—some complain that too much money is spent on it, but Head comments that the school receives help from the Friends of Lancing Chapel, Woodard Corporation and English Heritage, who paid 40% of recent restoration bills.

THE PUPILS About half from south east. Popular with ex pats. About 15 sons of daughters of clergy in the school at any one time. Polite and friendly. OBs: Trevor Huddleston, Peter Pears, Evelyn Waugh, not to mention Tom Driberg, who was expelled.

Entrance At 13 and 14 and some into Sixth Form (enter name three years before date due for girls). CE around 55%.

Exit Majority to degree courses. Fairly strong tradition of doctors and clergymen.

Bottom Line Offers 25 awards a year, including two clergy exhibitions and others for music and art.

Sensitive to those who have fallen on hard times.

Remarks Low key public school with strong Christian tradition.

LATYMER UPPER SCHOOL
King Street, London W6 9LR

TEL London (081) 741 1851

Pupils: 1000+ day boys (heaven knows how they fit them all in) • *Ages: 9-18* • *Size of Sixth Form: Approx 250* • *Non-denom* • *Fee-paying.*

HEAD Acting Head since Summer 1991 is Mr C Diggory. Previous Head resigned suddenly.

Academic Matters Results no longer look as though made up by a public relations firm: some worrying Ds and Es—which school categorizes as passes. Further Maths—good results in 1990, French not bad. Greek is now available to AS level, and the school has built a new Classics department since the last edition of this book. CDT to A-level. Computer network. Home/school liaison has been reinforced, with homework diaries right through GCSE.

Games, Options, the Arts Much stronger than most London day schools. Has two Olympic oarsmen at time of writing and comes regularly in top 10 schools in rowing—one of the three English schools which row from home—Eton and St Paul's are the other two. Impressive boathouse. Rugby—pretty solid results against interesting collection of schools eg All Hallows, Devon, Reigate GS, Lord William's Thame, Hampton etc. Music definitely strong—strings of pupils learning instruments, lively. Top performers have joint orchestra with Godolphin down the road (though otherwise the schools are hardly linked).

Background and Atmosphere School founded by one Edward Latymer, a lawyer who made provision in his will for the welfare of 'six poor aged men' and for 'eight poor boys' from the town of Hammersmith. Original brief also provided for 'some part of God's true religion', which nice high-sounding woolly approach has trailed down through the centuries. Buildings grammar-school type functional red-brick Victorian and later. Bulging. School sliced by Great West Road. Atmosphere extremely bouncy—to put it politely—beware boys cannoning into you.

THE PUPILS 'The big pots used to come here', said a local, 'MPs and things.' Still lots of MP OBs eg members for Dorset, Worcs, Bucks, Newham, Notts, Leics. Also some profs, actors, composers, conductors, hacks. Approx 18% second generation Asian immigrants at last count, 10%ish Jewish—sons of local middle class trades and professionals.

Entrance Registration up to 'any time in time for the administrative details to be worked out'. Exam to select 'pupils we think are going to do well here'. Age of entry, 11+, approx 44 from Latymer Prep Dept (*qv*) the rest from a staggering 160 or more primary schools—including 65% from state schools. No entry at 13—the latter (and, for all we know, the former) makes school a touch unpopular with prep school Heads.

Exit University, of course.

Bottom Line 50 Assisted Places 'which we go on giving off the top of the list until they run out'. Up to eight academic and three music scholarships per annum at 11+.

Remarks As we said before, first class grammar school type education and, like most such, strong all round.

LEEDS GIRLS' HIGH SCHOOL
Headingley Lane, Leeds LS6 1BN

TEL Leeds (0532) 744000

Pupils: Approx 949 girls • *All day* • *Ages: 3-18* • *Size of Sixth Form: Approx 151* • *Non-denom* • *Fee paying.*

HEAD Since January 1977, Miss Philippa Anne Randall (late forties), educated Christ's Hospital, LSE—BA History, etc. Described by educationalist as an 'intellectual hooligan'—certainly has no fear or favour. Nice sense of humour. Member of the Friends of Opera North, skis with the school every year, member of National and Yorkshire Women in Management. On sabbatical 1991/1992 when Deputy Head,

Marjorie Garner, in charge. School has high flown list of aims in handbook but basically, says Miss Randall, this is a grammar school foundation which 'gets them where they want to go'.

Academic Matters Outstanding. Hardly a D or below in sight, apart from in General Studies, Biology and French. Percentage of A-C passes at A-level averaged over years 1988-1990 was 96.5. In 1990, 61.4% A or B passes, most pupils taking four subjects. A small handful of keen Classicists. Most popular subjects: Physics and Chemistry, English and French. School does not offer exotica.

Games, Options, the Arts Also excellent, showing flair and imagination, and one pupil commented that her parents chose this school over others in the area 'because they encourage you to do things like art'. Very enthusiastic arts department under Mrs Fox. Five star new swimming pool. Music excellent and impressive music centre, also impressive list of activities, eg school is setting up exchange programme with the Kamazu Academy in Malawi (billed as the 'Eton of Africa').

Background and Atmosphere Founded in 1876, shares a foundation with the local boys' school (lots of scope for joint drama and General Study projects), ex direct grant. Pleasant grounds. Buildings varied from original to Sixties tat. Hall with organ and highly polished floor because pupils sit on it (no chairs). Atmosphere busy and purposeful. Prominently displayed motto—*age quod agis*, which girls all know how to translate.

THE PUPILS All sorts of backgrounds. One sixth Jewish. Brothers at Leeds Boys'. Many distinguished OGs including Catherine Pestell, new principal of Somerville, Oxford.

Entrance Interview, written exams and report from current school except for those entering at three-plus, who have an individual IQ-type test. Entry also at Sixth Form—exam and interview post mock-GCSEs.

Bottom Line Up to 15 Assisted Places per year for pupils entering at 11+. Unspecified music scholarships.

Remarks One of the best academic day schools for girls in the country.

THE LEYS SCHOOL
Cambridge CB2 2AD
TEL Cambridge (0223) 355327

Pupils: 321 boys, 67 girls (all in Sixth Form) • *Approx 296 board, 92 day* • *Ages: 13-19* • *Size of Sixth Form: 200* • *Methodist Foundation/Interdenom* • *Fee-paying.*

HEAD Since Summer 1990, the Rev John Barrett MA Cantab, formerly Headmaster of Kent College, Pembury. Educated at Culford School and University of Newcastle-upon-Tyne, followed by an MA in Theology at Cambridge. On the steering committee of the Bloxham Project, is British Secretary of the World Methodist Council, and has a long string of posts and activities to his name. Hobbies—golf, water colour painting. Married with one son, one daughter. With the Headship goes one of the nicest houses in the business—Regency, large garden, centre of Cambridge but secluded.

Academic Matters Considers itself academic but 'not a hothouse'. Master commented perhaps they used to concentrate too much on the middle and bottom ability pupils (NB there is one member of staff dealing with dyslexic problems). Renowned for Science, but, because of geographical position, tends to take Science for granted. 'We have a Senior Science Society,' said a master, 'which meets every other Wednesday, and every other speaker seems to be a Nobel prizewinner who arrives by bicycle.' Modern Languages strong, but small. Geography gaining ground since new Head of Geography appointed 1986.

Games, Options, the Arts Deadly rivals to Felsted. Generally good at sports, also play cricket, hockey, rowing—and now has international oarswoman on staff (NB sponsor needed) and considering adding girls to tennis team. Tends to come in top 10 at Bisley, plays squash, rows on Cam, is in University league for squash, also National School Clay Pigeon Champions for 1984, 1985, 1986. CCF voluntary and 'oversubscribed'. Visiting debaters high powered—like visiting scientists—Shirley Williams, Jeffrey Archer, Mary Whitehouse etc. Their indoor heated swimming pool opened in 1904, chapel opened 1905. Has v modern Design Centre with workshops, ceramics, sculpture, design, fine arts, electronics, printing press, cooking, computing etc. Fairly strong music, keen drama, and NB has schools' social event of the area—The Leys Summer Ball—rumoured to be as good as a May ball.

Background and Atmosphere Founded 1875, rather heavy red-brick houses. Each house has approximately 68 boys in it. Sixth Form girls' house, Granta, opened in 1984. Atmosphere unremarkable. Being in Cambridge, school agreed they were 'very vulnerable' to the drug problem and worked closely with the police and kept the boys very busy. Also, boys not allowed to go into pubs—school does pub checks with escalating fines for miscreants. Girls gradually being assimilated.

THE PUPILS Cambridge professionals' sons, some dons' sons. Old Boys include Alastair Burnet, lots of distinguished academics and professors, the Prince of Tonga and James Hilton, who based *Goodbye Mr Chips* on this school.

Entrance CE or scholarship exam. Sixth Form entry. Registration at any age. Popular place for girls—the Cambridge connection.

Exit Gets about nine into Oxbridge (out of 70+—school not large). Approx 80% go on to university of some kind, another 10% to further education, 10% to jobs.

Bottom Line Assisted Places; up to 14 awards per year including music and art, scholarships of up to 50% of fees. Also one or more scholarships into Sixth Form of up to 50% of fees.

Remarks City public school with girls in Sixth Form. No radical change at time of writing. Geographical position means school is able to get amazingly highly qualified staff (even the assistant groundsman has a degree in Natural Sciences), and this makes for strong all-round performance.

LORD WILLIAMS'S SCHOOL
Thame, Oxfordshire OX9 2AQ
TEL Thame (084 421) 3681

Pupils: 950 boys, 870 girls ● *All day* ● *Ages: 11-18* ● *Size of Sixth Form: 300* ● *Non-denom* ● *State.*

HEAD Since 1985, Mr David Kenningham MA (fifties). A Physicist who started his career in industrial management, switched to teaching in independent sector (Marlborough College), then to selective education (Royal Grammar School, High Wycombe), finally to comprehensive system (as Deputy Head, Whitley Abbey School, Coventry, followed by nine years as head of Cheney School, Oxford). A forceful, widely experienced Head with a strong belief in comprehensive education.

Academic Matters Good Maths at GCSE. Emphasis on non-academic subjects eg Child Development, Keyboarding, Food and Nutrition. After GCSEs, first year Sixth pupils take 'mature GCSEs' eg Science in Society, Health Studies, Sociology. At A-level languages are quite successful, though not very popular. Geography the popular A-level subject (three As and 13 Bs in 1990), also Maths and Physics. Strong management, a marked sense of purpose, well-structured curriculum, with much thought and discussion given to content, materials, input. Staff are actively encouraged to look positively at coursework on offer—nothing stands still or is taken for granted.

Background and Atmosphere A vast school formed in 1971 by the amalgamation of the ancient Lord Williams's Grammar School and the Wenman Secondary Modern School. Now on three sites in a bleak setting compensated for by acres of open space. Sports and Arts Centre offers some of best facilities in Oxfordshire. Rugby is possibly strongest sport; close links with Massachusetts school (Head taught in Massachusetts). Masses of extra-curricular activities from juggling to dry-skiing, and tradition of strong links with parents. Former boarding house now being used for Sixth Form.

THE PUPILS A complete cross-section—no creaming by any other school—from offspring of

Oxford dons (a few) to pupils whose families have lived here in rural Thame for generations.

Entrance Via primary schools in Thame, Chinnor and Tesworth in Oxfordshire and Brill and Long Crendon in Buckinghamshire. The only school for this area.

Exit Between three and five to Oxbridge each year, and 50 to 60 to universities, polytechnics and colleges. To all parts of the (UK) compass.

Remarks Interesting example of the amalgamation of grammar and secondary school elements. Close enough to Oxford to feel its influence and to attract teachers of high calibre.

LORETTO SCHOOL

Musselburgh, East Lothian, Scotland EH21 7RE

TEL Edinburgh (031) 665 2567

Pupils: 270 boys, 36 girls (all in Sixth Form) • *296 board, 10 day* • *Ages: 13-18* • *Size of Sixth Form: 140* • *Also has own prep school, the Nippers, ages 8-13 with 68 boarders, 24 day boys* • *Ecumenical* • *Fee-paying.*

HEAD Since 1984, The Reverend Norman Drummond MA BD (thirties) educated at Merchiston and Fitzwilliam, Cambridge, where he read Law. Ordained at New College, Edinburgh. Rugby blue. An unorthodox appointment, as Head was previously chaplain to the Parachute Regiment, the Black Watch and at Fettes, but has proved a tough, charismatic leader, concerned with the spiritual growth of his pupils as well as the academic (which is rare). Ten out of ten to the governors. Head insists on 'Loretto being too special to increase in size', and cultivates friendly atmosphere: punctiliously polite. Has four children, they live on campus. One of a growing number of distinguished Normans.

Academic Matters GCSE in Fifth Form, followed by by A-levels and some Scottish Highers. Huge Industry and Business Centre combining Computers, Economics, Politics, Business Studies and Modern Language labs—everything for the little European. Results not published.

Games, Options, the Arts Rugby school, highly competitive, plays every Scottish school in sight. Also keen cricket, re-vamped swimming pool, ski boots under every bed, golf on nearby links, dinghy sailing. CCF from second year. New music centre opened in 1990—part of the Head's £2.5 million building programme)—including a three manual pipe organ. Strong choral tradition—all members of the school sing as the choir—has recently been recognized by live broadcasts by ITV and BBC Radio. Pipes and drums are flourishing and have recently toured the USA.

Background and Atmosphere Sited on edge of Musselburgh links in a collection of sand-coloured school buildings, linked by a tunnel below the A1 with haunted stone-built Scottish baronial-type Pinkie House with fabulous painted ceiling. Founded 1827, and in 1862 was purchased by Hely Hutchinson Almond, a distinguished scholar of strong and unconventional convictions. Boys are divided into four houses, graduating via dormitories and studies to study bedrooms. Each boy responsible to his tutor. Girls live in old san (made obsolete, like elsewhere, thanks to penicillin), with panic buttons by each bed. (Why?) Charming war memorial chapel used daily and, says Head, 'is of particular significance to past and present Lorettonians'. *Cf* also page 23 of the prospectus. Boys confirmed in Anglican/Presbyterian service. Strong Lorettonian network.

Discipline 'No trouble' with drugs. Fines for smoking, suspension for going OTT followed by dismissal for repeated offence.

THE PUPILS A third from south of the Border, many OLs' sons, some ex pats, strong on Scots. Politer, tidier and kinder since the advent of the present Head. OLs: Norman Lamont; Headmasters Mavor and McMurray; MP Nicholas Fairbairn; Denis Forman; Hector Laing.

Entrance More than 50% CE. Non-prep entrants have special exam and interview. Has own prep school—the famous Nippers. Sixth Form: six GCSEs plus interview. Head comments that the school is 'now seriously selective'.

Exit Annually 80-90% to university or further education (in 1989, 60 out of 68). Pupils go on to be industrialists, engineers, a sprinkling of academics, many professors of medicine.

Bottom Line Heavily endowed throughout the school from scholarships to Nippers, via total academic scholarships, to bursaries for those who 'have deserved well of Loretto' to help through university and beyond (impoverisheds please note). Strong North American influence from OLs.

Remarks Tip top Scottish public school, bursting with life and interest.

MALVERN COLLEGE
Malvern, Worcestershire WR14 3DF
TEL Malvern (0684) 892333

Pupils: Approx 600 boys ● 560 board, 40 day ● Ages: 13-18 ● Size of Sixth Form: 240 ● C of E, but all faiths welcome ● Fee-paying.

HEAD Since 1983, Mr R de C Chapman (St Andrews). Mid-fifties, seems younger (perhaps because of the squash he plays). Taught Modern Languages at Glenalmond and Marlborough and was Rector of Glasgow Academy before Malvern. A busy (chairman of Common Entrance Board, on Committee of Headmasters' Conference etc), fluent, determined man.

Academic Matters   Science/Maths/Economics most popular; History, English, Modern Languages doing well. A-level pass rate regularly high around 95%, but some subjects rather low on A grade passes. Good GCSE results.

Games, Options, the Arts Keenly gamesy school—all those playing fields spilling down the hill—boys in various county teams plus one in England Under-15 Hockey and one in England Under-16 Rugby. Football is main game of autumn term, with rugger come the spring term. Offers all the usual games/sports options plus rackets, fives, canoeing, climbing wall on smart sports centre, cottage in Brecon Beacons for adventure training (compulsory at some point for all, unlike—for the first time this year—Combined Cadet Force, now an option with Community Service, Duke of Edinburgh's Award Scheme and Environmental Service). Exotic Sixth Form summer expeditions alternate annually with climbing ones.

Music, based in converted Victorian monastery (monks' cells—practice rooms) is plentiful. High turn over of Heads of Art, despite ritzy art block. Pioneers of the work experience, co-ordinated by three-man careers team—ranging from architecture to fisheries protection to fashion to Tesco. Technology needs building up, and an appeal just launched for new Technology Centre, staff already on stream.

Background and Atmosphere Large Victorian pile in hilltop quietude of Malvern. Houses ('One' to 'Nine' plus School House) form horseshoe interspersed with other buildings of campus. Malvern has solved co-ed question by combining, academically only, at Sixth Form level with Ellerslie School, just down the road, and for CCF and D of E with Lawnside Girls. Plenty of social life (dinner parties more in than discos). Sixth Formers have own study-bedrooms. In Sixth, boys select their own tutors (though they don't always get their choices).

Discipline Occasional drug related expulsion, but school has intricate house and tutor system 'so between us we should pick up any problems'.

THE PUPILS Sons of solid professional classes, and to the professions they will (probably) return. Many from west side of England, a number of non-nationals including Hong Kong Chinese contingent, whose results are excellent. Ex-OMs include Denholm Elliott, Jeremy Paxman, and, more typically, MPs, also the Speaker, Bernard Weatherill, supermarket chairmen, judges, lawyers etc. C S Lewis went here.

Entrance Registration and CE or separate test for state school entrants. Head wants to find ways to increase day boy element. Sixth Form entry by GCSE, interview and tests.

Exit 15-20 annually to Oxbridge and between 80%-90% to degree courses.

Bottom Line Assisted Places. Just added two more scholarships to the 21 academic ones (ranging down from a maximum of 75% of fees) already available, to encourage day boys. Plus scholarships/exhibitions for music and art, and one Sixth Form scholarship.

Remarks Traditional broad-based and caring public school but some disquieting reports.

MALVERN GIRLS' COLLEGE

15 Avenue Road, Malvern, Worcestershire
WR14 3BA
TEL Malvern (0684) 892288

upils: 520 girls • 460 board, 60 day • Ages: 11-18 •
ize of Sixth Form: 180 • C of E • Fee-paying.

HEAD Since 1986, Dr Valerie B Payne, MSc, PhD, (forties), educated Taskers High School and Imperial College, London. Head of Physics at Malvern Girls' College for 16 years; involved internationally with science curriculum development, and participation of women in Science. Member of the Common Entrance Board. Somewhat reserved, slightly daunting. Considers confidence the essential ingredient for girls to learn via education. 'A woman must be able to express what she wants, without demanding.'

Academic Matters Strong. Pace rigorous and intense. All-round academic strengths. Good History and Modern Languages. Both parents and girls clear they are 'not pressurized', but very definitely work hard, and expectations are high. Extra tuition on hand for strugglers, though parents of less bright consider another school might have suited better'. Wide General Studies for Sixth Formers, also one-year GCSE options are drama, Italian, and Environmental Science studies. Three A-levels the norm, and wide choice AS-levels. In addition there is a fast stream taking French A-level in one year.

Games, Options, the Arts Strong on lax field (NB Chinese contingent un-gamesy). Much used circular sports dome a controversial 1987 innovation ('How many sports do you actually play in the round?' laughed other schools), and all-weather pitch has improved the games facilities. Indoor pool, (with fine and changing cubicles). Very good music, hordes of orchestras, fine choir, music standard generally enhanced by annual music festivals and the Elgar connection. Definitely a Christian school, emphasis on community service, lively Grab-a-Granny scheme. Own mini enterprise; D of E Award. Design Technology recently innovated; cooking on offer. Some drama and music—and socializing—with the Boys' College.

Background and Atmosphere Huge and forbidding Victorian block, close by the railway, converted from the Imperial Hotel. Very institutional, strongly house oriented: all meals in the house (mixed ages). A member of staff has been appointed with specific responsibility for the weekend programme—previously a weakness. All middle school houses are locked at all times for security reasons. Middle school no longer wears ties and may wear slip on shoes. No uniform for Sixth Form. Splendid library (with 21,000 vols). Busy and purposeful. Also tough and worthy. Girls encouraged to learn from their mistakes. Head claims, now, 'People feel free to express ideas—and discuss them with me.'

THE PUPILS The first woman officer in the Household Cavalry is an Old Girl, also editor of English *Vogue* at time of writing. Interesting cross-section, socially, ethnographically and academically. Locals, Glos, Wales, the Wirrall, London; popular with professionals and farmers. The late Dame Elizabeth Lane, first woman county court judge is an Old Girl; so are Barbara Cartland and Elizabeth Tilberis—editor of *Vogue*.

Entrance At 11+, 12+, and 13+; between 10-15 at Sixth Form (filling post GCSE leakage).

Exit Around 90% go on to degree courses (between five and eight to Oxbridge); careers taken very seriously. Engineering now popular, also medicine, the City, Foreign Office.

Bottom Line Five academic scholarships and exhibitions at 11, 12 or 13 available, and three scholarships (internal or external) at Sixth Form. Also two music scholarships.

Remarks Very traditional girls' all round boarding school. Solid and strong, but perhaps lacking in imagination.

THE MANCHESTER GRAMMAR SCHOOL

Old Hall Lane Rusholme, Manchester
M13 0XT
TEL Manchester (061) 224 7201/2/3

Pupils: 1,400+ boys • All day • Ages: 11-18 • Size of Sixth Form: 400 • C of E links but basically non-denom • Fee-paying.

HEAD (High Master) Since Michaelmas 1985, Mr Geoffrey Parker MA Cantab (fifties), ex-Head of Wakefield, before that taught History at Tonbridge School. Married with grown up family. Relaxed, forthright, runs the most dynamic school in the country with a flourish. Aims to keep school in its pre-eminent position 'and improve it if he can', but says that, since we last saw him, he is 'even more certain of the dangers of complacency' in a successful school and it is 'vital to watch out for it'. Head is flanked by two long-serving deputies 'Surmasters', Mr Philip Schofield and Mr Peter Laycock, who head a terrific support team.

Academic Matters Outstanding in everything they do. Staff consider pupils 'often' more intelligent than they are themselves, but here this is modesty. One commented 'let me put it like this…what we achieve together far exceeds the sum of our individual efforts'. One of very few places you will find staff discussing merits of different Oxbridge colleges in the way prep school Heads discuss public schools.

Examination results are always at or near the top of the league tables. Small long standing Russian department. All Sixth Formers study English and Philosophy, and the school produces a booklet of General Studies on offer, eg new languages (but has dropped Japanese), Sociology, Applied Engineering and advanced Computer Programming. Two busy libraries with many boys helping, and a splendid bookshop.

In the Lower School, headed by Mr Ian Thorpe, the 'good learning' set as an objective by the Founder 'happens—and at a pace'. Pupils and staff work on a broad general curriculum for four years before GCSE choices are made.

Games, Options, the Arts Does not set out to be a games school, but surprises itself by doing rather well on the games field—the more so as all representative teams are composed of volunteers. All major and some minor sports represented. Music was described as 'good in parts': one pupil said concerts were 'as good as going to the Halle any day'. Younger boys regularly sing with the Halle, and school has a fine new Peter Collins organ. 1990 A-level art results not good. No sports centre. No house system—boys play against each other in years; pastoral care unit is the form. Strong crafts department and school does excellent silverwork with their own hallmark, MGS.

The MGS Dramatic Society has an 'active membership' of several hundred boys, and produces approx five major productions a year. Has its annual dramatic exchange with an American school, and counts among its 'Old Boys' not only Michael Wood, but Ben Kingsley, Robert Powell and RSC director Nicholas Hytner.

Lots of fell walking, trekking and mountaineering—six such holidays yearly, plus numerous weekends. Young boys start with weekends at the 'Owl' Nest' at Disley and at the school's barn at Grasmere.

Background and Atmosphere Founded in 1515 by Hugh Oldham, Bishop of Exeter, a year before he founded Corpus Christi College Oxford (with which the school has links), to educate able boys regardless of their parents' means to go on to university and the professions and open what the founder called the 'yate of knowledge. Moved to present purpose-built site in Fallowfield (three miles from City centre) in 1931—huge red brick based round central quad with heavy high portals, institutional green tiles to half-way up the walls. New boys are given a map to find their way about. Atmosphere dynamic, bursting with energy, particularly mental energy. Although day, it feels very much like a boarding school. Uniform for the main school is blue jackets—sometimes a little scruffy. Sixth Formers wear their own 'sensible' clothes—jacket and tie—and have their own common room.

THE PUPILS Cream of intelligentsia from Buxton to Blackpool—not necessarily middle class. 'People often come here as a last resort', said a master 'because their child is bright and bored and losing spark in his present environment.' Bright as bush babies; maybe a bit uncouth, but polite and considerate, and discipline not a major struggle though boys do get picked on if non-Mancunians. Famous Old Mancunians: dozens of these including Michael Atherton, John Ogden, Thomas de Quincey. More contemporary examples historian Michael Wood. Also 'rows of FRS' including Sir Michael Atiyah. Several members of Sieff family including Israel Sieff (a major benefactor of the school, which has the Sieff Theatre) and Simon Marks. Large Jewish element—approximately 15% of the school—and special assemblies are held for them and for Muslims and Hindus. Many pupils travel daily from Sheffield, Stoke-on-Trent, Blackburn etc.

Entrance Difficult, as you might imagine, indeed the High Master said MGS was 'arguably the most selective school in the land' and he could be right. Holds its own exam in February for following September in two parts: first part sieves out the non-starters with Qs, eg 'A maggot doubles its weight every day. On March 1 it weighs a quarter of a gram. Write down the date on which it weighs 64 grams.' You can apply for entry right up to the exam.

Exit 95% of Sixth Form go on to study for a degree. Regularly gets 50 or so pupils into Oxbridge. They also go to Leeds, Sheffield, Manchester etc. Squads of OMs go into the Civil Service, also to research, business, banking.

Bottom Line 40 Assisted Places each year, plus five into the Sixth Form. Bursary fund for keeping children in reduced straits at school and extending number of Assisted Places. (NB for historical reasons only the Bursar is called the Receiver.) Fees of £1,000 a term make this school still a bargain.

Remarks Marches strongly on. Still top equal with Eton as the strongest, most outstanding academic school for boys in the country. Not the place for late developers or those in need of social status, and has been described by staff of (jealous?) neighbouring schools as 'the sausage machine'. The only thing they lack is social polish.

MARLBOROUGH COLLEGE
Wiltshire SN8 1PA
TEL Marlborough (0672) 515511

Pupils: 660 boys, 220 girls ● All board ● Ages: 13-18 ● Size of Sixth Form: 400 ● C of E ● Fee-paying.

HEAD The Master, since 1986, Mr David Cope MA (forties), educated Winchester and Cambridge.

Remarks Not easy to comment constructively at the

moment. Still works for the well-motivated and self-disciplined but complaints have been heard from parents about problems with discipline and pastoral care.

THE McLAREN HIGH SCHOOL
Mollands Road, Callander, Perthshire FK17 8JH
TEL Callander (0877) 30156

Pupils: Approx 700 boys and girls ● All day, except for one boarding house for 12-15 pupils from outlying districts ● Ages: 11-17/18 ● Size of Sixth Form: 180 ● Non-denom ● State.

HEAD Rector, since February 1985, Mr H A Mathie MA, MEd (fifties). Read Classics at St Andrew's University and has taught in state system all his life. Married with three children. Quiet but impressive, confident and outspoken. Involved in church activities, plays golf, played hockey at university. Comments, 'we try to cater for individual pupils at their own level, helped now by the new exam system which has credit level, general level and foundation level, where before there was only "pass" and "fail"…Also obviously we try to make the school a community…with a nice atmosphere…and …prepare pupils for the world outside.'

School comes officially under the Director of Education, Central Region.

Academic Matters 58 staff, 18 subject departments. All mainstream subjects, including wonderful Classics teacher—second year Latin oversubscribed. Gaelic offered—about 10 take it. Good language lab facilities. Follows Scottish exam system only. Careful setting. Good results. Points system for good work.

Games, Options, the Arts Taking part in the European Legends Project in Paris with other countries (hands across sea)—doing eg *Rob Roy*. Groups go abroad to eg Turkey—very popular. Lively orchestra which stages concerts after school. Lots of clubs and activities in the lunch hour, but frequent complaint is that since the teachers' strike of 1985, the staff have stuck very much to their union rules, and there are not nearly enough extras after school—the school's biggest weakness. Not much emphasis on competitive team games—official line is that all must be catered for, not just the first 11 etc. Very keen music, with festivals and overseas trip every other year to with school orchestra. All manner of musical tuition offered, including the bagpipes. Art and Design strong. Canoeing, skiing trips. Good stage.

Background and Atmosphere Glorious setting below Callander in the Trossachs. Sixties buildings have received civic trust award—though they have a slightly bleak look. First class library served by Central Region Library Service—though some limitations on use of it. Room for wheel chairs through the school, including staircase lift, ramps. Pupils wear uniform, though this is not immediately apparent as they are invariably swaddled up in the latest plush slinky anorak, and white socks.

Foundation dates back to 1844; endowed by Callander philanthropist Donald McLaren in 1850 with a view to providing a 'salary of sufficient amount to induce men of superior talents and acquirements to become and to continue Teachers in the said School…'. School dux (leader) boards going back to 1909 on the walls. Motto: *Ab origine fides.*

Atmosphere slightly institutional—smell of Jeyes fluid—but optimistic (like Jeyes fluid), enthusiastic and children nice.

Discipline Usually punishment exercise, and the occasional detention. 'Basically' says Head, 'it's a question of contact with the parents.' He comments that parental control over children in general is not what it used to be and even in the comparative calm of Callander 'we feel ripples'. Anti-smoking crusade.

THE PUPILS All sorts, from a catchment area of 400 square miles—which obviously makes organizing extra-curricular activities difficult.

Entrance By registration.

Exit Farming, university, the arts—total cross section. One or two to Oxbridge. Glasgow, Edinburgh, St Andrew's and Bristol universities particularly popular.

Remarks Something of a showcase for the Scottish state system. Very sound academic school, much admired not only by locals, but by professional educationalists and education authorities.

MERCHANT TAYLORS' SCHOOL
Sandy Lodge, Northwood, Middlesex
HA6 2HT
TEL Northwood (09274) 21850

Pupils: 720 boys ● *70 board, 650 day* ● *Ages: 11-18* ● *Size of Sixth Form: about 230* ● *C of E* ● *Fee-paying.*

HEAD From September 1991, Mr John Gabitass, MA Oxon (forties), previously Second Master at Abingdon. No relation of the educational agency—observe the spelling.

Academic Matters Head reports teething troubles with GCSE now sorted out. 1990 A-levels reported as the 'best in the recorded history of the school'—at least as far as AB and C grades were concerned. Serious work ethic. School runs a full six day week—most unusual for a predominantly day school.

Games, Options, the Arts Seriously gamey, a lot of time and energy devoted to sport. Endless sea of rugby posts. Plays every school in sight—see fixtures list. Lots of after school clubs including debating, bridge, snooker, chess, war games etc. New swimming pool, also a studio/theatre. Three lakes in the grounds—one for field studies, one for fishing and one for sailing. CCF prominent.

Background and Atmosphere Founded in 1561. Moved from the City of London in 1933 to purpose-built school in deep suburbia. Building is a monument to early Thirties sobriety ((RIBA medal winner). The great hall stretches into gloomy infinity and library is replete with musty dignity. One of the original 'Clarendon Nine' schools, which included Winchester, Eton etc.

THE PUPILS Commute along the Metropolitan line from St John's Wood to Amersham. Nickname—the Merchant Failures. A tolerant, multi-racial community with a tradition for admitting refugees—post-war offspring of Polish and Russian refugees and post-1956 Hungarians, Kenyan and Ugandan Asians etc. 'Even 400 years ago, the school was for boys of every race and creed' said the Head.

Entrance At 11 and 13 via CE.

Exit 75-80% to higher education. 20 or so to Oxbridge. Thereafter civil service, accountancy, law, hotel management etc.

Bottom Line Assisted places at 11, 13 and 16.

Remarks Good local school.

MERCHISTON CASTLE SCHOOL
Colinton, Edinburgh EH13 OPU
TEL Edinburgh (031) 441 1722

Pupils: 375 boys ● *310 board, 65 day* ● *Ages: 11-18* ●
Size of Sixth Form: 130 ● *Non-denom* ● *Fee-paying.*

HEAD Since 1981, Mr David Spawforth MA (fifties) educated at Hertford, Oxford and former BP Educational Fellow, Keble Oxford. Previously House-master at Winchester and Wellington. Linguist, teaches French and German. Believes in 'tempting boys to explore different intellectual avenues' rather than confining them to set courses. Lives on campus with wife.

Academic Matters Mainly A-levels, but Scottish Highers offered as an alternative. Strong on Sciences. Private tuition available in most subjects. Achieve-ments important to Merchistonians: only French, Ger-man and Spanish languages offered, though specialist staff can be co-opted. Japanese being introduced. Gold and silver awards gained in British Physics Olympiad and the National Mathematics Competition. Some dyslexia treatment available, and splendid exam advice. Three-weekly reports for younger boys, discussed with boy; half termly assessments for Sixth Form.

Games, Options, the Arts Very strong on Rugby—almost a religion: 1989/1990 season played 19 matches, won 16, lost three. First 15 toured Japan and won all matches. Cricket: undefeated on Scottish circuit at time of writing. Athletics—gold and silver medals in the Scottish Schools Championships. Own golf course, squash, sub-aqua. Keen music and choir—recorded for the BBC in 1989 and toured the Far East in 1990. Skiing at Hillend and the real thing. Outward Bound. CCF compulsory for two years and can then opt out for Community Service, but CCF is key to shooting, etc.

House and school drama—regular Edinburgh Fes-tival fringe production—country dancing is popular (Edinburgh schools provide partners). Clubs for everything. Splendid multi-purpose building, housing gym, a theatre, computer rooms and classrooms, recently completed. Good links with industry—every-one does a one week course. Computers everywhere—in every house and classroom, and personal computers litter domitories.

Background and Atmosphere Merchiston (pro-nounced as in 'murky') Castle School was founded 1883, moved to purpose-built rather bleak buildings in grounds of Colinton House 1930. Non-denom school, though Church of Scotland-influenced services in Memorial Chapel.

School divided into houses laterally with boys moving up each year. Junior school, Pringle House, reserved for 11-12 year olds, run by Mr Rainy Brown (no longer a bachelor, no more bits of string in pockets). Boys progress from dormitories via study cubicles to study bedrooms. Boarding houses were definitely bleak, however refurbishment programme is under way. Games rooms with ping pong, etc. Boys' kitchens everywhere. Highly successful cafeteria-style feeding in the dining room, popular with staff and boys.

Discipline Head a disciplinarian, 'letters home' for smoking, gatings for drinking (though boys may consume up to two half pints of lager in strictly supervised Sixth Form club at weekends). 'No drugs problem' at time of writing.

THE PUPILS 60% Scots, lots of OBs' children, well mannered. A quarter ex pats.

Entrance At 11/12 via special exam and interview. At 13, CE for ex-prep school entrants—55% pass mark required, special exam for non-prep school entrants. Entry possible throughout school for right child. More in than out at Sixth Form.

Exit Approx 70% make university with a further 12% going to polytechnics, one or two to art college, a few do a 'gap' year.

Bottom Line Scholarships available at every level.

Remarks Tough middle class middle-of-the-road public school, training up pupils to take their part in tomorrow's world.

MILLFIELD SENIOR SCHOOL

Street, Somerset BA16 0YD

TEL Street (0458) 42291

Pupils: *Approx 750 boys, 480 girls* ● *970 board, 270 day* ● Ages: *13-18* ● *Size of Sixth Form: 440* ● *Non-denom* ● Fee-paying.

HEAD and chairman of executive group (governing gang of four), since September 1990, Mr Christopher Martin (fifties) MA, CBE for services to education. Educated Westminster School and St Andrew's University. Previously Head of Bristol Cathedral School. Says he agrees with the school's philosophy of finding something every child can be good at, but adds that the child must be made aware 'how this gift can make a contribution to the common wield and what that will mean'. Also says that there is, 'no dust here. The atmosphere is electrifying. The school is interested in evolution and understands it—sees it as essential: I love it.' In the interests of evolution he has already started on a series of changes that is leaving even Millfield gasping a bit, though his colleagues are so far impressed.

Takes over from the Principal, Mr C R M Atkinson, and from his Headmaster Mr Brian Gaskell.

Academic Matters Head defies us to find any school with as wide a range of subjects on offer—choice includes Japanese, Hindi, Dutch, Norwegian, communications studies, theatre studies, philosophy etc. Gets a steady 24 into Oxbridge and results, given mixed and large overseas intake, are impressive. Teaching varies from the highly eccentric and inspired to mediocre. Very hard working. School streamed with lots of small A and B groups, plus remove forms for pupils needing extra tuition. Ratio of staff to pupils is 1:8. School famous for its remedial department. Particularly strong in visual subjects and in Mathematics and Sciences.

Games, Options, the Arts Outstanding—if anything, says Mr Martin, 'better than ever', and the school's top teams tend to be playing county and professional teams (eg they were off to play Watford Under-19s the day we visited) rather than those of

schools. If pupil is tired of extras at Millfield then he is certainly tired of life, though there have been complaints that only the 'professional' squads of games players are keenly taught—others may be subjected to 'constructive dismissal'.

'Communal' games are athletics, cricket, hockey, netball, rugby and soccer, but if pupil is a 'star' his services to these will be minimized. School has full-time tennis pro, also full-time swimming and riding pros—and dozens of part-timers. Extras legion—fully equipped video recording studios, indoor riding school (under the famous Major Burke), own polo team, special summer vacation courses for the public. NB: All extras are not always available to everyone.

Background and Atmosphere Founded in 1935 by 'Boss' Meyer, who evolved a philosophy of putting the individual's needs before those of the school, and adopted an aggressive marketing atttitude which has now—reluctantly—been copied by the rest of the private sector. Atmosphere well described by new Head (above), and the feeling that all things are possible. Five-star groundsman has turned the basic rows of unprepossessing teaching huts into a pleasant and coherent whole.

Discipline School popularly supposed to be liberal, but in actuality disciplinary measures are 'vigorously applied'. Recent expulsions for drugs, bullying. No san, and children have been known to struggle on in illness as well as health.

THE PUPILS A carefully contrived 'mix' of rich, athletic, academic etc. Popular with film stars (if only because they have heard of it), the media, powerful Third World families and poverty-stricken Welsh owing to geographical position. 19% non-Brits. OBs: Duncan Goodhew, Mark Cox, Chris Law, Gareth Edwards.

Entrance Currently on interview only, though exam may be coming soon, according to member of staff.

Exit Widely differing careers reflecting widely differing children. Most go on to higher education. 'Gap' encouraged.

Bottom Line Can claim to be a genuine charity. School spends a staggering £1.4 million-plus a year on scholarships and bursaries, and at last count over 40% of pupils received financial assistance of some sort. School no longer the most expensive in the country but 'extras' not covered by the fees now proliferate.

Remarks Has been 'rudderless' for 18 month

owing to outgoing Principal's illness, and has suffered as a result. Now coming back on course with much admired new Head. School perhaps now a bit too big?

MILL HILL SCHOOL
The Ridgeway, London NW7 1QS
TEL London (081) 959 1176

Pupils: 490 boys, 50 girls (all in Sixth Form) • *Just under half board, rest day* • *Ages: 13-18* • *Size of Sixth Form: 240* • *Non-denom* • *Fee-paying.*

HEAD Since 1979, Mr A C Graham MA, FRSA (fifties), educated at Winchester and Cambridge, previously Housemaster at Eton. Suave, he enjoys unusual popularity among pupils, who deem him 'fairminded'. His aims for them: 'To exercise the best potential and exorcise the worst.'

Remarks Founded (1807) by nonconformists, once a traditional but now innovative and unfashionable independent school; on the edge of London with five pupils per acre of parkland yet within a dozen miles of metropolitan theatres, museums etc. (The school also owns a house in Dentdale, W Yorks, used for field studies etc.) Although maintenance of listed buildings and exceptional grounds places disproportionate burden on budget, *very* considerable improvements of facilities and appearance have banished the 'down-at-heel effect' reported previously. Academic standards improved drastically under present Head, expectations far higher. 'Education is about setting the right expectations,' he firmly believes. Natural Sciences, Business Studies and Modern Languages consistently the success stories at A-level (not least because many parents believe these subjects are useful, notes Head). Section Bilingue (established 1969) pioneered teaching History and Geography in French, but sadly disallowed by GCSE.

Rich and regular drama programme (leading to eg an award at Edinburgh Fringe Festival, and entry to RADA); music flourishing, and much encouraged—school gives biennial concerts at Queen Elizabeth Hall, has had three Distinction grade eight instrumentalists simultaneously, has a new pipe organ in the chapel. Strong tutorial structure ensuring academic supervi-

sion and pastoral care; enlightened management structure involves pupils eg Monitors and School Council. 80% of Sixth Formers go on to higher education; careers in law, engineering and medical profession popular. Francis Crick, Nigel Wray, Simon Jenkins and Denis Thatcher among Old Boys, along with lots of worthy judges and businessmen.

A school which inspires fierce loyalty among pupils and community.

MILTON ABBEY SCHOOL
Nr Blandford Forum, Dorset DT11 0BZ
TEL Milton Abbas (0258) 880484

Pupils: 285 boys • *All board* • *Ages: 13-18* • *Size of Sixth Form: variable, between 88 and 100* • *C of E.* • *Fee-paying.*

HEAD Since September 1987, Mr Robert H Hardy JP, MA Oxon (fifties), educated Winchester and Oxford. Previously Housemaster at Eton. Some parents find him short on imagination and humour, though others deny this vehemently.

Academic Matters Unlike some other schools specifically aiming to help less academic boys, dyslexics are integrated with the rest, (remedial help where needed). No class has more than 20, boys are setted for everything, except RI, General Studies and PE. Tutorial systems, whereby each subject master is available for two periods each week to give extra one-to-one help, 'Quite well used', say staff. Most boys stay for at least two A-levels, and get them in the end.

Games, Options, the Arts Much store is set by these: lively societies and activities, with coercion during first two years. Outstanding Natural History club (virtually all boys members), with own moth trap, lepidopterists etc. Good art studio and theatre, enthusiastic Department. Good boating (canoeing and sailing); CCF popular (school has strong links with Royal Armoured Corps at Bovington, also with the Navy). Good sports facilities, Rugby the main game; newly built golf course and new indoor heated swimming pool. Computing popular.

Background and Atmosphere Immensely beautiful listed Grade I building (begun by Sir William Chambers and taken over by James Wyatt), set in fold of valleys and Dorset hills. Modern blocks cleverly hidden; stable block cleverly converted into light classrooms and culture centre. Daily worship in the ravishing Abbey. Centrally run, with all five Houses in the main building each with its own territory. All Housemasters are married, family atmosphere pervasive, all boys know each other, 70% have study bedrooms, the rest sleep in dormitory/common rooms, ie with working spaces by the beds. Prefects are called pilots; atmosphere is structured and disciplined, good manners and consideration for others noticeable. Exeats minimal. Boys are kept occupied in this isolated school. Lovat sweater uniform. School founded in the mid-Fifties.

Discipline   Strong no smoking rule, drugs means instant dismissal (Dorset Drugs Squad regular visitors with videos and talks). 1991 dismissal for holding cache of firearms; also drugs expulsion.

THE PUPILS   Particularly nice lads, courteous, relaxed and friendly, with a sense of fellowship. Cohesive (backgrounds and IQ), geographically homes are widespread. Monthly rendezvous for Old Boys at Duke of Wellington, Eaton Terrace.

Entrance   Via CE. From everywhere, including all the top preps.

Exit   The Services, the land (farming, estate management), the City, estate agencies, family firms; variable numbers go on to further education.

Bottom Line   Up to eight scholarships, at least three for music, from 25–75% fees, also Lower Sixth scholarship.

Remarks   Good school which specializes in getting less academic pupils through A-levels. Beginning to suffer the consequences of this rather depressing image—and might benefit by building up excellence in other spheres.

MORE HOUSE SCHOOL
22-24 Pont Street, London SW1X 0AA
TEL London (071) 235 2855

Pupils: 240 girls • All day • Ages: 11-18 • Size of Sixth Form: 57 • RC. • Fee-paying.

HEAD   From September 1991, Miss Margaret Connell BA (forties), previously Deputy Head of Bromley High.

Remarks   In a state of flux, but parental confidence appears undimmed. New Head takes over from predecessor who left at short notice after only one year, and was successor to the excellent Mrs Pauline Mathias—a hard act to follow. London's smallest—cramped—academic day school is good for girls who need a cosy, happy, personal uninstitutional atmosphere.

MORETON HALL
Weston Rhyn, Oswestry, Shropshire
SY11 3EW
TEL Chirk (0691) 773671

Pupils: 350 girls • 325 board, 25 day • Ages: 11-18 • Size of Sixth Form: 100 • C of E. • Fee-paying.

PRINCIPAL   Interregnum until 1992 (asked to stay longer, but would prefer to hand over): Mr Michael Maloney MA Cantab (late fifties). Early retirement of Mr Jim Cussell and tragic death of excellent Deputy made this necessary. See *Who's Who* for potted biog of Mr Maloney, who has spent a lifetime in education, including being Head of Kamazu, the Eton of Africa in Malawi.

Academic Matters   Academic perfomance and emphasis is rising, though the school is mostly chosen for its personality; gives a sound middle-of-the-road education. Day recently re-structured to give time to activities without interrupting academic periods.

A-levels might include Home Economics or Dress-making alongside a few high-fliers aiming for Oxbridge. Good Life Skills course for Sixth Formers. Good dyslexic unit, but anxious to play this down as 'school is best for the bright ones'.

Games, Options, the Arts Gamesy school whose teams win lacrosse matches regularly. CDT and art both good, and drama gaining strength. Excellent careers department, very good at finding suitable work experience via a far-reaching network. Good music, some with Shrewsbury boys. Sixth Formers run Moreton Enterprise, their own business scheme, with outstanding success, and display shrewdness. Community minded girls. Strong connections with Shrewsbury School include social activities, lectures etc.

Background and Atmosphere Very friendly, uninstitutional, complex assortment of buildings. Pastoral weekend care and activities continue to be erratic, according to several parents. Flexible exeats a bonus for ex-pats. New magnificent sports hall finished in 1990. Two professional tennis coaches, indoor court etc.

THE PUPILS Mixed bunch, geographically and socially (school is well placed for Birmingham and Manchester areas, the Wirral and points north and west). Has reputation for taking on girls that other schools have chucked out or written off—produces open, friendly, chatty girls. Thea Musgrave, the composer, the best known Old Girl.

Entrance Own entry text and interview. Some come in at Sixth Form. Getting choosier. First registration for the year 2000 received at time of writing.

Exit 75% to higher education, art colleges very popular choice. Girls typically end up working in the media, where their persuasive and social skills are to the fore.

Bottom Line Two academic scholarships at 11 or 13, one at Sixth Form; one music scholarship; bursaries available.

Remarks Gives a rounded education in a rural area. Unpretentious and untraditional. Might suit misfits, although Head asks: would they get in nowadays? Appears strong enough to ride out recent tricky situation.

THE MOUNT SCHOOL
Dalton Terrace, York YO2 4DD
TEL York (0904) 654823

Pupils: 280 girls • 225 board, 55 day • Ages: 11-18 • Size of Sixth Form: Approx 85 • Quaker • Fee-paying.

HEAD From 1986, Miss Barbara J Windle MA Cantab (forties), formerly Head of English Sixth Form and Senior Tutor at Bolton School (Girls' Division). A Quaker, though not aggressively so, she rules the school with charm, humour, and a core of steel. Aims: 'To ensure that every child is conscious of being valued and finds something in which she achieves, and that would include extra-curricular as well as curricular activities.' Still busy kicking the school into 1990s.

Academic Matters Classes go from 14 to 20 pupils. Streaming in Maths and French; a School Inspectors' report complimented the school on 'the best resourced English Department'. Computers everywhere, Geography greatly improved, library good, GCSEs 'quietly confident, assessments are under control'. Splendid Maths, Art, Science Centre with smart red doors.

Games, Options, the Arts Marvellous maintained 20-acre oasis in the middle of York, with tennis courts everywhere, gym, large pool, standard collection of all-weather pitches (hockey or tennis). Clubs for everything from micro-electronics to creative writing via pottery. Masses of drama. Rock climbing is popular, own D of E's Award centre.

Background and Atmosphere The only all-girl Quaker school in the country but only 15% practising, a further 15% have Quaker 'links'. Quaker values are fostered, and 'Assembly is held Quaker style with the emphasis on silence in a non-denom format.' Emphasis on religious background: family meals are held in large dining room, preceded and ended by a silent grace. New 'healthy eating policy means less stodge'. New girls are allocated a mentor or 'nut-cracker' to show them round. Mixed-age bedrooms with own duvet covers. Sixth Form have study bedrooms (posters). Girls do a housework chore, and elect own head girl and her three deputies. Pupils tend to refer to staff by their full Quaker title, ie 'Barbara Windle', but call her Miss Windle.

THE PUPILS   The Christian belief that God is in everyone manifests itself in obvious inner calm. Grey uniform with coloured shirts. The Sixth Form wear mufti.

Entrance   Own entrance exam similar to CE, but, 'we help if they get stuck, it's the potential, not the results that we are examining'. More join for Sixth Form than leave after GCSE.

Exit   Practically all girls go on to further education.

Bottom Line   Assisted Places scheme at 11+.

Remarks   Famous Quaker school, well organized and friendly.

NORTH FORELAND LODGE

Sherfield-on-Loddon, Basingstoke,
Hampshire RG27 0HT
TEL Basingstoke (0256) 882431

Pupils: Approx 188 girls • *All board* • *Ages: 11-18* • *Size of Sixth Form: 48* • *C of E* • *Fee-paying.*

HEAD   Since 1983, Miss D L Matthews BA (forties), appointed from the Abbey School, Reading, where she was Senior Mistress and Head of History. Firm, sensible and keen on aim for school as stated by the school's first Head, Miss Wolseley-Lewis, who said her object in founding the school was to prepare the girls to be 'good citizens'. Apart from Miss Matthews, the schools has had only three Heads (not counting an interregnum) since its founding in 1909. Miss Matthews teaches herself, which she considers 'important'.

Remarks   Originally not an academic school and still not exactly a hothouse, but GCSE results are looking better, and 80% of Sixth Form go on to higher education, most doing a 'gap' year first. Strongest on French, English, but Science facilities are gradually being built up. Not a school which loses any sleep if it doesn't win interschools tournaments, but plays lacrosse and netball and is terrifically keen on tennis. Keen fencing (compulsory for one term). New sports hall opened in 1990.

School moved from North Foreland in Kent (hence name) to present gracious private house surrounded by 70 acres of grounds, and site is near enough to village for girls to make frequent visits. Sixth Form has a separate annexe and girls are encouraged to live together as 'flat-mates'—though a member of staff is responsible for overseeing. Otherwise, girls all more or less under one roof, winding up into the attics of the house.

House system only operates for games, but senior girls have very solid responsibilities including being 'room-warden'—ie sleeping in dormitory with six/seven juniors and no privacy. School has tradition of cleaning and wax polishing with 'christophers' and 'rollock' (polish)—no one knew why they were thus called—emptying 'waggers', tidying up and waiting at table (ie shades of finishing school). This takes about 20 minutes a day.

Pupils: upper and upper middle class, but also professional, diplomatic, services and bankers. Famous OGs: Sarah Churchill and the Queen of Denmark. No scholarships or bursaries though Head commented 'we would never hurl a girl out into the street'.

This was formerly one of *the* pukka non-academic girls' boarding schools with able pupils often choosing a career of social whirl rather than academe. Now the emphasis has shifted slightly to a bit more academic, a bit less pukka, though parents report it all feels exactly the same—happy and relaxed.

NORTH LONDON COLLEGIATE SCHOOL

Canons, Edgeware, Middlesex HA8 7RJ.
TEL London (081) 952 0912

Pupils: 700 girls • *All day* • *Ages: 11-18* • *Junior School 190, ages 7-11* • *Size of Sixth Form: 220 with 24 entering from state and private sector* • *C of E* • *Fee-paying*

HEAD   Since 1987, Mrs Joan Clancy MA (early fifties). Handsome, softly spoken Scot, also quick minded, with delightful sense of humour. This is her second Headship.

Academic Matters   Formidably strong with languages an outstanding strength. Some 99 'A' grades at A-level from 80 candidates at last count—small numbers opting for Greek A-level all passing with distinction. No impression of an academic hothouse in operation, nor of an arrogant elite, no complaints from children of any pressure. Class sizes cut down from 30 to 23/24 in response to GCSE: 'You have to cut down with so much individual work, so much oral and role play. We threw a lot of money at it. I just think it's so important. You've got to have lavish provision. I don't want that yoghurt-pot mentality around. It's no good being brave and "darned"—the boys' school aren't like that.'

Games, Options, the Arts Definitely not a sporty school. Head amused by lack of deadly serious attitudes on the game field, but in spite of the missing competitive cutting edge, their performances locally are very respectable. Lacrosse team touring Australia in 1991. Music a great strength, with a number of music scholars coming in at age 11. Design and Technology Department. Much affection for drama with pupils mounting their own productions in recently built and quite stunning studio theatre. Occasional collaboration with Harrow School.

Background and Atmosphere Along with Cheltenham Ladies' College, NLCC is the oldest of the endowed girls' schools, founded by the redoubtable Frances Mary Buss, a pioneer in the field of women's education, who broke with the tradition of rote learning and encouraged middle class women to free themselves from stiflingly narrow lives. In 1929 school moved to the former home of Lord Chandos. The buildings and, in particular, the grounds, are very fine, with 30 acres of parkland and two very large flower-filled ponds with newish art studio perfectly situated alongside one of these. An oasis in a beastly part of outer London. There's a relaxed, friendly atmosphere about the place; an awareness, too, on the part of the pupils that they are incredibly lucky to spend their school days in such beautiful surroundings. NLCC broke away from sister school, Camden Girls', in 1976, with the latter opting for the state system.

THE PUPILS Mainly the articulate pleasant offspring of wealthy north London intelligentsia (professional) and business community, with strong Jewish and Asian representation and a small Greek community. OGs: Esther Rantzen, Eleanor Bron.

Entrance Around 400 applications from north London suburbia vie for 70 places although some double booking, with strong competition from Haberdashers' Aske's and South Hampstead High. Entry at 11 via strongly competitive exam and interview; or at seven into junior school (which boasts a new building in the grounds), although transfer to senior school is not automatic.

Exit Around 20% to Oxbridge, and significant numbers to medicine, law and engineering.

Bottom Line Around 15 Assisted Places—but only 10-12 taken up. Very generous bursary fund with around 100 beneficiaries.

Remarks Strong school—one of London's top four academic schools for girls—with wonderful facilities, a friendly atmosphere and all this in a beautiful setting.

NORTH WESTMINSTER COMMUNITY SCHOOL
Penfold Street, London NW1 6RX
TEL London (071) 262 8000

Pupils: 1,700 girls and boys ● Ages: 11-18 ● Size of Sixth Form: approx 250 ● Non-denom ● State.

HEAD Michael Marland CBE, MA, Professor of Education, Warwick University, leading educationalist, skilful PR man, prolific author. Man of enormous energy, great administrative ability—revels in initiating radical programmes.

Remarks School offers biggest range of subjects in the capital—from Chinese to dance, stagecraft to Malay. Possibly over-ambitious, as exam results have demonstrated. One of the largest and most interesting state schools in London. Entry is close to 300 pupils a year; large numbers have English as a second language. A polyglot place. Some excellent members of staff.

THE NORWICH HIGH SCHOOL FOR GIRLS

Eaton Grove, 92 Newmarket Road, Norwich NR2 2HU

TEL Norwich (0603) 53265

Pupils: 600 girls in Senior School • All day • Ages: 11-18 • Size of Sixth Form: 160 • Junior School (Stafford House): Approx 220 girls • All day • Ages: 7-11 • Non-denom • Fee-paying.

HEAD   Since Autumn 1985, Mrs V C Bidwell BA (thirties). Brisk, business-like and hot on discipline, tidiness, shoe laces done up etc.

Remarks   The one and only serious academic girls private day school in Norfolk—huge catchment area and consequent pressure on places keeps standards reasonable. Strongest on three Rs. Gets one or two, sometimes more, into Oxbridge each year.

Keen on gym, swimming (has more than 260 Royal Life Saving Society awards) and Duke of Edinburgh-ing and does concerts in the glorious Norwich Cathedral. All this however comes very second to book work, and school is not known for excellence in extra curricular activities. Music considered strong, also art. Fourth of the Girls' Public Day School Trust schools, founded in 1872, and has the strengths of association with other such schools throughout the country. Grounds not large. Atmosphere is of hard-working grammar school.

Pupils are a mixture of solid middle class, bright working class seeking for self-improvement, sprinkling of upper middle who just manage to get in by skin of teeth after extensive coaching. One or two begin to show slight signs of being intellectually over-cooked at top end of school. Entrance by exam at eight-plus, 11+ and 12+; also at 16+ depending on GCSE results. Easiest way in is via the middle school at 8+; competition fiercest at 11+, when parents suddenly wake up and realize there is nowhere else comparable to go. Gets nought to nine into Oxbridge each year. About 90% to further education of some sort. Up to 30 Assisted Places and has scholarship and bursary fund for pupils at 11+, 12+ and in Sixth Form.

Excellent junior school, tails off slightly further up.

OAKHAM SCHOOL

Chapel Close, Oakham Rutland LE15 6DT

TEL Oakham (0572) 55238

Pupils: 498 boys, 498 girls • Approx 581 board, 415 day • Ages: 10-18 • Size of Sixth Form: Approx 260 (ratio of boys to girls 60:40) • C of E • Fee-paying.

HEAD   Since 1985, Mr Graham Smallbone MA (fifties), educated Uppingham and Worcester College (Haddow music scholar). Distinguished musical career—has done everything (see *Who's Who*) including Precentor at Eton. Quiet. Aims to 'create and maintain a community and fulfil pupils' talents as we find them, whatever they happen to be'. A Head's Head. Popular.

Academic Matters   Reasonable, given wide ability intake; bias to Science and Economics. Girls apparently take Arts and Science in equal numbers with boys at top of school. Keen on computers—much used.

School has special separate Oxbridge swot house started by Chris Dickson, so potential candidates get suitably hotted up. Oxbridge house is a ghetto blast free area. Occasional comments from parents that social life has greater priority than work.

Games, Options, the Arts   Keen music and at time of writing has three in the National Youth Orchestra. NB gives *free* music lessons if you pass grade five with merit. Otherwise stronger on games—major and minor. Keen on squash and shooting—regularly wins Squash National School Championships. Lots of Duke of Edinburgh Gold Awards. Enormous range of extras on offer, but pupils commented that the school did not always have the proper coaching back up and the danger was you got overwhelmed, flying off in too many directions at once. New shooting range now completed and Astroturf pitch.

Background and Atmosphere   First of 'new wave' of post-war co-eds (first wave being Millfield etc). Was local grammar school and still has humblish reputation in national terms. Slick public relations outfit, however, which raises profile in the media, and eyebrows in other schools. Changed from Direct Grant school of 400+ boys to full-blown co-ed almost overnight in 1970 with loads of Japanese-based lolly.

Cosy stone, with bits and bobs all over the place. Atmosphere v difficult to pin down as school very large and fragmented. Co-ed activities of second year Sixth make eyes pop out of visiting children from single sex schools.

THE PUPILS Less spotty than many co-eds, but some on the wild side. Smart checked kilts for girls up to 'Seventh' form (ie Upper Sixth—Oakham has rudimentary language of its own). Pupils come from East Anglia and 'up and down the A1'. 25% of boarders are foreign or ex pat. Pupils from a hodge podge of backgrounds, a fair number from London. Famous Old Boys: Thomas Merton the Trappist monk plus Matthew Manning the faith healer.

Entrance At 10 (though this is not publicized), 11, 13 and to Sixth Form. School sets its own exam for pupils from state sector; CE for the others—50ish pass mark but 'other factors are always taken into account'.

Exit 80% to higher education, many to red bricks and polys, roughly 20 to Oxbridge a year.

Bottom Line £400,000 per year in scholarships and bursaries.

Remarks Large co-ed establishment. All things to all men. 'I wouldn't contemplate sending a child here,' said a prep school Head, 'who was not very highly motivated'.

OBAN HIGH SCHOOL
Soroba Road, Argyll PA 34 4JB
TEL Oban (0631) 64231

Pupils: 1,025 boys and girls • Mainly day, but boarding hostel available • Ages: 11-18 • Size of Sixth Form: 60 • Non-denom • State.

HEAD Rector, since 1990, Mr B R Mitchell BSc Edinburgh (forties), formerly Deputy and Assistant Rector in this school. Takes over from Mr Twatt, who was Rector for 18 years.

Remarks Very large catchment area with 26 associated primary schools covering North Argyll and Islands. Pupils from distant mainland and islands board in the school hostel, which has four care staff on evening duty and academic staff on hand to help with

studies. Eight-class intake, staff of about 80—very good staff/pupil ratio. Staff is a 'good blend of youth and experience'.

Good arts department, Gaelic available, brilliant computing, secretarial course. Extra curricular activities which fell away during the teachers' strike have recovered somewhat. Pastoral care from eight guidance teachers to deal with pupils' problems. School is in a nuclear-free zone.

THE ORATORY SCHOOL
Woodcote near Reading, Berkshire RG8 0PJ
TEL Checkendon (0491) 680207

Pupils: 415 boys • 330 board, 85 day • Ages: 11-18 • Size of Sixth Form: 127 • RC • Fee-paying.

HEAD Since January 1989, Mr Maurice Lynn MA Oxon (forties); bachelor, Modern Linguist, previously Head of French at Westminster, before that taught at Radley and the Oratory.

Academic Matters Generally good for 'middle of the road academics'. A-level pass rate 1989, 96% and 1990, 98%, reflecting this school's rising academic stature. Flexible curriculum means almost any subjects can be linked; boys have their own individual prep times peppered throughout the day—'an impetus for boys to be self-organizing' comments one parent. French, Spanish, German, Italian, Portuguese, Latin and Greek available to A-level.

Games, Options, the Arts Superb cricket pitch giving view right across Berkshire, 14 tennis courts, good indoor swimming pool, squash courts, gymnasium. Shooting, rowing and sailing at nearby Goring and Theale. New sports complex with first Real Tennis court to be built in the UK for 80 years. Rowing now a major sport. Former gym/theatre now refurbished exclusively for drama. Music as vibrant as ever. Young instrumentalists in demand for orchestral work at nearby Oxford. Design and Technology rapidly expanding. Admired Head of Music and wife. School boasts a 'Palm Court' type orchestral group playing Twenties' music. Evenings used for sports coaching, music, rehearsals, societies.

Background and Atmosphere Originally founded in Birmingham in 1859 by the nineteenth-century Catholic educationalist (and putative Saint) Cardinal Newman, to prepare Catholic boys for university, it is now situated on a remote spur of the Chiltern Hills. The main house is stone-faced in imposing Georgian style and the cluster of new buildings around it, in which boys live in five houses under the care of Catholic lay (mostly married) Housemasters, are politely described as functional. Regular retreats and daily Mass for those who want it—'religion is not too obvious, but it is taken seriously', says one parent. Smoking now banned but boys of 18+ still allowed to visit local inns. School recently acquired property near Bayeux for linguistic and other educational trips.

THE PUPILS Mostly from either nearby or from London, though a few overseas, including some from Ireland, by and large from the Catholic middle classes, popular with parents of mixed marriages suspicious of 'monkey business', to quote one. NB 20% of pupils are non Catholics. OBs include Hilaire Belloc, Lennox Berkeley, Michael Berkeley. Gerard Manley Hopkins taught here.

Entrance Presents no particular problem; regular intake from own prep school.

Exit Claims to produce 'more top grades at A-level than any of the other Catholic public schools'. Two-thirds normally proceed to university, around 10 to Oxbridge.

Bottom Line Major scholarships at £2,955pa; others between £2,955—£1,476pa and exhibitions and awards in Mathematics and Modern Languages.

Remarks One of the few RC public schools run by lay staff. Smallish, solid, average establishment producing responsible citizens reportedly 'well balanced and good mixers', though it is doubtful it could set the nearby Thames on fire.

OUNDLE SCHOOL
Oundle, Peterborough PE8 4EN
TEL Oundle (0832) 273536

Pupils: Approx 720 boys, 43 girls (more coming) • *All board* • *Ages: 13-18 (but see Laxton School below)* • *Size of Sixth Form: Approx 300* • *C of E* • *Fee-paying.*

HEAD Since 1984, Mr D B McMurray MA Cantab (early fifties), formerly Head of Loretto (and he was a pupil there too) and before that taught at Fettes. Very tall. Comments that if Oundle produces a 'type' then he will have failed. Keen on scuba diving. Good reports from round about on his progress. Jolly Australian wife. Comments on school's recent move to co-education, 'to try to inculcate sensible attitudes to and expectations of the opposite sex, while keeping those sexes separate, is like teaching people to swim without allowing them to get wet'.

Academic Matters School has been famous for Sciences for decades and they are still infinitely more popular than Arts at time of writing. History Department still strong. Languages Department small, but getting good results. School pioneered CDT and the idea of learning through doing at the turn of the century. Boys all take four days out of each term's lessons—the 'block release system'—to disappear into the school's magnificent workshops and construct something—atmosphere here more like a factory than a school, with foundry (worth cultivating an Oundle boy to run up that wrought iron garden chair you want matching). 11 full-time female academic staff, plus two to three part-timers at time of writing.

Games, Options, the Arts 50-yard swimming pool kept constantly in the 80s. Three climbing walls, new sports centre, running track, two rifle ranges, grounds stretching as far as eye can see. The rugger coach, ex-Lions captain Terry Cobner, brought Oundle to the top position in 1989/1990 season. Good rowing tradition. Other games results very creditable, though a master commented that they would never come first in swimming as they do not have the Olympic squads of some schools—the idea being all-round excellence rather than specialization. Average Oundelian considered a 'pretty competitive animal', however.

First years exposed to all manner of options—known as FYTU (pronounced Fight You)—First Year

Training Unit. Pupils 'can't escape Oundle without some music' as it is compulsory for first year. School's 'Big Band' toured Europe in 1990. School bought local church in main street and turned it into the Rudolph Stahle Theatre, which puts on both professional and school productions—good way of getting some of pro expertise to rub off on boys. Massive Frobenius organ in school chapel—pause here a while and look at the John Piper windows and sad monuments to boys fallen in war. New Information Technology room and the installation of more computers in the Technology centre in the race for schools' technical supremacy.

Background and Atmosphere One of largest boys' boarding schools in the country. Ancient and interesting foundation. Founded by local lad, Sir Wm Laxton, who made good in the City, became eight times Master of the Worshipful Company of Grocers, and Lord Mayor of London, left provision in his will to endow his local grammar school, which was already in existence in 1485. Beautiful mellow buildings—see Pevsner— scattered all through the town of Oundle, with boys scurrying to and fro like university students: furthest boarding house a good 10 minutes hike to central quad. Wonderful avenue of trees, games fields stretching as far as eye can see. Massively built boarding houses (seven-man dorms mostly) 'which,' said a shocked mum 'look like something out of Florence Nightingale'. Girls' house however looks like an American Hilton—designed more with conferences in mind than girl boarders (architects Berry Bros & Rogen Hanson). One house, The Berrystead, for 11-13 year olds. Girls wear rather smart pin-stripe culottes.

Laxton School School divided into two in 1876— Laxton Grammar School for inhabitants of town who did not want classical studies; Oundle for sons of gents who did. Today two schools co-exist with separate Heads (Laxton Head: Bob Briggs) and activities, but do academic studies together. Laxton School is day school with approx 130 boys, plus girls in Sixth Form. Laxton Junior School started in 1973.

Discipline 'Pupils need to have clear cut boundaries' says the Head, 'but push those boundaries out as far as they dare'. Drugs: the 'instant out'. Drink: 'a can of beer is a different matter from being blotto'. For alcoholic offenders it's the 'one two three out system', ie 1) gated 2) rusticated 3) expelled. School has a few lively offenders.
  Not without problems.

THE PUPILS Large percentage—20-25—of sons of Old Boys—many Oundle families with father, uncles, cousins etc all here. 10% from overseas, approx 25 with non-British passports, including sons of Malaysian PMs and ambassador of Pakistan to Court of St James. Boys polite, but with air of some strain about it as though they had not been polite for long. Lots of stripey shirts. OBs: Arthur Marshall, Peter Scott, Cecil Lewis, A Alvarez, John Michael Lyons of Jaguar, Godfrey Messerry of Lucas etc.

Entrance 11+ or CE at 13. Assessment day for borderline cases—Head comments he would like to see 140 boys sit for 140 places—not have people sitting who will not get in. IQ wide fluctuations, but a 'switched on' IQ of 110 would probably get in, depending on demand: some would-be pupils sitting on the back burner reserve list have, as we write, just been taken off it and offered places.

Exit Gets a fair number into Oxbridge. Approx 75-80% go on to degree courses. Boys thereafter go on to be captains of industry, yuppies and engineers.

Bottom Line Rich, well-endowed—the grocer connection. Many scholarships including academic, art, music and Sixth Form, also 'continuation scholarships'—awards given to boys still at preparatory school who will then continue, with their awards, to Oundle—sort of cradle snatching.

Remarks Firing on all cyclinders and well spoken of by prep school Heads. However, girls still at guinea pig stage—school is still very much a boys' school, with a few girls in it.

OXENFOORD CASTLE SCHOOL
Pathean, Midlothian, Scotland EH37 5UD
TEL Ford (0875) 320 241

Pupils: 81 girls • 72 board, 9 day • Ages: 9-18 • Size of Sixth Form: 8 • Non-denom • Fee-paying.

HEAD Since 1979, Miss Mary Carmichael B Mus ARM (forties). Aims to 'make the most of every girl'.

Remarks Popular, a gentle school, the only girls' boarding school in Scotland for those who need cherishing rather than kicking on. A good fall-back for posh Scots. Ancestral pile. Probably the best needlework of any girls' school in Scotland.

OXFORD HIGH SCHOOL FOR GIRLS
Bellbroughton Road, Oxford OX2 6XA
TEL Oxford (0865) 59888

Pupils: 550 girls • All day • Ages: 11-18 • Also 90 girls in Lower School, ages 9-11 • Size of Sixth Form: 150 • Non-denom • Fee-paying.

HEAD Since 1981, Mrs J Townsend MA Oxon, MSc in Maths, educated at Wigan High and Hawarden Grammar School, and previously Head of Maths at St Helen's in Abingdon. Mrs T claims to have 'chalk in the blood'. Husband teaches in Shrivenham. Since her arrival she has transformed the pastoral side, employing former tutors, and made things 'better for the less clever'. Not 'the hothouse the myth has it'. Hopes that girls will 'have something to offer' and 'that they shall go out with confidence and own individual strengths developed'. Not universally popular.

Academic Matters Strongly academic—the Oxford environment. 'The brains are hanging off the wall', said a visiting parent. Streaming in Maths, Languages (French, German, Russian, Spanish, Latin, Greek). Compulsory to take two English, a Language, Maths, and two Science GCSEs. Brilliant teaching ('don't single out any one Head of Dept; unfair on the others'). Girls taking GCSE 'in their stride', though there are problems 'with over-articulate parents'. Computers everywhere and in subject rooms.

Games, Options, the Arts Games up to Upper Fifth; music magical, very strong drama; lively art (murals everywhere—even on the ceiling). Very stimulating. Trad games, sports hall, swimming pool, rowing, weight training, trampolining etc.

Background and Atmosphere Pretty grizzly boxes surrounded by garden, filled with herbs and games pitches. Ecumenical and sparkly assemblies and outlook on life, combined with laid-back underlying discipline. Girls required to do regular self-assessment.

School uniform includes navy cord trousers.

THE PUPILS 50% from Oxford, masses of dons' daughers, local schools pride themselves on the number of girls who get places here. Pupils have been known to come from as far as Reading.

Entrance Queues of keen local applicants. Apply one year before the September term of entry. Written exam on Maths, English and verbal reasoning, backed up by interview when encouraged to bring examples of hobbies or art. Sixth Form entry on good GCSE results plus previous Head's report (20 annually).

Exit Eight to 16 may leave after GCSE, otherwise approx one-third annually to Oxbridge, a half to other degree courses. Old Girls include Miriam Margoyles, Josephine Barnes, and Maggie Smith.

Bottom Line Good value. 20 Assisted Places at 11+, and five for girls in the Sixth Form. Bursaries for brains, music, scholarships.

Remarks A challenging, demanding and exciting school which offers consistently good results—and so it should, given the intake. Number one academic choice for Oxford and roundabout.

PANGBOURNE COLLEGE
Pangbourne, Reading RG8 8LA
TEL Pangbourne (0734) 842101

Pupils: 390 boys • 320 board, 70 day • Ages: 13-18 • Size of Sixth Form: 130 • C of E • Fee-paying.

HEAD Since September 1988, Mr Anthony Hudson MA, Dip Ed educated at Tonbridge, Grenoble University and Lincoln College, Oxford. Institute of Education (London University) for Dip Ed. Previously Sub-Warden at Radley.

Remarks Originally set up in 1917 as the nautical college for boys going on to Merchant or Royal Navy. Reputation for strict discipline is exaggerated, but underpins tough outward-boundish type activities the school is so good at; remnants of naval traditions linger on in dress eg epaulettes on sweaters, brass-buttoned jackets, and language eg Mess Hall = dining room; cabins = studies. Strong (voluntary) CCF, including (oversubscribed) Marines detachment; weekly parade and marchpast—led by the military band and guard—very popular.

Strong sports (matches played against far larger schools), notably water sports—always at forefront at Henley, boys have represented Britain in junior teams rowing and water-skiing. Well equipped and good facilities throughout; surprisingly sensitive art, music and drama. Film studies are on the curriculum, school has its own film unit, and has produced several award winning films. Two part time teachers for 'additional English'. Generally stimulating atmosphere for boys who fare best in smallish school. Suits the active. 'Be a doer' is the unwritten motto. 'Very handy', said a parent 'for dropping children off on your way to the station en route for the City.'

Seventeen new younger staff have been appointed over the last two years, out of a total of 38. National Curriculum has started at lower end of school. CDT has started—centre to open in 1991.

THE PERSE SCHOOL FOR GIRLS

Union Road, Cambridge CB2 1HF
TEL Cambridge (0223) 359589

Pupils: Approx 550 girls • All day • Ages: 11-18 • Junior School: Approx 160 girls, ages 7-11 • Size of Sixth Form: approx 140 • Non-denom • Fee-paying.

HEAD Since June 1989, Miss H S Smith MA Oxon (forties), educated at King Edward's Birmingham and St Hilda's Oxford where she read Mathematics. Appointed from within—she was previously Head of the Mathematics Department. Miss Smith comments that she aims to 'carry on running a school that remains successful' and she would like pupils to be 'ready for Europe, to do more with the Perse and even more music'.

Academic Matters One of the country's stronger Languages Departments— all pupils do a second language and Russian, Classics and Italian are on offer, as well as French, German and Spanish. The school has set up a highly popular exchange visit with Russia. Maths and Chemistry also currently strong. Non-academic

subjects the poor relation here. Wonderful, much-prized Head of Computer Studies, Mrs Handcock is so enthusiastic (*everything* in the school is being produced on computer or with the aid of one), that it has been known for her to be accidentally locked in the building at night. New art and CDT facilities, excellent dark-room. Wonderful electronics room replacing one destroyed by fire.

Staff in general of high calibre—thanks to presence of the university and other educational establishments in the city. Excellent overall. Some dyslexia dealt with on an individual basis.

Games, Options, the Arts Not a school that goes overboard on games, however the Head points out that they have currently got 10 hockey players in county squads—can't call that nothing. Keen swimming—in The Leys swimming pool and elsewhere—also cross country. Divided into houses for games and some games compulsory. Playing fields a brisk 10-minute walk down the road. Short on exciting extras—this, as Head points out, is basically an academic school

Background and Atmosphere Cosy, rather sedate institution with carpets, polish, wallpaper and good pictures on the wall. Buildings themselves 'are rather cramped,' says Head 'but by no means awful' (we said they were awful in the last edition—with some parts deeply reminiscent of the worst of St Trinian's, which is said to have been modelled on the Perse). School started in a private house near the Perse School for Boys in 1881 and spilled over to the next etc. Looks like students' digs, overlooked by the university chemistry lab. Still short of space, but the new five-floor building (drama, CDT etc) has done much to help.

Discipline Each child has a form teacher and a head of year. Head comments that they don't have much problem with discipline 'though we are introducing detention for next term'.

THE PUPILS Dons' daughters and distinguished academic names litter the school list. Also a 'number of farmers' daughters and people on bursaries you wouldn't otherwise expect' said a girl. Solid middle class academe. Old Girls: Lady Wootton is considered a particularly good example—'high powered, sceptical, detached, non-conformist'; also Jean Rhys, Philippa Pearce.

Entrance Registration any time before the December of the year before pupil is to come. Examination followed by interview—all on the same day - 'we have to be sure a child can cope academically'.

Exit Continuing fine record of getting pupils on to

next rung of academic ladder. Many opt for 'gap' before university. Rare to find pupil headed for secretarial college.

Bottom Line   A number of bursaries for pupils whose parents are in financial need. Large number of Assisted Places—most at 11+, also at Sixth Form (and some up Head's sleeve in case of need).

Remarks   Straight academic city day school. Perhaps a bit lacking in bounce and imagination in some areas, but NB, the Head comments that she still isn't sure she would recognise the school from our description.

PIMLICO SCHOOL

Lupus Street, London SW1V 3AT

TEL London (071) 828 0881

Pupils: 1,100 pupils in all, slightly more boys than girls • All day • Ages: 11-18 • Size of Sixth Form: 180 • Non-denom • State.

HEAD   Since September 1991, Miss Kathleen Wood BA (forties). Takes over from the remarkable Miss Gittins.

Academic Matters   Sixth Form consortium with Grey Coats and Westminster City School bumps up numbers to 500 and means the school can offer a much wider range of subjects than it could on its own. Excellent 1989 A-level results—40% As and Bs (though NB of 44 candidates, only 99 subjects were taken), 25% As/Bs for 1990, GCSE less impressive. Pupils taking all manner of exotic subjects at GCSE, eg Turkish, also Swedish and Portuguese (but no Greek). Sciences relatively weak (integrated Science at GCSE).

Games, Options, the Arts   School admits 15 promising young musicians each year to follow Pimlico Musicians' Course and music is very enthusiastic—rooms bursting with pupils plugged into Roland synthesizers. Art excellent, even outstanding and imaginative use of textiles. Everybody participates in PE (mixed sessions, 'except when they don't want to')—hall used non stop, also more room than appears at first glance in the grounds surrounding the school, including games pitch. Computers popular and two sessions a week are for girls only, as boys tend to hog

the machines otherwise. The school magazine *Pimlico Matters* won the *Daily Telegraph* national school newspaper competition for the second year running in 1990.

Background and Atmosphere   Dynamic, and consequently appealing to children, though makes mothers a bit nervous. Award-winning building arouses strong feelings, pro or anti. Feels like a Channel ferry, with staircases in the middle and 'bridges' at intervals. Rooms all have glass walls which makes for easy patrolling. Light airy and very badly in need of redecorating. Large windows with lots of space for pot plants. School opened as a comprehensive school in its present building in 1970, to great excitement and high hopes from educationalists—alas to be dashed in the first instance.

Entrance   'We are not a neighbourhood school, but a London one.' From over 70 primary schools, just over 40% from Westminster. Input from 'all points of the compass'. The criterion is distance, not residence in Westminster.

Exit   Large percentage leave after GCSE; replaced by Sixth Form intake who then scatter to universities and polys all over the country, plus some to art foundation courses and a number to 'gap'.

THE PUPILS   Ability banding no longer applies. Mixture of working class, impoverished middle class, and some non-nationals. Very lively indeed, and still some complaints from local residents about bad behaviour in the streets.

Bottom Line   Pimlico now manages its own budget of nearly £2 million, and the governing body has set up four sub-committees covering staffing (the big one), the curriculum, premises and finance. Already the school is feeling the benefit of not being centrally run.

Remarks   A dynamic and exciting inner city school, which has been getting better and better under outgoing Head.

PUTNEY HIGH SCHOOL
35 Putney Hill, London SW15 6BHs
TEL London (081) 788 4886

Pupils: 600 girls • All day • Ages: 11-18 • Size of Sixth Form: 145 • Also 225 girls in Lower School, ages 5-11 • Non-denom • Fee paying .

HEAD From September 1991, Mrs Merchant, previously Deputy Head of Latymer Upper School.

Academic Matters More all round than most of GPDST schools, and also less formal. Nineteen subjects offered at A-level, including History of Art, Economics and Italian (also at GCSE) and A-level. Nine basic subjects at GCSE plus Greek, German, Computer Studies, DT and Classical Civilisation options.

Games, Options, the Arts School has its own boat and girls row from Thames Boat Club and take part in regattas, but otherwise sport not high profile. Drama is good, also music, and girls collaborate with Tiffin Boys', King's College Wimbledon and Emanuel for concerts, plays and via the Christian Union. Good art results recently.

Background and Atmosphere Secretive, purple-clad profile. Suburban feel. Hidden cluster of basically two large Victorian houses surrounded by pleasant gardens with tennis and netball courts etc. As elsewhere, GPDST has been putting money into new buildings, and fresh lick of paint.

THE PUPILS A school for Putney locals and those from surrounding areas of Richmond, Twickenham, Fulham. Parents from professions, plus lots of media parents, 50% via junior school, a fair number from state schools. Amanda Waring is an OG.

Entrance By exam and interview and competitive.

Exit Significant number do 'gap' year. Secretarial college, art schools, polys and universities.

Bottom Line Generous Assisted Places, bursaries and half fees open scholarship at 11, as well as a half fees music scholarship. Assisted Places and a small number of scholarships and bursaries are also offered to Sixth Form entrants.

Remarks Girls' day school much sought after in the early Eighties, now more run of the mill.

QUEEN ANNE'S SCHOOL
Caversham, Reading, Berkshire RG4 0DX
TEL Reading (0734) 471582

Pupils: 400 girls • Approx 300 board (including a few weekly boarders), 100 day • Ages: 11-18 • Size of Sixth Form: 100 • C of E • Fee-paying.

HEAD Since 1977, Miss Audrey M Scott BA (fifties), state educated and previously Head of Limuru Girls' School, outside Nairobi (for ex pats etc) and Westwood House School, Peterborough. Teaches 'top and bottom' Divinity and Life (called Way of Life for Upper Sixth). A terribly nice Head, realistic, 'not a pusher', popular with staff and girls, great fun and a good communicator; very keen on 'what's best for the girls', thinks it 'important that a child wants to come to boarding school' and that pupils 'are happy with what they are doing' (particularly after they leave). Commenting on educational choice 'There is a hierarchy in Heaven, so what are we doing down here, trying to destroy it?' Not madly keen on exams, no exams in December for anyone and 'I can't see why we shouldn't do away with them altogether for the Junior School.' Everyone is addressed either as 'my dear' or 'ladies'.

Academic Matters Standard setting as per GCSE requirements for English, Maths, French, German and Spanish. Brilliant new language lab, Classics and Greek on demand. Keen Science and lots of engineers. CDT, not, as yet, computer linked, but that's in the pipe line, as is computer linkage throughout Geography etc. 96% get A/Cs in nine-plus subjects at GCSE ('too easy isn't it?'). Mild dyslexia catered for ('IQ must be over 125'). Four libraries, including one super new octagonal double decker showpiece; the old library is now a lecture hall.

Games, Options, the Arts Schools Lacrosse Champion for five of the last seven years—silver everywhere and serious tennis coaching (with ball thrower) even in early January in the frost. All-weather tennis courts. Fabulous new swimming pool with underwater lighting and music. Music on the up, regular tours round southern cathedrals and trips abroad including Hungary last year. 'Concerts now more enjoyable for adults' was Miss Scott's saying of the year. Drama good, lots of external activities, particularly at weekends—skating, dry skiing, sailing. Strong art department, good 3D textiles, home sciences, and with girls making ball gowns and the like. Good careers advice.

Background and Atmosphere Umbilically linked to Westminster, and immensely well-funded, QA is the country arm of the original Grey Coat Hospital (now in the state sector), although currently they only join up for conferences and the occasional drama workshop. First year pupils from Grey Coats spend a week each summer at Queen Anne's. Purpose built in 1894 (centenary celebrations in hand) the charming red brick complex sprawls round two sides of the 40 acre grounds less than five minutes from the centre of Reading. Massive games fields. Girls flow happily in long red cloaks throughout the campus, and graduate from 30 in the baby house to houses of 40/50.

Sixth Formers have own house and wear mufti (not jeans for lessons), give dinner parties and stay out later than rest of school. Boys welcome for tea in house, and girls all have own rooms (head girls have either private shower or bath). Visits to Reading allowed on basis of responsibility via 'The List', but only Sixth Formers can go there on Saturday afternoons ('the whole place changes'). School does an enormous amount of charity work and were knitting natty tank tops for Rumania when we visited. Hot on caring, particularly with anorexics, and those whose fathers were in the Gulf. Whole school attends chapel every morning.

THE PUPILS From within 50-mile radius. Home Counties. Delightful, bubbly, outgoing, mainly 'the unmentionable middle class, good solid citizens whosed values are straight'. 40/50 non Brits, (stiff English exam), and similar number of ex pats. Famous Old Girls: cartoonist Posy Simmonds, Jenny Seagrove.

Entrance Mainly 11+, rest 12 or 13+, CE and interview. Pupils come from local schools, and prep schools such as Godstowe, Maltman's Green etc. Six scholarships, but under review. Six or seven places usually available at Sixth Form level.

Exit Small leakage post-GCSE but not many to boys' schools. 95% go to university or polys, 13 to Oxbridge 1990.

Remarks Traditional girls' boarding school which is moving with the times. Steady on the academic and sporting fronts. Going well.

QUEEN ETHELBURGA'S SCHOOL
Harrogate, North Yorkshire, HD3 2SG.
TEL: Harrogate (0423) 64125

Pupils: 195 girls • 110 board, 85 day • Ages: 4-18 • Size of Sixth Form 30 • C of E • Fee-paying.

HEAD Since 1988, Mrs J M Town BA Oxon (fifties). Previously Deputy Head; teaches Maths, took over from Mrs James, now Headmistress at St Leonard's. Likes to see 'children with confidence in themselves'.

Remarks School was founded in 1912, purpose-built in congolomerate of red-brick buildings linked by open cloisters, situation on edge of Harrogate (can be chilly)—Lord Mountgarret, whose grandfather donated land, still plays a paternalistic role. Three boarding houses of mixed ages, 50 in each, girls sleep in dormitories divided into cubicles. Smashing Sixth Form house with study bedrooms. Strong on Art and Design, leading into Technology, good in music (ensembles not orchestras) and French, German, Latin. Excellent sports facilities. Computers essential. Girls learn typing and Information Technology in Sixth Form (as many come as leave). GCSE Fifth Form followed by AS and A-levels. Lots of locals. 13 scholarships. At one time the best private northern school for girls. Numbers slightly down, probably owing to demographic trend, and exodus to boys' boarding schools.

QUEEN MARGARET'S SCHOOL
Escrick Park, York YO4 6EU
TEL Escrick (090487) 261

Pupils: 360 girls ● *325 board, 35 day* ● *Ages: 11-18* ● *Size of Sixth Form: 90* ● *C of E* ● *Fee-paying.*

HEAD Since 1983, Mr Colin McGarrigle MA (forties), educated at Radley and Trinity College, Dublin. Previously Headmaster at Bramcote—and in a sense runs this along prep school lines. Lateral thinking, dynamic, terrifically enthusiastic (politics, music, sport are his hobbyhorses): 'You love him or loathe him', say parents frankly. Delightful wife, Morag, with a keen eye for detail and her finger on the pulse. She runs (among many other things) school shop, selling wrapping paper, tuck, make up—'I get the vibes daily.'

Academic Matters Good all round, English and Arts strong. Overall results are not especially impressive—there are good years and bad years, and last year (1990) seven girls went to Oxbridge, normally it is one. French is very well taught (Head of Department positively dislikes language lab system). 75% on average stay till Sixth Form: Head likes movement at this stage, and is considering expanding here. Good one-year General Studies course for Lower Sixth (popular with in-coming Europeans) includes Business Studies, typing, modern History, modern English. Not pressurized, but work ethic is firmly established. Science labs needed. Sound teaching—'and girls are certainly taught how to study', commented a parent.

Games, Options, the Arts Very successful games teams (Head coaches hockey); new squash courts (and handsome young male coach); nine-hole golf course (built by Head and family); riding school next door, and some girls' ponies kept in situ. Very good art, new Design and Technology centre; cooking and dressmaking for all at some stage 'because girls must'. Gym doubles up as theatre hall and also, surprisingly, as chapel. Choral music is strong.

Background and Atmosphere Dramatic parental takeover from Woodard Foundation in 1986. The school was founded in Scarborough in 1901, moved to Escrick in 1949, fine John Carr Palladian house, set in 50 acres of parkland—a lovely setting. Victorian additions, and some very clever conversions and recent additions (including new teaching 'cloisters' block). Sixth Formers live in little cottages, some linked to main school buildings. Unusually uninstitutional—lots of chintz and oak panelling and silk flowers ('If you give girls an attractive environment they'll look after it, and it gives you ammunition when you tell them to take their feet off the sofa,' says Mrs McGarrigle.) Circular dining hall, previously indoor lunging school, has hopeless acoustics, self-service to detriment of girls' manners, parents note. Library housed in wonderful panelled room (concerts held here), with huge windows, sofas, log fires and new full-time librarian. School diaries kept very full. Lots going on at week ends.

THE PUPILS Increasingly broad catchment area—Scotland, Peterborough, the south, locals, some foreigners, popular with farmers. Girls are assured and friendly and unspoilt. NB They move horizontally in year groups—Head thinks it highly unsuitable for 12-year olds to tune into 15-year olds' boyfriend talk—'This means girls have a chance to grow up less quickly than at some schools.'

Entrance By CE at 11+, 12+ and 13+, and at Sixth Form.

Exit Wide variety—A-levellers mostly to higher education (nursing colleges, poly or university); others to secretarial, technical, domestic science colleges.

Bottom Line Scholarship at 11, 12 and 13, also Sixth Form; music scholarship at 11. Limited bursaries.

Remarks An interesting and lively school, with deservedly high morale and a lot going on—and no clones.

QUEEN MARY'S SCHOOL
Baldersby Park, Topcliffe, nr Thirsk, North Yorkshire YO7 3BZ
TEL Thirsk (0845) 577425

Pupils: 225 girls ● *145 board (40 board weekly), 80 day* ● *Ages: 7-16* ● *C of E* ● *Fee-paying.*

HEAD Since 1978, Mr Peter Belward (fifties), educated Coleshill Grammar; and Mrs Mary Felicity

Belward, Cert Ed, educated at St Elphin's, Derbyshire. He teaches Maths, and she Art and Primary.

Remarks Small, friendly school with no Sixth Form: all but a handful (who go on to do other things) take A-levels elsewhere, 99% at boys' schools, eg Oundle, Uppingham, Lancing, also Gordonstoun. A nucleus leave at 11 to go to Tudor Hall, St Mary's Calne. Mixed ability intake: school says IQs vary from '140 down to the seventies', and this should be taken into account when looking at the results. Streaming and setting. Good German and French; weakness has been Physics and Maths, but new Physics teacher just appointed. School has a good unit for 10 dyslexic children.

Does well at games; good art. Baldersby Park (BP to those in the know) is an imposing Palladian mansion which wows the fathers. Girls live in converted flats with posho bathrooms and good sized dormitories; super conversions of old farm buildings and out-houses. Pupils are primarily Yorkshire and Scottish from landed families. Lively, and enjoy a prank or two. A happy school, though as an educationalist commented, 'the problem with having no Sixth Form is that the youngest use the 15- to 16-year olds as their role models—and this gives the latter an inflated sense both of their own importance and their achievements at a damn silly age!'

A likely choice for Yorkshire landed families, though not a good idea for high fliers.

QUEEN'S COLLEGE
43-49 Harley Street, London W1N 2BT
TEL London (071) 580 1533

Pupils: 398 girls • All day except for 13 weekly boarders • Ages: 11-18 • Size of Sixth Form: 135 • C of E. • Fee-paying.

PRINCIPAL Since January 1991, Lady Goodhart MA Oxon (fifties), an impressive lady (daughter of the missionary Lord Hemingord) with finger in many pies, keenly political, on endless committees—currently she is, among other things, chairman of Youth Clubs UK, and of the London Marriage Guidance Council, a trustee for the Protection of Rural England; stood as

cadidate for SDP Liberal Alliance in General Election in 1983 and 1987 etc, etc. Husband is a QC. Three children, youngest came here. Lady Goodhart taught here herself (part time) and also at Westminster Tutors. Passionately believes in girls getting qualifications as well as university degrees, 'because it is very important to be able to mix marriage and bringing up children with a career'. Says it is vital to see university as a stepping stone, not the be-all and end-all, and stresses (re Oxbridge) that 'what you read matters far more than which university you go to—because if you're really interested in your subject then it leads heaven knows where'.

Academic Matters Strong Modern Languages department, Classics small but good. A-level computing just introduced (expensive on time), 'Girls with computing knowledge much sought after at university', according to Mr Hurtchinson, gem of a senior tutor (runs his own software company). Several new part-timers on staff (Head, not surprisingly, keen on them). Staff cheerfully admit they are now 'working more than twice as hard'. Science being licked into shape, refurbishing programme apparently to be completed by September 1991. Outstandingly good careers advice, department run by American Mrs Maclennan—staff often consult her for their own children, 'because she does a vastly superior job to any other school'.

Games, Options, the Arts Very strong fencing (Olympic fencer is head of Geography), Regent's Park not far away but *not* a gamesy school. Good Art; clubs, societies etc during lunch break and not at the end of the day to ease commuters' strain.

Background and Atmosphere Founded in 1848 by F D Maurice, Professor of History at King's College, as 'the first institution to provide a sound academic education and proper qualification for women'—all the best governesses clutched Associateships from here. Very un-institutional, battered and lived in and loved; no prizes, no competitions. But Lady Goodhart is 'not keen on sloppiness'—academic or social—and the message is getting through. Lovely library (proper mahogany furniture), teeny-weeny playground, elegant staircases and buildings go back as well as sideways, but this is not a school you choose for gleaming modern facilities. Good set-up (underused—there are places for 20) for weekly boarders at top end of the school. No uniform.

THE PUPILS A good cross-section—30% on some kind of bursaries, 20% on Assisted Places, also a few super rich and ethnic minority groups. Old Girls include Gertrude Bell, Harriet Cass of the BBC, Katherine Mansfield, Emma Freud not to mention Miss Buss and Miss Beale.

Entrance Competitive exam and interview, and some at Sixth Form (school expands slightly here).

Exit 80% to degree courses, eight-10 Oxbridge. Good track record of ex-pupils setting up on their own in due course.

Bottom Line Generous funds, divided according to need. Nearly 25% of pupils are on some sort of scholarship, bursary or Assisted Place.

Remarks Interesting place—you love it or loathe it, not for the very conventional. Now beginning to move with a firm sense of direction.

QUEEN'S GATE SCHOOL
133 Queen's Gate, London SW7 5LF
TEL London (071) 589 3587

Pupils: 307 girls • All day • Ages: 4-18 • Size of Sixth Form: 40 • Non-denom • Fee-paying.

HEAD (Principal) Since 1987, Mrs A M Holyoak, Cert Ed (who says, re age 'Oh I've been 23 for ages'). Elegant, efficient and energetic. Lavishes enthusiasm and concern on the whole school, from tops to teenies. Has good sense of humour. Believes 'very, very strongly that girls should be educated to the epitome of their potential'. Was previously Head of Queen's Gate Junior School.

Headmistress of Senior School: Miss Skone-Roberts, who has study near Mrs Holyoak's.

Academic Matters Not noted for these and does not produce table of results, but has outstanding French staff, including the great and bilingual Miss Singh, who in 1989 got an A grade in GCSE for every single one of her pupils—17 at the appointed time and seven early. Italian also good (nine out of 11 As GCSE 1989). History of Art excellent with Miss de Leeuw, an ex-pupil with bags of oomph. The problem with Science, says Mrs Holyoak, is getting pupils to opt for it—at the moment so few do, they get practically one to one teaching—and do well. Some teaching appears to lack energy.

Games, Options, the Arts Art excellent, lots of trips to study abroad. School draws continually on resources of nearby museums and art galleries (V & A, Natural History etc). Small gym in basement. Shares swimming pool with St Paul's, goes to Battersea Park for netball and lacrosse, but you don't feel the heart of the school is in this. Enthusiastic aerobics club at lunchtime.

Background and Atmosphere School housed in three enormous Victorian South Ken mansions. Quite well off for space inside; no playground—small patio for sitting out on and for the garden club (which wins prizes). Founded 1891. Civilized atmosphere, with children beavering in small groups. Black gloss painted dining room for seniors, with red curtains and antique dresser. Food good. Front of school currently being restored to look shiny new for centenary in 1991.

THE PUPILS London upper-middle class. Old Girls: the Redgraves, Sieffs, 'lots of Foreign Office wives, judging by the Old Girls' lists', and 'arty' people.

Entrance School unusual in London in that it does not do IQ tests at four-plus and has no plans to change this—'how do you know how they are going to turn out?'

Exit All in Sixth Form currently going on to further education, some after 'gap' year. Steady flow to art college (Wimbledon and Chelsea last year), two or three to London University.

Bottom Line One scholarship for a third of fees at eight-plus; two internal scholarships for Upper Sixth, to encourage able girls to stay on.

Remarks Excellent choice for parents who want something other than the inner London girls' school rat race. Well-run, friendly, cosy, and is achieving Mrs Holyoak's stated aim.

QUEENSWOOD

Shepherd's Way, Brookmans Park, Hatfield,
Hertfordshire AL9 6NS
TEL Potters Bar (0707) 52262

Pupils: 395 girls ● *Mainly boarding, but day girls accepted from September 1991* ● *Ages: 11-18* ● *Size of Sixth Form: 111* ● *C of E* ● *Fee-paying.*

HEAD   Since 1981, Mrs Audrey Butler MA (early fifties), educated Queenswood, and St Andrew's (where she read Geography and Political Economy). A spokeswoman—on all manner of educational committees. Also a sportswoman (hockey and tennis blue, county golfer). Wonderful woman. Forthright, firm, extremely approachable, humorous, popular on all fronts. Previously at Lancing, where she was the girls' (Sixth Formers') first Housemistress.

Academic Matters   Maths probably the strongest subject; setting in Maths, French and also English (all GCSE English results As and Bs), though Head mindful to avoid categories, so there is no one fast stream, 'What counts is confidence in the classroom.' Nonetheless, academically a competitive school where high expectations are fostered. Staff are *very* lively, and Head has taken much trouble to find people who can 'turn the key—though they're like gold dust'. Good computing (they run a staff training centre). All girls asked to bring Walkman for Modern Language work. Sixth Formers all have to study a Modern Language and Current Affairs/General Studies alongside their A and AS levels; weekly visiting lecturer on anything from genetic engineering to glasnost (followed by dinner with Head and speaker, girls by rota). Enormous library.

Games, Option, the Arts   16 all-weather outdoor tennis courts, also strong on hockey. Indoor swimming pool, huge sports hall. High powered drama, ditto music; musical tradition goes back a long way, Ernest Read was Head of Dept for many years, though music later went seriously downhill, but in recent years has gathered momentum; choirs especially strong and visited Moscow 1990. Good dance, nice art. Weekends full of practices on music, games, drama fronts. Duke of Edinburgh awards scheme; regular Art History trips to Continent; keen exploration society - Queenswood Raven Exploration Society has regular canoeing and caving expeditions; thriving Engineering Club. Seniors distinctly articulate, and heed Head's advice, 'Challenge everything, don't accept anything.' Girls raise between £5,000—£7,000 for charity each year.

Background and Atmosphere   Only just out of suburbia, set in 420 acres of farmland, woodland and sportsfields. Founded in Clapham in 1884, moved to these purpose-built neo-Tudor beamed blocks in 1925. Parts warren-like, parts, eg the academic facilities, are first class, with 22 new classrooms from 1991, including eight departmental suites filled with all the latest equipment, even satellite access. Sixth Form common room has the anonymity of an airport lounge. The school is functional throughout (unprepossessing huge plastic rubbish bags much in evidence). Sleeping quarters up in the eaves much the most successful, nick-named by girls the 'West End'. Purple, maroon and grey uniform. Purposeful, get-on-with-it atmosphere; disciplined and institutional.

THE PUPILS   Solidly middle class, with 25% from abroad, including 16% non-Brits (European, American, Chinese, African and Carribean). Popular with the forces. Very friendly, very career-minded.

Entrance   Via CE at 11, 12 and 13, and a few at Sixth Form: selective.

Exit   90% to university and polytechnics. Two to six to Oxbridge. Vocational courses discouraged in lieu of good degree. Noticeably increasing numbers go on into business and commerce, fewer into the professions.

Bottom Line   Two Sixth Form scholarships, three academic scholarships (for 11, 12 and 13 year olds); two music scholarships; two *tennis* scholarships please note; bursaries.

Remarks   Still solid and thorough, highly structured, active, busy producing good and bouncy citizens for tomorrow's world.

RADLEY COLLEGE

Abingdon, Oxfordshire OX14 2HR

TEL Abingdon (0235) 520294

Pupils: 600 boys • *All board* • *Ages: 13-18* • *Size of Sixth Form: 240* • *C of E* • *Fee-paying.*

HEAD The Warden, from September 1991, Mr Richard M Morgan JP, MA, educated at Sherborne and read law at Gonville and Caius College, Cambridge, takes over from Mr Dennis Silk, who is acknowledged as the outstanding public school Headmaster of his generation.

Mr Morgan was previously Head of Cheltenham College, which he succeeded in restoring to health—a Herculean task. After Cambridge, Mr Morgan went into the City, then left because he 'wanted to do something more worthwhile' and went to Radley, where he was a very successful Housemaster. From Radley he was appointed to Cheltenham (in 1978), left Cheltenham in 1990 to have a sabbatical year (gardening and things), before taking up his Radley appointment. Acknowledged by prep schools as an excellent Head, 'I prayed he would get Radley', said one, though cuts a more controversial figure among parents, as he is apparently extremely outspoken and has a sense of humour with it. Comments that he 'still believes that (too much) pocket money is the root of all evil', and that the 'greatest crime is underachieving'.

Academic Matters Definitely among top 10 most academic schools. A-level results consistently high, Sciences and Arts can be combined (neither predominates), Business Studies a popular choice. Classics strong, also English, History, Maths and Science.

Strong emphasis on learning to work, boosted by general attitude of structure and discipline. (Masters are called Dons, university style.) Reading positively encouraged, reading lists etc, outgoing Head very keen on grammar.

Games, Options, the Arts Strongly sporting, Wellington the oldest rivals, also Bradfield, Harrow, Sherborne. Rowing cups galore, rarely lose at hockey, school has its own nine-hole golf course and its own pack of beagles. Facilities much used by local community. Strong debating and wide variety of options, activities, societies on the whole well attended. CCF compulsory for a time. Boys are kept very busy, and staff are eagle-eyed. Sewell Centre, which houses Art and Design Technology, has been extended to accommodate more Engineering Design work, reflecting increasing response to industrial careers.

Background and Atmosphere Main block is the Mansion, red brick 1720, much of the rest Victorian Gothic, all set in 700 flat acres, with lake, the school surrounded by playing fields on all sides. Houses are called Socials, Housemasters are Tutors, prefects Pups.

A very hierarchical establishment: new boys (Stigs) given chores (including waking everyone up in the mornings, the least popular job: NB breakfast starts at 7am, last chance at 7.45). Staff lean heavily on Pups, whose status, responsibilities and privileges much sought after. Staff and their wives incredibly committed. Atmosphere is very definitely structured (probably one of the most structured of all boys' schools), and high-pressured throughout. Boys wear undergraduate-style gowns. Compulsory evensong daily. Some criticism from boys that school puts too much emphasis on competition.

Discipline Firmly under control under outgoing Head.

THE PUPILS Relaxed—despite the tight discipline—and civilized, keenly aware of their pecking order, traditionalists, self-confident and purposeful (NB thus irritating some non-Radleian peers). One or two leave, unable or unwilling to cope with the tight discipline. Plenty of the upwardly mobile. From far and wide. Sample Old Boys: Mark Carlisle, Lord Scarman, Christopher Hibbert, Ted Dexter.

Entrance Booked solid till 2002 ('and cocky with it,' said a disappointed parent) with waiting lists. Caldicott a closely linked prep school, boys from the Dragon, Winchester House, Cothill, Summerfields and many others. TV series on Radley (1979) *still* packs 'em in.

Exit All to further education, 75% university (about 25 each year to Oxbridge), polytechnics etc, followed by industry, the services, farming and all the traditional public school careers.

Bottom Line Up to 12 academic scholarships and exhibitions, plus three other (eg artistic, athletic). Five music scholarships, two art scholarships and several exhibitions.

Remarks Once at the bottom of the second division public schools league, now at the top of the first division. New Head chosen to carry on the good work.

RANNOCH SCHOOL

Rannoch, Perthshire PH17 2QQ

TEL Kinloch Rannoch (088 22) 332

Pupils: 235 boys, 60 girls ● *All but one or two board* ● *Ages: 13-18* ● *Size of Sixth Form: Approx 84* ● *Junior School of 45 boys and girls, ages 11-13* ● *Non-denom* ● *Fee-paying.*

HEAD   Since 1982, Mr Michael Barratt MA (forties). Educated Merchiston, St Andrews and Oxford (English). Previously Housemaster at Strathallan. Wife plays significant part in school affairs—Froebel trained, helps Home Economics and is the Round Square rep, liaising with parents. Barratt hopes to run 'a happy school, fulfilling pupils' potential'.

Academic Matters   Very small classes and occasionally gets spectacular exam results with even the most unpromising of its pupils. The school has a reputation for employing gifted if unorthodox teachers, most of whom also have some outdoor skills. Highly professional remedial teaching, including extra remedial staff for Maths and English, and scribes and dictating machines for exams. GCSE and SCE—Higher and/or A-levels taken depending on results. Leaning towards Science As, but also Geography, Geology and a couple of years ago even an O-level in Swahili. Computer studies, Metalwork, CDT to GCSE and Scottish O grade.

Games, Options, the Arts   Very muscular and gamesy: the kit list includes a rucksack as well as a winter-weight sleeping bag. Excellent sports hall, rugger, basketball, squash, hockey, athletics, water sports, skiing, six-hole golf course. Rannoch marathon now a regular event. Duke of Edinburgh Award plays prominent part in school activities—compulsory to bronze level, thereafter voluntary but considerable number achieve gold (300 since school's founding) and gold winners painted on panelling—not Oxbridge gongs. Recent major expedition to rainforests of Venezuela.

True to Kurt Hahn principles, strong emphasis on community service—fire fighting, mountain service, ambulance service, and loch patrol. Also the school has a building service (pupils actually put one brick on top of the next)—which helped with the beautiful chapel and art/music complex, and helping with the interior of the new service station. Mostly creative work but

before open days slave labour used for spit and polish. Many weekend expeditions. Orchestra and trips to theatre at Pitlochry. More boys than girls do Home Economics 'because we can eat it afterwards'.

Background and Atmosphere   Founded in 1959 by Mr A J S Greig and two colleagues from Gordonstoun. Beautiful Highland setting but *very* remote. Member of Round Square. Houses very scruffy and beautiful panelling marred by graffiti. Girls' boarding house is new. Staff room gives impression of outward bound course—plaid shirts, sturdy shoes and weather-beaten faces. Complaints of cold in winter and midges in summer. FP said 'I don't *mind* the snow on my bed except when it melts.'

THE PUPILS   Children of artisans to aristocracy but predominantly farming and business (hoteliers are one of their largest parental groups). Large proportion of pupils from Scotland. Many ex pats but also Europeans and Africans. Happy, well adjusted, self-confident but without arrogance. 80% first generation fee payers.

Entrance   By interview to Junior School. CE at 13 from every sort of prep school, and a steady trickle from the south. Very low IQ not admitted as 'they need special schools'. More girls than boys at Sixth Form entry this year.

Exit   Considerable career advice, ISCO. 10% leave at GCSE. Last year 23 out of 35 offered further education places. Some go back to family farm, bum for 'year out'. Have just got their first pupil—a girl—into Cambridge—to read veterinary medicine.

Bottom Line   Average termly bill at time of writing £2520—a bit of a bargain. Extras: dry cleaning, skiing, music, charge for books, beginning and end of term travel. Several academic awards of 50%, five Assisted Places per year.

Remarks   Still *the* Scottish public school for those of non-academic bent or those requiring some form of remedial teaching. Excellent at bringing out the best in the least academic. Relaxed, happy, energetic, tough—*not* a softies school. Going from strength to strength.

REPTON SCHOOL

The Hall, Repton, Derbyshire DE6 6FH
TEL Burton on Trent (0283) 702375

Pupils: Approx 500 boys, 61 girls in Sixth Form with girls' boarding house • 413 boys boarding • Ages 13-18 • Size of Sixth Form: 262 • Christian foundation, but other faiths welcome • Fee-paying.

HEAD Since April 1987, Mr Graham Jones MA (forties), educated Birkenhead and read Economics at Fitzwilliam, Cambridge. Came from being House-master of Daviesites at Charterhouse.

Academic Matters Appear to be slipping some-what, and not a startling collection of results recently—rather an alarming number of Ds and below in Maths and English in 1990, and only Classics achieved 100% A/Bs (eight candidates in all for this). Computers now integrated into the timetable. Progress monitored monthly in lower school.

Games, Options, the Arts Consistently outstand-ing tennis school—at time of writing five players in the school were ranked among the top 10 under-16 players in the country's national ranking list— and is the school recommended by the LTA to tennis-mad parents. Has two indoor tennis courts. Also good at cricket (school has produced more test cricketers than anywhere except Eton and Winchester, according to Head) and practises indoor cricket during the winter months. Good active music, also drama. Short on exotic extras. Some CCF compulsory. Boys will be found on games field every afternoon, girls at present more likely to be doing community service, or possibly CCF.

Background and Atmosphere Bloody Mary Foundation—school has long and interesting history and the medieval monastery is still very much part of the school. Overlooking the Trent, gas coolers in background, glorious pink stone, huge beams and, said a master, 'enormous charisma'. Founded 1557 by executors of one Sir John Port; has some hereditary governors. School has Sir John Tooley on the govern-ing board. Atmosphere pleasant, informal (no school uniform except ties), but purposeful. Mr Tim Scott's house, The Hall, claims to be biggest boys' boarding house in country—103 boys.

THE PUPILS Large numbers from the big indus-trial conurbations of Sheffield, Leeds, Bradford and Doncaster. Also sons of farmers, ex pats, bankers, mostly within two hours' drive of school. Pupils gentle and unspoilt. Old Boys: C B Fry, the Palairets, an Archbishop (Michael Ramsey), Roald Dahl (who made it sound ghastly), Harold Abrahams (of *Chariots of Fire*), Christopher Isherwood—and more. 54% of Reptonians are first generation public school; 15-20% Old Reptonians' sons. Approximately 20 'Medes and Persians' including 15 Hong Kong Chinese. PS The school has had two archbishop Headmasters.

Entrance Registration and CE. Demand for girls' places highish - competitive procedure, registrations up to January 1st for September of that year. School has its own prep school, Foremarke Hall. Feeds: Arnold Lodge, Yarlet Hall, Stafford, St Anselm's, Smallwood Manor, plus local choir schools.

Exit Most to Leeds, Birmingham, Loughborough and other midland/northern unversities, and to polys. Also 'gap', one or two to Oxbridge, and one or two to management courses. Go on into business, Church, the services, medicine.

Bottom Line Maximum of 40 Assisted Places in school at any one time, small reduction for sons of clergy; up to nine scholarships and nine exhibitions every year, biggest is 50% of fees, plus up to five music awards and awards for art 'if work of sufficient merit is offered'. Bursary fund for hard-up.

Remarks A pleasant place, though not currently setting the world alight. Going fully co-educational in 1992.

ROEDEAN SCHOOL

Brighton, East Sussex BN2 5RQ
TEL Brighton (0273) 603181

Pupils: 480 • All board • Ages: 11-18 • Size of Sixth Form: 150 • C of E, but other faiths also • Fee-paying.

HEAD Since 1984, Mrs Ann Longley MA (forties), educated Walthamstow Hall School and Edinburgh University, taught in Australia, also Head of Vivian Webb School, California. Widowed, with three chil-dren. Charming, impressive speaker, hot on PR, serves on committees, spends much time talking to potential parents. A very strong administrator, she has stream-lined school management (much-needed), American style. 'My aim here is to build up the confidence and self-esteem of the girls so they develop all round as a person, and can participate fully in life, enabling them to integrate having a career with having a family.' Some criticism from girls that Head dazzles parents, but does not know individual pupils nearly well enough.

Academic Matters   Exceptionally strong Sciences (long-standing tradition). Outstanding Head of Physics, Dr Bailin (Indian, and very glamorous), is responsible for encouraging girls to make electronic car, satellite dish, laser photography etc. Head con-siders eight or maximum nine GCSEs enough, advises quality not quantity (stressing As and Bs for univer-sity)—and to leave time for other activities. At A-level, one-third of pupils study Sciences, one-third Arts subjects, one-third mix Sciences with Arts (usually a language). Strong Modern Languages, small but thriv-ing Classics department (new Head of Department from Camden Girls). Several staff from Sussex University. Very flexible time-tabling.

Games, Options, the Arts   Wide and flourishing options; very active and successful Duke of Edinburgh Award Scheme participants (nine *gold* medals per year not unusual), enthusiastic Young Enterprise busi-nesses; good drama, also music—some pupils involved wih local youth orchestra. New CDT Centre, Art department includes fabric design. A keenly and successfully sporty school (the jolly hockey image dies hard, famous for smutty games song), enormous new and much used indoor sports hall. One of rare girls' cricketing schools, lots of lovely matches with local prep and boys' schools.

Background and Atmosphere   Bracing sea air blows up treeless cliffs to forbidding pebbledashed buildings (windows and roof severely damaged by hurricane of 1987), set in 118 acres, just east of Brighton. Built in 1885 by three sisters, the Misses Lawrence, modelled on a boys' public school. Work has started on major development plan. A new Medical Centre and Humanities Department have already been completed and in mid-1991 extending facilities for music, drama and dance to include a theatre. Also a new library/resource Centre. Flexible and informal within a traditional and structured setting. Sixth Formers are increasingly involved on school committees, Head considers it vital for them 'to learn leadership and committee skill.' Junior house (apart from the huge

main block) is very cosy. Other houses (in main block) somewhat scruffy and Sixth Form house has the usual semi-detached air of domesticity with clothes drying etc. Strongly international flavour apparent through-out the school—multi-racial, multi-national— 'Though we don't really make enough use of it', says Head, determined to do so. Good pastoral back-up. Something indefinably chilly in the atmosphere, not just the sea air.

THE PUPILS   Open, friendly girls, fairly unsophisticated, supportive of each other, 'the global environment breeds tolerance', observes a parent. One third live overseas, (FO, Services etc) 20% non-nationals (including girls from EEC countries, Can-ada, USA, Africa—dwindling numbers nowadays— Middle Eastern countries especially Jordan, Malaysia, Hong Kong, Japan, and from Roedean's sister school in Johannesburg). Old Girls include Lynda Chalker MP, Sally Oppenheimer, MP, Verity Lambert, Dame Cecily Saunders (founder of the Hospice Movement).

Entrance   CE or own exam. 'We're looking for girls with a *wide* range of interests.' NB Major intake at 13, lots from co-ed preps. Sixth Form entry increasing soon (house currently being enlarged), to cope with this: new capacity will be for 160 girls.

Exit   Six to 12 to Oxbridge; also London, Bristol, Durham, Edinburgh, St Andrews' the most popular universities; also medical schools, art and design, and drama college; a few to US universities. Rare for a pupil not to pursue further education.

Bottom Line   About four per cent of fee income goes towards scholarships, approx 35 scholars/exhibi-tioners in school at any one time, including music scholars, plus another 10 or so receiving bursaries. Small endowment fund to help parents on hard times.

Remarks   One of the country's most famous girls' public schools. Fairly low profile but in good working order.

ROSSALL SCHOOL
Fleetwood, Lancashire FY7 8JW
TEL Fleetwood (0253) 873849

Pupils: 336 boys, 144 girls • 385 board, 95 day • Ages: 11-18 • Prep school: 215 boys and girls (60% boys, 40% girls, half board, half day), ages 7-11 • Pre-prep: 120 boys and girls (50% boys, 50% girls) • Size of Sixth Form: 175 • C of E • Fee-paying.

HEAD Since 1987 Mr R D W Rhodes JP, BA Durham (fifties). Previously Head of Arnold School and educated at Rossall. Tall, down to earth Historian, much respected. Firm but fair. Two grown up daughters.

Academic Matters Reasonable results, bearing in mind comprehensive intake.

Games, Options, the Arts Still strongly gamesy and fairly tough—Rossall hockey on the beach hugely popular (for three days each fortnight, due to tides), fives, keen CCF (boys and girls); Home Economics fairly popular with boys. Rossall Award is the home-grown D of E equivalent, very popular and challenging, undertaken by everyone. Instilling of leadership much valued. Good on trips. Daily chapel.

Background and Atmosphere Bracing—school is set on the coast with unlovely Fleetwood and Clevelys nearby. Founded in 1844, grim collegiate red brick buildings, huge dining hall, dorms recently divided to smaller size (16), a popular move, 'and we've got our carpet squares'. Girls' house pleasantly refurbished. Boy Sixth Formers spread (with privacy) among younger pupils, without resentment, and Monitors have fairly heavy responsibilities. Everyone does chores: discipline fairly firm, though staff still do pub crawl, according to pupils: Sixth now have own Club.

THE PUPILS 20% ex pats, including 22 foreign nationals, otherwise mostly northerners. Decent, polite, neat. Pupils very supportive of each other. Rossall hockey regularly draws Old Rossallians. OBs include Sir Thomas Beecham and David Brown of Aston Martin fame—and several Headmasters.

Entrance Own exam—increasing numbers come in via school's own prep, and Head happily notes pre-

prep is bulging too. Girls' numbers vastly increased since last edition.

Exit 65-75% go on to degrees. Wide variety of careers, business much favoured.

Bottom Line Assisted Places, 15 scholarships and some bursaries.

Remarks All round traditional northern public school, that breeds strength and loyalty.

ROYAL GRAMMAR SCHOOL
High Wycombe, Buckinghamshire HP13 6QT
TEL High Wycombe (0494) 24955

Pupils: 1,115 boys • 45 board, 1,070 day • Ages: 12-18 • Size of Sixth Form: 370 • Voluntary controlled state grammar school.

HEAD Since 1975, Mr R P Brown MA Oxon, JP (fifties), Barrister-at-Law. Previously Head of King Edward VI, Nuneaton. Serious and thoughtful with a certain gravitas as befits his legal background.

Academic Matters School has the strongest record for sending pupils to Oxbridge in the state sector. Formidable academic results, with several pupils getting five A-levels, a lot with four, eg Physics, Maths, Further Maths and English—this is not the soft option. Amazing. GCSE record equally impressive. NB Buckinghamshire one of the few counties to retain grammar schools through thick and thin. Weaker on Arts than Sciences. 20 women teachers, and one of them has written a wonderful account of being one of the few females in the 1990 Wycombiensian.

Games, Options, the Arts Strong on games, though typically of state day schools, they do not devote very much time to it, high record of wins. In the last year, nine international representatives spread over five different sports. Soccer, sailing, fives, fencing, golf, shooting competitions etc. Huge sports hall. Good music. Successful chess.

Background and Atmosphere Established in the

reign of Edward VI, school was granted a Royal Charter by Queen Elizabeth in 1562. Main school on 22-acre site north of High Wycombe, built shortly before First World War and many later additions. New Library and resources centre. Head comments, 'The library should be at the heart of the school'. Overwhelmingly masculine environment, and solid with it.

THE PUPILS Sons of motivated professionals, some of whom have moved here specifically for the education. Well-mannered.

Entrance At 12. No exam; part of the Buckinghamshire transfer system—about 32% of children are given a place in their grammar schools, but IQ levels for the county are much higher than the average. 15-20 come from other schools at Sixth Form.

Exit Large numbers to Oxbridge; lots to Southampton, Birmingham, lots of medics, rarely to polys. Philosophy, economics and law, all popular.

Bottom Line Cost of boarding confined to food and accommodation; tuition fees paid by the local authority providing parent or guardian is resident or a rate-payer.

Remarks As strong as ever: the Manchester Grammar of the state sector.

the brightest 10% from a juicy catchment area— Kingston the nearest academic boys' school; many come in from own prep, lots from state sector. Science and Maths traditionally strongest subjects, and substantially more boys take Science rather than Arts subjects at A-level. 20 to Oxbridge annually (30 in a good year recently), Oxford or Cambridge certainly the main aim here. Head feels 'We're selling parents short if there isn't rigour', but whereas five years ago emphasis was exclusively on academic success this is no longer true: sporting side is developing (though grounds are two miles away) and this is Bob Willis' old school. Sailing Club is 'embarrassingly successful' and has load of cups, shooting is good. Nice little drama studio. School does well in public speaking competition. Car maintenance, ballroom dancing (local girls' school corralled in), bachelor cooking are popular activities. Parents of Fourth and Fifth Forms warned their nice son will soon turn into a monster. One expelled 1990 for drugs. School tries to give parents guidelines, keen on good citizenship.

School founded in 1509 in centre of the town in a delightful tall white building, now used by Sixth Formers. Main teaching block across the road is a faceless Sixties hulk, Science and Technology block currently being added here. Like other grammar schools, this one gives a good education—but it is not glamorous.

THE ROYAL GRAMMAR SCHOOL

High Street, Guildford, Surrey GU1 3BB
TEL Guildford (0483) 502424

Pupils: 800 boys • All day • Ages: 11-18 • Size of Sixth Form: 240 • C of E • Fee-paying.

HEAD Since 1977, Mr John Daniel, MA (fifties), educated Truro School and Oxford. Modern Linguist; a tall thoughtful soul, who came in originally as Deputy Head, and saw the school switch over from Voluntary Controlled to Independent.

Remarks Another extremely strong grammar school—Head notes school's results marginally below Westminster's as published on *FT* index (and miffed not to have been included on this list). Happily creams

ROYAL GRAMMAR SCHOOL

Eskadale Terrace, Newcastle upon Tyne NE2 4DX
TEL Tyneside (091) 281 5711

Pupils: 990 boys • All day • Ages: 11-18 • Size of Sixth Form: 306 • Junior School: 165 boys, ages 8-10 • Non-denom • Fee-paying.

HEAD Since 1972, Mr A S Cox MA (fifties), tall, thoughtful and fair-minded, constantly tinkering with the school, careful over details. Enormously keen on AS exams.

Academic Matters High on national academic

league table. *The* Tyneside Grammar School (400 years old), with outstanding academic record (including remarkable record of awards to Oxford and Cambridge). All boys take 10 GCSEs, 30% of A-level results at A grades is the norm here. Powerful Economics, very strong Science tradition, good on all practical matters. Geography Department is good, but French, according to some parents, could be better. Market leader on the AS front, with everyone doing some. Classes of 30, with 15 per Sixth Form group. Boys kept to rigorous programme.

Games, Options, the Arts National recognition on the sports front—boys often run for England. School chess team frequently reaches finals of *The Times* School Tournament, often up against Manchester Grammar, and finally beaten by St Paul's. Drama quite keen, with girls drafted in from Central High, over the road. Art ('Pathetic 20 years ago' according to the Head) is now much encouraged—and good. High-powered computing newly developed. Duke of Edinburgh and Young Enterprise both popular.

Background and Atmosphere Coherent set of handsome buildings, with playing fields at the back. Good functional and stylish new additions. Music room built when slice of land removed for building of motorway. Fine old school hall with pews, organ and honour boards. Lively noticeboards. £1 million recently (well) spent updating swimming pool, and lecture room also cleverly revamped. Northern work ethic evident—but also liberal tradition (parents warned from the start boys need to be self-motivated) and some complaints beyond the school gates of adolescent loutishness.

THE PUPILS Lots of first-time buyers, regional accents, occasionally accused of arrogance by other schools. Boys travel in from as far afield as Durham (one hour); very good local transport links.

Entrance Unashamedly selective and highly competitive, via own exam or CE at eight, 11, 13. At Sixth Form, with interview and school report.

Exit Vast majority to university, impressive numbers to Oxbridge.

Bottom Line Very low fees (lower than many other less good day schools). Assisted Places, over one quarter of parents pay less than full fees (some none at all).

Remarks Extremely strong school, that benefits from being big and is not a sausage machine, preparing citizens for the twenty-first century.

THE ROYAL SCHOOL
Lansdown Road, Bath, Avon BA1 5SZ
TEL Bath (0225) 313877

Pupils: 386 girls, 17 boys ● 241 board, 162 day ● Ages: 3+-18 ● Size of Sixth Form: 80 ● C of E ● Fee-paying.

HEAD Since 1987, Dr Judith McClure (forties), educated Newlands Grammar School, Middlesbrough, (was briefly a nun), studied Law, later took First in History at Oxford; has been a lecturer at both Liverpool and Oxford universities. Jolly, dynamic, encouraging, carries all before, excited about education, has expanded and reorganized the school to incorporate the National Curriculum. Very anti academic hothouses, believes creative and practical aspects of education both equally important. Always wears gown. Dr McClure's husband is a historian, specializing in seventh to ninth century Spain.

Remarks Happy and friendly school, not renowned for its academic achievements, with strong army links (four generals on the board of governors). Originally founded in 1860s for orphaned daughters of army officers. Wide range of ability, including seven per cent gifted, seven or eight Euro boarders, individual needs well catered for (eg EFL, dyslexia etc). One-year Sixth Form course available for non-academic girls, and all Sixth Formers do a business course, also philosophy, and are encouraged to organize everything—parties to activities, and have their own block. Sciences and Technology emphasised now. High ratio of staff to pupils (1:8). Saturday morning school recently introduced.

Good extracurricular activities: very sporty, they win most matches—lacrosse, hockey, tennis and squash all keenly played; strong drama and high standard of needlework. Duke of Edinburgh, Young Enterprise. Firm pastoral care. School is on the records of achievement scheme— Head comments, 'the worst thing is a sense of failure.' Strenuous efforts to keep girls busy at weekends. Goodish use of cultural life of Bath: 10 minutes walk from the centre, set in acres of space, the main block is your archetypal Gothic school edifice, with high windowed attics recently converted into split level study bedrooms. Small, though gradually increasing, number of leavers go on to university. Nursing and secretarial colleges popular. Head wants girls to leave 'Capable of being independent and standing alone, feminist—but not to look down on men, to accept to be equal and different.' And she hopes girls will have seen enough women with families and careers during their time at her school to see that it is possible to combine both. Own pre-prep (co-ed) on the campus (opened September 1988). Definitely a caring school, good on individual attention, suitable choice for girls who might feel swamped in more competitive establishment, under an impressive Head.

RUGBY SCHOOL
Rugby, Warwickshire CV22 5EH
TEL *Rugby (0788) 543465*

Pupils: 590 boys, 105 girls (all in Sixth Form) • *510 boys boarding, 80 day boys; 90 girls boarding, 15 day girls* • *Size of Sixth Form: 350* • *C of E* • *Fee-paying.*

HEAD   Since September 1990, Mr M B Mavor CVO MA (forties). Educated at Loretto and Cambridge. Previously Head of Gordonstoun (got his gong for supervizing the schooling of HRH The Duke of York and HRH the Prince Edward—no mean task). Keen fisherman. A five-star Head—particularly good at public relations and has massive mother-appeal. 'He had everything,' commented a fellow Head who was at school with him 'he was bright, good at sport and popular.' Enjoys a challenge. Already attracting punters to the school.

Academic Matters   Results not startling, though sprinkling of bright pupils, and in 1990 got 25 into Oxbridge. Economics, History and English currently most popular. Huge new Design and Technology centre in process of going up, and Mr Mavor plans to 'do an Oundle'—throwing every pupil into it for a week, in order to get real, solid hands-on experience of a practical subject. Some very professional staff, possibly overkeen on talk and chalk. NB only four female members of staff at time of writing.

Games, Options, the Arts   Traditionally sporty school—rugby training starts at the end of the summer term, good hockey, girls regularly represent county at hockey and lacrosse, keen cricket. Smart new sports

centre recently opened, also used by the town. Keen CCF. Business course is part of General Studies for all upper school pupils. Strong drama, with at least three school plays a year, plus house plays and visiting professional productions in school's own theatre. Some useful visiting speakers. Music still reported as 'really quite good'. Rustled up a polo team with Cheltenham for the Independent Schools Polo Challenge—and beat Eton and Millfield.

Background and Atmosphere   Founded in 1567 but metamorphosed as a Victorian 'railway' school in the 19th century. Home of the famous Dr Arnold of *Tom Brown's Schooldays*. Head still uses study at one end of which is a door leading to a staircase built by Dr Arnold through which boys could slide in without having to run the gauntlet of the school secretary. It is still used and, 'I try to guess what they are coming for—whether it's good news or bad' says the Head, though he added that any flogging 'would have taken place in the Birching Tower'. Strong traditional atmosphere. Imposing buildings joining the town and non-stop traffic on one side, and running away into playing fields on the other. Feels rather like north Oxford. Girls live in very civilised houses, boys less so, though programme of refurbishment now 'more or less' completed. Girls eat main meals in boys' boarding houses. Rugby is one of the very few schools which still has separate dining rooms for each house (lots of wood and polish and noticeboards of dear departed) and this makes an incredible difference to the atmosphere—both the pupils who showed us round commented that they chose the school 'because of the friendly feel' which resulted from this dying practice. School much harmed by TV programme depicting pupils as insensitive ill-mannered snobs.

Discipline   Has been a problem. Boarding houses have been run very largely by boys on traditional lines, and this gives scope for abuse of privileges, bullying etc (girls as well as boys). Head says he is changing this—'centralizing' discipline, and 'it is important to have guidelines *and to stick to them*'. Also: 'the only thing that matters is how pupils behave to each other'. New generation of Housemasters coming in (contract 12 years)—six since publication of last edition of book.

THE PUPILS   Mainly from Midlands, a sprinkling from overseas, also from Yorkshire etc. OBs: Rupert Brooke (a girls' houses is named after him), Salman Rushdie, Hugh Montefiore, Ian Lang, Robert Hardy, Tom King. OBs as a whole show tremendous sense of loyalty to the school, and regard it with nostalgia.

Entrance   By registration and entrance exam (no

stiff in the least). Choice of house may be deferred until near time of entry.

Exit All over the shop—mostly to university (Edinburgh and London particularly popular at time of writing), eight per cent to polys.

Bottom Line 16+ academic scholarships were offered in 1990 and five 16+ music scholarships. Also help for the needy, and for sons of Old Rugbeians etc.

Remarks Famous traditional boys' public school which has been very iffy, but which Midlands prep school Heads now note is 'the one to watch'. Going fully co-ed in 1993 (aiming for 500 boys, 250 girls) and squeals of protest about this are being made by pupils and Old Boys at time of writing, though this is a case of opening the stable door after the horse has arrived, as there are already girls in the school. Huge changes afoot—and not before time.

ST ANTONY'S-LEWESTON SCHOOL
Sherborne, Dorset DT9 6EN
TEL Holnest (096 321)691

Pupils: 390 girls ● *300 board, 90 day* ● *Ages: 11-18* ● *Size of Sixth Form: 95* ● *RC* ● *Fee-paying.*

HEAD Since 1983, Mrs P Cartwright BSc, MA (forties), educated Ursuline convent Brentwood, previously has worked in maintained schools, most recently as Deputy Head of girls' school in Oxfordshire. Firm believer in single-sex education. Very sensible and very straight-forward. Aims to 'turn out decent human beings'.

Academic Matters Competent all round, Maths good. Theatre Studies popular A-level. Setted for Maths, French, English. Pressure put on girls to stay, but at last count 25 out of 70 left for Sixth Form elsewhere. One-year Sixth Form course on offer for non-academic girls. Good remedial English department for dyslexia etc (all tested first term, in case some have slipped through).

Games, Options, the Arts Squash popular; karate, outdoor pool, athletics, keen games of all sorts. Indoor

sports hall (pre-dating most other schoools'). Good drama, CDT block a new addition and this is strong, with very promising jewellery-making, wood and stone carving.

Background and Atmosphere Fine old house much jigged about, bought by Canadian steel magnate in the Twenties who inserted marble and art deco staircase with green glass bannister rail, giving ocean liner appearance. Massive space for conferences. Belgian nuns originally, far-seeing, judging by size of dining room which still contains whole school despite jump up in numbers. Convent attached, so nuns occasionally seen. Hideous chapel built in 1968.

Older girls sleep in much coveted study bedrooms (walls papered with pages from the glossies), younger ones in pine bunk beds. Long mirrors everywhere, also reproductions of paintings from our national collections, which Head firmly hopes girls absorb by osmosis. Recent introduction, and proving popular with staff and pupils and parents, are Profiles. Pastoral care is good, and works horizontally; personal and social education, a weekly slot on health, current affairs etc, 'Very useful', say staff. Last GSG comment on lack of activity at weekends caused much offence, and weekend activities have increased—though pupils still complain, and school tends to empty out over weekends, as many parents are within easy striking distance.

THE PUPILS About half RC, the rest a cross section of Christians, including Anglican Vicars' daughters. Wide social mix, well balanced, chatty and friendly.

Entrance Not a problem. By CE; some at Sixth Form.

Exit Higher education—degrees (after a year off), a few to secretarial.

Remarks An unpretentious school, considered by locals to be less stuffy than neighbouring Sherborne or St Mary's Shaftesbury.

ST BEES SCHOOL
St Bees, Cumbria CA 27 ODU
TEL Egremont (0946) 822263

Pupils: 200 boys, 160 girls • 180 board, 180 day • Ages: 11-18 • Size of Sixth Form: 120 • C of E • Fee-paying.

HEAD Since 1988, Mr Paul Chamberlain BSc (forties), formerly Housemaster at Haileybury.

Remarks Founded as grammar school in 1583, set in 150 acres of rural splendour, close to coast and Lake District. The school has a good A-level pass rate, with 95% each year progressing to further education, including four to seven to Oxbridge. Lord Whitelaw is chairman of governors, visits often.

A Business Management Centre serving the community as well as the school now under construction. Drama is popular, with annual school play, Sixth Form play, junior play and full-scale Gilbert and Sullivan. Also lots of concerts, keen art and design. School has excellent reputation for Rugby, hockey and athletics, and outdoor pursuits. Hardy pupils set up camp at weekends and head for the Lake District. Windsurfing, sailing, canoeing. St Bees possesses the most northerly of Eton fives courts. CCF and D of E. School is very popular with the residents of Cumbria, who may get bursaries if they play their cards right, and generous numbers of academic scholarships. 84 Assisted Places.

ST CHRISTOPHER SCHOOL
Letchworth, Hertfordshire SG6 3JZ
TEL Letchworth (04626) 79301

Pupils: Approx 292 boys, 222 girls • 224 board, 290 day • Ages: 3-19 • Size of Sixth Form: 90 • Non-denom • Fee-paying.

HEAD Since 1981, Mr Colin Reid MA (forties), read History at Cambridge. Wife Betsy teaches Humanities and Geography at the school. A quiet, confident Head, realistic in outlook.

Remarks An 'alternative' co-educational school for children of all abilities. Good exam results: pupils are encouraged to go for what is right for them. Founded as a progressive school in the Twenties, now housed in a Thirties mansion surrounded by spacious grounds. Very family atmosphere. All meals vegetarian—excellent and varied. Attracts staff who are interested in the all-round approach to education as well as academic excellence—they consider it 'a way of life'. All the usual games—some on the premises, others, such as squash, tennis, golf and riding, within easy reach. Good theatre and drama. Emphasis on arts and crafts. Splendid cooking classes. Parents on the whole the 'caring' type, looking for something different.

Entrance by interview not test, most leavers go on to further education, many to degree courses. Not for those seeking conventional public school education—but don't imagine that it is chaotic here. Breeds tolerance, open minds and teaches the young to value their peers, whatever their background or abilities. Several parents have reported that they are 'very happy' with their children's development at this school.

ST COLUMBA'S SCHOOL
Duchal Road, Kilmacolm, Renfrewshire
PA13 4AU
TEL Kilmacolm (050 587) 2238

Senior School: 120 boys, 185 girls • All day • Ages: 11-18 • Junior School: 225 boys and girls, ages 4-11 • Nursery School: 20 boys and girls ages 3-5 • Size of Sixth Form: 65 • Non-denom/C of E • Fee-paying.

HEAD Rector since 1987, Mr Andrew Livingstone BSc (Hons) Aberdeen, Dip Ed Glasgow (forties), educated at Campbeltown Grammer School, previously Deputy Rector of Paisley Grammer School. An educationalist (he served on the Scottish Exam Board), he is greatly enjoying the challenge of being the first Rector of this previously traditional girls' school which went co-ed in 1978. Believes that children 'should be encouraged to develop their personality to complement their academic abilities'.

Academic Matters Reputation enhanced by new Economics, Accountancy and Secretarial departments.

CDT. Pupils take Scottish 0–grades moving to Standard, with Highers the following year and either CSYS or A-levels. University entrance after either first or second year Sixth Form. Computers and videos are the norm. Excellent careers advice.

Games, Options, the Arts Games are played either on Birkmyre Park, or on the Ashes nearby, which currently boasts all-weather hockey pitch and tennis courts. Sports hall at Junior School. Orchestra is popular, masses of choral work, good drama, art and pottery above the old gym. D of E Award Scheme.

Background and Atmosphere Original school was founded in 1897, red brick. Quite strict, if informal, discipline. Very tidy. Junior and Nursery School in Shallot, the former boarding house, with trees, tennis courts, and flower beds. Senior school is cramped, but games area is couple of hundred yards away.

THE PUPILS Local professional families and bussed in from all over Renfrewshire and North Ayrshire. Approx two to three per cent ethnic.

Entrance From Junior to Senior school is no problem. Waiting list at ages 10, 11, 12. Own test and interview. Two classes, maximum 26.

Exit Occasional one after O-levels, otherwise either to university with Highers, or A-levels and CSYS. Approx 60% to university and degree courses, with one or two to Oxbridge.

Bottom Line Scholastic and musical scholarships. Assisted Places available.

Remarks No change. Useful local school.

ST DAVID'S COLLEGE
Gloddaeth Hall, Llandudno, Gwynedd,
North Wales LL30 1RD
TEL Llandudno (0492) 75974

Pupils: 201 boys • *140 board, 61 day* • *Ages: 11-18* •
Size of Sixth Form: 55 • *Non-denom* • *Fee-paying.*

HEAD Since January 1989, Mr B T Culan Morris MA Oxon. Teaches Biology. Formerly a Housemaster at Eastbourne College.

Remarks Founded in 1965, initially with 37 boys, stupendous setting on the edge of Snowdonia. Boys from all parts of the UK, much emphasis on building up self-confidence and self-reliance, initiative and individualism, the school has a deservedly high reputation for helping boys with difficulties—including dyslexia, late developers, etc (though these boys are always in a minority). Lots of care and understanding, a good place to gain maturity through outward-bound activities, challenge of hill walking, tough outdoor pursuits, eg sailing 3,000 miles to the Azores. Falconry on offer, with two buzzards being trained. Travel scholarship for a 'holiday which involves a purpose'. Two Welsh national athletic champions in 1990, and board sailors representing Wales. Also keen art, strong Technology and Computing. Small groups (18-20 is large) for academic work. Dyslexic unit much in demand and very good, early registration essential, but numbers overall falling. Each year a handful of boys go on to university, the majority to polytechnics and technical colleges. Muscular Christianity.

ST DENIS AND CRANLEY SCHOOL
Ettrick Road, Edinburgh EH10 5BJ
TEL Edinburgh (031) 229 1500

Pupils: 215 girls • *90 board, 100 day* • *Ages: 9-18* •
Small Lower Junior School: 25 day girls, ages 5-8. • *Nursery:*
20 boys and girls, ages 3-4. • *Size of Sixth Form: 45* • *Interdenom* • *Fee-paying.*

HEAD Since 1984, Mrs Jennifer Munro MA, Dip RE (fifties), came to St Denis and Cranley in 1970 and was previously Deputy Head of History. Educated at St Denis, a quietly charming Head who believes in encouraging each person.

Remarks School could be a ringer for Miss Brodie's: gentle, comfortable with good academic facilities. A successful mix of day and boarding. Surprisingly large number of pupils are from abroad; mostly ex pats, but also Americans and Pakistanis. School has strong links with La Maison d'Education de la Legion d'Honneur at St Denis in Paris. St Denis merged with Cranley School in 1979, the junior house was subsequently discontinued, but, having refused to die, is now under active resurrection.

Cosily encampused in Morningside's splendour, with eight acres of gardens housing six Victorian villas, tennis courts, new games hall, theatre, Science and Technology building etc. The school makes much use of local facilities: the Young Engineers' Club at Napier College, the swimming pool at Merchiston Castle, as well as theatres, etc, in Edinburgh.

Good remedial. School takes both English and Scottish exams—mostly Scottish. Biology popular. Most girls go on to colleges of further education or university. OG: Hannah Gordon. A quiet, gentle school but, says Head, 'They can also be vets and engineers, diplomats and social workers, who get their hands dirty, or find themselves in sticky situations and succeed.'

ST EDWARD'S SCHOOL
Woodstock Road, Oxford OX2 7NN
TEL Oxford (0865) 515241

Pupils: *Approx 525 boys, 50 girls (all in Sixth Form)* • *475 board, 100 day* • *Ages: 13-18* • *Size of Sixth Form: Approx 240* • *C of E* • *Fee-paying.*

HEAD Warden, Mr D Christie BSc Econ London, BA Strathclyde. Previously Head of Economics at Winchester. Kindly Scot, enjoys a debate, sees the world as a meritocracy. Keen to broaden entry base of school, also keen on promoting three-way communication despite boarding environment: pupils/school/parents.

Academic Matters Traditional belief that St Edward's is more brawny than brainy is dying, if not dead, disproved by recent results, easily on a par with other middle-ranking boarding schools. Does not offer every A-level under the sun (and has just dropped Business Studies, though Economics remains a large department); General Studies course for all Sixth Formers, plus one period a week on religious/moral issues. Some help for mild dyslexia in first year.

Games, Options, the Arts In line with brawny/brainy upheaval, has taken to losing (especially cricket)

matches, but sports are nonetheless extremely well-served: very pleasant pitches (hockey and rugby official games), classy sports centre (though indoor pool could be improved), water sports, especially rowing, a speciality. Activities, from archaeology, archery and (extra) art via science and engineering society to theatre crew, windsurfing and (extra) woodwork, spelt out in efficient little booklet given to newcomers. A good deal of high-standard drama and ditto music. New art and design centre. Week's management course and debating. CCF compulsory until proficiency, active Duke of Edinburgh Award scheme. Good library.

Background and Atmosphere A mile from the dreaming spires, tucked into the homelier Summertown district of north Oxford; playing fields run down to canal on other side of busy Woodstock Road from school (connected by underpass). Boarding houses: some comfy old, some very sparkling new. Daily life in them features large amounts of (popular) sliced white bread delivered for toasting. Send your own wholemeal. Not a school for special smartness and style, social or otherwise, of pupils ('and they don't go there to learn manners', remarked a parent tartly). Girls have their own boarding house, boys not allowed in, full stop. But day girls and boarders work in boys' study dorms. More women teachers than some public schools. Bar (with parents' permission) offers senior pupils beer and cider. Day pupils stay until 9pm.

THE PUPILS Mainly professional middle classes. Old boys: Sir Douglas Bader (who was largely excused his fees), Lord Olivier.

Entrance Down-payment of £250 at 11 guarantees place on successful passing of CE (minimum 50%)—book tends to close completely about a year later. Test and assessment for state school entrants.

Exit 90% of the Sixth to higher education, 70%-75% to university, 15-20% to polytechnics. The remainder, drop-outs apart, to armed forces, family and other businesses.

Bottom Line Fairly plentiful help. Up to 13 scholarships and exhibitions, two service exhibitions, 30% bursaries for sons of clergy, music and art scholarships (numbers vary from year to year), four continuation scholarships offered with a group of prep schools, plus Dragon/St Edward's School scholarship for a nine-year old at state school. Newly introduced with Save & Prosper: Arkwright Design scholarship for 16-year old.

Remarks A worthy middle-ranking school, which deserves to be taken more seriously than it has been in recent years.

ST ELPHIN'S SCHOOL
*Darley Dale, Matlock, Derbyshire, DE4
2HA*
TEL Matlock (0629) 732687

Pupils: Approx 360 girls ● 130 board, 230 day ● Ages: 3-18 (boys aged 3-7) ● Size of Sixth Form: Approx 68 ● C of E ● Fee-paying.

HEAD Since 1979, Mr Peter Pollard BA Liverpool and PGCE Cantab, read English (early fifties). Comments (in prospectus) that school 'is small enough for every pupil to feel at home'. Widower.

Remarks School was founded in Warrington in 1644 and named after a little known saint who perished in battle in the seventh century. Moved to Derbyshire countryside in 1904, now on A6, has a huge chimney stack in the background. Small classes, wide range of ability intake. No streaming in first year, but thereafter streamed and setted according to ability in Maths and French. All girls take French, and Latin and German are on offer. About 50% of girls go on to university. OG—Richmal Crompton, creator of *Just William.*

New junior school block in process of being built. Swimming for all at the nearby Matlock Lido, good range of playing fields including all-weather games pitch. Keen charity workers and fund raisers. School is represented at the annual Buxton Festival of Speech, Drama and Music. Some excellent and lively art. Girls wear smart kilts. Friendly, with good pastoral care. Fees reasonable and good range of scholarships on offer, including two of full fees and two of half fees.

School fulfils a need in an area not noted for private schools, but, notes a local educationalist, 'ambitious parents still send their children south'.

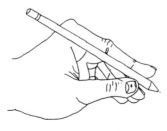

ST FELIX SCHOOL
Southwold, Suffolk IP18 6SD
TEL Southwold (0502) 722175

Pupils: Approx 350 girls ● 290 board, including 20 weekly boarders, 60 day ● Ages: 11-18 ● Size of Sixth Form: Approx 80 ● Non-denom ● Fee-paying.

HEAD From 1991, Mrs Susan Campion MA Cantab (forties), previously Head of Woodford County High School, London Borough of Redbridge. Bilingual, read Modern Languages at Girton. Married with two young sons and husband is an inventor. Takes over from Miss Claydon, who has left to marry the Head of nearby Orwell Park (*qv*).

Academic Matters No streaming, but sets for Maths, Latin (Latin no longer compulsory at any stage), Modern Languages. Results average, but with a fair number going for tough options. One or two doing Latin and Greek, three or four Chinese. GCSE results similar, plus strong CDT and computer study group.

Games, Options, the Arts PE compulsory throughout the school, but after three years options widen and girls may choose to sail, play golf, squash, badminton. School has produced the only woman golf blue in history of Cambridge (in 1986). Also the only girls' school to have produced a (male) boxing blue. Keen and growing music department.

Background and Atmosphere Lovely secluded site not far from the North Sea, surrounded by 75 acres of own land, soothing atmosphere, though trees have that wind-blown look. Victorian brick buildings—not a pre-fab in sight. Dorms no longer cramped, posters still standard James Dean. School has non-teaching Housemistresses. School's star-shaped dining room (cafeteria feeding) is now run by a vegetarian and complaints about food have tailed off.

THE PUPILS 20% Essex, 30% Suffolk, 18% Norfolk, six per cent non-nationals (some of the brightest and best), eight per cent ex pats. Pupils good at marrying well. Famous Old Girls: Olga Detterding, Mrs James Prior, Lady Waley-Cohen.

Entrance CE exam at 11+, 12+ or 13+, but school always willing to see people at any time. School is fed by adjoining prep school St George's.

Exit   70% to university and polys (some do 'gap' first), remainder to art schools, para-medical training, occasionally to secretarial. Some leakage to boys' Sixth Forms and to state-maintained Sixth Form colleges.

Bottom Line   Well-endowed, which is *most* unusual for a girls' school—by gravel pits and farmland income. Four scholarships and four exhibitions a year on academic merit, also bursaries for those fallen on hard times, plus music scholarship. Scholarships worth 35-50% of school fees and may be bumped up 'in certain circumstances'. Percentage of fee income which goes towards scholarships raised from three to five—is this a record for girls?

Remarks   Gentle girls' boarding school at which numbers are sadly dropping as girls move on to boys' schools and life.

ST GEORGE'S SCHOOL
Ascot, Berkshire SL5 7DZ
TEL Ascot (0344) 20273

Pupils: 280 girls • 196 board, 84 day • Ages: 11-18 •
Size of Sixth Form: Approx 65 • C of E • Fee-paying.

HEAD   Since January 1989, Mrs Anthea Griggs BA (fifties), educated North Foreland Lodge, Homerton College, Cambridge, and Edinburgh University. Previously Upper Sixth Housemistress and careers adviser at Harrogate Ladies' College. Pleasantly firm, slightly confiding manner.

Academic Matters   GCSE results surprisingly good for mixed ability intake (deliberate policy here), and A-level results back up Headmistress's assertion that they are just as proud of the girl who got two Es, but tried her best, as of the ones hung with laurels. Classical Civilization a popular A-level. One-year Sixth Form course for GCSE re-takes, typing etc.

Games, Options, the Arts   *Lots* and lots going on: zest is the watchword. Public performance cherished (regular winners of area finals in English Speaking Union); lively drama (budding actresses occasionally borrowed by Eton), debating usually with boys'

schools; keen D of E, YE and energetic charity fund-raising. Plenty of sport available, aerobics, squash and year-round tennis perennially popular.

Background and Atmosphere   On the Windsor Great Park edge of bustling Ascot, set amid rhodo-dendron and pine acreage. Homely jolly dorms vary in size, graduating up to privacy and study-bedrooms. Houses arranged by year group. Sixth can entertain boys in common room (dinner parties are fashionable), and though there is a background social whirl of school dances etc, discipline and sense of social usefulness hovers. Sensible system of increasing privileges for 'good citizenry'. Fierce no smoking rule (one girl expelled, four suspended on this count in last 18 months). Day girl element prevents claustrophobia.

THE PUPILS   Majority from the south, rather than London; popular choice for expatriate and service families; handful of foreigners.

Entrance   CE, mixed ability, essentially girls who have something to offer, assessed via time spent at the school a year before entry.

Exit   85%-90% to higher education (Bristol and Exeter favoured). Might end up in PR, advertising, teaching, •nannying, business, nursing, doctoring, archaeology.

Bottom Line   Reasonable fees for the area. Bursaries for emergencies.

Remarks   Steady all round performer.

ST GEORGE'S SCHOOL FOR GIRLS
Garscube Terrace, Edinburgh EH12 6BG
TEL Edinburgh (031) 332 4575

Pupils: 850 girls • 100 board, 750 day • Ages: 5-18 •
Size of Sixth Form: 140 • Non denom • Fee-paying.

HEAD   Since 1986, Mrs Jean Scott BSc (forties), educated at Wellington School, Ayr and Glasgow University, previously Deputy Head at Ipswich High. Very sensible, straightforward and popular.

Academic Matters   Impressive: most girls take

Highers in *one* year, A-levels the following year. 98% A–C A-level pass rate must be among highest anywhere. Sciences, (notably Chemistry) and Maths consistently the main strengths, French and History also very good. No academic prizes, no class orders, 'But they all know where they stand', commented a member of staff. Mrs Scott has introduced a broader General Studies programme for Sixth Form, and, most importantly, encouraged the girls to think for themselves and answer back—a harder task to change staff to this way of working than girls, observes the Head.

Games, Options, the Arts Games taken seriously—loads of cups for them—and school has been Scottish lacrosse champion for the last three years. Sports grounds surround school buildings, huge indoor sports hall. Good new music centre (600 musicians), and art is strong, housed in another new building. Lively debating, emphasis on D of E, computers everywhere. Head runs good programme, getting young (under 30) women in management in to talk to top of the school. Also makes admirable attempts to educate parents of day pupils on drugs, Aids etc, 'Girls tend to think they know all about this, and say 'Oh, not again!''

Background and Atmosphere Founders at forefront of campaign to admit women to university. Present premises purpose-built in 1912 (E-shaped building) for 250 but, with great foresight, hall still big enough to take greatly increased numbers. Fine view over the city. Much recent additional building and improved facilities for centenary. Purposeful atmosphere.

THE PUPILS Polite and hard-working. Wide social mix, school popular with Edinburgh Sloanes. If they come in at five or at eight, inevitable complaints about being in the same place too long.

Entrance Very carefully screened at five, thereafter by exam. Competitive.

Exit Degrees and higher education of all sorts—all over the place Scottish law a popular degree as a stepping stone into business, market research etc. Some leakage at Sixth Form.

Bottom Line Assisted Places and a few scholarships at Sixth Form.

Remarks Strong and popular school under very capable Head. Some parental grumbles.

ST LEONARDS SCHOOL
St Andrews, Fife KY16 9QU
TEL St Andrews (0334) 72126

Pupils: 378 girls • 293 board, 85 day • Ages: 11-18 • Size of Sixth Form: 134 • Junior School (St Katharines) in grounds: 43, ages 8-11 • Non-denom • Fee-paying.

HEAD Since 1988, Mrs Mary James BA (forties), headhunted from Queen Ethelburga's where she had been Headmistress for four years after teaching at Sedbergh and Casterton. First-class History Honours at York, followed by post grad at Oxford, married to fellow historian author Lawrence James; two sons. Charming, efficient, devoid of Head's usual clichés, extremely articulate and enthusiastic. Old Girl (Senior) of St Leonard's. Wants girls 'to discover their own bent and grain and build confidence and have a sense of who they are'. Keen for them to leave feeling, 'there is nothing they can't do—if they really want to', and equally keen for them to make happy marriages and have a balanced attitude about careers.

Academic Matters Definitely strong; many staff have links with university, and recently school is making more use of university facilities, eg on research science projects, classical meetings, debating. Strong careers department (starts as early as 13). New General Studies course for Sixth Form. In 1990: 98% pass rate at A-level, with 75% grades A-C. Staff 'fight like fury', to quote Head, over own territory and push for facilities.

Games, Options, the Arts Keenly gamesy, though essential games only twice a week; athletics popular; good pool, tennis courts everywhere, three squash courts, skiing, sailing club now in operation, also golf. Splendid music department. Computing, IT, cooking. Very good art (new Head of Department). Aesthetic Hour each day, to do nothing or read or listen to music, 'because girls need time to be reposeful', thinks Head, actually also used for choir/team practices and somewhat mocked by pupils 'Synthetic Hour'.

Background and Atmosphere Founded in 1877, mother school of Wycombe Abbey (*qv*), purpose-built with many additions, very near the sea—bracing air—and the university. Golf, riding and the beach, as well as trips into town, popular at weekends. High expectations almost tangible. Civilized houses, simple, fairly cosy, flowers, with mixed age dorms (very popular). Girls do own laundry (and iron clothes) except sheets. New Upper Sixth house opening September 1991, mid-construction now. Ghastly brown uniform on way out, strong green one (by Chris Clyne) on way in. Lower Sixth wear uniform. Massive medieval wall, library housed in Queen Mary's House, which boasts fascinating Maryana.

THE PUPILS Around 60% Scots, eight to 10% foreigners and ex pats. Upper crust. Lots of daughters of Seniors. Articulate and unspoilt, and allowed to be feminine (unlike some academic girls' schools). Famous Seniors: Betty Harvey Anderson, Dame Kathleen Ollerenshaw.

Entrance CE at 11, 12 or 13, own exam. for maintained school entrants; St. Katharine girls take 12+ CE (NB: revolutionized under new young Head and his wife and children).

Exit 85% on to university or polys, always around six to Oxbridge; Newcastle, Bristol, Exeter and Scottish universities popular. Slight leakage post GCSEs.

Bottom Line Well endowed for girls' school; rich in scholarships—for music, Seniors' daughters, older pupils etc.

Remarks A very strong school under exceptional Head—knows where it is going. Far less nervy sophistication than at many southern academic establishments.

ST LEONARD'S-MAYFIELD SCHOOL

The Old Palace, Mayfield, East Sussex
TN20 6PH
TEL Mayfield (0435) 873652

Pupils: 540 girls • 360 boarders, 180 day • Ages: 11-18 • Size of Sixth Form: 170 • RC • Fee-paying.

HEAD For many years, Sister Jean Sinclair BSc—1986/7 President of the Girls' School Association. Shy, humorous, gentle and popular. A Mathematician and former athlete, she is a convert to Roman Catholicism educated at Wycombe Abbey—strongly against personal publicity.

Remarks A large, low profile academic school which suits the motivated. Almost any subject can be studied.

Sciences strong: Mathematics and English competently taught and streamed from Third year. Strong hockey, tennis, netball. Lots of tennis courts, stunningly situated games pitches. New covered swimming pool designed by nun-architect. Excellent national competition-winning gymnastics.

Inter-house drama popular—likewise art and pottery. Some complaints from parents that cultural outings and field trips are in short supply 'though there is plenty on offer in the area' said one mother tartly.

Music outstanding under redoubtable Kenneth Pont, founder of the Gibbons Consort and editorial adviser to Oxford University Press. Four choirs, who perform regularly with local Glyndebourne soloists and London orchestras.

Beautiful situation with austere thirteenth-century chapel (restored by Pugin) and well kept grounds. One of the last convent schools with a religious community still supplying teaching nuns—though no habits worn and dearth of new vocations. Spartan boarding houses.

Girls (broad social and geographical mix) are mutually supportive but the shy, disorganized or unmotivated will not survive here. Complaints reach us from parents worried by 'too much change' among staff.

ST MARGARET'S SCHOOL EDINBURGH

East Suffolk Road, Edinburgh EH16 5PJ
TEL Edinburgh (031) 668 1986

Pupils: 830 girls, 18 boys ● *82 board, 748 day* ● *Ages: girls 3-18, boys 3-8* ● *Size of Sixth Form: 180* ● *Non-denom* ● *Fee-paying.*

HEAD Since 1984, Mrs M J Cameron MA Oxon (fifties), comfy no-nonsense Head who sees it 'like it is' and enormously 'enjoys teaching children to be individuals', and encouraging them 'to be people'. Doesn't believe in pushing so hard that they can't manage; came up via state system and relishes the discipline which private schools are allowed to instil.

Remarks Boys only to eight, pupils mainly come from local middle-class Edinburgh (and surrounding Mid and East Lothian), though influx (often from abroad for a year or two) to Senior College in the former three-star Oratava Hotel, where boarders live in luxury, Senior girls share a bedroom with private bath, while Fourth Form girls have to suffer three to a room (with private bath). Two good computer rooms (usually locked—pupils can't play with the machines), and usual domestic science, science and biology labs, business studies in (fancy machines), and gym above music studios in converted church. Good-ish art, and inspired ceramics. Over 70 staff, many part-timers. Can't do wheelchairs, but will accept moderate physical handicap. Remedial teaching at all levels. Good games and regular swimming. 75 unconditional university places offered including 13 in England. Pupils do Standard Grade, followed by Higher at Lower Sixth; A-levels at Upper Sixth.
Massive bursaries and family reductions. Assisted Places from age 10.
Conveniently placed for Newington, school attracts a wide range of parents; ranging from those who work in Edinburgh but live on 'the Southside', the better to get to their borders estates; to those whose children serve at the local supermarket. Massive recent expansion following merger with St Hilary's, and school is possibly less academic than formerly. Does well with a wide ability range. Good letting prospect during Edinburgh Festival.

ST MARY'S SCHOOL

Ascot, Berkshire, SL5 9JF
TEL Ascot (0344) 23721

Pupils: 330 girls ● *320 board, 10 day* ● *Ages: 10-18* ● *Size of Sixth Form: 85* ● *RC* ● *Fee-paying.*

HEAD Since 1982, Sister M Mark IBVM, BA, PGCE (forties) educated at St Mary's Ascot and London University. Comments on this book that she has 'never met a parent who has taken your Guide seriously.' Firm, tireless Head. Shrewd business woman. Likes skiing, dog walking, doing tapestries, reading and Scrabble.

Academic Matters Good exam results, though some queries about the breadth of education. Almost all pupils take Religious Studies at GCSE and, at time of writing, do very well in it. Otherwise, it's mainly the core subjects, with science coming a poor second to the arts. Most popular choices at A-level are history of art, ancient history and French. Almost certainly the most academic Catholic girls' school in England.

Games, Options, the Arts Good art, drama (including house plays), community service, not to mention dressmaking, computers, fencing etc. Tennis the top game, and keen coach is at the nets morning noon and night.

Background and Atmosphere Purpose-built in 1885 and extended since in similar red-brick Gothic. Impeccably kept buildings and grounds. School is run by nuns (though nuns who teach are a rare teaching commodity these days) of the Institute of the Blessed Virgin Mary, founded in the seventeenth century by Mary Ward, one of the great English educationalists.
Civilized bedrooms for older girls, and even dorms are more like rooms, with much privacy. Houses are given the responsibility of running the school in rota, and this system helps break school age barriers vertically. No uniform for Sixth Form, who live apart (Sixth Form block in process of being built when we visited), though by comparison with other Sixth Forms still in a highly structured timetable, without many privileges or stepping stones to life outside. No alcohol—the place for smoke and drink is down in the woods. Very friendly school. Soothing chapel and

slightly cloistered feel, a wonderful sanctuary from the shrill world outside.

THE PUPILS Top Catholics. Charming. A few smart foreigners, diplomats' daughters, OGs' daughters etc. 20% from overseas, mainly ex-pats. OGs include Caroline of Monaco, the Spanish infantas, Sarah Hogg.

Entrance By registration—lists close 18 months ahead of entry at time of writing.

Exit Some leave after GCSE, otherwise universities, including Manchester, Leeds and UEA, polys, secretarial, art colleges, nursing, teaching. Careers in the City, law, advertising.

Bottom Line OG scholarship for Sixth Form entry. Discretionary bursaries for pupils currently in the school. Schools reckons to be most expensive in the area—fees 'as high as the market place will allow'.

Remarks Excellent establishment with a quiet sense of community and purpose. An oasis of tranquility—which has changed remarkably little over the decades despite all.

ST MARY'S SCHOOL
Calne, Wiltshire SN11 0DF
TEL Calne (0249) 815899

Pupils: 312 girls • *281 board, 31 day* • *Ages: 11-18* • *Size of Sixth Form: 72* • *C of E* • *Fee paying.*

HEAD Since 1985, Miss Delscey Burns BA, MSc Oxon (thirties), educated at St Michael's Petworth and York University, previously Head of English at St George's Ascot, and has also taught in the state system. Shaping up to be an institution—and pretty with it. Keen that pupils should do well at their work and pick up some other skills on the way, and that they should be 'competent, flexible, cheerful and realistic'. Runs the school with a very light touch. Disarming concern about her 'flippant tongue' which, she says, has been known to get her into trouble. Has been known to get into her green Audi Quattro at the end of a difficult day and drive away the tensions. Lives in house attached to main school building.

Academic Matters Staggering improvement over the last five years, and excellent in any context. Pupils do well, says Miss Burns, they are in the top third ability band 'and they jolly well ought to'. Mainstream subjects only—school is too small for exotic languages etc. Some excellent staff plus one or two half asleep as we went round. History of Art is the pupils' choice. Latin for all at 11 and 21 in the current GCSE group. Class size 18-20. No streaming. Girls work like crazy—lots of talk and chalk teaching.

Games, Options, the Arts Two international lacrosse players on the staff at time of writing and six girls in the Wiltshire junior team—such enthusiasm here that girls get up at seven to put in extra practice. Four Duke of Edinburgh gold medallists. Lots of riding and 12 tennis courts, including four all-weather ones. Domestic science not taught—there was a choice between cooking and computers, and computers won, though all First years and many older girls do cookery as an 'activity'. Keen photography. Music strong, with new rabbit warren building (including a recording studio) and new Head of Music—Mr Abrams from Cranleigh. Whole school does 'dorm plays' and sings in carol competition. Eton and Radley send a side to the school to play hockey and lacrosse respectively.

Background and Atmosphere Founded in 1873 by Canon Duncan, the Vicar of St Mary's Church in Calne and school still uses church for high days. Situated in 25 acres in the middle of Calne—security a bit of a headache. Buildings functional, even hangar-like (breeze-blocks), though dormitories friendly. Houses divided horizontally and pupils move each year. 11-year olds go into 'school house' which is so cosy and has so many posters no one ever wants to go on to next house. There are 'companies' (houses) for games, singing etc. Slight murmurings about school grinding to a halt at weekends, but Miss Burns believes this is no longer the case—there is always plenty to do, excursions, art room open etc, dance with eg Radley. Good food (kitchen might even rise to a Chinese nosh), and there is a clocking-in system to make sure each child at least gets as far as the dining room.

THE PUPILS 24% London smart, also Yorkshire and Scotland ditto: 'It's a social ghetto', said a parent. All called Sophie and all the parents know each other. A few local farmers, etc. No ex pats. In the first division for hair flicking and giggling, though girls quite friendly and good-mannered with it. Very feminine school—and they enjoy it. Well-known locally as the place from which Mick Jagger's daughter was expelled.

Discipline Non-teaching Housemistresses, one tutor allocated to each child to supervize welfare throughout school career—which makes it easy for parents, but not so brilliant if child and tutor do not hit it off. Shopping privileges in Calne. Drugs—out; alcohol 'very serious trouble'; smoking 'is illegal under-16 anyway'. And: 'If I am in *loco parentis* I don't care how old they are, they are not allowed to buy alcohol.' And there is a 'sin book'.

Entrance Absolutely not a pushover, as so sought after. Potential pupils 'need to see us by the age of nine'. Entrance at 11+, and 12+ via CE.

Exit Small but consistent leakage post-GCSEs, usually to boys' schools. 26 to top universities in 1990, the rest to polys, secretarial courses and 'gap'ing. Head encourages pupils to get some sort of work or non-academic expeience before going to university 'partly to see how much they hate working nine to five, and then they'll make much better use of their time as students'. Horizons: law, art world, teaching, media, medical.

Bottom Line Academic scholarships at 11+ and 12+ for daughters of OGs, two at Sixth Form, also one music scholarship. No endowment.

Remarks Charming small girls' boarding school which sticks to the basics (both academically and otherwise) on the principle that it is better to do some things well, than many things badly. It is still *the* fashionable choice for smarter daughters. Rare to hear complaints, despite its limitations.

ST MARY'S SCHOOL
Shaftesbury, Dorset SP7 9LP
TEL Shaftesbury (0747) 54005

Pupils: 320 girls ● 210 boarders, 110 day ● Ages: 10-18 ●
Size of Sixth Form: 65 ● RC ● Fee-paying.

HEAD Since 1985, Sister M Campion Livesey MA Cantab (thirties) educated Lady Eleanor Holles and Cambridge. Clever, friendly, open, warm and relaxed, though some complaints from Sixth Form girls that 'she can't keep her distance'.

Academic Matters Sound, but 'teaching not always as good as hoped for', according to some parents. Strong Sciences and Modern Languages. About 23 girls per class (mixed abilities), setted for Maths, French and Latin. No Saturday morning school. Sixth Form non A-level curriculum includes two periods of General Studies, RE, PE, Art/Textiles or Information Technology, plus a single period of Careers and Current Affairs per week.

Games, Options, the Arts Flourishing games, including squash, judo, athletics, 'But far too few tennis courts', commented a parent. New Sports Hall. Good art and textile design, flourishing music department with good choirs which have given concert tours in Austria, Bavaria and Italy in recent years. Keen on Duke of Edinburgh Awards. Community service throughout the school.

Background and Atmosphere Large chateau-style Edwardian house converted some 40 years ago. Lots of space, well-used, well-kept with rolling Dorset/Wiltshire views. Previously a convent, now a Charitable Company, with separate legal existence from the Religious Community to whom it belongs. A few nuns still teach, but not for much longer. Religious education important—with emphasis on academic, emotional and spiritual aspects. Not tradition-bound in many respects, and certainly not 'fashionable' the way its sister school, St Mary's Ascot, is. Carpeted, curtained cubicle in dormitories, shared bedrooms from Fifth Form upward (not overly tidy), and *very* formal common rooms. Exeats flexible, which suits the numerous overseas contingent. House system recently introduced, partly for competitive purposes, which has had dramatic effect on weekends, now action-packed. ('Indeed, we may have to reduce some activities,' says Head). Older girls allowed to Shaftesbury, Bath, Salisbury. Nuns run soup kitchen, school front door kept locked against vagrants, sadly unwelcoming first impression to potential parents.

THE PUPILS 35% of boarders' parents are in the services, not necessarily living abroad. Large local element (not all RC). Some pupils financed by the local Wiltshire Education Authority.

Entrance At 10 and 11 by own exam, and at 12 and 13 usually by CE, own exam if girl not coming from prep school. Not as easy as it once was.

Exit 80-85% go on to degree courses. A steady stream follow careers in nursing, physio- or speech-therapy; foundation art course, drama or music school, secretarial college in trickles.

Bottom Line One music scholarship at 11, 12 or 13; one art scholarship at 13 or 14; two Sixth Form academic scholarships (all open externally and internally). Relatively reasonable fees.

Remarks Steady, un-stuffy school, previously a convent, soon to lose nuns—to the dismay of parents.

ST MARY'S SCHOOL
Wantage, Oxfordshire OX12 8BZ
TEL (02357) 3571

Pupils: 302 girls • All board • Ages: 11-18 • Size of Sixth Form: 69 • High Church Anglican • Fee-paying.

HEAD Since 1980, the Rev P H Johns MA (fifties), previously Senior Mistress and Housemistress at Gordonstoun. Widow, with two grown-up children. NB Strongly dislikes this book, did not allow us to see round the school or talk to girls, to which end we were seen off the premises by Head, 'Not that we have anything to hide'.

Academic Matters Not an academic hotshot, and pressure certainly not put on girls—even staff describe the attitude towards exams as laid-back. That said, results are reasonable, and are getting better. Pupils of widely ranging abilities. German is compulsory (no Italian or Spanish available at GCSE, more emphasis now on Science. Some good teaching, some cosy teachers. New male Deputy Head. Post-GCSE leavers diminishing slightly.

Games, Options, the Arts Traditionally strong lacrosse and tennis. Art has picked up recently, say parents. Good sports hall; music and drama popular, (occasionally with Bradfield and St Edward's, Oxford). Sewing and cookery strong.

Background and Atmosphere Founded by the Vicar of Wantage in 1873 to be run by Anglican nuns, who withdrew in 1972 (though school retains links with them), and spiritual atmosphere lingers tangibly. Buildings are cosy and domestic, hemmed in by main road whistling past windows. Very noisy dining room. Smart royal blue uniform and navy Batman type capes, much hated sensible brown shoes.

Discipline Has been iffy in the past....

THE PUPILS Live wires. Upper-middle class, many second and third generation pupils, parents all know each other, very happy girls who make friends for life. Old girls include Olivia Channon and Rosie Johnson.

Entrance Interview and CE.

Exit Some to university or polys, also History of Art, art school, music college, drama school, secretarial.

Bottom Line No endowments. One junior scholarship, two music scholarships, one Sixth Form scholarship.

Remarks Popular, cosy and happy as ever, and a good place to gain confidence.

ST PAUL'S SCHOOL
Lonsdale Road, London SW13 9JT
TEL London (081) 748 9162

Pupils: 750 boys • 120 board, 630 day • Ages: 13-18 • Size of Sixth Form: 300 • C of E • Fee-paying.

HEAD The High Master, since 1986, Canon Peter Pilkington MA (fifties) educated Dame Allan's, Newcastle and Cambridge. Taught at Eton, previously Head of the King's School, Canterbury. A delightful, popular, caring man, short, plump, twinkly, with tremendous humour, he is down to earth and perceptive. Emphasizes twin aims of academic excellence and pastoral care for individual pupil.

Academic Matters Outstandingly high numbers of A grades for both Maths and Physics. Curriculum recently revised, so that all boys have to take an option in a practical subject from second year. Most boys take GCSE French and Maths at end of second year, other subjects year following. 22 per class, with boys continually moving and shifting, depending on progress and motivation, kept stretched but not pressurized. High fliers flourish. Impressively long detailed reports each term can reduce non-brilliant to despair. Staff include Left-wingers, some parents bemoan lack of eccentrics and really sparky teachers, and also apparent lack of emphasis on English grammar.

Games, Options, the Arts Two-hour lunch-break daily during which boys are involved in a non-academic activity—eg rowing (impressive), music, swimming, games. Cricket currently strong. (NB Some, inevitably, hang around.) Enviable grassy acres plus the river, excellent indoor pool, fencing *salle* said to be best in Western Europe; fives a major game here. CDT flourishes, drama a great strength, also music. Newly enlarged musical facilities, much over-all refurbishing, resource centres. Long and varied list of visiting lecturers, who find boys' questions and attitudes challenging. Saturday school taken up with games, rehearsals, extras. Good art and pottery.

Background and Atmosphere Founded in 1509 by Dean Colet, friend of Erasmus and Thomas More, whose humanitarian principles still stand firm. Trustees of the Foundation: Worshipful Company of Mercers. School moved to its present site in 1968: hideous and faceless but compact pebbledash buildings with odd bits of old stained glass and statuary recalling former glory. Set in 45 acres (previously reservoirs). New boys coming from London preps find school life curiously unstructured, with little feeling of being part of a community. To participate in 'Apposition' is every boy's aim: (four outstanding pupils speak/make music etc to assembled distinguished visitors, governors and parents). Head keen on getting parents far more involved in educational developments.

Discipline Strong and well-used tutor system, whereby parents are asked to invite tutor (plus wife, if he has one) home for a meal: communication is intended to be frequent and open. However, many stories of wild behaviour on and off the school premises. Head commented on the question of drugs that each case is examined on its own merits. School has regular visits from psychiatrist/counsellor.

THE PUPILS Drawn from all around London and from as far away as Guildford and Windsor. Many from state schools, many from Colet Court. All sorts, no types. Very articulate. Old Boys include John Milton, Edmund Halley, Jonathan Miller, Peter Shaffer.

Entrance Tough: all but the brightest weeded out; intake is 150/160 per year. At 10 or 11, all prospective pupils and parents come to the school: Head interviews parents, the Surmaster sees the boys, and afterwards they compare notes. Main lists close then, and CE follows on as qualifying exam. Boys must perform well in every subject.

Exit Vast majority go on to university, 'They're more thoughtful about which university now', observes Canon Pilkington, 40-55 annually to Oxbridge and regularly to the Royal College of Art. Wide variety of careers eventually, marked emphasis on traditional ones—law, medicine, professions, services, the Church.

Bottom Line There are 153 scholars (as many as the miraculous draft of fishes—scholars wear a silver fish badge): scholarships are mainly awarded on entrance, some develop in the Eighth ie Sixth Form. Scholars integrated with the rest of the school. School caters for cases of genuine need. Assisted Places.

Remarks One of the two top London public schools. Less of a hothouse atmosphere than Westminster, with acres of space and facilities.

ST PAUL'S GIRLS' SCHOOL
Brook Green, London W6 7BS
TEL London (071) 603 2288

Pupils: 620 girls • All day • Ages 11-18 • Size of Sixth Form (known as Seventh and Eighth Forms): 214 • Anglican Foundation • Fee-paying.

HEAD High Mistress since 1989, Mrs Helen Williams MA (fifties), previously Headmistress of Blackheath High School. Educated Redland High School, Bristol, read English at Girton. Began her teaching career at St Paul's ('It's always been my model school'), then St George's Edinburgh, later a don at Edinburgh University. Has published work on *The Wasteland* by T S Eliot. Two grown-up sons. The antithesis of her predecessor, Mrs Williams is low profile, not one to project herself (girls are critical about this), accessible. Intends to challenge the 'race from goal to goal to deepening the process—I know it sounds woofy, but are they doing too much, too fast, and should they go deeper, have more time to read, to reflect, to question?

Academic Matters Outstanding—30-40% consistently go to Oxford or Cambridge. Traditionally strong in both the Arts and the Sciences. Maths, Physics, Chemistry *and* Latin are all compulsory.

Stimulating and demanding, the atmosphere is extremely conducive to learning, girls very keen on achievement (staff too). Head keen on AOs. Very closely advised on A-levels, also careers. Deputy Head Miss Gough described by one and all as 'brilliant teacher' (English)—and a major influence in the school, according to parents. Arts students are strongly advised to take a year out before university. Leakage after GCSEs (16 at last count)—but far more come in.

Preparing to introduce the school's own certificate in place of some GCSE certificates.

Games, Options, the Arts Olympic-sized swimming pool, two lacrosse pitches, multi-gym, eight tennis courts—and all used with panache, though music and drama are the most serious extras. Gustav Holst was once Director of Music (wrote the *Planet Suite* here). Splendid theatre built in memory of Old Paulina Dame Celia Johnson.

Background and Atmosphere Large red brick Edwardian building, distinctly spacious for a London school. Established this century as part of John Colet's Educational Foundation of 1509. Governing body is drawn from the Worshipful Company of Mercers, and Oxford, Cambridge and London University dons. No uniform. Occasional complaints from parents that the spiritual side of life is apparently sacrificed to the academic, especially at top end of the school. Humming with activity and energy all the time.

THE PUPILS Mostly middle class intelligentsia, currently 50 Jewish girls, 15 Muslims and numerous representatives of other faiths, in keeping with school's original intention. Highly articulate, highly motivated, highly self confident—often accused of arrogance. By far the most distinguished list of Old Girls of any girls' school—among them, Rosalind Franklin, Prof Joan Robinson, Imogen Holst, Baroness Stocks, Shirleys Summerskill and Conran.

Entrance Extremely selective, via school's own entrance exam. Potential is what counts. Well over 300 sit for 78 places; 25% from state primaries. Some places at 16+. Head tells potential pupils and their parents 'Stamina is absolutely essential—physical, intellectual and emotional stamina.'

Exit 90-95% to university, of which 30-40% go to Oxbridge. Law and Medicine currently high on Paulina career lists, also academia, publishing, art dealing, architecture.

Bottom Line Up to 15 Assisted Places each year, (including five in Sixth Form), also Foundation Awards for music and art. New bursary award named in honour of Heather Brigstocke, the previous High Mistress.

Remarks Enormously impressive—and still possibly the strongest academic girls' private day school in the country.

ST SWITHUN'S SCHOOL
Winchester, Hampshire SO 21 1HA
TEL Winchester (0962) 861316

Pupils: 433 girls ● *248 board, 185 day* ● *Ages: 11-18* ● *Size of Sixth Form: 103* ● *C of E* ● *Fee-paying.*

HEAD Since 1986, Miss J E Jefferson BA (forties), read History at Newcastle, did Dip Ed at Oxford. Aims for girls to leave, 'with the confidence and courage to challenge what is happening in the world'.

Academic Matters Excellent general course for Sixth Formers with outside speakers, followed by 'debriefings' and essays. Academic atmosphere, and impressive staff. Usual range of subjects at A-level, with some very good results. Development of Technology course since last edition of book, though it is still in its infancy. Classics particularly well taught, also Maths and strong Sciences with seven labs.

Games, Options, the Arts Wide ranging and energetic extras, including pre-driving course, scuba diving, dressage, aerobics, archery—to name but a few. Beefy lacrosse, netball—all very competitive and weaklings may get shovelled aside. Drama is good and large numbers of girls take the Guildhall drama exams. Good music, with chamber groups and two orchestras. Some joint activities (particularly drama) with Winchester College, though pupils report Wykehamists not always interested.

Background and Atmosphere Founded in 1884 now housed in large thirties Queen Anne-style purpose-built building, with lots of space, but rather bleakly set in green belt outside Winchester, with several addditions and extensions. Separate day and boarding houses, except for Upper Sixth, whose house is mixed day and boarding. Good libraries. New block housing crafts, technology and a language lab etc. Atmosphere generally one of work and purposeful ness, and sensible discipline. No Saturday morning school, but boarders are kept busy (see above).

THE PUPILS Mostly from within a 50-100-mile radius, including lots of day girl daughters of Southampton businessmen and fairly large contingent of ex pats. Beastly uniform—but none for the Sixth Form. OGs: Baroness Warnock and Prof Joscelyn Toynbee.

Entrance CE at 11, 12 and 13, some from St Swithun's own Junior School, some at Sixth Form.

Exit All to further education, mainly to university, a handful to Oxbridge.

Bottom Line One major, one minor academic scholarship, also a music school, some help for the needy and some Assisted Places at Sixth Form level.

Remarks Solid girls' school with slightly amorphous feel, owing to almost equal split between day and boarding pupils.

SEDBERGH SCHOOL
Sedbergh, Cumbria LA10 5HG
TEL Sedbergh (05396) 20535

Pupils: 490 boys ● 475 board, 15 day ● Ages: 11-18 ● Size of Sixth Form: 174 ● C of E and C of S ● Fee-paying.

HEAD Since 1982, Dr R G Baxter BSc, PhD (formerly Birmingham Grammar. Previously Under Master at Winchester where he taught Maths for 12 years, and lecturer in Applied Maths at Sheffield University. Dr Baxter has been a 'civilizing influence' on the traditional tough rugger-bugger image of Sedbergh. Sixth Form lunch with Head over the year, boys 'open and friendly and know where the line is drawn'. Authoritarian. PR possibly not his long suit.

Academic Matters 'Academically, the school needed pulling': there are now signs that it has been. Exam results improving. Essential GCSEs: two English, Maths, two Sciences, one Language. Strongest in Science and Maths; least popular—Modern Languages.

Games, Options, the Arts Famed for its rugger and the 'Wilson Run'—a 10-mile fell race open to ages 16+. Good CDT with interesting art and pottery. Magnifi-

cent music and a good drama school. Regular trips abroad with games—particularly cricket. 25-metre indoor pool, new sports hall, CCF (medals for shooting). Strong links with Navy. Excellent careers advice and superb interview experience (with FPs and parents). D of E awards.

Background and Atmosphere Founded in 1525 by Roger Lupton, a Provost of Eton, the original seven houses have been joined by a 'baby' house, Cressbrook, for state school entries at 11-13 (huge waiting list). Original traditional type dorms are being converted to study/bedrooms. Limestone houses throughout tiny town: music in former Bursar's house, Evans, on Main Street. Sixth Form bar in games pavilion next to Civic Medical Centre. Impressive conversion of Georgian building on site of Lupton's original school into Churchill Library (roof leaks). Good house system, with three or four Housemasters who are a 'match for any in the country' according to local prep school.

THE PUPILS Mainly local with a fair proportion from Scotland; 20 ex pats and ditto ethnic. 'Boys greet their Head in a variety of regional accents.' OBs: Brendan Bracken and Willy Carling.

Entrance Junior House via 11+ and interview. Otherwise CE from prep schools.

Exit A leak of 2% after GCSE; 80% to degree courses. Exceptionally good careers guidance, with FPs and parents forming serious interview panels.

Bottom Line Five Assisted Places for Junior House, also Scholarships, Assisted Places Sixth Form, bursaries and music scholarships.

Remarks Good reports on all sides—well-structured games-orientated school which has been dramatically renovated, and civilized.

SEVENOAKS SCHOOL
Sevenoaks, Kent TN13 1HU
TEL Sevenoaks (0732) 455133

Pupils: 550 boys, 360 girls • 160 boys board, 390 day boys • 146 girls board, 214 day girls • Ages: 11-18 • Size of Sixth Form: 400 • Non-denom • Fee-paying.

HEAD Since 1981, Mr Richard Barker MA (early fifties), educated at Repton, then Cambridge and Bristol universities. Ambitious. Strong on PR. Go-ahead, energetic, an innovator (eg introduced Business Studies at Marlborough while teaching there). Wide and forward-looking view at education, talks persuasively.

Academic Matters Determinedly up-to-date approach to teaching. Offers International Baccalaureate as an alternative to A-level (it has worldwide recognition as a qualification for university). Gathers in strength academically to reach high and broad standards at the top of the school. Three main and three subsidiary subjects are studied, including a Science, Maths, a Language and a national literature. In September 1991, 130 Sixth Formers were reading the full IB diploma. Very hot on all branches of Science (Astronomy on offer, and school has its own observatory).
Outstanding Modern Languages, with unusual ones, eg Dutch and Norwegian, on offer. Recent introduction of exchange visits during term to/from France, Germany, Spain, Eastern bloc.

Games, Options, the Arts Plenty of scope for budding musicians (Kodaly method of music taught). Thriving drama department (own theatre), a festival every year with 35 major productions (there is an annual performance of a play in a foreign language). All children have to do a creative subject (specialist craftsmen employed for this). School has a studio for budding TV reporters, actors and producers. National pioneers for the Voluntary Service Unit: boys and girls are much encouraged to be community minded. Rugger the main claim to fame on games field (*two* teams tour the world), sailing, shooting and tennis all strong (three covered tennis courts). CCF is voluntary and popular, and includes girls.

Background and Atmosphere Built in 1418 by Sir William Sevenoke, Mayor of London and a friend of Henry V as a thank you for his share in the victory at Agincourt. Borders on 1,000 acres of Knowle Park. Lots of new buildings, and purposeful air of efficiency pervades. Right in the main town of Sevenoaks, but spreads out into boskiness at the back. Fits a lot into a confined space. Strong support from locals. Some concern about standards at bottom end of school: '*Definitely* better at the top end', said a parent.

THE PUPILS Largely local, favoured by media parents. Many bilingual hybrids. 20% are non-nationals, many of them European, from as many as 37 different countries, attracted by Sixth Form International Centre, and unusually broad outlook of education here.

Entrance At 11 and 13, via school's own exam or CE. Pass mark now 'very close to 60%'. 80 pupils come in at Sixth Form.

Exit Consistently good A-level results. Oxbridge 'expecting 25 a year from now on', and London School of Economics, plus an exceptionally wide variety of universities (including overseas). Polytechnics popular for business-type courses. Medicine and engineering favoured careers.

Bottom Line Offers 50 academic scholarships a year and five Assisted Places at last, after years of lobbying.

Remarks International Bac and European links now the envy of other schools. Essentially a day school (except at Sixth Form), with a strong Sixth Form intake.

SHEFFIELD HIGH SCHOOL
10 Rutland Park, Sheffield S10 2PE
TEL Sheffield (0742) 660324

Pupils: Approx 520 girls in Senior School; 190 in Junior Department • All day • Ages: 4-18 • Size of Sixth Form 120 • Non-denom • Fee-paying • Girls' Public Day School Trust.

HEAD Since September 1989, Mrs Margaret Houston BA (late forties), educated St Hilda's Whitby, Barnsley High and Leeds University (English). Ha been teaching all her life, mostly in comprehensives in the area, formerly Deputy Head of Harrogate Grammar. Married with two children; husband is a lecturer in local Sixth Form College. Untalkative. Comments that a 'good academic education is of value to girls in itself, and in order to provide them with the necessary tools for life...we're not about flower arranging and elocution'.

Remarks Useful if uninspiring private academic girls' day school, in an area not noted for these. Betjemanesque buildings. Register asap, entrance by exam at 11+ and interview/test at other ages (including at three-plus). Currently very good at tennis (runners up for Northern Championship, 1990), hoping to send riding team to Stonar for one-day event, also hot on voluntary service (the area is bursting with charity shops). Three-ish to Oxbridge a year, Durham popular, 'vast majority' go on to higher education. The Trust to which the school belongs has recently spent money 'upgrading the entrance' and in expanding buildings to provide extra form in junior department in September 1991 and two more forms gradually thereafter. Some 'leakage' at Sixth Form—one or two to boys' schools, some to the state sector. 17 Assisted Places in each year. Strong languages (French and German). OGs: Margaret Drabble and the creator of Rupert Bear.

SHERBORNE SCHOOL

Sherborne, Dorset DT9 3AP

TEL Sherborne (0935) 812646

Pupils: 650 boys ● All board ● Ages: 13-18 ● Size of Sixth Form: 260 ● C of E ● Fee-paying.

HEAD Since 1988, Mr Peter Lapping MA (forties), educated at St John's College, Johannesburg, University of Natal(where he read History) and Lincoln College Oxford (for PPE). Previously Head of Maiplake College. A nice man, easy and gentle, though reputedly steely qualities too. Keen on producing balanced boys who will look you in the eye, roll up their sleeves and get on with it'.

Academic Matters Strengthened considerably under previous Head. Very sound teaching all round, and steadily good results. Specialization left late. Changing list of non-specialist subjects at A-level might include Tragedy, Architecture, Investment, Ecology, and some studies are done with Sherborne School for Girls. Modern Languages (housed in impressive new block) and History good. Non-workers 'asked' to leave (rare but not unheard of).

Games, Options, the Arts Outstanding games record—playing fields cover 50 acres with 11 cricket pitches, athletics track, 10 hard tennis, eight grass tennis courts, 16 rugger pitches, all-weather pitch etc, plus indoor sports centre (used by locals as well), with gymnasium, squash courts, swimming pool. Compulsory games until 16. Flourishing Technical Activities Centre, CCF of high repute, a major (voluntary) activity, all three services, and boys often end up with pilots' licence, and experience in parachuting. Drama keen and good, smaller productions are often run entirely by boys, major ones can occupy 200 boys (electricians, painters etc), and some joint productions with Sherborne Girls. Powell Hall, the theatre, is also used by visiting theatre groups. Very strong Debating Society (has provided several Presidents of Union at Oxbridge). Talks by visitors (and sometimes boys) often given in masters' drawing rooms. Good music, and art increasingly successful.

Background and Atmosphere Delightfully set in the shadow of the Abbey (much used by the boys), founded by Edward VI as Grammar School in 1530, glorious library with famed hammer roof, the main bulk of the building, including the courts and chapel, carried out in 1870s. No campus—many of school buildings are scattered through the town. Nine houses, 70 boys in each, with Housemaster plus three tutors, means someone is always on parade (NB not true of all schools, by a long way). Tenth house being built in order to decrease numbers of boys per house, thereby emphasizing pastoral care further. Refurbishment scheme afoot for all Houses, study-bedrooms on the increase now. Centralized feeding. Sixth Form centre where boys can entertain, some social mixing with Sherborne and Leweston girls. Traditional new boys initiation tests, but little bullying, if any. Fairly tight ship, day firmly structured, boys kept busy and well stretched from the start, generally purposeful, though as they go up the school some mutterings heard that city lights are far away. School recently left five-acre property in town centre by wealthy local coal merchant, Head enjoying toying with this.

THE PUPILS Relaxed, sensible, self-confident, a

fairly disciplined lot comment locals. School anxious to point out it is not *just* a West Country school—some come from East Anglia, Scotland, London home counties. Fierce loyalty from Old Boys, who include David Shepherd, Nigel Dempster, Jeremy Irons, John le Carre, A N Whitehead, Christopher Chataway, Richard Eyre and the King of Swaziland.

Entrance Registration by 10, preferably earlier; pass-mark at CE approx 55%.

Exit 80% go on to university (between 20 and 25 to Oxbridge). Also London, Exeter, Durham, Bristol, Manchester, Reading, Bath. Remaining 20% of leavers likely to go into services and traditional public school careers.

Bottom Line Wide range of generous scholarships, exhibitions and bursaries offered.

Remarks Traditional public school with high morale and rising profile, surprisingly civilized despite lingering gamesy image.

SHERBORNE SCHOOL FOR GIRLS

Sherborne, Dorset DT9 3QN

TEL Sherborne (0935) 812245

Pupils: 466 girls ● 460 board, 6 day ● Ages: 12-18 ● Size of Sixth Form: 155 ● C of E. ● Fee-paying.

HEAD Since 1985, Miss June Taylor BSc (forties), educated at Sherborne School for Girls and Sussex University. Totally home grown—Head girl, Maths teacher, then Housemistress for 15 years at Sherborne. Enthusiastic, capable, traditionalist. Not always easily available to parents. Aims for girls to 'develop their interests, do well academically—and enjoy life'. Speaks disparagingly about 'knowledge factories', and suspects that there is a 'misplaced belief in qualifications on bits of paper'.

Academic Matters Sound though not brilliant, work flow steady without being pressurized, all girls take three A-levels (a few, more). Study periods fall throughout the day (first lesson is at 8.35am), flexible timetabling essential because of music and extras

offered (eg squash coaching). English, Maths, Sciences all strong, also Modern Languages, with small but successful Russian department (available to Sixth Formers only). Teaching often thorough, but not exciting. Some Sixth Form options done with Sherborne Boys.

Games, Options, the Arts Outstanding music, quite the best in any nonspecialist girls' school, under Miss Augusta Miller, diminutive, dynamic, tireless and fun, a brilliant teacher and organizer, especially of choral activities. School music productions always *very* good, very varied—and not only for the most talented. Strongly gamesy, unusual number of Sixth Formers in school teams, win most matches at all levels (one of few girls' schools to play both lax and hockey, and first girls' school to put down all-weather hockey pitch). Sports complex includes squash courts and shower area ('car wash'). Excellent art centre, with much use CDT, takes on jewellery making, photography etc.

Background and Atmosphere Founded turn-of-the-century (not an architectural treat), on 40-acre site on outskirts of the town. Unusually strong (and very competitive) house system (leniency or otherwise of Housemistresses varies quite considerably); all meals eaten in their boarding houses ('good food', say the girls), ages mix freely, everyone does their own laundry (except sheets). Girls kept busy most of the time, strong sense of purpose pervades the school, structured day, fairly tight discipline, all the usual girls' boarding school complaints that 'not enough' happening at weekends. 'Cheapie walking' (Cheap Street) favourite Saturday afternoon outing. Upper Sixth have their own house and can invite Sherborne boys to their TV common room, aptly named 'the airport lounge'—anonymity the keynote of the whole house. All Upper Sixth allowed into town pubs for a meal.

THE PUPILS First choice West Country school for many, also Londoners, girls with brothers next door at Sherborne Boys'. Fairly wide social mix. Happy girls, very supportive of each other, sensible, not push ('Not pushy enough,' say critics). Recognisable by manner of mane tossing.

Entrance Two-thirds come at 12+ (younger, provided they have passed the 12+ exam), one-third 13+; approximately six at Sixth Form.

Exit 70% go on to degree courses, about eight or so to Oxbridge, others to Bristol, Exeter, Southampton, Manchester, Durham. Medical, paramedical, teaching, art college, cookery, bi-lingual secretarial courses, all popular.

Bottom line   Five scholarships (from two-thirds to one-quarter fees), two exhibitions, plus three music scholarships; also Sixth Form scholarship.

Remarks   Strong and good, traditional, all round girls' boarding school.

SHIPLAKE COLLEGE

Henley-on-Thames, Oxfordshire RG9 4BW

TEL Wargrave (0734) 402455

Pupils: 340 boys • *275 board, 65 day* • *Ages: 13-18* • *Size of Sixth Form: 100* • *C of E* • *Fee-paying.*

HEAD   Since September 1988, Nicholas Bevan MA (forties), educated Shrewsbury and Balliol College, Oxford. Soldiered for six years, before deciding to become a teacher (trained at St John's College, Cambridge). Taught at Westminster, then Shrewsbury, where parents latterly considered him one of the best Housemasters.

Academic Matters   Copes very well with less able boys and those with learning difficulties in English. Well spoken of by many preps, who use it as a standby for boys who cannot get into their first choice of academic school. The average boy can shine here, and particular help is given to dyslexics. Boys are not academically submerged, policy being 'to obtain the maximum results with the minimum of fuss', in the words of the late Head. 17 A-levels offered. No shame attached to any amount of exam retakes. Maths and Physics main strengths. Classical History has a high pass rate. New attention paid to French.

Games, Options, the Arts   Strong Arts still. Strong cricket tradition. Rugby doing nicely. Superb sports hall and boat house. Strong rowing school, and averages four international junior oarsmen a year. Flourishing drama and music.

Background and Atmosphere   Established 1959 in beautiful setting overlooking river Thames. Firmly traditional, with an emphasis on developing self-discipline. Senior boys run 'Junior Common Room' with bar.

THE PUPILS   Well-mannered and gentlemanly breed of chaps, often with a keen desire to make serious money. Stock Exchange and marketing are high on the list of job intentions.

Entrance   CE, plus the school's own English paper (no longer Maths). High attention is paid to prep school Head's report. Boys with difficulties in English need to book early; they are looked at for potential in that subject: 50% of the remedial English entry (16 are accepted each year) are turned away at interview—many are called, but few are chosen. NB Several pupils come in from the state system.

Exit   Typically, about 25% to university or polytechnics, rest spread to agricultural colleges, City, farming, services.

Bottom Line   Two scholarships awarded annually: one, the value of one term's fees; the other, half a term's fees. Two day scholarships, one for pupil under 14, one for pupil entering Sixth Form. Music scholarship, value £650.

Remarks   Super confidence-building establishment in the public school mould. Much sought after. Has style. Particularly competent at teaching children in need of remedial help.

SHREWSBURY HIGH SCHOOL

32 Town Walls, Shrewsbury, Shropshire SY1 1TN

TEL Shrewsbury (0743) 62872

Pupils: 600 girls • *All day* • *Ages: 4-18* • *Size of Sixth Form: 80* • *Non-denom* • *Fee-paying.*

HEAD   Since 1990, Miss Susan Gardner MA (forties). Strong academic day school, popular locally with wide catchment area from both sides of the Welsh/English border. Hard work and few frills, like most sister GPDST schools; some social intercourse with Shrewsbury School (brothers etc), just across the river. Gently expanding from the bottom up; new labs. Social Biology and Economics recently added to A-level syllabus. Assisted Places under used (a common cry). Good reports reach us.

SHREWSBURY SCHOOL

The Schools, Shrewsbury, Shropshire
SY3 7BA
TEL *Shrewsbury (0743) 344537*

Pupils: 668 boys ● 524 board, 124 day ● Ages: 13- 18 ●
Size of Sixth Form: 257 ● C of E ● Fee-paying.

HEAD   Since September 1988, Mr Edward (Ted) Maidment (forties), educated Pocklington School, Scholar and Choral Scholar at Jesus College, Cambridge. Read History for primary degree, then History of Literature and Sociology at University of London. Previously Headmaster of Ellesmere College. Bachelor, jovial, keen singer, larger than life, refreshing. Knows his pupils—and cares. Teaches some General Studies to Sixth Form, Divinity and History to Third and Fourth years. Has fished for staff from all over the place, and comments he prefers good teachers to buildings, taking his time over appointments still to be made, 'you wait for the right person'.

Academic Matters   A fairly wide cross-section of academic ability, well-coped with at all levels. Good balance of traditional and modern teaching methods. Very strong Sciences; possibly the best Biology department in the country, under Ian Lacey—A grades galore at A-level, and a pupil came top of exams, nationwide. Electronic microscope and amazing collection of pickled organs. Strong Maths. Languages 'improving', according to parents, (Mrs Thatcher's resignation first gleaned by pupils via French satellite news). At time of our visit, school advertising for European director, 'someone to network and not just talk about languages'. Sixth Form cover wide General Studies (including good Business Studies Course). Remarkable ancient library, one of the most important scholarly public school libraries.

Games, Options, the Arts   Famous for rowing (six OBs in the current Great Britain rowing squad), and strong on most games. Very good music, Department now headed by John Moore. Major achievement so far is production of a full scale opera composed by a present Sixth Form music scholar. Very good art and drama too, (despite tiny theatre). School strong on outward bound type of activities, also community work. Lots of visiting speakers. Strong careers depart-

ment, (Old Boys extremely helpful), strong industrial links. Flourishing school workshops.

Discipline   'Know your boys' is the Head's motto on discipline—to which end he has decreased size of houses to 55, and built a new one (the showpiece), and has introduced highly structured tutor system. Not many reports of wild behaviour.

Background and Atmosphere   Founded in 1552 by Charter of King Edward VI, and later in century reckoned to be the *largest* school in England. Samuel Butler revived it at the end of the eighteenth century, moved in nineteenth century from the town to its present splendid position across the river; buildings on 'the site' extremely spread out, boys run everywhere (rarely bike). Mothy outdoor noticeboards. Grounds superbly kept. Over £1 million spent updating and extending facilities over last 25 years. Day boys have a separate house; all houses eat at their own tables in communal dining hall (food claimed to be good), and are very house-conscious; breakfast and supper cafeteria style, but lunch is formal with tables set, grace, youngest boys serving the school from trolleys, Prefects giving out notices. Chapel three times a week. Boys mix with girls from Shrewsbury High; Moreton Hall girls come for careers lectures and some music and drama. School considered by parents to be 'very well run', plenty on offer, and boys are kept busy and challenged. 'Very good', report parents, 'for middle of the road boys—they're happy and self confident.'

THE PUPILS   Locals (huge catchment area), lots of sons of Old Boys. Old Salopians include most of the Private Eye team, also Michael Heseltine. Boys mainly well-mannered, with ease of manner and unpretentious. (Absolutely no intentions of including girls here.)

Entrance   Registration from birth; CE. Often from Abberley, Packwood, Moor Park, Prestfield, King's Grange, Malsis, Yarlet. Occasionally a few at Sixth Form.

Exit   20 a year to Oxbridge; 74% on to university, 13% to polytechnics for degree courses, a few to agricultural college.

Bottom Line   Generous scholarships—17 academic and two music.

Remarks   Now very strong under excellent leadership—good all round, a civilized traditional public school. Go and look.

SOUTH HAMPSTEAD HIGH SCHOOL

3 Maresfield Gardens, London NW3 5SS
TEL London (071) 435 2899

Pupils: 525 girls • *All day* • *Ages: 11-18* • *Size of Sixth Form: 150* • *Non-denom* • *Fee-paying.*

HEAD Since 1975, Mrs Averill Burgess BA (fifties), educated at a Leicestershire Girls' Grammar School, read History at London University. Previously Head of History at Wimbledon High School. Divorced. High profile Head, constantly in the thick of every educational argument, with hotly held views on single sex schools, to wit, that girls do better in them (but she would say that, wouldn't she, running a school packed with academic high flyers). GSA President 1989-90.

Academic Matters As the prospectus puts it, this school is 'unashamedly academic'. Arts extremely strong; English very good. Science the unloved relation. No choices until Fourth year. Grades have been abolished for routine written work in the first three years, 'to reduce the pressure for unrelieved A grades'—a nice swing against current educational trend. Expectations extremely high. 20 A-levels to choose from—main stream subjects only, nothing exotic. A and B grades at A-level were 74.8% in 1989/90, though, surprisingly, 61 candidates took only 176 subjects, ie under three each. Computer Studies a forte (not an exam subject); History and History of Art keenly followed. Pockets of brilliance noticeable among pupils, results, staff, though pace appears less pressurized than at some academic girls' schools. Non-examinable General Studies for all Sixth Formers; Current Affairs plays vital role. Girls must organize visiting speakers.

Games, Options, the Arts Strong music tradition, especially choral, also drama, some music and drama shared with neighbouring University College School boys, 'they grab us for their plays, but here we play boys' parts too'. Sport is serious, despite lack of facilities, regular winners of netball matches—came fourth in the Aberdair Cup. Good art (no pottery). Double-decker bus with computers, and CDT workshop comes once a week shared with sister schools.

Background and Atmosphere Founded in 1876, moved to present site in 1882, added to and adapted ever since—rabbit warreny. Dining area with circular tables, far friendlier than traditional school refectory tables. Space everywhere is at a premium, though adjacent Victorian building recently acquired. Every corner used, areas of the school down-at-heel, some austere and traditional old-fashioned classrooms. 'Everyone is good', is a conscious policy, thus no school prizes below Sixth Form (where there are endowments). 'There is always a danger of an academic school getting too hard-edged', thinks the Head. School exams are graded, not percentaged, without placings. Head abolished prefect system and gave responsibility to all the Sixth Form. Enhanced pastoral care system another of Head's innovations, with health education covering wide syllabus; and tutors to lend sympathetic ear to their needs. Sensible uniform allows choice of trousers or skirt.

THE PUPILS Daughters of locals (actors, professionals, intelligentsia), large bright Jewish contingent, and from farthest corners of north and north-west London; wide social mix. Friendly, quizzical, sensible, unpretentious. Old Girls include Rabbi Julia Neuberger, Helena Bonham-Carter, Glynis Johns, Dilys Powell.

Entrance Via school's own exam at 11: one-quarter from junior school round the corner, half of the rest from state schools, six children competing for each place. 'We're not looking for the standard child', explained Head, 'we're after alertness, curiosity and interest.'

Exit Practically every one to university, as you would expect, 17 to Oxbridge in 1991. They go on into law, medicine, accountancy, merchant banking, journalism—a preference for tough careers.

Bottom Line One or two academic scholarships (half or quarter fees), and 11 Assisted Places at 11+, five at Sixth Form; bursaries available. Like other GPDST schools, fees kept remarkably low.

Remarks Very strong local academic day school, popular with the 'chattering classes' of north west London. Offers slightly rounder education than most other GPDST schools.

STAMFORD HIGH SCHOOL FOR GIRLS

St Martin's, Stamford, Lincolnshire PE9 2LJ

TEL Stamford (0780) 62330

Pupils: Approx 745 in all • 100+ board; 30+ weekly board; remaining day • Ages: 11-18 • Junior School: 269, majority day, a few boarding, also 55 day boys, ages 4-11 (boys 4-8) • Non-denom • Fee-paying.

HEAD   Since 1978, Miss G Bland BA (forties).

Remarks   Still excellent reports from this largish high school for girls where, to quote an ex-pupil (now a Headmistress) 'I was educated in the very broadest sense of the word.' Entry by test and interview. Some Assisted Places. Founded 1877. Feed from Junior school.

STONAR SCHOOL

Cottles Park, Atworth, Melksham, Wiltshire SN12 8NT

TEL Melksham (0225) 702309

Pupils: Approx 500 girls • 290 board, 210 day • Ages: 5-18 • Size of Sixth Form: 102 • C of E • Fee-paying.

HEAD   Since September 1985, Mrs Susan Hopkinson BA (early fifties). Educated at Howell's School, Llandaff and at St Hugh's Oxford (History). Very enthusiastic and bubbly. She says: 'The experience of being at school should prepare you *realistically* for a career; I don't want to produce little misfits who can't get a job.' Runs school in a practical, business-like way and comments: 'Schools are in fact competitive small businesses and it is important to make them user-friendly and to give the customers what they want...' Aims to help girls develop an awareness of the possible conflicts that they may encounter over working and

bringing up a family. She herself is a mother of two, and her husband now runs the History and Politics Department at Stonar (pronounced to rhyme with don not stone).

Academic Matters   OK. Not a highly academic school; results creditable given intake. Good, modern Science facilities. Some subjects get one to one tuition at the top of the school. Staff-pupil ratio 1:10.6, 'including eight full-time males'. 63% A-C passes at GCSE at time of writing, 20% with grade A.

Games, Options, the Arts   Stabling for 40 horses and covered riding school with mini-Badminton cross-country course. Guinea pigs etc also welcome. School holds inter-schools one day event (for riding, not guinea pigs), which is becoming increasingly popular and competitors come from schools all over the country. Own covered swimming pool with resident coach, who has got girls into the inter-schools swimming tournament finals. Strong in cross country. Several county hockey players. New Head of Art from Bristol Grammar School. Music school nice but short on sound proofing. Enthusiastic and ambitious expeditions eg walking 200 miles from Kathmandu to the Everest Base Camp.

Background and Atmosphere   Charming neo-Gothic building, behind which lies a slightly scrubby collection of outer buildings, and a Bath stone fronted new junior school and purpose built Sixth Form complex on a collegiate model, all set in 70 acres of beautiful Wiltshire countryside.

Gentle, uninstitutional atmosphere, generally happy, homely, safe and relaxed. Sixth Formers voted to abolish their smoking room in 1990.

THE PUPILS   Some charming and gentle Sloane and half-Sloane souls—the sort of girls you would be happy for your daughter to mix with. Boarders mainly from southern counties and London, also weekly boarders (started 1986). Strong overseas contingent: 4 or so ex pats, small proportion from Japan and Hong Kong, a little Zambian contingent, and a number from service families.

Entrance   Nine years and over—school's entrance exam. 14 and over—interview plus report and recommendation from previous school.

Exit   Approx 12 to university a year, two or three to art college.

Bottom Line   Discretionary bursary for the lower school for a particular talent. Four Sixth Form scholarships—two for those already in the school—which helps stop the leakage to boys' schools. Half-fees scholarships available at 11+; music, riding and athletics bursaries. Enormous increase in numbers (150 more than in 1989) and this has made development of facilities possible.

Remarks Numbers have rocketed over past two to three years, mainly because the Head has built up a competent and efficient establishment in keeping with the requirements of pupils and parents in the 1990s. Ailing girls' schools would do well to study the role model. Excellent.

STONYHURST COLLEGE
Stonyhurst, Blackburn, Lancashire BB6 9PZ
TEL Stonyhurst (025486) 247

Pupils: 435 boys, 3 day girls • *All boys board* • *Ages: 13-18* • *Size of Sixth Form: 190* • *RC* • *Fee-paying.*

HEAD Since 1985, Dr Giles Mercer MA, DPhil (early forties), educated at Austin Friars, Cambridge and Oxford. Head of History at Charterhouse, then worked for Ministry of Defence. The first married lay Head of any Jesuit College in the English speaking world. Delightful, boyish, un-Headish.

Academic Matters Extremely thorough teaching commented on on all fronts by parents—study arrangements conducive to work: 8.15am daily prep time before classes begin, prep on both Saturday and Sunday. 1990 best A-level results on record (Head declares himself 'cautiously pleased'), wide programme for all to follow alongside A-level subjects. Japanese on offer. Outstanding Design and Technology Centre (won RSA design award): 30 boys currently studying Design & Technology for A-level, local schools, industries (including British Aerospace) use facilities. Sprinklings of young staff via far-flung Jesuit establishments. Exceptionally good careers department (uses ECCTIS 2000) and advice.

Games, Options, the Arts Strong games and outdoor pursuits tradition, including fishing on the Hodder for trout and salmon, fell walking, canoeing, sailing. Three boys recently played rugby for England under-19 team (one captained it), nine-hole golf course

(condition improved). Strong D of E, very strong shooting tradition etc, etc. Good music, with no individual instrument charge. (Holiday lets to the National Youth Orchestra.) School has its own observatory.

Background and Atmosphere Feels isolated. Daunting and imposing vast building—the largest boarding school under one roof, set in parkland. School founded in 1593 in France for RC boys forced to be educated out of England, moved here in 1794 into property belonging to the Weld family, with many additions. Magnificent collection of paintings (mainly early Italian), donated by OBs, and ethnographica collected by missionary Jesuits, acres of Dürer woodcuts—all manner of treasures. (When HM the Queen visited Stonyhurst in October 1990, the school presented her with a piece of tartan re-worked from Bonny Prince Charlie's kilt, from their collection.) Guts of teaching areas recently renovated. Vast cubicled dormitories (40 beds), generously large study bedrooms for Sixth Formers. Religion taken very seriously (and taught to question it). Prefects have more clout than at many public schools, though staff very definitely run the place. Centrally run—a rarity—with everyone sleeping under the same roof, and boys divided into year groups ('Playrooms'). No sleeping out exeats other than half term. Bar for Upper Sixth. Staff play cat-and-mouse game with smokers. Long tradition of charity work undertaken (often organized) by boys.

THE PUPILS Widely mixed socially and geographically: 10% from abroad (Spanish speaking world, Hong Kong, France, Hungary, often via other Jesuit colleges, all must speak good English); 60% UK residents from north of the Trent. Also from the south, Wales, Ireland. Old Boys include seven VCs, 11 martyrs (including three canonized saints); Arthur Conan Doyle, Charles Laughton, General Walters, Paul Johnson, Lord Devlin.

Entrance 55% passmark at CE (though a lower mark, plus strong school report might work), largely from own prep school St Mary's Hall, on the same campus, also St John's Beaumont, Windsor (both bulging). A few places at Sixth Form.

Exit 95% go on to degree courses, approximately 10% of annual leavers to Oxbridge.

Bottom Line Nine academic scholarships (depending on quality of applicants), several music scholarships. Extensive bursaries, Assisted Places at 11+, 13+ and 16+.

Remarks Impressively thorough in the best Jesuit belt-and-braces tradition. School poised for appeal and development scheme to celebrate 400th anniversary. Despite go-ahead lay Head's glasnost approach, this is nonetheless public school more as fathers— and even grandfathers—remember it.

STOWE SCHOOL
Buckingham MK18 5EH
TEL Buckingham (0280) 813164

Pupils: 583 including 80 girls in the Sixth Form, the rest boys ● Approx 40 day pupils, otherwise boarding ● Size of Sixth Form: Approx 240 (including the girls) ● Ages: 13-18 ● C of E ● Fee-paying.

Head Since September 1989, Mr Jeremy Nichols MA (forties), educated Lancing (captain of everything) and Cambridge, where he read English and Italian. Was previously one of Eton's brighter Housemasters. Golden family—a governor's dream. Good teacher. Keen on Dickens and has springer called Mr Boffin. Dynamic, driven, kind, keen on sport. Could be someone who spreads himself a bit thin.

Academic Matters Impossible to comment, owing to huge ability mix in school and current state of flux.

Games, Options, the Arts New (at time of writing) music director from Framlingham—ex-director collected large redundancy. Drama of long-standing excellence, particularly enthusiastically supported by the girls in the Sixth Form. Girls do community service while boys are playing rugger.

Background and atmosphere Five-star Grade 1 buildings, the beauty of which rubs off on pupils, though can daunt staff and a large personality is needed not to be dwarfed by the architectural magnificence. Garden follies now in the hands of English Heritage (new folly is in fact their ticket booth). Acres of roof currently being overhauled—and not before time— many reports of drips with buckets under them.

School founded in 1923 by, among others, Montauban (cf the school library, which is good), under first Head Roxburgh—one of the great Headmasters of his generation.

The Pupils Mixed, very. Colourful collection of Old Boys, including Nicholas Henderson, John Sainsbury and Alistair McAlpine, not to mention David Niven, Richard Branson.

Discipline An extremely colourful collection of antics.

Entrance From an amazing collection of schools, including Sunningdale, Sussex House and Wicken Park.

Exit 60-70% to degree courses. Keen Gappers.

Bottom Line Scholarships worth exploring—art, music as well as academic. Has had some horrific extras.

Remarks A school which should do well in about five years' time, if Headmaster doesn't wilt under the gargantuan strain of putting this once great public school back in place.

STRATHALLAN SCHOOL
Forgandenny, Perthshire PH2 9EG
TEL Bridge of Earn (0738) 812546

Pupils: 378 boys, 125 girls ● All board ● Ages: 11-18 ● Size of Sixth Form: 150 ● Non-denom ● Fee-paying.

HEAD Since 1975, Mr David Pighills MA Cantab (fifties). Still no plans to leave at moment, though admits 'there comes a time'. Teaches Biology, but is 'mainly a Headmaster'. Educated at 'an English public school' in North Wales and Cambridge. Unmarried.

Forceful and dynamic Head, who came to the school after 15 years as Housemaster at Fettes. Mr Pighills has totally revamped Strathallan. Shows prospective parents around with pride and humour.

Academic Matters 48 full-time staff, plus 12 part-timers. CDT has four full-time staff and produce Linley-quality furniture, as well as standard collection of metalwork and ingenious gadgets; computer-controlled design equipment and pupils working in their spare time. CDT is popular with girls. Separate computer room, with variety of computers. The school plays the system—all pupils take Higher English unless doing English A-level, otherwise pupils sit A-levels with Highers as an option. Breakdown of exam results not published.

Games, Options, the Arts Good music, excitement among music staff over installation of new Copeman Hart four manual organ; good art, pottery, good music, pipe band, Rugby, cricket, own golf course, skiing, CCF (boys only), hot on flying, gliding, sailing and fishing in own loch (when stocked), also 12 permits on River Earn. Girls do cooking. Lots of trips to Glasgow and Edinburgh for theatres and exhibitions.

Background and Atmosphere All pupils now have separate study bedrooms (with pantries everywhere) after second year. Attractive chapel and hideous dining room (not a Pighills product). Classroom complex is 300 yards from rest of school. School stands in own 150 acre grounds permanently filled with pupils 'doing things'. Girls are totally accepted and occasional liaisons seem to improve work output—against the national trend.

THE PUPILS Less than an hour from central Edinburgh or Glasgow, Strathallan is easily accessible for ex pats (20% of parents), as well as popular with native Scots. Trickles from the south. Girls have been brighter than boys, but this is now balancing out.

Discipline Drinking means rustication or gating (one boy kept back for a week of the holidays). Drugs are 'not evidently a problem'. Smoking: £10 fine. AIDS education from school doctor: the more academic video produces better discussion.

Entrance Usually either at 11 for Junior House (interview and test), then automatic or by CE (pass mark variable, child may have more than one attempt). Pupils can enter at other times, and Sixth Form, if places available.

Exit 90% to further education, mostly to Scottish universities (Edinburgh still top social university); a few to Oxbridge. 'About 15' leave after Fifth Form to try other spheres.

Bottom Line Scholarships for Junior School. Senior School entrances and Sixth Form (sympathetic bursaries for parents with unexpected financial hardships). Music Awards, Assisted Places. Discounts for siblings. Fees comparable with English public schools.

Remarks Acceptable alternative public school co-education, going from strength to strength.

STREATHAM HILL AND CLAPHAM HIGH SCHOOL
Wavertree Road, London SW2 3SR
TEL London (081) 674 6912

Pupils: 384 girls ● All day ● Ages: 11-19 ● Size of Sixth Form: 60-80 ● Junior School: 150 girls, ages 5-11 ● Non-denom ● Fee-paying.

HEAD Since 1979, Miss G M Ellis BSc (forties). Has transformed Streatham High from an inward-looking establishment to a school highly thought of by parents and children. Head is popular, committed and full of enthusiasm for her staff and children. 'If we do anything at all wrong we really feel we've let her down,' remarked one child.

Academic Matters Staff are hard-working, with tightly organized curriculum—Chemistry, Physics, Biology taught in main school as separate subjects from day one, compulsory until 16. Latin introduced in Second Year, German in Third Year. Creditable average of eight GCSEs per pupil. At Sixth Form level slight bias towards Science—possibly because Head is a scientist. All Sixth Formers now follow a language course, choosing from business French, German, Italian, Russian or Japanese.

Games, Options, the Arts Good at gymnastics and netball and and the new sports hall and dance studio has extended range of activities. Music considered very important, with orchestra, string and wind groups and two choirs. Art, also very good and original. Sixth Formers (no uniform) have much autonomy and some responsibility. Outside speakers, invited weekly, range from NATO official to Salvation Army officer. New library, and Head comments 'the girls make frequent requests for books and I have a policy of never saying no'.

Background and Atmosphere Barracks-like Fifties exterior (flying bombs destroyed most of school in 1944) belies a light, tranquil interior. 'Perhaps it's too nice, too secure,' said one girl. 'The real world isn't quite as I imagine it.' Parents and children like the size (small), atmosphere (tolerant and kindly), and the less-than-sophisticated environment. Very hard working, it's a long day, with many extras at the end of it.

'All I want to do is to sleep,' said a pupil turning down a treat on Sunday.

THE PUPILS   Culturally and racially very mixed, including offspring of professionals, teachers (numerous), shopkeepers, and many children on Assisted Places. 'We're not aware of class, nor that some children are very rich, others are not,' one pupil observed.

Entrance   Via relatively unpressurized exam at 11 and 20-minute interview with Head.

Exit   Around 70-90% to university and polytechnics, some straight into management training, average of two to four to medicine each year.

Bottom Line   Generous allocation of Assisted Places—22-24 out of an annual intake of 52.

Remarks   More obviously a 'family' girl's private school than many larger establishments. A steady performer.

bottom of cricket pitch in front of main school.

Founded in 1847 as school for children of dissenters—Baptists and Congregationalists—of which many in the south west. (Queen's Taunton was for Methodists.) All games fields are within walking distance. Polished wood corridors. Boys dorms have low wood cubicles. Girls houses squashed by comparison. Slight feeling of second class citizenship among girls. From 'all over', but most noticeable were locals. Sue Brown, the first female Oxford cox, is an OG. Entry is by CE or school's scholarship exam at 13, held in March. Also entry at Sixth Form. Gets a steady clutch into Oxbridge a year. Has five hefty open scholarships for academic ability; some 'local' schools, also 'ministerial' ones (children of ministers of the Protestant church); one music or art; a few Assisted Places.

Useful local school in which you can put your children aged three and leave them for the next 15 years.

TAUNTON SCHOOL

Taunton, Somerset TA2 6AD

TEL Taunton (0823) 276081

Pupils: Approx 599 boys, 450 girls   •   425 board, 624 day   •   Ages: 3-18 (school has two single sex prep schools; all move to senior school at 13)   •   Size of Sixth Form: 200+   •   Interdenom   •   Fee-paying.

HEAD   Since 1987, Mr B B Sutton MA (fifties), educated at Eltham College—which was evacuated to Taunton School in the War—then History at Peterhouse. Comes to Taunton from being Head of the Hereford Cathedral School.

Remarks   Traditionally stronger on Science and senior science master is a world authority on centipedes; past senior science master was Ernest Neale, the badger man. GCSE and A-level results spread right across the board (lots of Cs and Ds). Traditionally strong at Rugby. Proper facilities for girls to play games and they are expected to do two main sessions a week.

Excellent and enthusiastic CDT department—very on the ball—and Maths, Physics and Design is a popular option. Very keen CCF. Railway runs at

THOMAS MILLS HIGH SCHOOL

Saxtead Road, Framlingham, Suffolk 1P12 9HE

TEL Framlingham (0728) 723493

Pupils: 900 girls and boys   •   All day   •   Ages: 11-18   •   Size of Sixth Form: approx 250   •   Non denom   •   State

HEAD   Since 1985, Mr A J Leach BD (forties), degree in Divinity from London. Came to Thomas Mills from Thurlston High School in Ipswich.

Remarks   Alternative education for *Independent* readers' offspring. People—parents and teachers—buy houses in the area for the school. Excellent ex-grammar school which, under forceful and fearless Headship of previous Head, M J M Brown, managed amazing transition from grammar school to comprehensive with hardly a ripple on the surface of results (but do not expect force feeding). Strong Sixth Form covering a wide catchment (and one-third out of catchment) area. Brilliant Applied Arts department. Has the highest staying-on rate in Suffolk and a stable staff.

TIFFIN SCHOOL
Queen Elizabeth Road, Kingston upon Thames, Surrey KT2 6RL
TEL London (081) 546 4638

Pupils: 880 boys • *Ages: 11-18* • *Size of Sixth Form: 260* • *Non denom* • *Voluntarily controlled.*

HEAD   Since 1988, A M Dempsey BSc, PhD (forties), Scientist. Educated at Tiffin and Bristol University. Previously Deputy Head at Feltham Community School. Married with one son. Hobbies include walking and industrial archeology.

Remarks   Oversubscribed for 11+ exam by six to one. 240 pupils living outside the borough compete with in-borough pupils. A selective grammar school with an excellent record of academic success, sends large numbers to Oxbridge. Slight bias towards Science and Mathematics, with English, History, Geography and Languages strong. German, Spanish, Russian offered as GCSE options, also Greek to A-level. New building housing Technology, Music, Art and Drama. School has strong drama with occasional visitation/participation by Tiffin Girls'. Co-operation between the schools is still fairly thin on the ground, but is gradually increasing.
   School has outstanding record in choral work. Sport is also strong, with playing fields near Hampton Court and a boathouse on the Thames. Committed careers team. Much time given to pastoral work. Voluntarily controlled and not opting out.

TIFFIN GIRLS' SCHOOL
Richmond Road, Kingston upon Thames, Surrey KT2 5PL
TEL London (081) 546 0773

Pupils: 795 girls • *All day* • *Ages 11-18* • *Size of Sixth Form: 180* • *Non-denom* • *State.*

HEAD   Since 1989, Mrs S Buchanan BA.

Remarks   Hugely popular selective grammar school, with strongly competitive 11+ and consistently high reputation in all academic areas. Most go on to university, with Science notably stronger than Arts, though the arts have been undergoing a renaissance in popularity. Has averaged eight a year to Oxbridge. Excellent modern buildings. Well-equipped labs offer introduction to electricity, electronics, micro-electronics, structure, mechanisms, hydraulics, pneumatics and control technology. A-level subjects include Sociology, Theatre Studies, Computer Science and Business Studies.

TONBRIDGE SCHOOL
Tonbridge, Kent TN9 1JP
TEL Tonbrige (0732) 365555

Pupils: 650 boys • *⁎434 board, 216 day* • *Ages: 13-18* • *Size of Sixth Form: 270* • *C of E* • *Fee-paying.*

HEAD   Since 1990, Mr (J M) Martin Hammond MA (forties), educated Winchester (Scholar), Scholar of Balliol College. Previously Headmaster of City of London School, taught at St Paul's, Harrow and was Head of Classics, then Master in College at Eton. One of the most academically distinguished of all Heads, and one of the few who has experience as Head of Department, Director of Studies and Housemaster. Pipe smoking, positive and affable, ambitious for the school. Has been described by former colleagues as a man of 'iron determination' and 'creative ruthlessness'. On the alert to make changes ('I like making changes'), but finds few are needed, 'some prinking around the edges, nothing central', though he is now working on a huge re-development programme for the next seven years, shifting things around within the given space. Declares he is, 'Most interested in the ordinary guy, and what he gets out of it all.' Holds firmly to the principle 'If a thing is worth doing, it's worth doing well.'

Academic Matters Unashamedly academic (school narked not to have been mentioned in the *FT* top academic league, 'We would have tied eighth.' Hard to get in, very popular. Pass mark at CE is 60% and once in, a boy has to work. Good facilities, with each Department housed in its own area. Sciences, Economics, History and English all notably strong. Good Classics. Smallish classes in the lower school, and only 10 in the Upper. Boys say that the relationship with masters is excellent in the Sixth Form. Generously staffed and staff tend to stay put (too long, according to some parents). Good syllabus of non-examinable subjects for A-level students; impressive programme of seminar lectures (keeps Common Room happy) arranged by Dr Anthony Seldon, Head of History—speakers often remark on quality of boys' questions.

Games, Options, the Arts Powerfully gamesy, compulsory even for Sixth Formers, teams at many levels. Formidable cricket and rugger sides and boasts 100 acres of pitches. Offers 20 different sports including racquets, fives, sailing, golf and rowing. Marvellous all-weather athletics track with pole vaulting, shot putting and high and long jumps. Also two all-weather pitches. Strong music: two school orchestras, chamber orchestra and string quartets, wind ensemble, chamber brass and concert band. Fine Chapel Choir and Choral Society—the school prepares boys for university choral and organ scholarships. Drama good, with projected three-auditoria theatre

Background and Atmosphere Founded in 1553 and rebuilt in the nineteenth-century Gothic style in the centre of town. Chapel destroyed by fire in 1989: after much debate plans now implemented to restore it (at a cost of £6½ million, including £½ million for a new organ). Meanwhile temporary chapel (attended four times a week, plus Sundays) mars the sweep of well-kept building. Boys live and eat in their houses (this is very rare) which are scattered round the town, though most are very close. Very house oriented: quality of life, say the boys, depends on which house you're in. Day boys have their own houses. Very structured

environment prevails overall, and boys admit the pace is 'fairly pressurized.'

THE PUPILS A wide cross section socially due to the generous endowment of scholarships by the Skinner's Company which attracts bright boys (both academic and musical). Still essentially a 'local' school and not socially 'upper crust', though it is so academically. A robust, demanding school. Manners not brilliant, some boys 'hairy at the heel' and there is evidence of bullying. Draws from over 50 prep and state schools in southern England. Very few non English. There is now a Sixth Form bar and prefects can get beer once or twice a week. Most seem fairly happy with their lot. Old Boys include Colin Cowdrey, E M Forster, Sidney Keyes and Sir Patrick Mayhew.

Entrance Hard, though the Head is keen to play this down. Two-thirds come in from CE and a third through the scholarship exam (but not all with awards).

Exit Excellent results. Most go on to university, (a quarter to Oxbridge), fewer to polys. Roughly even Arts/Science bias, but within the latter, medicine and engineering are still the most popular choices.

Bottom Line Generously endowed—up to 25% of boys receive an award of some kind. 17 academic awards a year between full and one-quarter fees, as well as music and art. Extensive resources for the unexpectedly needy.

Remarks Traditional ruggy buggy public school with go-ahead Head. Good for the bright all rounder with stamina. Note large day/local element.

TRURO SCHOOL
Truro, Cornwall TR1 1TH
TEL Truro (0872) 72763

Pupils: 770 boys, 100 girls (all in Sixth Form) • Just under 300 boarders (boys and girls), both weekly and full time • Ages: 10-17 (15-18 for girls) • Size of Sixth Form: 320 • Also: 250 pupils at Treliske, the school's prep and pre prep on separate site, ages 3-11 • Methodist Foundation • Fee-paying.

HEAD Since autumn 1986, Mr B K Hobbs BSc ARCS (early forties). Read Mathematics at Imperial

College, London. Formerly Head of Torquay Boys' Grammar School, took over at Truro from Derek Burrell, who retired after being in the school for 27 years. Laid back, unpretentious, enthusiastic and quietly outspoken (Mr Hobbs, that is). Aims to run an academic establishment 'stretching each pupil to the limits of his/her ability—that's what it's all about...then of course there is social development...' Comes from Kent and is a Rotarian. Married with four children; wife helps in the nursery school.

Academic Matters Very strong in Maths (Head and Deputy Head are both Mathematicians) and Sciences in general—does not go in for Combined Sciences. Lots of geographers. Languages the poor relation. Solid and, in some areas, excellent results. 60-70 join the school at Sixth Form from other schools.

Games, Options, the Arts Dynamic and original projects and extras. This is *the* school for chess—had, until last year, Grand Master M Adams and even without him (he was competing in World zonal Championships in the Philippines) managed to come second in the country in *The Times* inter-schools competition. They also have a world karate champion. 120 pupils are doing Duke of Edinburgh gold medals (is this a school record?). Also into the Young Enterprise Scheme and were the first school to create a *real aeroplane* (in 1980, with sponsorship from BP) which was flown across the Channel. Strong cricket team—top eight. South west table tennis champions two years ago. Strong swimming (though pool in state of disarray when we visited). New theatre being built. The list of achievements and aspirations goes on and on...

Background and Atmosphere Glorious site 'on the ridge' overlooking the River Truro and the cathedral—a position which brings tears to the eyes of property developers. Grounds run down from the ridge, and playing fields stretch out at the back. Founded 1880. Part of Methodist Board of Management for Residential Schools and Colleges.

Rather lumpen school buildings as befits what was formerly the grammar school, with higgledy piggledy annexes and extra science labs etc. Large art block. School at present in process of rapid expansion, as has grown enormously, not least because of the demise of Truro Cathedral School. Boarding houses dotted around town, including one housed in an elegant mansion house with most beautiful grounds.

THE PUPILS Come from all over Cornwall, from Scilly to Saltash. OBs: Robert Shaw, Bryan Pearce, Michael Adams, also the ex world karate champion,

David Penhaligon, Ben Luxon, Alan Opie.

Entrance Own exam at 11—which ties in with state system—one of the very few schools which is thoughtful enough to do this. Grammar school ability required. Alternatively via school's own prep school of Treliske.

Exit 17 Oxbridge in 1989, a proportion to green wellie belt universities, one or two to Falmouth Art College, to banking, Scottish universities and to south west polytechnics—eg a dozen or so pupils at Plymouth. Some to Swansea University and Cardiff.

Bottom Line Best value in private boarding education in the country, apart from the (genuine) charity schools. A few scholarships, but the school is not endowed—they come out of fee income. Fees at time of writing £2,000 a term. Head comments 'Parents cannot afford as much here as at other places.'

Remarks Cornwall's only Headmasters' Conference Head school, traditional but liberal. Scores top marks for everything except buildings and grounds—place looks like a bomb has hit it with chairs stacked hither and thither and bulldozers churning up the athletics track.

TUDOR HALL SCHOOL
Wykham Park, Banbury, Oxfordshire OX16 9UR
TEL Banbury (0295) 263434

Pupils: 250 girls ● *233 board, 17 day* ● *Ages: 11-18* ● *Size of Sixth Form: 68* ● *C of E* ● *Fee-paying.*

HEAD Since 1984, Miss N Godfrey BA (forties), educated at Northampton School for Girls and London University. Taught at the Royal Ballet School, Abbots Bromley and Ancaster House (Deputy Head at both these). Shrewd and purposeful beneath a somewhat timid manner. Teaches something at all levels (English her real subject), 'If you're going to discuss pupils with your staff, you must know the pupils.' Very enthusiastic about theatre, also building, and extremely keen on the small school.

Academic Matters Steady and rising. Greek now on

offer. Economics and Maths consistently the strongest subjects; History and English very popular. Nice language labs, Spanish is on the curriculum and Sixth Formers can do crash course in Italian. Clever streaming and much encouragement given to pupils.

Games, Options, the Arts   Fairly gamesy, with both lacrosse and hockey, tennis courts in the old walled garden, one squash court, large indoor sports hall, outdoor swimming pool. Good art and needlework, big Home Economics Department (Sixth Formers do a 'hostess cookery' course). New CDT block opened by David Hicks. Riding available locally; typing course on hand (with word processing etc), driving lessons, Duke of Edinburgh's Award Scheme. Dabating is strong ('So they're prepared for public speaking', observed a pleased parent). Music school's rehearsal room is also used for drama workshops. New senior Russian club. Work experience post GCSEs. Good broadening studies for Sixth Formers; regular speakers drawn largely from Oxford and Stratford.

Background and Atmosphere   Very uninstitutional. Founded elsewhere in 1850, now in much-extended seventeenth-century manor and eighteenth-century house, set in pretty grounds; project in hand to restore the old Japanese garden; country house feel pervades. Rows of Huskies and green wellies. Recent building work in old stables area is very sympathetic with the rest, and has vastly improved academic facilities, and also given girls more breathing space in living quarters. Weekend activities and outings improving, observe parents, and Head has brought in more resident staff. Food is voted good. Girls live in houses by age, making friendships for life (and move house en masse each year). Vertical houses for competitive purposes. Sixth have swish quarters, plenty of privacy. Plans afoot for renovation (main building currently crumbly). A Woodard school.

THE PUPILS   Sloanes, pretty girls with soft hair and nice manners, unspoilt, friendly, practical, with a positive interest in life and life's good things, enjoyers who want to contribute. Head claims, with justification, Tudors have a go at most things, and are good mixers. 'I like to think that if there was a weeping five year old and an old granny present, our girls would be equally good with both.' Employable.

Entrance   High in popularity stakes, register early. Girls come at 11+, 12+ and 13+, and a few at Sixth Form, post GCSE drop-off. All rounders and joiners-in best suited to small school ethos.

Exit   Half to university, specifically the green welly ones, eg Exeter. The rest to polys, also art and design courses.

Bottom Line   One music scholarship.

Remarks   A truly nice school, beginning to flex a little academic muscle, where you would be confident your child would be safe and happy.

UNIVERSITY COLLEGE SCHOOL
Frognal, London NW3 6XH
TEL London (071) 435 2215

Pupils: 520 boys ● All day ● Ages: 13-18 ● Size of Sixth Form: 200 ● Non denom ● Fee-paying.

HEAD   Since 1983, Mr G S Slaughter JP, MA (fifties), educated at the Royal Masonic School and King's College, Cambridge. Historian, keen on theatre, cricket and family life; gives the apppearance of being on the defensive, though probably is not.

Academic Matters   Traditionally renowned for excellence in Classics, Maths and the Sciences—some feel to the detriment of other subjects eg Modern Languages: (surprisingly, in so cosmopolitan an environment, only French and German are offered, though performance rate in the former is excellent—101 out of 103 got an A or B in GCSE 1990, average number of subjects taken being nine). Teaching is seen as sound generally. Technology Department excellent.

Games, Options, the Arts   Good games facilities, especially given that this is expensive, built-up Hampstead; tennis courts, fives, squash, and an indoor pool all on the premises; own playing field and all-weather pitch nearby. Excellent well-equipped school theatre, regularly borrowed by professional theatre companies. Strong jazz tradition—David Lund, Head of English is a well-known jazz buff. Choral society very popular. Visiting speakers—particularly from the media (David Frost, Michael Grade etc)—a regular feature.

Background and Atmosphere   Founded in Gower Street in 1830 as part of University College, London, for non-Christians at a time when Oxford and Cambridge required membership of C of E as condition of entry. Arson attack in 1978 gutted the great hall—splendidly restored and rebuilt—and 22 classrooms. Religion is still not taught and a liberal outlook is still true of the school's educational policy. Emphasis on self-discipline, boys are given a good measure of responsibility for running activities outside the classroom. No bells. Masculine atmosphere.

THE PUPILS Solidly middle class, often rich (though mothers more intellectual and less designer dressed than other Hampstead schools). Strong Jewish element—lots of media brats—parents in journalism, publishing, showbusiness etc. Pupils accused of being 'cynical, self-assured, worldly wise'.

Entrance Two-thirds come from UCS's own excellent prep in Holly Hill (the much loved Mr MacGregor retires 1991). The others from preps and primaries all over north London.

Exit 75% of leavers go on to higher education. A great many lawyers, doctors, accountants and civil servants result. Also successful businessmen (often third and fourth generation at the school).

Bottom Line Exhibitions, bursaries at 13+. Also scholarships at 13+, are (largely) honorary. Assisted Places at 16+. School very quick to respond to parental financial crisis where appropriate.

Remarks Sound. Traditional liberal, understated—and secure in its own worth. Celebrating its centenary year and unlikely to alter dramatically in tone.

UPPINGHAM SCHOOL
Rutland, LE15 9QE
TEL Uppingham (0572) 822216

Pupils: • *Approx 680 pupils, 82 girls (all in Sixth Form)* • *All board* • *Ages: 13-18 (boys), 16-18 (girls)* • *Size of Sixth Form: Approx 322* • *C of E* • *Fee-paying.*

HEAD From September 1991, Dr S C Winkley MA (forties), educated St Edward's Oxford and at Brasenose College, Oxford. Doctor of philosophy. Previously Second Master at Winchester. Married with

young children. Well spoken of. Takes over from N R Bomford, who is now Head of Harrow.

Academic Matters Strong classical tradition. Good balance between Arts and Sciences. A number do Design A-level, of which school was pioneer in early Seventies. Setting. New Maths block built in 1989. Wildly fluctuating results—from 87% ABCs at A-level in Further Maths, to 15% in Geology and 43% in French—overall ABC percentage is 61. Outgoing Head comments on the school's weaker brethren (academically speaking) 'the wonder of it is that as many candidates actually achieve C grades, not how few!'

Games, Options, the Arts Outstanding music department—one of the strongest public school music departments in the country, under director Neil Page (distinguished tradition here—Douglas Guest was director from 1945-50), with seven full-time music teachers, string orchestra, alternative string orchestra, a chapel choir which 'keeps everyone singing', outside consultants such as Robert Tear, inter-house singing competitions. Is invited to perform at Snape (no mean honour). Concert choir puts on ambitious works such as Britten's *Hymn to St Cecilia* and Tippett's *A Child of Our Time* and, unlike many schools, performs them to a very high standard.

Excellent art and applied technology, with outstanding Head of CDT, Andrew Wilson. Workshops for wood and metalwork, also the Thring Centre, housed in an old manor in the main street, in which pupils can help make a film, or paint scenery for the theatre, or print etc. Two artists in residence. Competent computer centre, much used in the solving of design problems (AO-level computer studies on offer). Keen theatre with three or more major productions a year.

School has one of largest unbroken stretches of playing fields in the country—'the Middle'—and pretty bleak it is in winter with wind whistling in. Excellent shooting record—another regular winner at Bisley.

Background and Atmosphere Founded 1584, completely dominates Uppingham, a sleepy place, according to one or two pupils. School distinguished in present day terms by having a house system in which pupils eat in their own houses. This makes an enormous difference—friendlier, manners better, much stronger feeling of community, less likelihood of pupils falling by the wayside because they have gone to the wall/been overlooked. Two cooks to each house reflected in school fees however. There are two main clusters of buildings and 14 boarding houses, some of them a very brisk seven minutes' walk from classrooms. 'Nearly all' pupils have their own studies. Girls have been admitted since 1975—two houses. Tuck and coffee shop for all; bar for seniors—one hour, two evenings a week and Sunday mornings. Sombre black uniforms, tending to scruffiness.

Discipline Pastoral care reinforced by the strong house system. Little book of school rules makes no reference to sex. Could be safer from drugs here than most places, owing to steady middle classness of families and relative isolation. One or two mutterings about application of discipline.

THE PUPILS Straight up and down middle class—nothing flashy. Main catchment area: within two-and-a-half hours drive, including north Yorkshire and north London. Very polite and at ease, no neurotics. Approx 15% second to fourth generation Uppingha-mians. Strong overseas placements for 'gap' year activities, thanks in part to good Old Boy network.

Entrance BY CE. By exam results into Sixth Form. Also report from previous school and interview. About 25 prep schools regularly send on boys in quantity—Orwell Park a good example. 25 scholars from the choir schools at time of writing. Girls on interview—no competitive entrance exam, but they must have minimum five Cs at GCSE and there is no margin in this—register at least two years in advance.

Exit Approx 20 to Oxbridge a year, 70 to other universities, 36 to polys and some to 'some other form of tertiary level'.

Bottom Line Up to 24 scholarships awarded annually, both academic and music. No Assisted Places.

Remarks Could be just what you are looking for and haven't thought of—cosy, capable of producing As if your child is seriously bright. Excellent non-academic subjects.

WELLINGTON COLLEGE
Crowthorne, Berkshire RG11 7PU
TEL Crowthorne (0344) 772261

Pupils: 798 boys, 50 girls (all in Sixth Form) ● *670 boys board, 128 day; 45 girls board, 5 day* ● *Size of Sixth Form: 350* ● *C of E* ● *Fee-paying.*

HEAD The Master, since 1989, Mr C J Driver (Jonty) BA, BEd (Cape Town), MPhil Oxon, FRSA (early fifties). Educated at St Andrew's Grahamstown, South Africa and University of Cape Town where he read English, followed by an MPhil at Trinity, Oxford (he was President of the National Union of SA Students). Previously taught at Sevenoaks; was Direc-tor of Sixth Form studies at Matthew Humberstone Comprehensive, and Principal of the Island School Hong Kong.

An unorthodox appointment, he continually reminds one of the South African upbringing. A thinker—long pauses before he speaks—and great fun, the pupils find him 'only moderately approachable—not good at the quick chat', but he is disarmingly frank and much enjoys his new job. Possibly a bit disor-ganised. Lives on campus with his wife Ann, and has published a selection of novels and poetry.

Academic Matters Sound. History still tops, but good Maths and Science, super new building for IT ('comes out of your ears') and Microtechnology, children can learn video producing too, building never closed and out of hours work possible throughout on computers and in CDT workshop (not computer linked). Over a quarter of the staff teach Science—the place is stiff with text book authors. 20 labs. French and German taking an increasingly important role, with interesting exchange with new independent school in Bordeaux—Acadis, where Wellington pupils gain industry experience in France. Seminars on all sorts of subjects conducted in 'free' time; external examiners (usually Oxford or Cambridge Dons) set papers for History and other prizes. Streaming.

Games, Options, the Arts Seriously keen on games, especially rugger and hockey with brilliant new huge sports hall, big enough for indoor hockey (there is an Astroturf pitch). Blood matches with Harrow and Radley. 400 acres of pitches, and woods, and a lake which those on the Kings Leap run have to plough through (up to their waist) on the annual run. 'Great fun' said our guide. CCF compulsory for one year only. Each child must also play an orchestral instrument for his first year and will get free tuition (for a term) if he shows talent. Very strong drama, good jazz orchestra and travelling choir. High standard pottery and excellent art dept. School has own Industrial Liaison Officer and links with companies like EMI, Tate & Lyle. Founder member of 'gap', with a £5,000 bursary available, but reckons most contacts now come through old Wellingtonians.

Background and Atmosphere Conglomerate of John Shaw red and white brick building designed in 1854, plus lots of well-blended additions. Appointments of governors and any alteration to the Statutes have to be approved by Buckingham Palace. The College was founded in 1853 in memory of the Great Duke. Despite the new Master's assurances, the boys' dormitories (ie the houses within the College itself) are still hideously untidy (boys live in 'tissues'—a derivation from Partitions). Boys in College eat in the main school hall where they have canteen feeding ('usually quite good') with a vegetarian option. Gentle fagging system is employed whereby the younger boys in each house take it in turns to collect the newspapers, mail and milk for that house. Lots of staff houses in the grounds, with young children everywhere.
  Strong religious bias. The previous Master, Dr Newsome, had a wonderful crypt chapel for quiet thought constructed below the main (and very handsome) chapel by Sir Gilbert Scott (1863).

Discipline Automatic rustication for boys invading the girls' house, Apsley, otherwise sackings for bullying, drugs (calls the police), smoking equals fine ('usually part of a bigger picture'). Drinking for a first offender is 'Master fatigues' or gating, and thereafter rustication. (The Junior Common Room sells beer, and pupils over 18 can go into local pubs, the College supplies an Identity Card.) Sex equals instant dismissal. 1991 drugs sackings.

THE PUPILS Around 20/25% OWs' children, decent, purposeful, well-mannered chaps, possibly lacking in imagination, though there is plenty of artistic and external stimulation. Girls blissfully happy. Military names and decorations heavy on the ground, strong local trend, though many of the day boys do eventually board. Huge range of OWs, 15 awarded VCs, also among least likely, Robert Morley, Harold Nicolson, Clement Freud, Sebastian Faulkes, Rory Bremner and the Bishops of Ripon and Oxford.

Entrance Early registration via CE culls from 'over 200 prep schools' strong feed from Eagle House, Wellington's own prep. Girls (80-90 apply for 25 places) have interview and test. Five or six boys' places usually available for Sixth Form studies post-GCSE.

Exit Slight leakage post GCSE. 'Over 90% to university and polytechnics', 25-26 annually to Oxbridge, otherwise Durham, Bristol, Edinburgh, London, Nottingham, St Andrews and Bath. Strong medical bias. Average 15 army scholarships per year for university.

Bottom Line A dozen or so scholarships, plus bursaries, and five Assisted Places at 16 and three at 13.

Remarks Sound traditional public school education for the pupil who likes structure and discipline. Not good for free spirits. New Head is kicking life into the place.

WELLS CATHEDRAL SCHOOL
Wells, Somerset BA5 2ST
TEL Wells (0749) 72117

Pupils: Approx 294 boys, 292 girls • Boarding and day • Ages: • 11-18 • Size of Sixth Form: 155 • Junior School of approx 216 mixed, ages 5-11 • C of E • Fee-paying.

HEAD Since April 1986, Mr J S Baxter BA (forties) from Westminster School.

Remarks Many came in from school's very good prep. Specialist music school situated in shadow of the great and glorious Cathedral, round what Betjeman considered the 'most beautiful square mile of Britain'. Choristers are all together in one boarding house under the direction of the Master of Choristers and the Cathedral organist. Also 50 specialist music places—good choice if musical and general education is what you have in mind. Much of school fronts on to main road, but warren-like extensions sprout out behind, and include huge heated open air swimming pool and graceful stone houses. One of five Direct Grant schools left in country (the other four are Purcell, Yehudi Menuhin, Chetham's, Royal Ballet). Non-musicians welcome, and no longer feel like second class citizens.

Plenty of positive feedback from parents.

WEST HEATH SCHOOL
Sevenoaks, Kent TN13 1SR
TEL Sevenoaks (0732) 452541

Pupils: 170 girls • 150 board, 20 day • Ages: 11-18 • Size of Sixth Form: 45 • C of E • Fee-paying.

HEAD Since September 1987, Mrs L Cohn-Sherbok MA Cantab, MA Kent, (thirties). Former History teacher at King's Canterbury, small, alert, clever. Mrs Cohn-Sherbok is the wife of an American Rabbi—popular with the girls and known as 'Rabbi Dan'—who says grace at meals and interests himself in the girls and their activities when he's not lecturing · at Kent University.

Academic Matters Cosier and less academic than neighbouring Benenden. A tutorial system in place, the small classes are streamed and weekly tests given. Small Sixth Form, even faintly exotic mix at A-level cannot be coped with within the curriculum. Results not given.

Games, Options, the Arts Good for tennis (12 courts) (Annabel Croft is an old girl). The Rudge Sports Hall (opened by old girl HRH Princess of Wales) is a popular addition. Heated indoor swimming pool, lacrosse and netball pitches. Self-defence is on the curriculum. Music is keen here—madrigal singing was a passion of Miss Rudge's (the previous Head) and is still going strong, in addition to two choirs and a jazz group. Lots of concerts and school productions. Arts and Crafts department now expanded. All girls can take art, design, textiles and ceramics. Information Technology with open-access computer room.

Background and Atmosphere An austere though well-proportioned house, set in lovely grounds. Small, cosy and old-fashioned—dormitories of up to seven. 'That quote about pupils thinking of nothing but flower arranging was so true—though they do not like it said', according to a member of staff. Family atmosphere with old retainers looking after second generation girls. Fifth formers upwards have study bedrooms. First year Sixth live in 'cowsheds' (dormitory blocks), and Second year Sixth in 'colt houses', where they have their own study bedrooms and self-catering kitchen, though one meal daily must be taken in school. School meals served family style in Regency dining room.

The Pupils Traditional upper-middle and upper class daughters of stockbrokers, bankers, farmers both local and from Norfolk, Suffolk and Essex, with a contingent from Scotland. Lots of Old Girls' daughters.

Entrance By CE examination at 11+, 12+ or 13+—oversubscribed this year and getting tougher, but entry requirements not demanding.

Exit Some to university, some to polytechnics, secretarial colleges.

Bottom Line Academic and music scholarships are awarded internally.

Remarks Cosy, supportive and disciplined small-scale haven for the daughters of well-born conventional parents for whom the social result is still more important than the academic.

WESTMINSTER SCHOOL
Little Dean's Yard, London SW1P 3PF
TEL London (071) 222 6904

Pupils: 520 boys, 90 girls (all in Sixth Form) • Approx 300 day boys, 220 weekly boarders; 65 day girls, 25 weekly boarders • Ages: 13-18 • Size of Sixth Form: 290 • C of E • Fee-paying.

HEAD Since 1986, Mr David Summerscale MA (early fifties), formerly Master of Haileybury, educated Sherborne and Trinity Hall, Cambridge (played squash, tennis, cricket for university teams). French wife, two littles. Started teaching career in India at the University of Delhi and still has connections with the country. A gentle, civilized academic, who looks (although he does not agree with this) as though he has just been handed a wagonload of monkeys, and doesn't quite know not to do with them. Some complaints that

Head 'doesn't make his presence felt enough'.

Academic Matters   Traditionally one of the most high-powered schools in London, if not in the country. Academic pressure high and does not let up until pupil safely launched on next rung of ladder. Previously school used to boast image of little boys groaning under briefcases, then went through a fashion of pretending not to work at all, now more balanced. Geography now up and running under new Head of Department. CDT according to Head is no longer looked on as the poor relation. Fantastic Science block, still the envy of other schools, has injected energy into the department. English teaching outstanding as ever. The Common Room everyone high powered wants to be in, a real power house and bang in the centre of London.

Games, Options, the Arts   Music not as strong as it should be given the pool of talent. Debating, chess and other intellectual sports are popular. Sad-looking gym under cloisters with vintage smell of sock. Cricketers no longer too indolent to be seen in Vincent Square, water and fencing both successful at national and international level. Strong expedition society, compulsory for all lower school and part of Head's 'broadening' ethos—everything from white water canoeing to chamber music weekends for aesthetes.

Background and Atmosphere   Historic buildings umbilically tied to Westminster Abbey, in which school services are held thrice weekly, and Latin prayers once a week on Wednesdays. Founded 1560 by Queen Elizabeth I, following her father's provision for 40 King's Scholars at the Abbey. Cloistered as an Oxford College with the Dean's Yard standing in as quad, but not in the least calm—noisy, scruffy, tourists taking tea etc, though most boarding houses 'no longer squalid' according to Head. Constant complaints about persistently *ghastly* food.

Weekly boarding system takes the sting out of boarding—and what is done outside boarding hours is under parents' jurisdiction, for which staff still truly thankful.

THE PUPILS   Big social mix, middle class intelligentsia, offspring of ambitious parents, many two-income families, also high quota divorced and suburban. Also international set, bilinguals in profusion and rich Middle-Easterners. Majority from London and round about, though some as far afield as Brighton and Oxford. Pupils highly articulate, social, often have thin veneer of sophistication, nervously brilliant and difficult to teach. Brilliant and beautiful girls prone to wearing 'pussy pelmets'. Pupils still have greater awareness of the outside world than most other schools we have visited. Lots of famous OWs, including six prime ministers, Grosvenors, Wedgwood-Benn and Shane McGowan, lead singer of the Pogues.

Discipline   Surprising lack of awareness among some cynical staff of rough behaviour and victimizing. Masters possibly too lofty to understand the needs and ways of young boys? Lack of space for letting off steam and rabbit warreny layout may have something to do with the problem.

Entrance   Still one of the most fought-after schools in London. However, demographically speaking, it is now easier than it was even three years ago, and failure for even reasonably able pupils is rare. Put child's name down age 10, go for interview then CE or, for scholars, school's own exam. Approx 25% come from Westminster Under (*qv*).

Exit   Consistently sends large numbers (40–50) a year to Oxbridge. Most pupils go on to university and then become bankers, ad-men, lawyers, company men etc. Strong commercial streak here.

Bottom Line   Actual bill currently around £9,600 a year (£7,500 when we last went to print in 1989) for boarders; £6,400 (£5,000 previously) day pupils. 10 scholars a year—including two music—have half-price education. No official bursaries but Assisted Places taken over from Westminster Under.

Remarks   An adult and sophisticated school with a university ethos under a well-liked, though low-profile, Head. Westminster offers a more liberal and broadening education than academically comparable St Paul's Boys. Not for the faint-hearted.

WESTONBIRT SCHOOL
Tetbury, Gloucestershire GL8 8QG
TEL Westonbirt (0666 88) 333

Pupils: *276 girls* ● *237 board, 19 day* ● *Ages: 11-18* ●
Size of Sixth Form: *70* ● *C of E* ● *Fee-paying.*

HEAD   Since 1986, Mrs G Hylson-Smith BA Hons, (fifties), educated Wycombe Abbey and Leicester university, and aged 40 did a post-graduate degree at Hatfield 'because I thought my Classics were looking ropey'. Previously taught at Haberdasher's Aske's London, and has taught in boys' schools. Classicist. Tall woman, clear-headed, not one to trot out usual Head's clichés. Grown up children; she describes her husband, Bursar of an Oxford College, as 'a half-weekly boarder'.

Remarks   Back on the map as a school where middle brow girls can shine and gain confidence, but Head definitely wants girls who are 'sparky—who will jump in and have a go'—the usual cry of small schools. Hot (and not ashamed) on marketing, keen prep school visitor etc, dynamic Head has been/still is busy building school up (NB Sixth Form down to 20 when she arrived). Coming from pressurized London day school, fully aware that the bottom end tends to feel bad about themselves. 'Here I want girls to feel good about themselves—if they've got a D and go to agricultural college, that's great'.

Two-thirds go on to further education, mostly degree courses, art college, History of Art popular, some become bi-lingual secretaries. English followed by History of Art are favourite A-levels, Maths not brilliant, nor are Sciences say parents. Lots of new staff, (well paid) Housemistresses teach half a timetable ('if not, they're patronized in the staff room'). Girls encouraged to make own decisions early. D of E, Young Enterprise, good lax, golf course (with honesty box) down the road.

Girls coerced at weekends (too much hanging about previously), Sunday night aerobics, nice music, (in former camellia house), keen drama, with four plays a year. Lessons right through till 6.05, prep spread throughout the day (music lessons and practice during prep time). Evenings free for friends and clubs. A *Neighbours* watching school. Art Design Technology block opening in September 1991 (discreetly screened behind trees, in well chosen brick). Very good tutor system; record of achievement cards every term, on which child comments on teachers and goals set.

Most stupendous and impressive neo-Renaissance pile (built for Holford family), listed Grade I, wonderful grounds and gardens ('only four gardeners'), arboretum now in hands of the Forestry Commission. Beautiful library; some dorms boast fascinating original painted furniture, somewhat at odds with girls' bottle-littered dressing tables. Chaplain very well spoken of(Low Church). Girls come in at 11, 12 and 13, 10% daughters of forces, Sloanes, strong contingent of first-time buyers, girls from M4-run and London. Good mixers, ages mingle freely throughout school.

Well worth looking at if your daughter needs confidence-building, small community and emphasis on individuality.

WILLIAM ELLIS SCHOOL
Highgate Road, London NW5 1RN
TEL London (071) 267 9346

Pupils: 845 boys • All day • Ages: 11-18 • Size of Sixth Form: 225 boys in Joint Sixth Form with adjacent Parliament Hills Girls School—a total of 475 students • Non-denom • State (former grammar school, turned comprehensive 1978).

HEAD   Since 1988, Mr Michael Wheale MA (early fifties) sees school as part of the community and places much emphasis on communication with parents. He has the difficult task of educating boys of a very wide range of ability but is 'proud ' to be running a comprehensive school. Independent minded.

Academic Matters   117 boys took 702 GCSEs in 1990 and nearly 60% of the results were in the ABC grades (national average is 48%, and London appreciably lower). A-level results for 1990 down a bit on 1989, as pupils damaged by the 'uncertainty' of London state education percolate through. This should right itself in a year or two. Formal teaching and setting are mixed with individual learning and some all-ability classes. The more able boys are stretched in a variety of ways, including studying additional subjects beyond the end of the school day. Overall impression is of a school working flat out at many levels and standards still improving. Plenty of cross-fertilization of ideas and willingness to explore new teaching methods, and much energy devoted to curriculum development.

School has obtained funds from the Spanish government to run a course teaching Geography in Spanish—the first of its kind in the UK. Linked study programme in English, History and Geography—boys relish the stimulating, lively programme. Ellis possesses a brilliantly equipped TV studio - part of Department of Modern Communications—and pupils trained in the use of the studio and its equipment crew each other's productions. Their Media Resources department is also strong. Lovely watermill in Surrey—used for field studies, tutor group visits, chamber music weekends, and intensive A-level revision courses—has recently been extended.

Games, Options, the Arts Playing fields at Edgware and school has been represented internationally in athletics and soccer and at county level in Rugby and cross country running. Clubs are numerous; co-operation with Parliament Hill Girls' School clubs increases choice—cookery as well as electronics, table tennis as well as design and technology. Music department is traditionally strong with junior and senior orchestras; joins with Camden School for Girls to form North Camden Schools' Orchestra.

Background and Atmosphere Solid. Thirties building now cramped and scruffy, unpainted and bursting at the seams. There is a hyperactive buzz about the place, but also a feeling of intimacy and impressive levels of concentration in the classroom. Community liaison is taken very seriously, with Deputy Head in charge of this area of school life.

THE PUPILS Offspring of Fabians, Hampstead academics, journalists, and streetwise offspring from deprived inner-city areas. It's an electric mix—with 36 different mother tongues, and Bengali, Spanish, Greek and Cantonese lessons offered after school. Undoubtedly an outer layer of toughness is needed to survive but the highly-charged, energetic nature of the school produces resilient, confident children, aware of society's needs and very much part of their local community.

Entrance Via local primary schools at 11+. There is also entry to the joint Sixth Form from the state independent sector. Consideration is given to up to 12 boys with 'proven interest and commitment' in music (no geographical restrictions).

Exit Each year 35-45% to universities and polys.

Remarks Strong and popular boys' comprehensive state school in north London, blessed with large numbers of very bright, articulate pupils. Teaching is highly thought of.

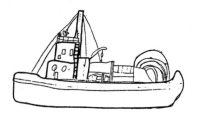

WIMBLEDON HIGH SCHOOL
Mansel Road, London SW19 4AB
TEL London (081) 946 1756

Pupils: 740 girls • *All day* • *Ages: 5-18* • *Size of Sixth Form: approx 120* • *Non-denom* • *Fee-paying.*

HEAD Since 1982, Mrs Rosemary Smith MA (fifties). Was herself educated at a GPDST School, Brighton and Hove High. Energetic, outspoken, very down-to-earth. Has previous experience in maintained schools. Very aware of preparing girls for the world they are going to live in. 'One of the sad things is that so often women will make two to three applications for promotion and then they'll give up.'

Academic Matters Large classes (28), with smaller groups for French, Maths, Science. Very good and solid academic record: 50 or 60 per year average nearly nine GCSEs apiece. School is especially strong in Maths and Science; also History. New block houses enlarged library and art studio.

Games, Options, the Arts Not fanatical about sport, but has a good representation in county teams. Upper forms have additional options of gymnastics, squash, badminton and self-defence. Sixth Formers join forces with local King's College School for drama, debating etc.

Background and Atmosphere Pleasant campus, slightly cramped, the red brick buildings look like a set for a Sherlock Holmes play.

THE PUPILS Wide catchment area, 50% live locally (parents move into the area for the school); lots of daughters of civil servants, and some with medical and university backgrounds.

Entrance Three-form entry at 11, half coming up from their juniors; 160 sit exam for 44 places (but lots also trying for St Paul's, Godolphin and Latymer, Tiffin etc); all children interviewed before exam.

Exit 60% to university, including 10% into Oxbridge—and virtually everyone else into further education including medical schools, usually five or six a year.

Bottom Line   GPDST school—good value. Assisted Places and bursaries also available.

Remarks   Very strong local school.

WINCHESTER COLLEGE
Winchester, Hampshire SO23 9NA
TEL Winchester (0962) 854328

Pupils: 650 boys • *635 board, 15 day* • *Ages: 13-18* • *Size of Sixth Form: 390* • *C of E* • *Fee-paying.*

HEAD   Since 1985, Mr James Sabben-Clare MA (forties) educated at Winchester and Oxford. Previously Head of Classics Department, and Second Master at Winchester. Taught at Marlborough before that. Keen on carpentry. His wife teaches Law in the school. Fantastically efficient, very strong on admin, and beneath the initial tight-lipped reserve, friendly. Home grown product, and as such an unusual choice of Head.

Academic Matters   Traditionally a power house, among the top boarding academic schools in the country. Background of bright but not exceptionally clever boys, says mother of one such. No hierarchy of subjects (questioning a group of Sixth Formers about their A-level subjects reveals wide variety). Recent increased emphasis on Sciences, fine laboratories. Russian something of a tradition—for the last 50 years a handful have taken it at A-level. Brightest boys spend first two years on GCSE, followed by transition—one year in broad studies without specializing. Teaching largely excellent—though again Old Wykehamist parents with sons now in the school keen to point out there seem fewer really brilliant and inspiring teachers than in their day. Nonetheless, boys live in constant atmosphere of erudition and mental stimulation. Academic analysis much prized. Boys taught to see all sides of an argument, 'The strength and the weakness, and why they can't run things', according to a disillusioned parent.

Games, Options, the Arts   Forceful in non-academic activities, a marvellous centre for all sorts of things. Sporting facilities are very good—mainstream games (Soccer, Winchester's own variety of football, cricket) not compulsory after first year. Famously beautiful cricket pitch. Long list of options, and minor sports are especially strong, with several boys competing in national teams (eg sailing, basket ball, water polo, cross country). Judo, fives, steeplechasing, karate etc all on offer. Boys encouraged to make their own choice, 'Informed decisions are what our education is about'. Also fishing—famous and flourishing fishing club, on the Itchen. CDT distinctly good (NB long established); fine large indoor sport centre, with pool. Magnificently light art school (converted from nineteenth century sanatorium), though by comparison with many lesser schools, underused, except for lively three-dimensional work. Strong drama, and splendid theatre, music is also very good indeed (two-thirds of boys learn an instrument), some co-productions with St Swithun's. CCF compulsory—and popular—for one year (army, Royal Air Force and Royal Marines sections).

Background and Atmosphere   Most beautiful setting—lovely mellow old buildings (some date back to fourteenth century), new additions spanning several centuries, are discreetly designed and placed. On one side the town, on another the Cathedral Close, and the rest stretches lushly across meadows and river and playing fields with poplars, willows and plane trees. Boarding houses (re-furbished) are set cosily along narrow, ancient lanes and backstreets, and some have strong family/domestic atmosphere. Houses are autonomous units (all meals in a boy's house, scholars live in separate house),—'College'—dates back to the fourteenth century—and exudes strong aroma of sock. Mr Sabben-Clare very keen to 'draw more of the threads into the middle', introducing, for instance, more staff meetings, more parent/staff get-togethers. Fine staff common room conversion, to this end, despite some resistance. System of young and old pupils working side by side in 'toys' (study cubicles) generally regarded as a Good Thing by all because newcomers are kept in sight. NB Winchester is thick with its own slang, 'notions'.

Discipline   Head has tightened up—again. Geography of school offers temptations to slip into pubs (who have been warned off), and Housemasters' task is a hard one. Part of the problem with Winchester appears to be that the previous Head ran the school altogether too much as a university campus, making very academic staff appointments. These staff are now moving up to be Housemasters, 'and', said a prep school head, 'they do not always understand the needs of young boys'.

THE PUPILS Tendency to cynicism, 'the by-product of lots of clever boys together'. School certainly continues to produce dry wits. Boys come in from a huge variety of preps, diminishing numbers of sons of Old Boys, increasing number of grammar school educated parents. Dozens of famous Old Wykehamists including Montague John Druitt, possibly Jack the Ripper, Sir Geoffrey Howe, Viscount Whitelaw, Hugh Gaitskill, Dick Crossman, Prof Freeman Dyson etc.

Entrance Registration on boys' eighth birthday, interview at 11, when candidates selected to take school's own entrance examination. Prep school heads tend to allow only suitable candidates to sit—which adds to the mystique .

Exit About 40-50+ to Oxford and Cambridge each year; the rest to other universities. Go on to be civil servants (fewer nowadays), City gents and experts.

Bottom Line About one-quarter of pupils do not pay full fees, and are supported by one or other of the school funds; 70 scholars; approx six Exhibitioners per year, plus up to six bursaries for boys from Hampshire state schools, plus up to six music exhibitions. Also five Assisted Places per year. Huge resources etc make it good value.

Remarks Not as popular with prep school Heads or with parents as it has been in the past. Lingering reputation for producing dry academics, possibly out of keeping with the tail end of the twentieth century. Projects rather a remote image.

WITHINGTON GIRLS' SCHOOL

Wellington Road, Fallowfield, Manchester M14 6BL

TEL *Manchester (061) 224 1077*

Pupils: 560 girls • *All day* • *Ages: 7-18* • *Size of Sixth Form: 130* • *Non-denom* • *Fee-paying.*

HEAD Since 1986, Mrs Margaret Kenyon MA (forties). Educated at Merchant Taylors', Liverpool, and Oxford. Previously at Cheadle Hulme in Manchester. She is also the school's Bursar. An attractive woman, positive, quick talking, who wants the girls to feel they have 'every right to approach the next stage of their life with confidence', and declares she would like the girls to feel 'that the world is their oyster'.

Academic Matters School has had emphasis on Science from the start, and still produces more doctors than anything else. At least one-third of Sixth take A-level Physics. Regularly *very* impressive results, with one-third taking Science, one-third Arts, one-third mixing (usually a Modern Language—another strong department). AS exams increasingly taken to complement/supplement. Thorough teaching on all fronts, and distinctly imaginative at junior end of school. Good careers department, links with industry, girls encouraged to organize their own work-shadowing. Speakers a regular feature, and often include senior hospital figures, who are sometimes parents.

Games, Options, the Arts Very good tennis tradition (Lancashire champions) also lacrosse; strong music (several parents in the Halle orchestra). Drama (under new member of staff) includes workshops, productions are now twice yearly and include involvement of half the school. Regular joint productions with Manchester Grammar School. Cultural life of Manchester well and regularly used, including going to some university lectures. Good art. Strong on scientific societies. Would like to do more with Manchester Grammar School but timetables rarely co-incide. CDT well established and IT has been extended downwards into the Junior School. Another new development is that the school's Head of Physics organizes a research project funded by the Royal Society to encourage the girls to take part in original research at school level. Girls are good fund raisers, with special Dr Barnardo's link.

Background and Atmosphere School founded in 1890 by a group of prominent Mancunians, original aims still hold good: to provide efficient and liberal education for girls; to make work interesting and stimulating in itself, eliminating prizes; to remain small; to stress importance of Natural Science. School set in large oasis of green (building on this is mercifully forbidden by Founders' order). Buildings airy and light. Well stocked Library. Not a hothouse atmosphere, though girls are unquestionably highly motivated. Entrepreneurial spirits encouraged.

THE PUPILS From a huge catchment area, wide mixture of backgrounds, races and creeds. School closes at 4pm, girls leave promptly to catch buses.

Agreeable and polite. Old Girls include many distinguished doctors who have become consultants, also: university professors, the first female director of Price Waterhouse in Manchester, C A Lejeune, Judith Chalmers, Catherine Stott.

Entrance   Own exam at seven, eight or 11 (appproximately 24 come in from own junior school, 40 from outside); some at Sixth Form.

Exit   Practically all go on to degrees, mainly university: Oxford the most popular choice always (about eight per year), three to six to Cambridge; at least eight per year to medicine. Engineering a popular subject.

Bottom Line   No scholarships, but 15 Assisted Places at 11, and three at Sixth Form.

Remarks   Small and very strong girls' day school, hotly sought after in its area that benefits enormously from educational resources of Manchester.

WOLDINGHAM SCHOOL

Marden Park, Woldingham, Surrey CR3 7YA

TEL Caterham (0883) 349431

Pupils: 450 girls   ●   360 board, 90 day   ●   Ages: 11-18   ●
Size of Sixth Form: 130   ●   RC   ●   Fee-payiing.

HEAD   Since 1985, Dr P Dineen (fifties), educated in Wales, also Cardiff and London Universities. Was a nun briefly, now married. Previous post: Head of co-ed comprehensive with 1,150 pupils. Business-like, very determined, somewhat abrupt in manner, she believes firmly in educating girls to use freedom.

Academic Matters   Fairly steady. Not a hothouse. Good Sciences, especially since new Science and Technology block went up (NB stage one of a 15-year development programme). Less motivated girls encouraged to leave and make way for self-starters to come in at A-level. Wide range of subjects (and mixtures of subjects) available. In the past, school has had reputation for encouraging girls to think for themselves.

Games, Options, the Arts   Good games (especially tennis), very good art (now with artist in residence) and drama too. Top end of the school is strong on outings—galleries, theatres, exhibitions, lectures. Flourishing debating. No formal lessons on Saturday mornings, but seniors' programme includes careers lectures, and there has been increased emphasis on extra curricular activities over last year or so, generally undertaken for one term, eg photography, fashion, cooking. Juniors' Saturday morning: study period, plus hair-washing period.

Background and Atmosphere   Glorious setting (though suburbia only a few miles off), with wonderfully kept grounds (one wonders why the girls do not have gardens of their own). Formerly a convent, now there are three nuns on teaching staff (in mufti), and a separate community has returned to live in bungalow on campus, and have set up a Centre for Prayer and Spirituality. Atmosphere is tolerantly Christian rather than dogmatically RC. Relaxed and gentle place, with underlying thread of self-discipline which is taken seriously. Policy-making councils for girls well used; 'Ribbons' (prefects) elected by pupils (a coveted honour), and much store is set by generous helping of both freedom and responsibility—producing maturer adolescents than at many girls' schools. Good career advice on hand. Exeats every weekend if wanted. London not far off and large day element creates some dilemmas. International dimensions of school building up—pupils tune into exchanges with students at Sacred Heart schools in most European countries, USA and Australia; twin school in Africa established to encourage need for social justice.

THE PUPILS   40% from overseas, mainly ex pats, of whom 16% are non-British. Breeds great loyalty among Old Girls down the generations. Articulate, enthusiastic girls, wide social mix.

Entrance   More selective now it can afford to be (registration not less than three years in advance). All girls interviewed before exam. Some at Sixth Form.

Exit   Just under 70% go on to a degree (reading very diverse subjects at equally diverse universities and polytechnics). Horizons: medicine, law, engineering, the City, teaching, art world, fashion.

Bottom Line   Nine scholarships (some academic, others music and art) plus three internal ones for Sixth Formers.

Remarks   Interesting and lively school trying hard to educate for the twenty-first century, though still mumblings of 'patchy' from parents reach us.

WORTH SCHOOL

Paddockhurst Road, Turners Hill, Crawley,
Sussex RH10 4SD

TEL Copthorne (0342) 715207

Pupils: 316 boys ● *All board* ● *Ages: 13-18* ● *Also 98 boys in Junior House ages 9-13, all board* ● *Size of Sixth Form: 115* ● *RC (Benedictine Foundation)* ● *Fee-paying.*

HEAD Since 1983, Downside educated Father Stephen Ortiger MA (forties), 'until I am told to go, either by the Abbot or God!' Red-haired, jolly, with a splendid twinkle and quick wit. Teaches RE. Parents report he is 'immensely caring', though advises 'benign neglect' initially while their son settle in. Hopes to produce 'intelligent, thinking, caring people'.

Academic Matters Better results than Downside. Teaching done by monks (mostly Oxbridge educated, some good-looking and glamorous in their sports gear) and laity. All boys study 10 subjects in their first year; fortnightly reports. Mathematics, English and Theology (this is taught by the inspirational Fr Christopher Jamieson) are the strongest subjects; Head comments that, 'the buzz word has got round that Theology is a streching and exciting subject- there's not any one answer, but an element of philosophy and it allows boys to ask questions'. All Sixth Form do General Studies and Computing (school has successfully developed some software for the handicapped). Aims at average boys academically, though increased number of scholarships attract clever boys, and those with learning difficulties helpfully handled.

Games, Options, the Arts New Sports Hall. Normal emphasis on games, though fencing has a very high standard and all boys in the first year do the Bronze for Duke of Edinburgh Award Scheme. Very strong on drama (recently written from within—music as well—about the murder of Archbishop Romero in South America): plays performed in circular abbey, school yearns for proper theatre. Emphasis on community work, 200 out of 320 boys help at 17 outlets—not for the faint-hearted. Out of school, keen skiing parties, camping and pilgrimages to Lourdes.

Background and Atmosphere Original building is Lord Cowdray's late nineteenth-century house in 500 acres of rolling Sussex parkland, with many additions and new buildings sympathetically designed. Founded (1933) as a prep school for Downside, Worth did not become a senior school until 1964. Since then it has steadily acquired a reputation for its happy atmosphere, good results and the pastoral care of which parents speak so highly, with the modest and reassuring Father Stephen at the helm.

Two Housemasters are monks, three are married lay-masters with the Benedictine tradition, the ethos of which underpins the School; notably good staff/pupil relations. Unwritten tradition that staff, monks in particular, come in to pupils' rooms without knocking and vice versa—a source of amazement and sometimes envy among some other public schools. Very strong positive drive to instil social responsibility and the right values. Thought provoking sermons actually listened to. Old Boys return for Midnight Mass and to be married in the Abbey. But Father Stephen is philosophical about the religious drop-out rate after school. 'It is jolly difficult today, but marriage and children refocus the faith wonderfully.' Sixth Form Society has common room and a bar where 17-year olds may use house ticket for alcohol. Fairly scruffy modest dorms, study beds at Upper Sixth (Prefects have an internal telephone). Fagging is alive and well—boys are paid to fetch newspapers, vacuum Prefects' rooms etc. Highly sociable boys—school holds record for having more dances than any other—once a fortnight with a selection of girls' schools (including Roedean, St Leonard's, Mayfield, Woldingham) for which tongue-in-cheek review on 'away' or 'home' fixtures are published in the school magazine.

THE PUPILS Well-placed for Gatwick (mercifully out of earshot) and takes approximately a quarter of boys of parents stationed abroad in the services or diplomatic. Others are mainly from the South. Friendly, rounded and unpretentious boys, tidy—and with nice manners, catered for very much as individuals without necessarily being high fliers, though some are.

Discipline Good with infringement of clear rules punished—the only case of drugs since the school's foundation was met with instant expulsion, though one mother commented that on the odd occasion 'a good kick where it hurts', might fill the bill better than the monks' Christian tolerance and endlessly constructive understanding. The Fast Set worries some parents.

Entrance Interview for the Junior School, CE for all with 55% pass mark, over-subscribed this year and with more awards offered.

Exit   At last count nine to Oxbridge, 42 to other universities, medical schools, polytechnics.

Bottom Line   Three scholarships of 50% fees and other awards together with one annually for candidate outstanding in Science, Maths and Classics.

Remarks   It has a deserved reputation for its pastoral care underpinned by the ethos of a religious community where the value of individuality is stressed regardless of status or ability. Getting steadily better. Seriously considering expanding to take in girls.

WYCOMBE ABBEY SCHOOL

High Wycombe, Buckinghamshire
HP11 1PE
TEL High Wycombe (0494) 20381

Pupils: Approx 500 girls   •   All board   •   Ages: 11-18   •   Size of Sixth Form: Approx 170   •   C of E   •   Fee-paying.

HEAD   From January 1989, Mrs J M Goodland BA (fifties), educated at Howell's Denbigh and Bristol University—read French and Spanish. Comments that we got the last entry on her completely wrong and so, with apologies, here is the definitive version. Divorced. One son and two daughters, all grown up. Previously Head of now defunct Scottish prep and has taught in several state schools ('your career path is always messy if you have children'), then at St Anne's Windermere, followed by Casterton; last post (since 1983) was Head of St George's Ascot. Takes over from Miss Lancaster, one of the outstanding Heads of her generation—'an impossible act to follow'. Comments that she feels very lucky to have been chosen and that it is fun.

Academic Matters   Fulfilling pupils' potential— hardly a D or E in sight at A-level, except for a few in Latin and Maths. Maths and Latin currently popular, also Religious Studies (16 took A-level Religious Studies in 1990) and English Literature. Some excellent teaching, with dedicated and loyal souls, some of whom have served the school for many years. Prefects

taken from first year Sixth so that exam-takers are not distracted (an excellent system).

Games, Options, the Arts   Drama appears to be taking over the school—first rate teacher and first rate theatre in new Arts Centre, which is a triumph of modern architecture and blends in well with the grounds. Very strong lacrosse school. Music strong (inspired concerts, lots of grade eights). Keen fencing. New dark room has inspired an enthusiastic photographic club. School currently also has successful poet, not to mention 11 in the Bucks squad. Solid programme of local community work.

Background and Atmosphere   School founded 1896 by Dame Frances Dove from St Leonard's in Scotland who came south. Still retains faint links with mother school (prays for it). Also one or two St Leonard's traditions such as 'book bags'—large bags for humping books round in. Buildings Gothic and much improved by redecoration in soft colours. Pleasant grounds on edge of High Wycombe. 'The Wall' which runs round the school, and used to be seen as symbolic of the school keeping itself to itself, now open to admit the world—in particular the police, who train their dogs in the grounds. The Sixth Form building—Clarence House—much mellowed but still 'not what one would have wished'.

THE PUPILS   Daughters of professional intelligentsia—civil servants, barristers, some landed. Drawn from huge number of different schools all over the country: 'it isn't every year' says Mrs Goodland 'that a school will produce a Wycombe girl'. Powerful council with Lord Carrington as President. Powerful OGs: Elizabeth Butler-Sloss, Elspeth Howe, Judith Chaplin, adviser to John Major, Delphine Gray-Fiske (senior pilot in Dan-Air as we write).

Entrance   CE at 11, 12 and 13; school is highly selective. Registration at any age. Interview beforehand—'I would hate someone to come who didn't like the school' (and presumably vice versa).

Exit   Regularly gets 17-20 pupils into Oxbridge. Also to Edinburgh, Bristol, Durham, etc. Medicine also popular, and girls tend to take secretarial or other such course as part of their 'gap' year.

Bottom Line   Generous numbers of scholarships and bursaries by girls schools' standards, including three per year of two terms' fees each, several smaller ones; two to three Sixth Form scholarships on full fees; one Sixth Form science scholarship. Bursaries from 'Seniors' (Old Girls, of which there is a thriving association) plus a trust for 'hard times'.

Remarks Once *the* smart power-house for girls. Now there are others contending for that position and the school also suffers slightly from the general drop in popularity of all-girls' boarding schools.

WYMONDHAM COLLEGE
Norfolk NR18 9SZ
TEL Wymondham (0953) 605566

Pupils: Approx 425 boys, 425 girls • *Approx 600 board (both sexes), 250 day* • *Ages: 11-18* • *Size of Sixth Form: 300* • *Non-denom* • *State, but element of fee-paying.*

HEAD Since 1971, Mr R Wolsey BSc (age not given), forthright, more at home in class than buttering up parents, taught at Charterhouse and Culford before appointed here. Has survived more policy changes than the Vicar of Bray. Led fight to resist closure of school, which resulted in large sums of money being raised and questions being asked in parliament. Says school has work ethos and pupils are *expected* to do well. Very interesting on the subject of co-education, at which he is highly experienced.

Academic Matters Good, considering some of the raw material. Head of one of the houses had exam results stuck on wall to cheer himself up when he was feeling down. One of the best school libraries in the country—over 14,000 useful tomes, large budget and excellent staff. Science is school's great strength.

Games, Options, the Arts Lots available but not much evidence of any. Certainly Sixth Form's one idea of extras was to 'get into Norwich as often as possible'. Strong CCF tradition, and it is taken very seriously—school was RAF base during war. Main games—soccer, cricket, rugby. Good art department. Lots of TV watching.

Background and Atmosphere Founded 1951 by Norfolk County Council Chief Education Officer, Sir Lincoln Ralphs, a man of vision who, it is believed, designed the boarding houses with two separate staircases so that—as now happens—boys and girls could reside under one roof *as though in a family*: being caught on wrong staircase means instant expulsion. This 'family' set up works much much better than segregation, according to Head—not so much chance to get steamed up when you see each other eyeball to eyeball over the cornflakes.

Teaching done in windswept Nissen huts—bleak, and no gesture is made to window dressing—Head's study furnished like an old folks' home. Atmosphere still pretty sexy and some pupils alarmingly precocious. (School is pronounced Wind 'em.)

THE PUPILS Rag bag. Social background 'very very mixed', said the Head. 'Some very low-income families plus pupils whose parents would prefer public school but send children here because it's cheaper.'

Entrance Single parent families get priority, though single parentness no longer automatic qualification for fees being paid.

Exit Reckons to get 12 people into Oxbridge a year and regularly gets a number of those fiercely fought over RAF scholarships.

Bottom Line State boarding school (one of few in the country) which has introduced element of fee-paying as the present intention is to make the boarding pay for itself. Fee-payers up to £2,600 a year at last count.

Remarks Claims to be largest co-ed state boarding school in Europe. Norfolk County Education Officer commented on last edition's entry on Wymondham that it was 'frankly banal, filled with inaccuracy and describes an institution which I do not recognise'. If you don't mind the humble surroundings and a slight tendency to rough manners, worth looking at. Unfortunately suffers from planning blight and County bureaucracy.

INDEX

REGIONAL INDEX